FROM
THOUGHT
TO
THEME

A RHETORIC AND READER FOR COLLEGE ENGLISH

NINTH EDITION

FROM THOUGHT TO THEME

A RHETORIC AND READER FOR COLLEGE ENGLISH

NINTH EDITION

WILLIAM F. SMITH
Fullerton College

RAYMOND D. LIEDLICH
Columbia College

Harcourt Brace Jovanovich College Publishers
Fort Worth Philadelphia San Diego New York Orlando Austin San Antonio
Toronto Montreal London Sydney Tokyo

Editor in Chief • Ted Buchholz
Acquisitions Editor • Stephen T. Jordan
Developmental Editor • Laurie Runion
Project Editor • Angela Williams
Senior Production Manager • Annette Dudley Wiggins
Senior Book Designer • Don Fujimoto

Address for Editorial Correspondence
Harcourt Brace Jovanovich, 301 Commerce Street, Suite 3700, Fort Worth, TX 76102

Address for Orders
Harcourt Brace Jovanovich, 6277 Sea Harbor Drive, Orlando, FL 32887
1-800-782-4479, or 1-800-433-0001 (in Florida)

ISBN: 0–15–500176–0

Library of Congress Catalogue Number: 92–70633

Printed in the United States of America

3456789012   090   987654321

CHAPTER 6   ARGUMENTATION   209

PART II   READER   *269*

CHAPTER 1.   Narration   271

CHAPTER 2.   Description   289

CHAPTER 3.   Illustration   305

CHAPTER 4.   Facts and Judgments   321

• Indicates selection new to this edition

Composition : PCA/CMB Graphic
Achevé d'imprimer par CPI Firmin Didot,
à Mesnil-sur-l'Estrée, le 14 novembre 2014
Dépôt légal : novembre 2014
Numéro d'imprimeur : 125350

ISBN : 978-2-7152-3541-0/Imprimé en France

266465

1 - 10 — 1968
2 - 8 — 1946

$$3417$$
$$- 1968$$

$$2949$$
$$- 1946$$
$$\overline{1003}$$

$$1003$$
$$1449$$
$$\overline{2452}$$

(1) 2482 — 6

hand with minimal assistance from the text. The help provided through the headnotes and follow-up questions for the first three selections in each group should enable students to approach the final essay in each section with confidence and to analyze it with minimal assistance.

Three indexes are provided for Part II—an Index to Reading Selections by Subject Matter, an Index to Reading Selections by Basic Rhetorical Type, and an Index to the Questions on Language and Rhetoric. The first will be helpful to those who use a thematic approach; the second and third will facilitate integration of the study of rhetorical principles in Part I with the analysis of rhetorical models in Part II.

Both rhetoric and reader concentrate on expository and argumentative prose because these are the forms of writing most essential to success in college studies and because they contribute to the development of responsible critical thought and expression. However, we have included a substantial number of readings and exercises in personal narrative and description because we believe these forms are initially more accessible to beginning college students.

From Thought to Theme was planned as a basic textbook to help students clarify, organize, and present their thoughts and feelings on paper. The rhetoric leads them through a sequence of lessons to an understanding and application of the principles that govern expository and argumentative prose. The readings have been selected and arranged to extend and expand those lessons. Although there are obviously many ways to help students improve their reading and writing, we believe that our emphasis on a sequential, structured approach is especially helpful to students with limited background or experience in writing. The reactions to previous editions have reinforced our confidence in the soundness of this approach.

We continue to be indebted to countless teachers and students in colleges and universities throughout the country for their responses to, and recommendations for, the various editions of this book. We are especially grateful to Linda Ford of Tacoma Community College and Sandra Hanby Harris of Tidewater Community College for their suggestions for revision of this edition. As always, we appreciate the assistance of our publisher through the efforts of Stephen T. Jordan, Acquisitions Editor; Laurie Runion, Developmental Editor; Angela Williams, Project Editor; Annette Dudley Wiggins, Senior Production Manager; and Don Fujimoto, Senior Book Designer. Finally and most importantly, we want to thank our wives, Dorothy and Martha, without whose support neither the first nor this ninth edition could have come to publication.

W.F.S.
R.D.L.

College composition courses have, in recent years, reflected a growing concern about critical thinking—about logic, the multiple dimensions of language, and the skills of persuasion. Such a concern is surely justifiable, because clarity and persuasiveness in writing are dependent on an underlying clarity and logical thought, a well-ordered structure, and an awareness of the writer's audience. Beginning with the first edition in 1965 and continuing in all subsequent editions, we have attempted to present in clear, simple terms the fundamentals of sound, logical thought. Chapter 6 focuses on these fundamentals and shows students how to apply them to their own writing. It also contains a full discussion of cause and effect relationships as a pattern for paragraph development, a subject introduced in Chapter 3 but given more complete treatment in Chapter 6 because of its connection to logical thinking.

Twelve sample multiparagraph themes and eighty-five sample paragraphs are used to illustrate the rhetorical principles presented in Part I. Approximately 70 percent of them are new to this edition. Most of these intrinsically interesting paragraphs are sufficiently self-contained to afford opportunities for discussion and writing. In addition to the illustrative paragraphs, more than seventy-five exercises are provided to encourage immediate application of the lessons as they are studied.

Part II consists of thirty-six reading selections arranged in nine sections of four each. As in the eighth edition, they are organized rhetorically. The first two sections deal with the narrative and descriptive modes both for their appeal and for their accessibility to students. The personal narrative provides an easy form for students to follow initially in preparing their essays. The descriptive mode calls for close attention to detail, the substance of virtually all effective writing. The next seven sections are arranged by basic patterns of development, each of which was presented in Part I. To avoid oversimplification, we have explained to students again and again through editorial comments and questions that patterns of development are rarely pure, that most writing incorporates a combination of patterns, and that writers choose whatever serves their purpose best.

Two-thirds of the selections included here are new to this edition. Approximately two-thirds of them are authored by women and minority writers. And as in the past, two-thirds of the readings are published here for the first time in any composition textbook.

The first three essays in each section are accompanied by headnotes that introduce each selection and point out rhetorical devices students should look for; related questions about the author's use of language and rhetorical choices follow these selections, along with a list of vocabulary items. Additional questions and exercises designed to stimulate student thinking, discussion, and writing complete the apparatus. Although some of these questions do not call explicitly for writing, most lend themselves to such assignments. The fourth and final selection in each group is presented without editorial apparatus in order to challenge students to demonstrate their mastery of the material at

PREFACE

The first edition of *From Thought to Theme* was conceived thirty years ago at one of those many informal meetings on the perimeter of the annual Conference on College Composition and Communication. We wanted a textbook that would serve the specific needs and interests of both our students and ourselves, one we were unable to find in any other form. Although our primary objective in developing the book was to satisfy ourselves, it became obvious following publication that many other teachers of composition were looking for the same kinds of things that we were. Three decades and nine editions later, we reflect less on its success and more on the reasons behind it.

What we were after was a textbook that would respect the background and abilities of students, regardless of their previous experience in the English classroom. Then, as now, our efforts have been aimed at

1. building on and enhancing their existing knowledge and skills
2. appealing to and expanding their range of interests
3. providing a sound structure for them to follow, while recognizing available alternatives
4. helping them to sort through their feelings, to think for themselves, and to come to their own conclusions, both as readers and as writers.

As in previous editions, the text is divided into two parts: Part I is a rhetoric and Part II is a reader. Chapter 1 presents a brief survey of the process of writing an expository theme, focusing on the important stages of that process. Instructors who focus on the multiparagraph essay immediately or who begin with the paragraph and work up to the longer composition should find this overview useful at the beginning of the book. Chapter 5 provides a fuller, more detailed discussion of these stages, especially prewriting and revision, that are crucial to the writing of clear, persuasive prose. Chapter 5 also introduces the principle of emphasis; it provides a series of steps to follow in preparing the final draft of the theme, as well as a summary of the important principles covered in the first five chapters.

Giving students a preliminary overview of the composition process in Chapter 1 should help them to understand the relevance of Chapters 2, 3, and 4. These chapters concentrate primarily on the paragraph, presenting it as a theme in miniature and providing explicit, detailed explanations of the important concepts of unity, development, and coherence as they relate to both the paragraph and essay.

CHAPTER **4**   COHERENCE   **105**

CHAPTER **5**   THE EXPOSITORY THEME   **141**

CONTENTS

RHETORIC

An Overview

The general purpose of this book is to help you to use and respond to language with greater assurance and skill. A more specific, practical purpose is to help you to write clear, coherent paragraphs and essays as well as to read and analyze expository prose more effectively. The discussion and writing assignments focus primarily on expository, persuasive prose, the kind of writing most frequently demanded of college students. As you develop greater skill in discovering, developing, and expressing your thoughts and feelings, you will also learn to think more clearly, more logically, since writing necessarily uses words, and most of our thinking is done with words. The ability to think and write clearly will be important to you in college because almost every subject you study will require writing in some form—essay examinations, laboratory reports, term papers, book reviews, and application forms of one kind or another. But the principles you will study, the skills you will acquire in reading, writing, and thinking more effectively, will have a broader relevance as well, for they will help you to function more successfully after college in your social, public, and professional life, as a citizen and human being in an increasingly sophisticated industrial society.

The first five chapters deal with rhetoric, the art of persuasive speech and writing. This subject has been studied by college students for hundreds of years; in fact, you have been using rhetoric in all your attempts at explanation or persuasion, in and out of school, whether you were aware of it or not. In these chapters we will concentrate on the basic principles of unity, development, coherence, and emphasis as they relate to the paragraph and essay. Chapter Six will take a brief look at some common problems of sentence construction beginning writers often encounter.

◙ THE EXPOSITORY THEME

In your college classes you will frequently be asked to write papers of several hundred words, compositions consisting of several paragraphs linked together in support of one central idea. Since the paragraph is the basic unit of expository and persuasive writing, in the next three chapters we will concentrate primarily on the paragraph in illustrating the principles of unity, development, and coherence. But since the paragraphs you write will generally be a part of a longer paper, we will begin here by presenting a brief preview of the process of writing the longer paper and then return to this subject in greater depth and detail in Chapter Five.

Many students who have trouble with writing assignments think that writing is simply an intuitive, inherited aptitude; that those who write well simply have a natural facility for it; and that if one lacks this facility, there is little to be done about it. To these students writing is the product of unconscious inspiration, a "bolt from the blue," and if one isn't blessed, well . . . that's that. The ability to write is, of course, enhanced by a natural aptitude for words and their arrangement. Some persons do seem to have a gift for language, an intuitive grasp of what might be called the "art" of writing that teachers and texts can't impart. But good writing does not result from natural ability alone; it is the result of thoughtful planning, intelligently directed effort, and the practice of writing and rewriting. These are matters of the "craft" of writing, and they *can* be taught and learned. And even those who have language in their bones do not simply reach for a piece of paper, tune in to some creative instinct, and write lucid, polished prose. They must think about their subject, explore their memory, their feelings, plan what they want to say, and revise their work carefully. In short, good writing doesn't demand genius, but a willingness to learn and a steady application of what has been learned.

There are no simple mechanical rules to follow in writing a theme; a system that works well for one writer may not work well for another. There *is* a uniqueness, an intuitive aspect, to all writing; but by following a series of steps, moving through a number of closely related stages in the process of writing a theme, you should be able to avoid many of the frustrations and false starts that plague and panic students who have no plan of procedure. These steps include (1) selecting a subject, (2) focusing your subject, (3) exploring your subject and developing a thesis statement, (4) devising a plan, (5) writing the first draft, (6) revising the first draft, and (7) preparing the final copy. The first four stages involve important pre-writing activities, the last three the writing itself.

(1) Selecting a Subject

The problem of selecting a subject is simplified when you are asked to write an expository essay on an assigned, restricted subject. In this case make certain you understand precisely what the subject, or question as in an essay examination, calls for and organize your material to focus on that subject. When you are given greater latitude in choice of subject, as for example when you are writing about a personal experience, and your own feelings, judgments, and attitudes are important, you will need to take more time to work up your subject, making certain it will have some interest and significance for your reader. When you have a choice, choose a subject you know something about or one you want to know more about. Don't undervalue the significance of your own experience, especially one that taught you something important about yourself or changed your life in some way.

(2) Focusing Your Subject

After you have decided upon a subject, you must limit it sufficiently so that you can deal with it satisfactorily within the length of the paper you intend to write. You could not write a 300–500 word paper on "The World of Work," but one aspect of it, the benefits college students gain by working while going to college, could serve as a more specific, interesting, and therefore more satisfactory topic for an audience of college students. Similarly, a loosely focused, autobiographical essay on your childhood, adolescence, and late teen years would be less successful than a paper limited to one experience that taught you something important.

(3) Exploring Your Subject and Developing a Thesis Statement

In this stage you begin to explore your subject, to think about what you want to accomplish in your paper, what effect you want to have on your reader. If, for example, you want to inform and persuade your readers of the benefits of foreign travel, you must ask yourself what information they'll need to understand and accept your ideas and opinions. Your own travel experience, your reading and observations, conversations with others—all will serve as sources of material. If your subject is a personal experience, you'll have to dig into your memory bank for material.

Formulate, at least tentatively, a thesis for your paper, one major point you want to get across, a central question you want to answer. Though you may change your thesis as your paper evolves, devising a thesis statement at this stage will give direction to your writing; it will provide a foundation upon which to build your detail. Purpose and thesis are related concepts, but they are not the same thing. Your purpose—what you want to do in a paper—provides an overall design, a basis for choosing the kind of detail and strategies you will use in organizing your paper. Your thesis statement, on the other hand, expresses your controlling idea, the point you want to make. It is useful to write them down at this stage so that you'll keep them in mind as you develop your ideas. For a paper on the benefit of foreign travel, they might look something like this:

Purpose   In this paper I want to inform and persuade my fellow students of the benefits I see in foreign travel.

Thesis   Foreign travel is an exciting, culturally enriching, and maturing experience for college students.

(4) Devising a Plan: The Scratch Outline

Having thought about your purpose and come up with a tentative thesis, you must now generate and organize ideas in support of that thesis. You must supply *enough* detail so that your readers fully understand your ideas and use the *appropriate* detail and strategies to persuade them of the validity of those ideas. The time you spend in pre-writing, in working up your detail—facts, illustrations, judgments—is time well spent, for it will make the later assembling of your sentences and paragraphs in their final form much easier.

As you think about your subject, jot down ideas that come to mind from your own experience and observations, and take notes on your reading as well. Then work up a brief scratch outline of your material, organizing the body of it around three or four main points that support your thesis. As you do this, *keep your readers in mind:* What do they already know about the subject? What do they need to know? What biases or prejudices might they possess that would shape their response to your subject? What do you expect them to learn from your paper? Such questions are important, for they will help you decide on the kinds of detail you'll include, the terms and concepts you'll have to define, the words you'll use, the tone you'll adopt, and so on. The more you know about your readers, the better you'll be able to stimulate their interests and satisfy their expectations.

A scratch outline for an essay on why big-time college sports programs need to be reformed might take this form:

1. Harm to athletes
   Insulated from mainstream of college life
   Demands on time and energy prevent serious study
   Intellectual development neglected
2. Harm to colleges
   Corruption of basic purpose—to educate and civilize
   Athletic department not integrated into total college program
   Purpose of college sports distorted—obsession with winning
3. Opposition arguments
   College sports provide entertainment and money
   Attract more students because of team publicity
   Special obligation to Black athletes
4. Conclusion—balance needed
   Obvious value of college sports
   Elimination of excess

(5) Writing the First Draft

Your material sorted into a scratch outline, you are now ready to write your first draft, to transform your notes into the sentences and paragraphs of your theme. The main headings of your outline will serve as the topic sentences of your paragraphs, each paragraph advancing the thought, supporting the thesis of your paper. Once you begin writing, move steadily onward. Worry about grammar, spelling, word choice, punctuation, and so on later when you revise. Remember, your outline is simply a framework, not an irrevocable contract. You can change it, adding or omitting detail, as your finished paper takes more definite shape in your mind. The following draft develops the thesis that emerges from the outline presented above: "High-powered collegiate athletic programs need to be reformed to reduce their commercialization and strengthen their educational values."

College Athletics: Profit and Loss

College athletes have traditionally been regarded as heroes who bring fame and glory to their teams and schools, but recent and continuing scandals involving big-time collegiate sports programs have brought renewed demands that those in charge clean up their act. Those demanding a clean-up point to the fact that the percentage of athletes who graduate is much lower than that of non-athletes. And in several instances athletes have graduated who have not attended class nor even learned to read. Repeated cases of recruitment violations, under-the-table financial inducements offered to star high school athletes, as well as gambling and drug scandals have added fuel to the fire. Recently the National Collegiate Athletic Association, the body that governs collegiate sports, attempted to redress this situation by Proposition 48, which establishes tougher academic standards for college athletes. But these new standards are too weak to be effective. Moreover, even this solution has aroused strong feelings on the part of those who favor maintaining the current level and focus of big-time college sports and those who demand more fundamental change.

College athletes have indeed brought fame and fortune to their schools but at a price both to themselves and their schools. The heavy demands on the time and energy of athletes make it difficult, if not impossible, for them to participate in or profit from the intellectual stimulus of academic life. Frequently housed in special dormitories and fed at training tables, they are isolated from the mainstream of college life. The heavy schedule of practice plus the road trips for out-of-town games seriously reduce time available for study. As a result, many athletes do not undertake a course of serious study. Instead they are guided into classes with such meager intellectual content that after four or five years they have received little in the way of an education. A few do go on into professional sports but only a tiny minority. All too often the athlete is exploited to fill the stadium on Saturday afternoon rather than encouraged and stimulated to develop his intellectual, moral, and spiritual capacities.

And the athletes are not the only ones affected. The institutions that support these sports factories sacrifice their integrity and corrupt their mission, which is to educate and civilize rather than provide profitable entertainment for alumni and fans. On these campuses the athletic department, instead of being integrated with other departments of the college, and so subordinated to its fundamental educational purpose under the guidance and direction of the college president, has become a separate corporate entity with its own budget. Coaches in such schools not infrequently earn more than the president and are accountable to alumni and booster groups rather than to the president and board of trustees. In such circumstances it is not surprising that the desire to win, and continue the cash flow that underwrites the program, is ultimately more important than the obligation to educate players. In a real sense, high-powered college sports programs have become farm systems for professional teams.

Those favoring continuation of the current system concede the fact that the system is not perfect, that it needs to be policed more effectively by the N.C.A.A., but they argue that its strengths outweigh its weaknesses. Major college athletic contests, they maintain, provide mass entertainment that earns much-needed money not only for the athletic department but for the whole college as well. Successful teams increase alumni donations that help all departments. Furthermore, they say, media exposure of team success publicizes the institution, attracting more students and thus providing a larger pool of applicants to select from. But perhaps the most frequent argument concerns Black athletes since many would be prevented from getting a college education and developing their athletic skills in preparation for a career in professional sports.

These arguments are not without merit. Winning teams do provide entertainment and make money; but providing entertainment is not the primary justification for college sports, and there are other ways to raise money than maintaining professionalized athletic teams. Ivy League colleges, for example, do very well without big-time sports programs. The argument that Black athletes would be denied an education and a chance to play professionally if all athletes had to meet the same standards as non-athletes and athletic departments integrated with other departments also needs examination. For one thing, Black athletes are more often exploited than educated, and after four years of play many do not graduate. Many are not prepared for the intellectual rigor of college study but are recruited primarily for what they can do for the college rather than for what the college can do for them. And, secondly, only a tiny minority actually make it in professional sports and those only for a few years.

The "professionalizing" of sports in many American colleges and universities is a serious problem that will require serious attention and, admittedly, painful adjustments. Although sports programs perform an important, legitimate function in higher education in America, they must be more directly related to the primary objective of colleges and universities, which is to develop the intellectual, moral, and emotional capacities of students, not to provide mass entertainment for profit. Sports contests do provide an emotional release from the grind of classwork and examinations, they do build school loyalty among alumni, and they do stimulate interest in colleges and universities on the part of the public at large. No, they should not be eliminated, but they must be brought into a sane balance with the educational purpose of higher education.

(6) Revising the First Draft

Here is a second draft of "College Athletics: Profit and Loss." Read it carefully. Note the changes that have been made.

College Athletics: Profit and Loss

Recent scandals involving college athletes have renewed demands for reform in big-time college sports programs. The continuing recurrence of the problem over the years raises the question, "Are big-time collegiate athletics consistent with the aims and values of higher education in America?" College athletes have traditionally been regarded as heroes who bring fame and glory to their teams and schools, but these benefits are costly. Those demanding a clean-up point to the fact that the percentage of athletes who graduate is much lower than that of non-athletes. And, they add, too many of those who have graduated have not been required to learn much, in some instances even to read. Repeated cases of recruitment violations, secret financial inducements offered high school athletes, and gambling and drug cases have sharpened the criticism. The National Collegiate Athletic Association, the body that governs collegiate sports, has recently attempted to redress the situation by establishing slightly higher standards for college athletes, but this "solution" has satisfied neither proponents nor opponents of reform. But however heated this argument has become, an objective assessment of high-powered collegiate athletic programs clearly indicates the need to reduce their commercialism and strengthen their educational values.

College athletes have indeed brought glory and recognition to themselves and to their schools, but at a price. The heavy demands on the time and energy of athletes make it difficult for them to participate in or profit from the intellectual climate of academic life, or even to graduate. Frequently housed in special dormitories and fed at training tables, they are often isolated from the mainstream of college life. The long hours of practice, extensive road trips, and post-season bowl games seriously reduce time for study. As a result, many, if not most, athletes do not undertake a course requiring concentrated study but are channeled into classes with meager intellectual content. Not surprising, after four or five years on campus they have received only a smattering of an education. And this, too, is not surprising because they were recruited for what they could do for the college—not for what the college could do for them.

And athletes are not the only ones adversely affected. Colleges and universities supporting these sport factories abdicate their responsibility and corrupt their mission, which is to educate and civilize, not provide profitable entertainment for alumni and the public. On these campuses the athletic department, instead of being integrated with the academic departments and thus related to the basic educational function of the school, often becomes a separate corporate entity with its own budget. In a very real sense the athletic program becomes a kind of farm system for professional teams. In such schools coaches not infrequently earn more than the president and are often more accountable to alumni and booster groups than they are to the president and trustees. Thus winning, and maintaining the cash flow that underwrites the program, takes precedence over any educational value.

Those favoring the continuation of the current system may admit that the system is not perfect, that it needs to be policed more effectively by the N.C.A.A., but they argue that its strengths outweigh its weaknesses. For one thing, they say, major college sports do provide entertainment that earns much-needed money not only for the athletic department but for the whole school. Furthermore, they add, media exposure publicizes the institution and attracts more students, thus providing a larger pool of applicants to choose from. But perhaps the argument most often advanced against reforming the system concerns Black athletes. Black leaders such as Jesse Jackson and Benjamin Hooks of the National Association for the Advancement of Colored People argue that raising standards would discriminate against Black athletes since they would be prevented from getting a college education and honing their athletic skills for a career in professional sports.

These arguments are not without merit. Winning teams do provide entertainment and money for the school, but supplying mass entertainment is hardly the primary justification for college sports. And there are other ways to raise money than professionalizing collegiate teams. Ivy League colleges, for example, do very well without high-powered sports programs—and they provide entertainment for their followers as well. The argument that Black athletes would be discriminated against, denied the chance of a college education and of playing professionally, also needs to be examined. To begin with, Black athletes are more often exploited than educated. Many Black athletes are not prepared for the intellectual rigor of college work and do not graduate after four years of college. The graduation rate for Black athletes nationwide is about twenty-five percent, and three-fourths of them have physical education degrees. Malcolm Gladwell, in an article in *The New Republic,* writes: "Memphis State University . . . has earned much fame and substantial television revenues for its successful basketball teams, but in the past 12 years not a single one of its many Black players has graduated."[1]

As for Black collegiate athletes succeeding as professionals, only a tiny minority do and those only for a few years. According to a recent survey, fifty-nine percent of Black high school athletes said they expected to play in college; forty-three percent thought they could make it as professionals. Actually, about one percent of Black high school athletes succeed in college sports; one in ten thousand play professionally.[2] Richard Lapchick, director of Northeastern University's Center for the Study of Sport in Society decries this unrealistic expectation: "It's something that we've sold to the Black community decade after decade . . . we have to get Black students to focus on alternatives."[3]

The "professionalizing" of sports in many American colleges and universities demands serious attention and, admittedly, painful adjustments. Sports programs perform an important, legitimate function in higher education: they provide fun and excitement for students, an emotional release from the grind of classes and examinations; they build school loyalty among alumni; and they stimulate interest in colleges and universities in the general public. But they must be more directly related to the primary objective of higher education—to develop the intellectual, moral, and emotional capacities of students. No, they should not be eliminated, but they must be reformed. Writes Congressman Thomas A. Luken from Ohio, universities ". . . should return to their traditional goal of helping youngsters become more creative, more intelligent, more compassionate, more civilized, and better citizens—rather than bigger, faster, and tougher. We must educate youngsters for life and not just for the pros."[4]

The opening and closing parts of the first paragraph have been revised in the second draft. Two sentences have been added at the beginning. The opening sentence is now shorter and focuses immediately upon the

---

[1] Malcolm Gladwell, "Dunk and Flunk," *The New Republic,* May 19, 1986.

[2] See n. 1 above.

[3] *Los Angeles Times,* November 15, 1990, p. C4.

[4] *The New York Times,* October 4, 1986.

two most important subjects in the essay, scandals and the demand for reform. The opening sentence of the original version is now the third sentence. A question has been inserted in the second sentence to arouse reader interest and to imply the thesis of the essay, that big-time collegiate athletics are not consistent with educational values. And the last sentence of the paragraph now specifically presents the writer's thesis.

The second paragraph has also been modified. Some changes in wording—"intellectual climate" for "intellectual stimulus," "long hours" for "heavy schedule," "extensive road trips" for "road trips for out-of-town games," "concentrated study" for "serious study," "channeled" for "guided," and a "smattering of an education" for "little in the way of an education"—have been made in the interest of precision and conciseness. Two sentences in the original draft—"As a result . . . study" and "Instead they are guided . . . an education"—have been reordered, the idea of meagerness of education separated to form one sentence for emphasis. The last two sentences of the paragraph have been eliminated. The sentence asserting that few athletes go on to play professionally has been placed later in the essay, and the final sentence has been sharply condensed and parallel structure added for emphasis. (Note the repetition of "not surprising.")

In the third paragraph of the first draft, the long sentence "On these campuses . . . with its own budget" has been condensed a bit and the last sentence moved up because its central idea, the college athletic program as a farm system for professional sports teams, is closely related to the idea of the athletic department as a separate entity. A transitional expression, "for one thing," has been added in the second sentence of the fourth paragraph. The sentence "Successful teams . . . help all departments" repeats, in large measure, the idea of the preceding sentence and has been eliminated. Reference to Jesse Jackson and Benjamin Hooks has been added for specificity.

The fifth paragraph has been substantially revised. The fourth sentence has been shortened to avoid repetition of thought. The fifth sentence has also been condensed to focus on just one idea, exploitation, to give it proper emphasis. The second half of this sentence, which concerns graduation rates, has been added to the sixth sentence in the revised version since that sentence deals with intellectual rigor, and graduation is directly related to this idea. The last sentence in this paragraph has been repositioned as the first sentence of the sixth paragraph because it focuses on the second issue regarding Black athletes, their hope to play professionally. Finally, a quoted passage concludes the paragraph to provide authoritative support for the argument about graduation rates for Black athletes.

The sixth paragraph in the second draft is new. It has been developed to deal more fully with Black athletes' hopes for advancement to the professional ranks. It is an important issue, but only one sentence was devoted to it in the first draft. This new paragraph supplies factual detail and expert testimony as supporting evidence. The concluding paragraph is basically unchanged. The sentence detailing specific values of college sports has been repositioned. It now follows the sentence asserting that college sports do have a legitimate function to justify that assertion more emphatically. And, as in preceding paragraphs, a quoted passage reiterates the primary function of a college education and rounds off the essay by answering the question posed in the beginning paragraph, "Are big-time collegiate athletics consistent with the aims and values of higher education in America?"

(7) Preparing the Final Copy

Suggestions for making up the final copy are presented on page 206 of Chapter Five.

CHAPTER

Unity

An essential quality of all good writing is _unity,_ or singleness of purpose. The paragraph is a unit of thought concerned with the exposition of a single idea, and if it is to communicate that idea clearly and
concisely, it must possess oneness. That is, all the detail—the reasons,
illustrations, facts—used to develop it must pertain to one controlling
idea. Consider, for example, the following paragraph:

> Though often defended as a painless way to avoid higher
> taxes, the use of state-sanctioned lotteries to raise funds for pub-
> lic purposes is pernicious. Advertising propaganda and news-
> paper accounts of ecstatic winners encourage the belief that
> players have a serious chance to win. In fact, more than 99.9
> percent lose. Gambling casinos and race tracks offer much bet-
> ter odds. And not only are players deluded into thinking they
> can win, they are drawn from the poorest segment of the popu-
> lation, those least able to afford the loss or understand the true
> chances of winning. Ticket sales are, thus, a tax, a regressive tax
> since it hits hardest at those least able to pay. But perhaps the
> most serious weakness of state lotteries is that they encourage
> gambling, the craving for easy wealth, wealth not related to
> work, discipline, and saving. As George Will comments,
> ". . . those who cherish capitalism should note that the moral
> weakness of capitalism derives, in part, from the belief that too
> much wealth is allocated . . . to people who earn their bread
> neither by the sweat of their brows nor wrinkling their brows for
> socially useful purposes."[1]

The controlling idea of this paragraph is contained in the first sentence, "Though often defended . . . is pernicious," and the following
sentences provide supporting detail. To justify his assertion of the evil
of state-sanctioned lotteries, the writer presents three arguments as
evidence: (1) such lotteries delude players, (2) they introduce a regres-
sive tax, and (3) they whet an appetite for easy riches.

[1] "Lotteries Cheat and Corrupt the People," _Hartford Courant,_ October 15, 1978.

15

■ THE TOPIC SENTENCE

The sentence that expresses the controlling idea of a paragraph is called the *topic sentence.* In the paragraph above, it is the first sentence, the sentence on which the unity of the paragraph is based. An important first step in achieving paragraph unity is to express your thought in a topic sentence and place that sentence at the beginning of your paragraph. A beginning topic sentence provides an organizational focus, a guideline that will help you to stick to your subject. It will not guarantee paragraph unity, however. The following paragraph, for example, begins with a topic sentence, but it does not prevent the writer from wandering off the subject.

> College dropouts have been a source of concern in recent years. To many people the high dropout rate, more than fifty percent before graduation, is a social catastrophe. But is it really? Some drop out because they can't cope with the intellectual demands of college level studies. In those state universities required by law to admit all high school graduates as many as thirty percent leave after their freshman year because they fail. But capable students also leave, many because of emotional problems. A third reason is that many students lack motivation; many in this group had no real reason for attending college in the first place. Students who drop out of college should not be stigmatized as losers. Though financial rewards are often cited as the primary justification for going to college, many successful persons do not have college degrees. And many famous writers, artists, composers— Hemingway, Picasso, Mozart, for example—did not possess degrees. In short, a student who does not graduate from college should not be considered irresponsible. Not everyone needs a college education to contribute something to society.

This paragraph lacks unity. The opening sentence focuses on the seriousness of the problem of college dropouts. The next two sentences reinforce this idea and lead the reader to expect an explanation of why the problem is serious. The following four sentences, however, shift focus to why students drop out, not why the problem is serious. In the remaining five sentences the writer offers an assessment of the problem, arguing that it is not a social catastrophe. In this paragraph the writer has spread himself too thin, attempted too much.

What has happened in this paragraph often happens in students' paragraphs. Although students place a topic sentence first, they may not use the controlling idea of that sentence to guide the thought of the sentences that follow. The topic sentence of this paragraph seemed broad enough to include material on why students drop and whether it is a "social catastrophe." Had the writer narrowed his focus in the topic sentence, he would have been less likely to lose control of the direction of his thought. Consider this revised version:

> Students who drop out of college, more than fifty percent before graduation, do so for a variety of reasons. Some drop out because they cannot cope with the intellectual rigor of college level studies. In those state universities required by law to accept all high school graduates as many as thirty percent or more are weeded out after their freshman year because they fail. But capable students also leave, primarily because of unresolved emotional problems. In this group are those who get married and leave school and those who cannot or do not wish to endure the dissatisfactions and frustrations inseparable from four or more years of concentrated mental effort. Many in the latter group are unwilling to postpone an immediate gratification of their desire for material comforts—cars, fashionable clothes, entertainment, vacation trips—and drop out to earn money to acquire them. And, finally, many students drop out because they had no real purpose in attending college in the first place. Some were pressured by parents, others by friends.

The topic of the revised version is more pointed. The original topic sentence has been modified to change the focus from college dropouts as a "source of concern" to the "variety of reasons" they do. Those sentences concerning the seriousness of the problem have been eliminated, and some have been added to illustrate the emotional problems students confront at college and the lack of serious motivation. Because the writer has now more tightly defined his subject and followed his topic sentence more carefully, the paragraph is more unified, more successful.

◼ THE CONTROLLING IDEA

In the preceding section we have referred to and briefly explained the concept of the controlling idea in the topic sentence, but something more needs to be said about it. Like all normal sentences, a topic sentence has a subject and a predicate. In the sentence

Traveling by train has several advantages over traveling by plane.

the controlling idea, *several advantages,* is part of the predicate. Most of the topic sentences you will write follow this pattern, with the controlling idea in the predicate. The topic sentences that follow do so. Occasionally, however, the controlling idea may be part of the subject of the topic sentence, as in the following:

> A number of methods for combating juvenile delinquency are now in use.

The controlling idea here is *number of methods.*

   Whether you include your controlling idea in the subject or the predicate, make certain that every topic sentence you write does contain a key word or group of words that expresses a dominant idea. A controlling idea will help you to limit your subject to one that you can deal with more completely in a paragraph, and to avoid the kind of broad, general topic sentence that tempts students to include a variety of detail only loosely related to their central idea. Here are some examples of such broad, general topic sentences with their suggested revisions. Each revision sharpens the focus of the original sentence by stressing a more specific controlling idea.

Original	Revised
1. Eastern Europe is a mess.	Rebuilding the economies of Eastern Europe will require massive foreign investment to aid manufacturing.
2. Installment buying is bad.	Installment buying can result in foolish purchases and a load of debt.
3. Big-time college athletics may not be good for athletes.	Big-time college athletics may hinder the athlete's intellectual development.
4. Maria del Monte is a neat girl.	Maria del Monte's wit, friendliness, and poise make her a popular girl.

   The revised sentence about Maria del Monte illustrates an important aspect of the controlling idea—it may contain more than one idea. Here is another example:

> The study of psychology is *interesting* and *useful.*

The two ideas in this topic sentence could be developed, although briefly of course, in a single paragraph. The controlling idea in this next sentence, however, is too comprehensive for development in one paragraph:

America is a *democratic society* based on a system of *free enterprise,* which emphasizes *individual initiative.*

Adequate development of the ideas in this sentence would require several paragraphs, for each of the italicized terms would have to be explained and illustrated. To attempt such a discussion in a single paragraph would create serious problems in unity, especially for an inexperienced writer.

EXERCISE 1

Underline the topic sentence and circle the controlling idea in the following paragraphs.

1. The dangers of scofflawry vary widely. The person who illegally spits on the sidewalk remains disgusting, but clearly poses less risk to others than the company that illegally buries hazardous chemical waste in an unauthorized location. The fare-beater on the subway presents less threat to life than the landlord who ignores fire safety statutes. The most immediately and measurably dangerous scofflawry, however, also happens to be the most visible. The culprit is the American driver, whose lawless activities today add up to a colossal public nuisance. The hazards range from routine double parking that jams city streets to the drunk driving that kills some 25,000 people and injures at least 650,000 others yearly. Illegal speeding on open highways? New surveys show that on some interstate highways 83 percent of all drivers are currently ignoring the federal 55 m.p.h. speed limit. (From Frank Trippett, "A Red Light for Scofflaws," *Time,* January 24, 1983.)

2. Above all others, the perseverance of La Salle in his search for the mouth of the Mississippi was unsurpassed. While preparing in Quebec, he mastered eight Indian languages. From then on he suffered accidents, betrayals, desertions, losses of men and provisions, fever and snow blindness, the hostility and intrigues of rivals who incited the Indians against him and plotted to ambush or poison him. He was truly pursued, as Francis Parkman wrote, by a "demon of havoc." Paddling through heavy waves in a storm over Lake Ontario, he waded through freezing surf to beach the canoes each night, and lost guns and baggage when a canoe was swamped and sank. To lay the foundations of a fort above Niagara, frozen ground had to be thawed by boiling water. When the fort was at last built, La Salle christened it Crevecoeur—that is, Heartbreak. It earned the name when in his absence it was plundered and deserted by its half-starved mutinous garrison. Farther on, a friendly Indian village, intended as a destination, was found laid waste by the Iroquois with only charred stakes stuck with skulls standing among the ashes, while wolves and buzzards prowled through the remains. (From Barbara Tuchman, "Mankind's Better Moments," *Practicing History,* Knopf, 1981.)

3. As it turns out, many joggers and runners do seem to require a certain amount of nursing, and the precise benefits of jogging and running are very much in the flux of controversy. As nearly as I can make out, internists appear to think jogging/running quite a good thing for circulation, respiration, general metabolism. Orthopedists, bone and joint men, appear to deplore it, citing its potential for injury: shin splints, stone bruises, tendonitis of the knee or ankle, spinal troubles. All physicians agree that great care must be taken, especially if one is past forty years

20

old, when too strenuous a running program can be dangerous. To die from a heart attack while jogging seems neither a glorious nor a philosophical death. The French used to speak of "stumbling toward eternity," which seems to me far preferable to running toward the same destination. (From Joseph Epstein, "Runners Vs. Smokers," *Familiar Territory: Observations on American Life,* Oxford University Press, Inc., 1979.)

4. The tensions and troubles of modern life often cause people, especially old people, to yearn for "the good old days," when life was simpler and therefore better. But was it? The truth is that life in America 150 years ago, before the beginning of the age of industrialization, was harsh for many people. Life expectancy was rather short, about 38 years for males and a few more for females. Farm labor was hard and never-ending, dawn to dusk, 72 hours and more per week for men; and women worked even longer hours cooking, scrubbing floors, feeding farm animals, making clothes, preserving food. And speaking of food, because of a lack of refrigeration there were no fresh vegetables in winter; as a result, vitamin deficiency diseases were common. In times of drought or insect invasions food supplies were scarce. Epidemics also caused heavy loss of life. Infant mortality was high and childbirth a serious business in isolated areas where doctors were few and midwives inadequately trained.

5. I was aware that many men who have accumulated more millions of money than they can ever use have shown a rabid hunger for more, and have not scrupled to cheat the ignorant and the helpless out of their poor servings in order to partially appease that appetite. I furnished a hundred different kinds of wild and tame animals the opportunity to accumulate vast stores of food, but none of them would do it. The squirrels and bees and certain birds made accumulations, but stopped when they had gathered a winter's supply, and could not be persuaded to add to it either honestly or by chicane. In order to bolster up a tottering reputation the ant pretended to store up supplies, but I was not deceived. I know the ant. These experiments convinced me that there is this difference between man and the higher animals: he is avaricious and miserly, they are not. (From Mark Twain, "The Damned Human Race," *Letter from the Earth,* Harper and Row, 1962.)

21

EXERCISE 2

A. The controlling idea of a topic sentence, as explained earlier, is the key word or group of words that expresses its basic idea. In the following sentences circle the word or group of words that contains the controlling idea.

   Example   For most people regular exercise is (beneficial.)

1. Investment in the commodities market is a (risky) venture.
2. Though popular with the public, federal insurance of bank deposits (contributed) to the savings and loan debacle.
3. Surviving the first year of college can be a (harrowing) experience.
4. Although the Declaration of Independence assures us that "all men are created equal," the meaning of the phrase needs (to be made (explicit) if fruitful discussion of the concept of equality is to take place.
5. A number of suggestions have been made by professional economists on reducing the federal deficit.
6. Recent studies have revealed the (danger) of living with smokers.
7. Professor Chun is a (lively, witty, well-informed) lecturer.
8. Centralized planning and bureaucratic inefficiency are (important causes) of the growing collapse of the former Soviet Union's economy.
9. College students display a variety of fashions in the clothing they wear.
10. There is a growing feeling in Japan and Western Europe that Americans may be (too self-indulgent) to seriously confront their economic problems.

B. Revise the following topic sentences to narrow the focus on a more specific dominant idea.

Example

   Original   The new Phaeton automobile is a fine car.
   Revision   Superior workmanship, beautiful design, and economical operation make the new Phaeton a fine automobile.

1. Professor Tweed is a problem for his students.

   _____

   _____

2. The nuclear energy industry is in trouble.

   _____

   _____

22

3. Aurora Dawn's new novel about Hollywood intrigues and scandal doesn't <u>do much for me</u>.

_____

_____

_____

4. Nigel Fabersham is a <u>sleazy</u> character.

_____

_____

_____

5. Maureen Rubin, the current district attorney, would make a <u>fantastic mayor</u>.

_____

_____

_____

6. Roland Curtin's latest book, *Inside Australia's Outback,* is an <u>interesting book</u>.

_____

_____

_____

7. The latest fashion in women's swimsuits is <u>really something</u>.

_____

_____

_____

8. The housing market for young, unmarried couples is a sad situation.

_____

_____

_____

9. Abraham Lincoln was a great president.

_____

_____

_____

10. Foreign students do not have an easy time at American universities.

_____

_____

_____

24

EXERCISE 3

A. Compose a precise topic sentence on each of the following subjects. Concentrate on *one* idea in your controlling idea and underline that idea.

> Example   *Subject*—high school dropouts
> *Topic Sentence*—Students who drop out of high school diminish their chances of finding well-paying jobs.

Person

1. A teacher who's made a strong impression on you

   _____

   _____

2. The former Soviet Union

   _____

   _____

3. Professional or collegiate sports

   _____

   _____

   _____

4. Family life

   _____

   _____

   _____

5. Environmental protection

   _____

   _____

   _____

25

B. Revise each of the topic sentences you've written in Exercise A above, this time including *two* ideas in your topic sentence. Again, underline your controlling idea.

> Example   Students who drop out of high school diminish their chances of finding interesting, well-paying jobs.

1. _____

_____

_____

2. _____

_____

_____

3. _____

_____

_____

4. _____

_____

_____

5. _____

_____

_____

C. Compose a paragraph using as your topic sentence one of the sentences you've written for A or B above. Work up a scratch outline for your paragraph, following the general procedure presented on pages 6–7 in Chapter One for developing a scratch outline for a theme. Below your topic sentence list the detail that might be used to develop your controlling idea. Make sure that your detail—facts, judgments, illustrations—are clear, concrete, interesting. As you consider your material, you may wish to modify your topic sentence. Don't hesitate to do so.

26

Check your detail once more to eliminate irrelevancies; then write your paragraph. Your plan might look something like this:

Topic—High school dropouts
Topic Sentence—High school dropouts have a difficult time finding satisfying jobs.

1. Financial
   minimum wage work
   meeting basic living expenses difficult
2. Psychological
   dull, routine work
   lack of advancement
   self-image diminishes
3. Social
   limited opportunities for social contacts in workplace
   difficulty developing social skills
   lack of stimulating, interesting peers

The numbered items under the topic sentence represent primary support; the items below each number provide illustration of the more general primary items.

27

■ PRIMARY AND SECONDARY SUPPORTING DETAIL

When your topic sentence is somewhat complicated, you will often have to develop your paragraph more extensively than when your topic sentence is simple. In this case, some of your sentences will contain more important ideas than others. That is, the detail in some sentences will directly support the controlling idea, whereas the detail in other sentences will explain and clarify these direct supporting statements. We can thus conveniently distinguish between *primary* support—detail that relates directly to the main idea of the paragraph—and *secondary* support—detail that explains and clarifies primary support. In the following paragraph the topic idea is supported by a number of primary statements, each of which relates directly to the controlling idea of the topic sentence—the different ways the strength of alcoholic drinks is measured.

> The strength of alcoholic drinks is measured differently in Britain, the United States, and France. In Britain the concentration of alcohol is designated by its "proof," a rather quaint system involving gunpowder. In this system "proof" refers to the concentration of alcohol in gunpowder soaked with it that allows the power to burn steadily—the higher the proof, the stronger the flame. In Britain 100 proof liquor contains, oddly enough, 57.1 percent alcohol. In the United States, however, 100 proof means a 50 percent concentration. That is, the percentage of alcohol in American liquor can be determined by dividing the proof figure in half; pure alcohol would be 200 proof. The French system is simpler and neater. The French measure percentage of alcohol by volume, as so many degrees Gay-Lussac: 100 degrees (100° Gay-Lussac) means 100 percent alcohol.

The topic sentence of the following paragraph is developed by four primary sentences and one secondary.

> The direct benefits of such a universal national youth service program would be significant. Every young man and woman would face a meaningful role in society after high school. Everyone would receive job training, and the right to earn assistance toward post-secondary education. Those going on to post-secondary education would have their education interrupted by a constructive work experience. There is evidence that they would thereby become more highly motivated and

successful students, particularly if their work experience related closely to subsequent vocational interests. Many participants might locate careers by means of their national-service assignments. (From Steven Muller, "Our Youth Should Serve," *Newsweek*, July 10, 1978, p. 15.)

An analysis of each of these two paragraphs illuminates this difference between primary and secondary supporting statements:

Topic Sentence   The strength of alcoholic drinks is measured differently in Britain, the United States, and France.

Primary Support
1. In Britain the concentration of alcohol . . . involving gunpowder.

Secondary Support
In this system "proof" . . . the flame.
In Britain 100 proof . . . alcohol.

Primary Support
2. In the United States, however . . . concentration.

Secondary Support
That is, the percentage of alcohol . . . 200 proof.

Primary Support
3. The French system is simpler and neater.

Secondary Support
The French measure percentage of alcohol . . . alcohol.

Topic Sentence   The direct benefits of such a universal national youth service program would be significant.

Primary Support
1. Every young man and woman . . . high school.
2. Everyone would receive . . . education.
3. Those going on to post-secondary . . . experience.

Secondary Support
There is evidence . . . vocational interests.

Primary Support
4. Many participants . . . national-service assignments.

When you have decided on a topic sentence, examine its controlling idea carefully. If it is fairly complex, you will need both primary and secondary support to develop it adequately. The writer of the following paragraph uses both primary and secondary support in developing the controlling idea.

> Automobile manufacturers have certainly catered to the public's love of comfort and convenience in designing the modern automobile. Ease of movement and relaxation of physical tension have been emphasized. Plush carpets, luxuriously padded seats curved to support the spine, and headrests enhance riding comfort. By simply touching a button, the driver can raise, lower, or tilt his seat forward or backward to obtain the most comfortable driving position. Tilt-away steering wheels also make it easier to get in and out of the car. Suspension systems have also been greatly improved to smooth out the bumps on the roughest of roads. Soft coil springs, heavy duty shock absorbers, gas- and air-filled shocks, stabilizer bars—all of these options let buyers choose their level of comfort. Efficient air conditioning and heating systems let riders control the temperature. No longer must they freeze in winter nor roast in the summer. Visual and audio discomforts have also been reduced. Windows can be raised or lowered electrically to shut out external noise and tinted to cut down on glare. Stereophonic tape players and AM-FM radios provide listening pleasure to occupants as they glide along the highway. Even telephones can easily be installed to accommodate busy salespeople and executives who want to keep in touch with clients or the home office without having to waste time stopping the car to use a pay phone.

The controlling idea of this paragraph is contained in the first sentence: "Automobile manufacturers have certainly catered to the public's love of comfort in designing the modern automobile." Six primary statements support the controlling idea. What are they? Which sentences provide illustration and clarification of these primary statements? An understanding of the way this paragraph is assembled will provide practical guidance when you need more than primary support to develop the controlling idea of a paragraph.

This discussion of primary and secondary detail is intended to clarify a basic characteristic of the structure of the expository or argumentative paragraph. As you will discover in your reading and writing, however, this distinction is not precisely applicable to every paragraph of this type. That is, every sentence of such a paragraph does not necessarily add a new primary or secondary supporting detail. Occasionally, a writer begins a paragraph with one or more sentences that lead in to the topic sentence, as is the case with the paragraph on pages 37–38. And in a paragraph that is part of a longer composition, one or two sentences at the beginning may refer to an idea developed in a preceding paragraph. You will also discover that one sentence may simply repeat, as a means of emphasis, an idea in a preceding sentence of the same paragraph.

In the following excerpt from Will and Ariel Durant's *Caesar and Christ,* the third volume of their monumental *The Story of Civilization,* the first two sentences of the second paragraph continue the thought of the first paragraph—that Christianity, in the mind of the "greatest of historians" (Edward Gibbon, author of *The Decline and Fall of the Roman Empire*), caused the fall of Rome. The first sentence, "There is some truth in this hard indictment," iterates the idea in the topic sentence of the preceding paragraph and thus helps to tie these two paragraphs together. The next sentence, "Christianity unwillingly shared in the chaos of creeds that helped produce that medley of mores which moderately contributed to Rome's collapse," expands upon the idea of the preceding sentence by elucidating the element of "truth in this hard indictment," that Christianity did unwillingly contribute to the "medley of mores" which moderately contributed to Rome's fall. And the third sentence, "But the growth of Christianity was more an effect than the cause of Rome's decay," contains the controlling idea that the sentences following it develop.

Topic
Sentence   The greatest of historians held that Christianity was the chief cause of Rome's fall. For this religion, he and his followers argued, had destroyed the old faith that had given moral character to the Roman soul and stability to the Roman state. It had declared war upon the classic culture—upon science, philosophy, literature, and art. It had brought an enfeebling Oriental mysticism into the realistic stoicism of Roman life; it had turned men's thoughts from the tasks of this world to an enervating preparation for some cosmic catastrophe, and had lured them into seeking individual salvation through asceticism and prayer, rather than collective salvation through devotion to the state. It had disrupted the unity of the Empire while soldier emperors were

struggling to preserve it; it had discouraged its adherents from holding office, or rendering military service; it had preached an ethic of nonresistance and peace when the survival of the Empire had demanded a will to war. Christ's victory had been Rome's death.

Linking
Sentence

Topic
Sentence

There is some truth in this hard indictment. Christianity unwillingly shared in the chaos of creeds that helped produce that medley of mores which moderately contributed to Rome's collapse. But the growth of Christianity was more an effect than a cause of Rome's decay. The breakup of the old religion had begun long before Christ; there were more vigorous attacks upon it in Ennius and Lucretius than in any pagan author after them. Moral disintegration had begun with the Roman conquest of Greece, and had culminated under Nero; thereafter Roman morals improved, and the ethical influence of Christianity upon Roman life was largely a wholesome one. It was because Rome was already dying that Christianity grew so rapidly. Men lost faith in the state not because Christianity held them aloof, but because the state defended wealth against poverty, fought to capture slaves, taxed toil to support luxury, and failed to protect its people from famine, pestilence, invasion, and destitution; forgivably they turned from Caesar preaching war to Christ preaching peace, from incredible brutality to unprecedented charity, from a life without hope or dignity to a faith that consoled their poverty and honored their humanity. Rome was not destroyed by Christianity, any more than by barbarian invasion; it was an empty shell when Christianity rose to influence and invasion came. (From Will and Ariel Durant, *The Story of Civilization,* Volume Three, *Caesar and Christ,* Simon and Schuster, 1944.)

EXERCISE 4

A. Read the following paragraph carefully and pick out the topic sentence, the primary sentences, and the secondary sentences. Write them in the blanks provided. Reread pages 28–30 and study the process presented on those pages.

   Public transportation in the United States is in trouble, deep trouble. And the solution is not in sight. The more serious problem is funding. Mass transit is largely dependent upon government financing—local, state, and federal money provides 56 percent of current operating expenses—and that funding is being reduced in accord with the public demand to trim government spending. Equipment, fuel, and maintenance costs continue to rise; but raising fares is politically unpopular, so transit systems' woes increase. New York City, which has the largest system, needs more than $14 billion for repair and improvement of equipment. Mechanical failure also complicates the problem. *Newsweek* magazine reports that half of Houston's 760 buses are idled by breakdown and one quarter of New York's subway cars are out of commission at any one time.[2] The new Grumman Flexible bus, in use in more than 30 cities, was supposed to increase ridership with its modern innovations in comfort; but it has spent about as much time in the repair shop as on the road. But transit unions, in the opinion of many observers, represent the chief obstacle to progress. Big city transit workers are more generously paid than other government workers—in Chicago, for example, a bus driver can make $25,000 a year in 3½ years and in Boston the average salary is $33,000. Since unions resist attempts to lower operational costs by employing part-time drivers during rush hours, to eliminate unnecessary personnel, and to curb wage demands in troubled transit districts, the outlook for any improvement in the public transit system is bleak indeed.

Topic
Sentence _____

_____

Controlling _____
Idea

_____

Primary Support

1. _____

_____

[2] "Can't Get There from Here," June 1, 1981, pp. 44–45.

33

Secondary Support

———————————————————————————

———————————————————————————

———————————————————————————

Primary Support

2. ————————————————————————

———————————————————————————

Secondary Support

———————————————————————————

———————————————————————————

———————————————————————————

Primary Support

3. ————————————————————————

———————————————————————————

Secondary Support

———————————————————————————

———————————————————————————

———————————————————————————

B. In the following exercise a topic sentence and some supporting sentences provide the framework for a paragraph on sports fans. Supply the primary and secondary support needed to develop the controlling idea in the blanks provided.

    Topic   Scanning a crowded football stadium, one can quickly dis-
    Sentence tinguish three types of male sports fans.

34

Primary Support
1. The true sports enthusiast is easily spotted.

    Secondary Support

    a. _____

       _____

    b. _____

       _____

Primary Support
2. The casual, mildly interested fan is also conspicuous.

    Secondary Support
    a. He is usually well dressed, accompanied by his wife or girlfriend and another couple.
    b. He wants the home team to win, but he is not a fanatic, and he chats amiably with his companions during the course of the game.

    c. _____

       _____

Primary Support

3. _____

    Secondary Support

    a. _____

       _____

    b. _____

       _____

C. Using the detail and framework you've developed for Exercise A, and any additional detail you wish to make it more interesting, colorful, and specific, compose a 100–150 word paragraph on sports fans.

▣ PLACEMENT OF THE TOPIC SENTENCE

We have suggested that you place the topic sentence first. This advice is especially valid for inexperienced writers, for a beginning topic sentence provides the best guideline and the most effective check against irrelevant matter. However, as you gain skill and experience in writing lucid, well-developed paragraphs, you may occasionally wish to place the topic sentence elsewhere. For example, you may use it not to announce your main point but to introduce it at the conclusion of your paragraph as a means of emphasis.

The following paragraph is from an essay titled "Work," written by Bertrand Russell, a famous British mathematician-philosopher. In the first part of the paragraph, Russell focuses on the difference in men's ability to "regard their lives as a whole" and the direct connection between this ability and happiness. In the fifth sentence he relates this ability to wisdom, morality, and education. But not until the final sentence does he present his basic point . . . that consistent purpose, the ability to regard life as a whole, is most fully realized in work.

> Human beings differ profoundly in regard to the tendency to regard their lives as a whole. To some men it is natural to do so, and essential to happiness to be able to do so with some satisfaction. To others life is a series of detached incidents without directed movement and without unity. I think the former sort are more likely to achieve happiness than the latter, since they will gradually build up those circumstances from which they can derive contentment and self-respect, whereas others will be blown about by the winds of circumstances now this way, now that, without arriving at any haven. The habit of viewing life as a whole is an essential part both of wisdom and true morality, and is one of the things which ought to be encouraged in education. Consistent purpose is not enough to make life happy, but it is an almost indispensable condition of a happy life. And consistent purpose embodies itself mainly in work. (From Bertrand Russell, "Work," *The Conquest of Happiness,* Liveright Publishing Corporation and Unwin Hyman, Ltd., 1930 and 1958.)

Another method is to begin and end with a topic sentence.

> There's little question that employment patterns are shifting and will continue to shift throughout the world. Take agriculture. When Ronald Reagan was born, almost one-third of America worked down on the farm. Now, barely one out of 30 works

the land in the U.S. The same trend is true in Europe and Japan, where one out of 20 work on a farm. The mechanization of the American farm led the American worker to heavy industry in World War II, then to the service industry after the postwar period. Nowadays, one out of three American blue-collar workers are in services, meaning they don't manufacture anything. They simply service the machines and people who do the manufacturing in the blue-collar industry and the machines and people who grind out the paperwork in the white-collar industry. This shifting trend will continue as robots take more of the jobs in manufacturing and computers take more of the jobs in the office. (From Marvin Cetron and Thomas O'Toole, "Jobs for Tomorrow," *Encounters With the Future: A Forecast of Life into the 21st Century,* McGraw-Hill Publishing Co., 1982.)

⌐ In some paragraphs you may need two sentences to express your central idea. In the paragraph below, the first two sentences convey the main idea, that avarice is worse than either untidiness or vanity as a vice among the aged.

Among the vices of age are avarice, untidiness, and vanity, which takes the form of a craving to be loved or simply admired. Avarice is the worst of those three. Why do so many old persons, men and women alike, insist on hoarding money when they have no prospect of using it and even when they have no heirs? They eat the cheapest food, buy no clothes, and live in a single room when they could afford better lodging. It may be that they regard money as a form of power; there is a comfort in watching it accumulate while other powers are dwindling away. How often we read of an old person found dead in a hovel, on a mattress partly stuffed with bankbooks and stock certificates! The bankbook syndrome, we call it in our family, which has never succumbed. (From Malcolm Cowley, *The View from Eighty,* Viking Penguin, Inc., 1976, 1978, 1980.)

The topic sentence of this next paragraph is the third sentence, "Such concern is justifiable, of course. . . ." The first two sentences lead into this sentence, and the sentences following it develop its controlling idea—the increase in thievery and fraud in the United States.

Judging from the fervor with which candidates for public office ally themselves with efforts to reduce crime and punish criminals, Americans are deeply disturbed about the rising level of crime in this country. They want the Mafia exposed and destroyed; they want murderers, muggers, rapists, dope peddlers off the streets and into prison. Such concern is justifiable, of course; but other types of criminal activity, common thievery and fraud, are more common and ultimately more destructive. That many Americans routinely falsify their income tax reports is well established. Hundreds of millions of dollars earned by small business operators, self-employed workers, waiters, or taxi drivers, for example, go unreported. The General Services Administration, the agency that purchases supplies for the federal government, is being investigated because of reputed kickbacks and bribes in the awarding of contracts to suppliers. Investigations have also revealed chiseling by doctors, pharmacists, nursing home administrators, and laboratories in overbilling the government for services provided under the Medicaid program, fraud amounting to hundreds of millions of dollars. According to a governmental report, as of July 1977, 12 percent of college students who had obtained federally insured loans have defaulted on their loans, leaving the federal treasury $500 million poorer. And private industry suffers substantial losses every year, from executives who pad their expense accounts and use company cars and planes for their own use, from factory workers who steal tools and material, and from hotel and motel guests who pilfer towels and bedding. This decline in personal honesty is not yet epidemic, but it is growing. If it becomes the rule rather than the exception, if everyone cheats or steal because "everybody else is doing it," Americans will face a bleak future in moral and economic terms.

In some paragraphs, particularly narrative and descriptive paragraphs, the topic idea may be implied rather than explicitly stated. The implied topic idea of the paragraph below is a description of a Hindu prisoner, who is being taken from his cell to be hanged. Notice how carefully George Orwell selects his details to render a unified impression of the scene.

One prisoner had been brought out of his cell. He was a Hindu, a puny wisp of a man, with a shaven head and vague liquid eyes. He had a thick sprouting moustache, absurdly too big for his body, rather like the moustache of a comic man on the films. Six tall Indian warders were guarding him and getting him ready for the gallows. Two of them stood by with rifles and fixed bayonets, while the others handcuffed him, passed a chain through his handcuffs and fixed it to their belts, and lashed his arms tight to his sides. They crowded very close about him, with their hands always on him in a careful, caressing grip, as though all the while feeling him to make sure he was there. It was like men handling a fish which is still alive and may jump back into the water. But he stood quite unresisting, yielding his arms limply to the ropes, as though he hardly noticed what was happening. [From George Orwell, *Shooting an Elephant and Other Essays,* Harcourt Brace Jovanovich, 1945.]

◼ THE CONCLUDING SENTENCE

Be careful not to introduce a new idea or point of view at the end of your paragraph. Under pressure to develop an idea fully, students occasionally add in the final sentence an idea that is only loosely related to the controlling idea and so dissipate the unified impression they have labored to effect. Consider, for example, the following paragraph:

> Travelling and living in Europe have become increasingly popular with Americans since the end of World War II. Some seek escape from the hurry and worry of contemporary American life, the rat race for material reward. They seek the more leisurely, culturally richer life, which they hope to find in such cities as Vienna, Paris, Rome, and Brussels. The increase in the number of American businesses and factories in Europe has dramatically increased the size of American "colonies" in foreign countries. In fact, American businessmen and their families comprise the largest group of Americans living in Europe. A third group consists of United States government employees, technical experts, researchers, and so forth, those sent to administer trade and aid programs. And, finally, college-age youths travel to Europe for study, fun, adventure, for a final fling before going to work. This influx of Americans, however, has not been universally welcomed by the people of the host countries. In fact, some European critics complain that this new American "invasion" is corrupting European life.

The writer's controlling idea, expressed in the first sentence, is that Americans are increasingly attracted to travelling and living in Europe. Four primary sentences provide basic support for this idea. In the last sentence, however, she disrupts the unity of the paragraph by adding a new idea, the feeling among some European critics that the American "invasion" is corrupting European life. These last two sentences should be omitted here and the idea they introduce reserved for another paragraph.

One final suggestion: if you are writing a single paragraph, especially one that is rather long or complex, you can improve its unity by reinforcing the controlling idea in your concluding sentence, as does the writer of the following paragraph:

Sport may be the toy department of life, but one of its abiding compensations is that, at least on the field, it is the real thing. Much has been done in recent years in the attempt to ruin sport—the ruthlessness of owners, the greed of players, the general exploitation of fans. But even all this cannot destroy it. On the court, down on the field, sport is fraud-free and fakeproof. With a full count, two men on, his team down by one run in the last of the eighth, a batter (as well as a pitcher) is beyond the aid of public relations. At match point at Forest Hills a player's press clippings are of no help. Last year's earnings will not sink a twelve-foot putt on the eighteenth at Augusta. Alan Page, galloping up along a quarterback's blind side, figures to be neglectful of that quarterback's image as a swinger. In these situations, and hundreds of others, a man either comes through or he doesn't. He is alone out there, naked but for his ability, which counts for everything. Something there is that is elemental about this, and something greatly satisfying. (From Joseph Epstein, "Obsessed with Sport," *Harper's Magazine,* July, 1976.)

EXERCISE 5

A. In the following exercises there are three topic sentences, accompanied by a number of supporting sentences. Most of the accompanying sentences directly support the controlling idea of the topic sentence; others are irrelevant. Eliminate the irrelevant sentences and organize the remaining sentences into a paragraph, adding whatever detail may be necessary.

1. Though censorship is widely regarded as a sin in democratic societies, some censorship of the mass media seems reasonable.
   a. Billboards and public galleries usually avoid such images as well.
   b. One reason is that newspaper publishers and television networks don't want to assault the sensibilities of unwitting readers and viewers.
   c. Scenes of violent, intimate homosexual or heterosexual behavior or lovemaking don't usually appear in prime time television programs.
   d. Another reason is that words and images can not only inspire and ennoble but also degrade and demean.
   e. For example, newspapers don't usually show pictures of shocking, violent crimes of mutilation, especially in their front pages.
   f. Libertarians reject this argument because they believe it justifies censorship; they argue that art never corrupted anybody.
   g. In fact, many psychologists and sociologists believe that the increasingly violent crimes being committed by young people are partly the result of having been fed a steady diet of violence in films and on television.
   h. Of course, censorship of the media can be carried too far.
   i. But even those who share this view not infrequently decry the violence on television, an art form, because of its putative, harmful effects on youth.
   j. It is wise to remember that the first objective of any aspiring dictator is to seize control of newspapers and radio and television stations.
2. Professor Todd is a lively, eccentric little man.
   a. He stands five feet five in his bare feet.
   b. When he smiles, his mouth stretches from ear to ear.
   c. When he lectures, he paces back and forth behind the lectern, his eyes glued to the floor or gazing out the window.
   d. His principal interest outside of school is bird watching.
   e. In fact, he has published two books on the subject.
   f. He seldom looks at the faces of his students when he lectures, but if a student asks what he considers an important question, his eyes light up and fasten intently on the questioner.
   g. If a student asks him an interesting question after class, he grasps the student firmly by the elbow, knits his brow in furious concentration as he responds to the question, and then relaxes into that wide grin, eyes sparkling, as the student nods his head in understanding.

41

h. When, however, he is irritated or angry at student inattention to his lecture or lack of participation in class discussion, his lisp grows more pronounced, and he begins to stutter a bit.

i. He is genuinely concerned about students learning his subject, spending long hours in his office helping them to understand the material and offering wise counsel on other problems as well.

j. This is his last year, for he is now seventy and must retire.

k. His students will miss him; in fact, many have petitioned the Board of Trustees to allow him to continue teaching beyond seventy.

l. A professor's mental competence and teaching capability, not his age, should determine whether he should retire.

3. Stocks, municipal bonds, and real estate have been perennial favorites with investors for many years, but each has its drawbacks.

a. Over the years stocks have proven a good investment for the wise investor.

b. Investors have made money on dividends, stock splits (additional shares of stock given shareholders when profits are high), and sale of stock.

c. Municipal bonds provide a good return for the long-term investor because the interest earned on them is tax-free, and this locked-in interest yield is a decided plus during periods of low inflation and low interest rates.

d. Inflation, however, erodes the value of bond yields over the years; and though bonds can be sold, because of their long-term maturity, owners often lose money in such sales.

e. But what goes up also comes down and shareholders lose money when the market falls or stagnates.

f. Some critics complain that since municipal bonds are tax-free, they provide an unfair advantage for wealthy people who invest in them and thus pay no income tax at all.

g. But this advantage must be weighed against the disadvantage that if this tax-free aspect of municipal bonds were eliminated, many cities, states, and school districts would have to pay more in interest to finance their various projects.

h. And that's because interest rates on such bonds would have to be substantially increased to compensate for the tax loss potential buyers would sustain.

i. But real estate requires maintenance, which can be a headache, and the money saved in tax deductions is not really voided, simply deferred.

j. Real estate has attracted investors because of the steady appreciation in the value of such assets between the time of purchase and sale and the tax deductions owners can take.

k. Moreover, real estate is not easy to sell in periods of recession or high-interest mortgages; and such investments often tie up money for extended periods of time.

42

B. In the following paragraphs the beginning topic sentences have been omitted. Read each paragraph carefully; then construct a sentence that conveys the main idea of the paragraph, one that could serve as its topic sentence.

1. Never for one minute did he look at the world or at people, except in relation to himself. He was not only the most important person in the world, to himself. In his own eyes he was the only person who existed. He believed himself to be one of the greatest dramatists in the world, one of the greatest thinkers, and one of the greatest composers. To hear him talk, he was Shakespeare, and Beethoven, and Plato, rolled into one. And you would have had no difficulty in hearing him talk. He was one of the most exhausting conversationalists that ever lived. An evening with him was an evening spent in listening to a monologue. Sometimes he was brilliant; sometimes he was maddeningly tiresome. But whether he was being brilliant or dull, he had one sole topic of conversation: himself. What *he* thought and what *he* did. (From Deems Taylor, "The Monster," *Of Men and Music,* Simon and Schuster, 1937.)

_____

_____

2. It's especially damaging for young children because they lack the moral judgment of adults. Many children are only dimly aware of the consequences of their actions, and, as parents know, they are excellent mimics. They often imitate violence they see on TV, without necessarily understanding what they are doing or what the consequences might be. One five-year-old boy from Boston recently got up from watching a teen-slasher film and stabbed a 2-year-old girl with a butcher knife. He didn't mean to kill her (and luckily he did not). He was just imitating the man in the video. (From Tipper Gore, "Curbing the Sexploitation Industry," *The New York Times,* March 14, 1988.)

_____

_____

3. They find working under pressure or against deadlines highly stimulating, providing the motivation to do their best. And they rarely succumb to adverse stress reactions. To slow such "racehorses" down to the pace of a turtle would be as stressful as trying to make the turtle keep up with the horse. Yet others crumble when the crunch is on or the overload light flashes. Some take life's large and small obstacles in stride, regarding them as a challenge to succeed in spite of everything. Others are thwarted

43

by every unexpected turn of events, from a traffic delay to a serious ill-ness in the family. (From Jane Brody, "Stress: Some Good, Some Bad," *The New York Times Guide to Personal Health,* The New York Times Co., 1982.)

_____

_____

4. There is the meaning given to the word by the anthropologist, in which all social habits, techniques, religious practices, marriage customs, in fact everything—including the kitchen sink—is examined to throw light on how a particular society lives and moves, or just exists. Then there is "culture" in a narrower sense, in which we are concerned not with mate-rial techniques, not with the social organization that holds society to-gether, but with the ideas, the aesthetic experiences and achievements, and the philosophical or religious ideas that affect and are affected by the aesthetic experiences and achievements of a given society. A special vari-ant of the last sense of "culture" is the narrow identification of the word with the fine arts and the implicit relegation of the fine arts to the margin of life, to what is done in leisure or for leisure. [From D. W. Brogan, *America in the Modern World,* Rutgers University Press, 1960.]

The word culture has many denotations and conotations.

C. Examine the following paragraphs for unity and be prepared to point out the specific weakness of those that lack unity and to explain how they might be improved. Check to see that each sentence in the paragraph sup-ports a controlling idea in a topic sentence. As an aid here, enclose the topic sentence of each paragraph in brackets and underline its controlling idea. In those paragraphs that contain primary and secondary support, make certain that each primary statement directly develops the controlling idea and that each secondary statement provides a relevant explanation or clarification of each primary statement. Place a capital P before each pri-mary statement and a capital S before each secondary statement. Before every irrelevant sentence place an I, and place an RTS before any state-ment that reinforces the topic sentence.

1. _____ Americans' love affair with the automobile has been a costly ro-mance. _____ Perhaps the most obvious negative effect has been the pol-lution it has created. _____ Of the 200 or more million tons of waste spewed into the air each year in the United States, automobiles contribute 94.6 million tons. _____ Another problem is simply the space gobbled up

44

by the automobile. _____ In Los Angeles, a city that couldn't function without the automobile, 60 to 70 percent of the space is devoted to cars in the form of streets, freeways, and parking lots. _____ The citizens of that metropolis are hoping to ease the problem with an underground railway and perhaps a light-rail system. _____ These additions should help, but they won't alleviate the problem completely. _____ Reliance on the automobile has also produced two other negative effects. _____ It has diminished people's desire to walk, reducing the opportunity for healthful exercise in this flabby age. _____ And, by using up so much urban space, it has made it more difficult for people to find a place to walk. _____ This latter result is socially undesirable, for it reduces the opportunity for people to mingle, to get to know each other at least by sight. _____

2. _____ The results of the barbarian conquest were endless. _____ Economically it meant reruralization. _____ The barbarians lived by tillage, herding, hunting, and war, and had not yet learned the commercial complexities on which cities thrived; with their victory the municipal character of Western civilization ceased for seven centuries. _____ Ethnically the migrations brought a new mingling of racial elements—a substantial infusion of Germanic blood into Italy, Gaul, and Spain, and of Asiatic blood into Russia, the Balkans, and Hungary. _____ The mixture did not mystically reinvigorate the Italian or Gallic population. _____ What happened was the elimination of weak individuals and strains through war and other forms of competition; the compulsion laid upon everyone to develop strength, stamina, and courage, and the masculine qualities that long security had suppressed; the renewal, by poverty, of healthier and simpler habits of life than those which the doles and luxuries of the cities had bred. _____ Politically the conquest replaced a higher with a lower form of monarchy; it augmented the authority of persons, and reduced the power and protection of laws; individualism and violence increased. _____ Historically, the conquest destroyed the outward form of what had already inwardly decayed; it cleared away with regrettable brutality and thoroughness a system of life which, with all its gifts of order, culture, and law, had worn itself into senile debility, and had lost the powers of regeneration and growth. _____ A new beginning was not possible: the Empire in the West faded, but the states of modern Europe were born. _____ A thousand years before Christ northern invaders had entered Italy, subdued and mingled with its inhabitants, borrowed civilization from them, and with them, through eight centuries, had built a new civilization. _____ Four hundred years after Christ the process was repeated; the wheel of history came full turn; the beginning and the end were the same. _____ But the end was always a beginning. (From Will and Ariel Durant, *The Age of Faith,* Vol. IV of *The Story of Civilization,* Simon and Schuster, 1950, p. 43.)

3. _____ The American businessman has certain remarkable qualities in an exceptional degree. _____ His vitality is extraordinary. _____ He lives

his business from morning to night; he gives to it the devotion that a medieval saint gave to his religion. _____ He is almost always experimental about it, eager to take a chance, anxious to change from one vocation to another if the latter seems to offer additional opportunities. _____ He believes profoundly in the possibilities of machinery; and he is almost always willing to take the long rather than the short view. _____ He knows, as no other people but the Germans and, since 1917, the Russians know, the value of expertise and research. _____ He assumes that success in a business calling is of itself a title to influence, and since there are few men who do not desire influence, he agrees with but little difficulty that the successful businessman ought to be respected. _____ There is, indeed, an important sense in which it is true to say that for most Americans the acquisition of wealth is a form of religious exercise; that is why, perhaps a well-known advertiser could write, in the twenties, of Jesus Christ as a successful businessman without the public feeling that there was some incongruity in the thesis. (From Harold Laski, *The American Democracy,* The Viking Press, Copyright 1948, p. 169–70.)

4. _____ Not all thinking is of the same kind. _____ Much of our thought consists simply of feelings and recollections, a free association of ideas concerned with the self in the form of reverie, daydreaming. _____ It consists of hopes, fears, a remembrance of things past, perhaps a half-conscious sense of contentment. _____ Walter Mitty, a character in one of James Thurber's stories, comes to mind. _____ To cope with the dull routine of his life, he imagined himself in various dangerous situations in which his daring and ingenuity saved the day. _____ He is one of Thurber's most successful creations. _____ Rationalization defines a kind of thinking in which we seek reasons to justify our actions, to defend our beliefs when we feel ourselves challenged _____ Much of what passes for serious thinking, psychologists tell us, is of this type. _____ Critical thinking, a third type, produces solutions to problems, for it has direction. _____ It aims at truth, at an unbiased view of a problem and a sensible way of coping with it. _____ Critical thinking deals realistically with facts to arrive at a conclusion to account for them.

5. ___T___ The serious depletion of oil and natural gas reserves in the United States has prompted investigation of a number of new energy sources. ___P___ One of the most promising of these is the fast breeder nuclear reactor. ___S___ The conventional nuclear power plant taps only 1 percent of the energy produced by the splitting (fission) of uranium atoms; and uranium 235, the fuel used, is scarce. ___S___ The fast breeder reactor, however, by a process of transforming uranium into plutonium, produces more fuel than it consumes and therefore virtually eliminates the problem of the scarcity of nuclear fuel. ___P___ An even more fantastic machine now being experimented with is the fusion reactor. ___S___ It combines heavy hydrogen atoms to produce helium atoms, releasing nuclear energy that can be converted into electricity. ___S___ Because the

46

fusion reactor uses for fuel an element contained in sea water, the successful development of this device would solve humanity's energy problems for a long, long time. _RST_ Other promising sources of energy are contained in sunlight, subsurface heat, ocean tides, and everyday trash. _P 3_ Various experiments are under way to trap sunlight to create heat energy that can be used in boiler turbines to produce electric currents. _P_ Geothermal power is produced by drilling holes into the earth and forcing cold water into one hole. _S_ As it comes into contract with hot rock four or five miles below the surface, the water is heated and fractures the rock. _S_ The hot water then rises to the surface in another hole and is used to drive a turbine to produce electricity. _P_ In several regions of the world, the ebb and flow of the tides could be harnessed to produce electrical power, as they are on the Rance River estuary in France. _P_ And, finally, the lowly trash Americans accumulate in ever-increasing quantities, about 2½ billion tons a year, should not be overlooked. _S_ Experts estimate that if it were burned in power plants, enough electricity could be generated to take care of 50 percent of this country's current energy needs.

D. In the following short theme a student describes a crossing guard who, over a period of years, escorted her and her friends across a busy intersection as she walked to school. Read the composition at least twice, making certain you understand the dominant impression conveyed by the writer. Then read it over again, this time noting the specific details that communicate this impression.

Cliff

I remember vividly my first day of school, for on that day I met Cliff, the crossing guard at the intersection in front of Lincoln Elementary School. Cliff was an important part of my life for the next twelve years. He was sixty-one, gray-haired, with a mustache and a smile to warm the heart of any frightened five-year-old. No school ever had a more friendly, gracious host to welcome the pupils each morning and escort them safely across the busy boulevard every afternoon. Cliff invented a little hand-clapping game to greet his children. He would put out his right hand, palm up, and the children would laugh and clap his hand. Then they would put up their hands, and he would clap them resoundingly. All of us, big and small, enjoyed this greeting immensely.

Nine years and thousands of handclaps later when I was graduating from junior high school, Cliff decided to retire. He told us all that he was getting old and tired and wanted to do some fishing. One day in June at a flag ceremony in front of the school, the principal announced Cliff's decision. Many of us

47

had moist eyes that day as Cliff walked up to thank the principal for his kind words. He waved to all of us and thanked us for being such good kids. And we all waved back, cheering lustily and clapping our hands furiously. We all loved Cliff and told ourselves that school just wouldn't be the same without him.

The summer passed all too quickly, and on my first day of high school I approached the crossing where Cliff had welcomed me my first day of elementary school nine years before. "It won't be the same with Cliff gone," I thought. But glancing up, I recognized that familiar yellow jacket, the wide smile, and the outstretched palm. Cliff hadn't retired after all. He couldn't, not while there were children to brighten his lonely days. He simply missed them too much.

Cliff is seventy-four now and still straight and tall. Last week I drove past my old friend at the old, familiar crossing. He was surrounded by his many new friends on their way to school. I honked my horn, and he waved his hand and gave me a smile that would warm the heart of any frightened eighteen-year-old on her way to her first day of college.

The central impression here is that of a friendly, gracious, warm-hearted older man. This controlling idea is expressed in the fourth sentence. The preceding three sentences provide background information. Succeeding sentences contain the details that convey the impression of a friendly, enthusiastic older man with a love for and need of children in his life. The writer tells us about his dignified, friendly appearance and manner, his hand-clapping game, his smile, his desire to retire, and the children's response to his friendliness. Think back over your own experiences, and select a person who has made a strong impression on you—a relative, a friend, a teacher, an employer. Write a short theme of one to three paragraphs in which you present a unified impression of that individual. Choose your details carefully, using only those that directly relate to the impression you wish to convey.

E. Read the following poem carefully, at least twice. It is carefully constructed to present a dominant impression of a man, Richard Cory. Though he is shown to have several admirable qualities, they are all related to one overriding quality. What is that quality? What adjective best describes him? Bear in mind that you are not asked to relate the message of the poem, its central idea, but only the dominant quality of Richard Cory. Is the name Richard Cory well chosen? Why? How does it reinforce his dominant quality?

48

RICHARD CORY

Whenever Richard Cory went down town,
We people on the pavement looked at him:
He was a gentlemen from sole to crown,
Clean favored, and imperially slim.

And he was always quietly arrayed,
And he was always human when he talked;
But still he fluttered pulses when he said,
"Good-morning," and he glittered when he walked.

And he was rich—yes, richer than a king—
And admirably schooled in every grace:
In fine, we thought that he was everything
To make us wish that we were in his place.

So on we worked, and waited for the light,
And went without the meat, and cursed the bread;
And Richard Cory, one calm summer night,
Went home and put a bullet through his head.

EDWIN ARLINGTON ROBINSON

◼ SUMMARY

The most important quality of good writing is clarity. To achieve clarity and conciseness in your paragraphs, you must make sure they are unified. The following suggestions will help you write unified paragraphs:

1. Be sure that each paragraph has a controlling idea expressed in a topic sentence. As a check against irrelevancy, it is helpful to place this sentence at the beginning of a paragraph, but occasionally it may be placed elsewhere—at the end of a paragraph, for example, to summarize rather than to announce a topic.
2. Make certain that primary supporting detail focuses clearly on the controlling idea.
3. If the central idea requires more than primary support, make certain that secondary supporting detail explains and clarifies the primary detail.
4. Be especially careful to avoid inserting a new idea in the last sentence of the paragraph.

CHAPTER

Development

A second important quality of an effective paragraph is *completeness.* A major weakness in student writing is the underdevelopment of paragraphs, the failure to supply sufficient detail to clarify, illustrate, or support the controlling idea. Because the paragraph is an organic entity—a group of related sentences that develop a single idea—it must be reasonably complete if it is to communicate this idea satisfactorily. Consider, for example, the following paragraph:

> Undergraduate education in America, particularly in large public universities, needs to be improved. First- and second-year students are usually herded into such large classes that individual attention and encouragement are all but impossible. Furthermore, the more distinguished professors primarily pursue their own research and writing relieved of the necessity to do much teaching, especially on the undergraduate level. If the quality of undergraduate education is not to deteriorate, changes must be made.

This paragraph begins with a clear, concise topic sentence, but the paragraph lacks development. Only two primary supporting sentences are offered to defend the proposition that undergraduate education in America needs improving: that the size of freshman and sophomore classes is too large and that these beginning students are denied the stimulation of contact with experienced, senior professors. Each of these primary supporting judgments needs secondary detail, and perhaps another argument as well, to develop the controlling idea more fully. The writer of this paragraph has simply not said enough about the controlling idea. By adding further supporting material, he or she could have made the thesis more persuasive. Note the changes in this revised version:

> Undergraduate education in America, particularly in large public universities, needs to be improved. For one thing, first- and

51

second-year students are usually herded into such large classes that individual attention or encouragement are all but impossible. And these students need such attention to help them acquire the skills and discipline to adjust to the intellectual rigor of university studies. This help and guidance is especially important today when so many students must work part-time with less time and energy for concentrated study. Another reason is that the more experienced, distinguished professors typically avoid teaching lower-level students. Primarily pursuing their own research and writing, they seldom teach more than one or two classes a semester, or year, and those usually on an upper division or graduate level. Many students who could benefit from the challenge and stimulation of such teachers at the beginning of their university studies are denied the opportunity. In place of professors, teaching assistants, graduate students working on advanced degrees, provide much of the teaching in these first two years; and though they are frequently able, competent instructors, their primary interest and energy are not devoted to teaching but to their own studies. The increasing impersonality of university education engendered by large classes and the increasing expense of hiring high-powered scholars to pursue research rather than teach will not increase public confidence in higher education, confidence that will be sorely needed as tuition costs continue their spiral upward.

This second paragraph is more persuasive because its controlling idea has been more fully developed. The two primary judgments have been clarified by additional detail, and a third idea, the decline in public confidence as tuition costs increase, has been added.

The more fully developed the paragraph, the longer it will be, as in the example above; but there is no set length for a paragraph. In expository writing the majority of paragraphs consist of clusters of sentences that develop one idea. The writer, having finished with one aspect of the subject, moves on to another aspect in a new paragraph. Occasionally, however, factors other than movement of thought influence paragraph length. Newspaper paragraphs, for example, often consist of only one sentence. The narrow-column format makes it necessary to reduce paragraph length to make it easier for the reader to digest information. Considerations of rhythm and emphasis may also dictate shorter paragraphs, particularly in the longer essay or article. In a term paper of fifteen to twenty paragraphs, for example, a short paragraph sandwiched between longer ones may provide a change of pace, a chance for readers to pause slightly and assimilate what they have read before continuing; or it may underscore an important point, the contrast in paragraph size focusing reader attention. And introductory or concluding paragraphs in an essay of five or six paragraphs may also be somewhat shorter for similar reasons. The kinds of expository paragraphs you will be required to write, however, usually demand 100 to 150 words (6 to 10 sentences) for adequate development. But regardless of paragraph length, your main concern will be to include sufficient detail so that your readers can comprehend your meaning without having to supply their own information.

The ability to write well-developed paragraphs requires a good deal of practice in thought development. The quality of your paragraphs will depend largely on your ability to think of effective ways to illustrate and support your ideas. A ready supply of ideas is therefore a basic asset to any writer. However, this supply is seldom available to the average college freshman. You are certainly not abnormal, therefore, if you have had trouble finding material to support your ideas in a written assignment. But you can do something about it. You can increase your stock of ideas and your fund of information and thereby facilitate your thinking and your writing.

One way of doing this is through reading—newspapers, weekly news magazines, books. Your studies will provide ample opportunity for improving your reading skills, but you will find that the news and editorial sections of first-rate newspapers and news magazines are especially valuable sources of ideas and information. When you need information on a specific subject, consult the *Readers' Guide to Periodical Literature,* a library reference work that alphabetically lists magazine articles by subject and by authors' last names. Listening to radio and television news commentators and conversing with persons knowledgeable in particular subjects will also provide information and insight.

Your choice of method in developing a paragraph will usually be determined by your topic sentence. That is, a well-written topic sentence generally implies a method of development. Consider the following topic sentence:

> Deficits in the federal budget of the United States have been increasing dramatically in recent years.

This statement obviously calls for factual detail to support it. The following sentence

> Slang is frequently vivid and expressive.

needs illustrative detail. The sentence

> The political labels "conservative" and "reactionary" are frequently confused in political discussions today.

clearly requires a combination of definition, comparison, and contrast for adequate development.

In the following pages you will be introduced to a variety of ways to develop the expository paragraph. The purpose of exposition is to explain the logical relationships between things, relationships involving the general and the specific, similarity and difference, the part and the whole. The patterns of development that will be discussed and illustrated—illustration, facts, judgments, comparison and contrast, analysis, definition, cause and effect, and combination of methods—all deal with these basic relationships. Illustration, facts, and judgments are the basic materials of which most expository paragraphs are constructed. The others represent common methods of organizing facts, judgments, and illustrations to construct a paragraph. Developing a paragraph by showing cause and effect relationships will be considered later in a discussion of the argumentative paragraph. This chapter does not include all the possible methods of developing paragraphs, but it does offer a variety of the most frequently used patterns.

◼ ILLUSTRATION

An easy and effective way to support an idea is by the use of examples. In his topic sentence the writer makes a general statement and then clarifies it through specific illustrative detail: he points to a specific occurrence, condition, or fact that concretely illustrates his idea. A writer using this strategy often begins with a general statement, explains and elaborates upon that statement in a following sentence, and then provides examples and illustrations to support his controlling idea. The exemplification in such paragraphs may consist of one detailed example, as in the paragraph below:

> A number of studies have shown that while people may protest about some social change, when the change actually takes place most will fall silently and willingly into line. It's the rare examples of change being resisted with violence that unfortunately receive most publicity. A psychologist interested in this phenomenon once made an amusing study of the differences between what people say they'll do and what they really do in a particular situation that evokes prejudice. Travelling across the country with a

Chinese couple, he found that the three of them were received in 250 hotels and restaurants with great hospitality—and only once were refused service. When the trip was over, he wrote to each of the hotels and restaurants and asked if they would serve Chinese people. Ninety-two percent of those who had actually served them said they would not do so! (From Ian Stevenson, "People Aren't Born Prejudiced," *Parents Magazine,* Parents Magazine Enterprises, February, 1960.)

Or it may consist of several examples, as in the following paragraph about the occasionally humorous ambiguity of the English language:

Isn't English wonderful? It is wonderfully confusing—and among the confusions is something called *amphiboly.* To quote *Webster's Third,* an amphiboly is an "ambiguity in language; a phrase or sentence susceptible of more than one interpretation by virtue of an ambiguous grammatical construction." Example: *Nothing is too good for my mother-in-law.* There's also the advertisement that tells us, presumably unintentionally, that *nothing is more effective than Esoterica.* A friend in Fort Lauderdale, Kathryn Passarelli, was impressed by the ad. "Naturally, I use nothing," she said. My own pet amphiboly became a popular song toward the end of the 1970s: *If I said you had a beautiful body, would you hold it against me?* An Indianapolis newspaper item reported that a suspect had been arrested "for entering a bedroom of the opposite sex." [From James Kilpatrick, "Fun and Games from the Watched Pot of Language," *Smithsonian,* April 1984.]

In general, several examples are more convincing than one. But a carefully chosen example, one that clearly illustrates and is honestly representative, is preferable to a series of superficial, atypical ones. If your controlling idea is fairly complex, it is probably better to use one extended example so that you have ample opportunity to develop your idea fully. In either case, the important point is that your examples be clear, relevant, and specific.

Narrative can also be used to illustrate a point. In the following short essay, the writer relates a personal incident that taught him a truth about racial prejudice—one isn't born with it.

One of the significant, and encouraging, things about racial prejudice is that it is learned, absorbed, not inherited. People aren't born with a bias against minority groups. Whatever prejudice they have, they have acquired from those around them as they grew older. An incident from my own life made this fact clear to me.

For the first seven years of my life, we lived next door to a Black family, the Walkers. Mrs. Walker and my mother were especially good friends, helping each other in hundreds of ways the way good neighbors do. I often played with Marian, the Walkers' daughter, from the time I was two until I was seven, when we moved down to Pine Street into a better neighborhood. I liked Marian a lot; she taught me how to roller skate, to play marbles, and even how to read a little. Whenever my mother was gone, Marian took care of me. As I've said, I liked Marian, and I don't remember ever being concerned with, or perhaps even aware of, the fact that she was Black and I was White.

After we moved, I didn't see Marian again until the night I graduated from high school, ten years later. After the graduation ceremony that night, I hurried back to meet my mother and family friends with my girlfriend before we left for a party. Marian and Mrs. Walker were there with my mother, smiling and congratulating me. Marian gave me a present and a big hug, and I remember how embarrassed I was in front of my girlfriend and other friends who had come up to congratulate me for having won a scholarship award. I excused myself quickly, ignoring my mother's slightly pained expression, and hurried off with my friends on the way to the party.

The next morning at breakfast I began to think about the previous night, about graduation, the party, and then about the Walkers, Marian's present, and my mother's disappointed look. My thoughts wandered back to the time when Marian and I were children, and I began to feel ashamed, really ashamed, of the way I had acted the night before. I realized then what had happened to me. As a child I was free of prejudice; but as I'd grown older, I picked some up along the way.

The next two paragraphs use some form of illustration to develop their thought. The first, written by a student, is about the comforts of the modern automobile.

Until today I've never thought much about the many comforts and conveniences my new car provides. It's a scorching afternoon, 101 degrees in the shade, and yet I sit in comfort in a velour, cushioned, adjustable seat. I'm listening to the stereo sound of my own live orchestra while the air in my royal cocoon is automatically kept at a cool and refreshing 74 degrees. And it's all happening at 55 miles per hour in the fast lane of Interstate 5—amazing. As I whistle along in this almost surrealistic environment, I notice a hill ahead, and as I begin the ascent, the cruise control automatically maintains the speed uphill. As I glide on further down the road, the onboard computer reassures me that I have 85 miles left until I reach my destination and that with ten gallons of fuel remaining, I will arrive home with a comfortable margin. Sure enough, here's my off ramp, and as I ease the car down the street and into the garage, I push one button, and all the doors unlock simultaneously, another and the antenna retracts. Ah yes, I wonder what it was like in the old days.

In this next paragraph the writer provides three examples to support his controlling idea. Note again the common pattern of paragraphs using examples to develop the main idea. The second sentence introduces the main idea (the first sentence is simply transitional, linking this paragraph with a preceding one), that things American appeal to a closed or oppressed society; the third sentence presents a reason to support this judgment; and the remaining sentences contain the examples.

Yet there is to all this another dimension, and a more interesting one. For, the more closed or oppressed a society, the greater its hunger, or so it seems, for things American. And this is not just because nothing excites the appetite like prohibition; it is, rather, because America is still in many respects a symbol, and one with a hopeful ring to it. Michael Jackson in Havana means something different from Michael Jackson in Encino. Watching him in Cuba becomes a way of making contact with a world of possibility, affiliating oneself with a land that seems fresher and more open than older or more established cultures. I once saw a dissident intellectual in Havana scrawl passionate political appeals to Mr. Jackson all over the album cover of "Bad." The people who spend a week's wages to visit the Kentucky Fried Chicken outlet in Tian An Men Square are not there just for the Colonel's secret recipe; they are buying into something more, not unlike the students who erected a Statue of Liberty nearby last year. In Thailand, McDonald's franchises feature floor-to-ceiling windows so that customers can be seen by their envious friends paying three times more for their burgers than they would elsewhere. Those of us who covet Gucci, Mercedes and Dior can hardly scoff. (From Pico Iyer, "The World's Taste is All-American," *Los Angeles Times,* December 16, 1990, p. M7.)

EXERCISE 6

A. Choose one of the following topics and write a paragraph or a short essay using examples to develop it.

1. the plusses or minuses of waiting on tables as a part-time job
2. an incident that taught you something important (Use a narrative to illustrate your central idea, as in the short essay on pp. 55–56.)
3. slang as a vivid, expressive form of language
4. Americans' love of violent action as reflected in various forms of popular entertainment
5. the effects on divorce on (pick one) children, parents, or society
6. variety in college students' dress
7. risks of investing in the stock market, real estate, gold, etc.
8. the joys or sorrows of owning a sports car
9. apartment living for the college student—joys or sorrows
10. Americans' increasing interest in healthful living

   If you are planning to write a paragraph on one of these topics, transform the topic into a sharply defined, specific idea and express it as your topic sentence. Then list the examples that might be used to develop your controlling idea. After examining your supporting detail, you may wish to modify your original topic sentence. Do not hesitate to do so. Formulating a topic sentence at the beginning is simply a way of ensuring unity. Eliminate the irrelevant items from your list; then write your paragraph, using examples from your list. Make sure your examples are clear, concrete, and interesting. After some time has elapsed, look over your paragraph and revise it if necessary, adding or deleting detail to ensure unity and good development. Your preliminary plan might look something like this:

   Topic—the role of sex in selling
   Topic Sentence—Sex plays an enormously important role in selling.

   1. Men's and women's toiletries
      aftershave lotion, men's cologne
      perfume, lipstick, toothpaste, lingerie
   2. Front pages of tabloid newspapers and magazine covers
      National Enquirer, Vogue, Cosmopolitan
   3. Sex in selling—cheesy but sleazy
      Gross, crude
      Too often too little subtlety

58

Here is a first draft:

Add a Transition Here

It's no secret that sex plays an enormously important part in selling. Sometimes its use is obvious and explicit, at other times suggestive and symbolic. Sex is often used to promote the sale of men's and women's toiletries. Well-known athletes and handsome movie stars tout the sexually enhancing powers of aftershave lotions and colognes in television commercials. Joe Namath, for example, spoke glowingly and knowingly of

Add a Phrase Here

Brut cologne to enhance young men's sexual appeal. Perfume commercials put beautiful women in seductive poses wearing loose-fitting, suggestive clothing, while a voice in low, hushed tones suggests that love and romance await those who put just a dab behind the

A Transition Here, Too

ears. Tabloid newspapers frequently feature racy headlines and sensational stories of love and lust on their front pages to catch the eyes of supermarket shoppers

Needs Examples Here

as they go out the checkout counter. And popular women's magazines—for example, *Cosmopolitan, Vogue, Mademoiselle*—display beautiful, scantily clad, well-nourished young women on their covers. The message is thus pretty clear. Sex sells. And what sells stays.

Condense Here

One may, of course, deplore the crudity, the tastelessness of many sexually suggestive advertisements; but

Too Much Comment

advertisers are not, in this day and age, going to give up a good thing to please the purists. Subtlety and discretion may be extolled as virtues in our private lives; they are seldom practiced in the market place, however.

This first draft is generally well organized and developed, but it needs some revision. A third example to support the controlling idea would flesh it out a bit; and the last few sentences, which present the writer's opinion of sex in selling, begin to shift the focus of the paragraph and need to be condensed. Some comment to conclude the paragraph would work, but it shouldn't be too involved, or it will weaken the unity of the paragraph. Note the changes made in the revision.

59

First Primary Sentence

It's surely no secret that sex plays an important part in selling. Sometimes its use is obvious and explicit, at other times suggestive and symbolic. For instance, sex is often, if not invariably, used to promote the sale of men's and women's toiletries. In television commercials, well-known male professional athletes and handsome movie stars tout the sexually enhancing powers of aftershave lotion and men's cologne. Joe Namath, for example, spoke glowingly and knowingly of the potency of Brut cologne to lure the ladies. To promote the sale of perfume, television advertisers photograph beautiful women in seductive poses, wearing loose-fitting, suggestive clothing, while a voice in low, hushed tones suggests that love and romance await those who put just a dab behind the ears.

Second Primary Sentence

Sex is also used by tabloid newspapers, which frequently feature racy headlines and sensational stories of love and lust on their front pages to catch the eyes of supermarket shoppers as they scan the newspaper rack checking out. The *National Enquirer, Globe,* and the *Star Reporter* are good examples. And popular women's magazines—such as *Cosmopolitan, Vogue,* and *Mademoiselle*—display scantily clad, well-nourished, beautiful women on their covers.

Third Primary Sentence

But perhaps the most interesting use of sex in selling was evident in the introduction of the hardtop convertible a few decades back. A convertible in dealers' showrooms drew in male customers, but they usually bought a four-door sedan. The convertible, supposedly, had associations of youth, adventure—a mistress; but the sedan was the girl one married, one who would be a good wife and mother. To combine the appeal of mistress and wife, auto manufacturers brought out the hardtop convertible. It was an instant success. The message is, thus,

60

pretty clear. Sex sells. And what sells, stays, regardless of its occasional tastelessness or lack of subtlety.

The plan for this paragraph could also serve as the foundation of a longer essay. In this case each of the three primary supporting sentences in the revised version could be transformed into a topic sentence for a full paragraph. (See Chapter Five for a further discussion of the process for developing the multi-paragraph essay.)

B. The following quoted statements contain interesting subjects for paragraphs. Select one, explain its meaning, and provide illustrations to support your interpretation. Use your first sentence to introduce the passage, your second to explain its meaning, and the remainder of the sentences in the paragraph to provide needed exemplification.

1. A man's character is his fate.—Novalis
2. Learning should be a handshake instead of a kiss.—Steven M. Weiss
3. When all you've got is a hammer, everything looks like a nail.—Anonymous
4. One who speaks the truth should have one foot in the stirrup.—Turkish proverb
5. He who leaps high must take a long run.—Danish proverb
6. He who sups with the devil hath need of a long spoon.—English proverb
7. Living well is the best revenge.—Spanish proverb
8. Never send a goat to guard a cabbage patch.—Russian proverb
9. If you can't stand the heat, get out of the kitchen.—Harry Truman
10. The man who marries for money will earn it.—Jewish proverb

▣ FACTS AND JUDGMENTS

Factual detail is often used to support an idea. The writer may begin a paragraph with a topic statement and then support that statement with facts and statistics. Or the writer may present the details first and place the topic sentence at the end as the logical conclusion to be drawn from the evidence. The following paragraph is arranged with the topic idea at the beginning.

> But the problem of multiple murder is not confined to the nation's penitentiaries. In 1981, 91 police officers were killed in the line of duty in this country. Seven percent of those arrested in the cases that have been solved had a previous arrest for murder. In New York City in 1976 and 1977, 85 persons arrested for homicide had a previous arrest for murder. Six of these individuals had two previous arrests for murder, and one had four previous murder arrests. During those two years the New York police were arresting for murder persons with a previous arrest for murder on the average of one every 8.5 days. This is not surprising when we learn that in 1975, for example, the median time served in Massachusetts for homicide was less than two-and-a-half years. In 1976 a study sponsored by the Twentieth Century Fund found that the average time served in the United States for first-degree murder is ten years. The median time served may be considerably lower. (From Edward I. Koch, "Death and Justice: How Capital Punishment Affirms Life," *The New Republic,* April 15, 1985.)

Because both facts and judgments are useful in supporting topic sentences, and because confusion about them sometimes weakens student writing, a brief explanation of their differences should be instructive. A fact is a report, a statement of what has actually happened or of what actually exists. It can be verified: one can test the accuracy of the report through one's own observation or computation or by consulting a reliable source. For example, the following statement is factual:

George Bush defeated Michael Dukakis for the Presidency.

A judgment, on the other hand, records a personal opinion. It indicates approval or disapproval. Unlike a factual statement, it cannot be proven true or false. The following statement is judgmental:

Winston Churchill was England's greatest prime minister.

Many statements, however, cannot be so precisely differentiated as these two examples. The following statement involves both fact and judgment:

> Mountain climbing is an arduous activity.

It can be verified to an extent, and yet it clearly includes judgment.

In your writing make certain that your paragraphs do not consist solely of judgments unsupported by facts. Judgments can serve both as topic sentences and as supporting detail, but they need to be grounded in and illustrated by facts if they are to be convincing. The student who wrote the following paragraph, for example, relied too heavily on judgment unsupported by fact to prove his point.

> Plea bargaining, a negotiated agreement between the lawyer of the accused and the prosecuting attorney whereby the accused agrees to plead guilty to a lesser crime than the one he or she is charged with so as to avoid a possibly stiffer sentence, is corrupting the administration of criminal justice in the United States. Supporters of this practice claim that it is an efficient technique, saves the cost of a trial, and gives the defendant a break. In fact, however, it is simply a perversion of justice that puts criminals back on the streets to prey on society. The criminal justice system in the United States is in a mess because of plea bargaining. Those who defend the practice must bear a good share of the blame.

Such words and phrases as "corrupting," "perversion of justice," "prey on society," and "must bear a good share of the blame" express the writer's judgment. This judgment is not supported with facts, however. A revised version, with factual statements added, is more persuasive.

> I do not believe that plea bargaining represents a step forward for criminal justice in this country. This practice, whereby the accused agrees to plead guilty to a lesser crime than the one he or she is charged with so as to avoid a possibly stiffer sentence, has become an integral part of the administration of American criminal procedure. In 1974, for example, almost 68 percent of the criminal cases handled by the Los Angeles Supreme Court, 13,294 out of 19,608, were processed by means of plea bargaining.[1] Those who defend the practice—a group that includes

[1] Gene Blake, "Trial System Debate Is On in California," *Los Angeles Times,* November 9, 1975, Sec. VIII, p. 5.

numerous courts, the American Bar Association, and legal commissions—argue that plea bargaining is an efficient technique,
saves court costs, and gives the defendant a break. It is true that
eliminating plea bargaining would increase the cost of criminal
justice: it has been estimated that the number of judges, prosecutors, public defenders—all those needed to try a defendant in
a public trial—would have to be more than doubled.[2] The cost
of such an increase, it must be admitted, would be substantial;
but the present system, which puts criminals back on the street
sooner, is, in the long run, far more costly to society. And this
cost includes more than the loss or destruction of property. It
includes the loss of innocent lives as well. The argument that
plea bargaining gives the defendant a break is undeniable. But
the "break" he or she gets in the form of more lenient treatment
from prosecutors and judges is not a break for society, whose
interests also deserve to be protected. And, finally, plea bargaining distorts justice because it is removed from public view
in an open court where the interests of society and the rights of
the defendant can be more effectively protected. "Too often,"
writes Gene Blake, a legal affairs writer for the *Los Angeles
Times,* "some private defense lawyers who depend on a volume
of small criminal cases for their livelihood and public defenders
with too many cases to handle may urge guilty pleas which are
not in the best interest of possibly innocent clients."[3] The best
that can be said of plea bargaining is that it compensates for the
failures of an inefficient criminal justice system. If this system is
to function effectively in the future, however, other means must
be found to sustain it.

The central proposition is more soundly argued in this revision, for
several facts have been supplied to bolster the judgments of the original. Although readers may still reject the proposition, they are aware
of the evidence that led the writer to his conclusion.

In the following three paragraphs, facts and judgments support the
controlling idea. In the first paragraph, facts and judgments are combined.

A report prepared for President Carter by the State Department and the Council on Environmental Quality reveals that
time is running out for action to prevent the world from becoming unlivable by the year 2000.[4] Population pressures, dwindling

---

[2] Blake, p. 5.
[3] Blake, p. 5.
[4] "Earth: Scarcely Livable by 2000?" *International Herald Tribune,* Paris, July 25, 1980, p. 1.

food supplies, environmental pollution, and depleted natural resources will, according to the report, seriously diminish the quality of life on this planet. The world's population is expected to increase from 4 billion in 1980 to 6.35 billion in 2000. Mexico City, for example, will add 20 million inhabitants by 2000. World food production should increase about 90 percent in the next 20 years, but this increase will occur in countries whose diets are already good, not in the underdeveloped nations now suffering from malnutrition and starvation. In addition, the price of food will rise 100 percent in the next 20 years. Air and water pollution are likely to worsen as increasing quantities of coal and oil are burned. Deforestation of the world will continue, with stocks of wood throughout the world expected to decline by 47 percent by 2000. Fresh water shortages will increase also because of rising levels of human, agricultural, and industrial consumption. These gloomy forecasts may prove inaccurate if technological progress can solve some of these problems, but recent studies made by other agencies, American and international, reach similar conclusions.

In the next paragraph facts provide the sole support of the controlling idea.

But time and economic forces are sweeping the last of the old ways from Daufuskie [an island off the South Carolina coast], thought to be a Yemassee Indian word meaning "field of blood." Its cash crops—cotton and oysters—are gone, victims of disease and pollution. As men left for work on the mainland, the post-Civil War population of mostly 1,200 ex-slaves dwindled. Now, less than a quarter of the island's 181 full-time residents are black. A development boom is likely to complete the exodus. Two posh resorts have opened recently, part of a projected 20-year, $500 million transformation that will leave Daufuskie a manicured enclave of golf courses and waterfront homes—not unlike Hilton Head, its neighboring island to the east. Two civil-rights groups, the NAACP and the Christic Institute, charge that the boom is snuffing out a once vital African-American culture. (From Howard Manly, "An Island's Vanishing Culture," *Newsweek,* January 14, 1991.)

And in this last paragraph judgments provide the foundation for the writer's point.

The amusements of modern urban populations tend more and more to be passive and collective, and to consist of inactive observation of the skilled activities of others. Undoubtedly such amusements are much better than none, but they are not as good as would be those of a population which had, through education, a wider range of intelligent interests not connected with work. Better economic organization, allowing mankind to benefit by the productivity of machines, should lead to a very great increase of leisure, and much leisure is apt to be tedious except to those who have considerable intelligent activities and interests. If a leisured population is to be happy, it must be an educated population, and must be educated with a view to mental enjoyment as well as to the direct usefulness of technical knowledge. (From Bertrand Russell, "Useless Knowledge" from *In Praise of Idleness and Other Essays,* Unwin Hyman, Ltd., 1935.)

EXERCISE 7

A. The controlling idea in each of the following sentences could be developed by factual detail. Consult reference works in the library and supply four primary factual details to support the controlling idea. List your data in the spaces provided.

1. The American Civil War was a costly, brutal conflict.

_____

_____

_____

_____

2. In the past twenty years health care costs have soared in the United States.

_____

_____

_____

_____

3. Top-flight professional athletes are well paid.

_____

_____

_____

_____

4. Drug addiction is a serious health hazard.

_____

_____

_____

_____

67

B. Select one of the four topic sentences given in 7A, and, using the factual information you have listed, write a paragraph of 100 words or more.

C. The following subjects are often the bases of sharp differences of opinion. Select one and develop a paragraph in which you argue one side of the question. In your topic sentence make clear the position you favor, and support your controlling idea with judgments.

 1. State-sanctioned lotteries as a means of raising revenues
 2. Quotas as a means of achieving racial equality in the job market
 3. Professional boxing
 4. AIDS testing
 5. Population growth
 6. Hunting as a sport
 7. Compulsory universal service for American youth
 8. Jogging
 9. The American love of spectator sports
10. Paying salaries to college athletes

▣ COMPARISON AND CONTRAST

In paragraphs of *comparison* writers point out similarities between two or more things. In paragraphs of *contrast* they point out the differences. As a student, you will frequently be asked to compare or contrast philosophical ideas, historical figures, characters in a novel, or political parties. By studying these two patterns carefully and by practicing the techniques involved, you can improve your ability to develop and communicate your thoughts clearly.

The supporting material for comparison or contrast frequently consists of factual details, judgments, or examples. In the following paragraph the writer contrasts a current American attitude toward deferred gratification with an older one. Factual and judgmental detail provide support for this contrast.

> *Now instead of later:* Once upon a time Americans understood the principle of deferred gratification. We put a little of each paycheck away "for a rainy day." If we wanted a new sofa or a week at a lakeside cabin, we saved up for it, and the banks helped us out by providing special Christmas Club and Vacation Club accounts. If we lived in the right part of the country, we planted corn and beans and waited patiently for the harvest. If we wanted to be thinner, we simply ate less of our favorite foods and waited patiently for the scale to drop, a pound at a time. But today we aren't so patient. We take out loans instead of making deposits, or we use our VISA or Mastercard to get that furniture or vacation trip—relax now, pay later. We buy our food, like our clothing, ready-made and off the rack. And if we're in a hurry to lose weight, we try the latest miracle diet, guaranteed to shed ten pounds in ten days . . . unless we're rich enough to afford liposuction. (From Janet Mandell Goldstein, "The Quick Fix Society," *The Macmillan Reader,* ed. Judith Nadell and John Langan, Macmillan Publishing Co., 1990.)

In this next paragraph the writer uses contrast to support his point that loose-fitting clothing is sexually appealing.

> As Herrick [an English poet] points out, looseness and disorder in dress are erotically appealing. Soft, flowing, warm-hued clothes traditionally suggest a warm, informal, affectionate personality, and the garment which is partially unfastened not only reveals more flesh but implies that total nakedness will be easily achieved. Excessive neatness, on the other hand, suggests an

excessively well-controlled, possibly repressed personality. Tight, bundled-up or buttoned-up clothes (if not figure-revealing) are felt to contain a tight, erotically held-in person. Hard, crisp fabrics—gabardines and starched cottons and stiff synthetics— also seem to deny sensuality, and so do grayed, dull colors. When drab-colored clothes are both unusually tight and unusually neat, observers will suspect not only sexual disinterest but impotence or frigidity. [From Alison Lurie, "Fabric, Fur, and Skin," *The Language of Clothes,* Random House, 1981.]

The pattern of development of the following paragraph includes both comparison and contrast. The writer discusses the similarities and contrasts of two of her teachers.

Two of my professors this semester, Dr. Henshaw and Mr. Johnson, are very different in personality and temperament but alike in love of their subject and concern for students. To begin with the differences: Dr. Henshaw is always well-organized and prepared. He arrives at class on time, impeccably dressed, eager to begin. His lectures are clear and coherent, and he speaks articulately. After lecturing, he probes student understanding with precise, well-focused questions. He is serious and intent, all business. Mr. Johnson, on the other hand, is more laid-back. He is often late to class, ambling in with books and papers jumbled together in general confusion. His clothes are a decade out of date. His lectures are rambling affairs, punctuated with jokes and anecdotes, as he paces behind the lectern mumbling. However, he encourages lively class discussions, occasionally interrupting them to emphasize a point. In spite of these differences, both teachers obviously love teaching and want their students to learn. Dr. Henshaw, though occasionally pained by poor performance, is quick to praise good work, reading well-written essays in class; and he spends a good deal of his time helping students in his office. Mr. Johnson is always chatting with students after class, lending them books from his own library, and encouraging and helping students who are having trouble in the course.

Arrangement of Supporting Material

You may arrange the supporting material for a paragraph based on comparison or contrast in a variety of ways. If, for example, you are contrasting two opinions on a subject, as does the writer of the paragraph on deferred gratification on page 69, you may focus on one opinion in the first four or five sentences and on the other in the remaining sentences. Another method is to alternate between subjects in successive sentences, as does the writer of this next paragraph, who illustrates the differences in current American and British English with reference to the automobile and related experiences.

Vocabulary differences in current American and British English can be illustrated by recounting the same experience as it happens on both sides of the Atlantic. An American driver pulls his *sedan* into a *gas station* to buy *gas,* get his *windshield* cleaned, and have the attendant look under the *hood* to check the electrical system. A British driver drives his *saloon car* into a *petrol station* to buy *petrol,* get his *windscreen* cleaned, and have the attendant look under the *bonnet* to check the electrical system. The American attendant *checks the battery,* tests the *generator,* and examines the *spark plugs* and the spare *tire* in the *trunk.* His British counterpart *tops off the accumulator,* tests the *dynamo,* examines the *sparking plugs,* and checks the spare *tyre* in the *boot.*

Before he leaves the station, the American driver takes a map from the *glove compartment* because he knows he has to take a *detour* at the next *corner* to get back to the *freeway.* Similarly, the British driver takes his map from the *cubby locker* because he knows he has to take the *road diversion* at the next *turning* to get back to the *motorway.* The American motorist looks for a *turnout* on the *divided highway* before the *overpass;* his British cousin looks for a *lay-by* on the *dual carriage way* before the *flyover.* On his way out of the station, the American sees other drivers *lining up* behind him, honking their *horns* for service; a *dump truck* leaking oil from its *pan;* a *station wagon* with a smashed *fender* and bent *bumper;* and a *convertible* with its *top* down and *muffler* dragging. As he leaves the station, the British driver observes other drivers *queuing up,* honking their *hooters* for service; a *tipping lorry* leaking oil from its *sump;* a *utility car* with a smashed *mudgard* and bent *overrider;* and a *drop head* with its *hood* down and its *silencer* dragging.

A third method is to alternate between subjects within the same sentence, as the writer of the following paragraph does in a contrast of Robert E. Lee and Ulysses S. Grant.

The two generals who led the Confederate and Union forces in the American Civil War, Robert E. Lee and Ulysses S. Grant, present a study in contrast. Though they were both strong men, their strengths represented two conflicting traditions in nineteenth-century American life. Lee was an aristocratic

Virginian, Grant the son of a tanner on the Western frontier. Lee symbolized landed wealth, a privileged class at the top of a hierarchical social structure, Grant the self-reliance and rough-and-tumble democracy of frontier men. Lee stood for the noblest elements of a transplanted English aristocratic ideal—family, culture, a sense of obligation to one's community characteristic of the country squire; Grant embodied the frontier men for whom traditional forms and social patterns meant little. Whatever privileges a man might enjoy, he would have to earn them himself. Grant was, in the words of Bruce Catton, ". . . the modern man emerging . . . ," a precursor of "the great age of steel and machinery. . . . Lee might have ridden down from the old age of chivalry, lance in hand, silken banner fluttering over his head."

In a composition of several paragraphs, you will have a similar choice in arranging detail. For example, if you were contrasting liberal education with career education on the bases of purpose, historical development, and benefits, you might focus on liberal education in the first few paragraphs, each paragraph dealing with one of these three points, and then consider career education in the remaining paragraphs; or you might discuss purpose, historical development, and benefits in this order, shifting your focus between liberal education and career education as you progressed. In long compositions it is probably more effective to use this alternating focus. The steady comparison or contrast of detail keeps the purpose of the paper more clearly and forcefully in the reader's mind.

Analogy

A special kind of comparison is the *analogy,* a comparison of two things that are unlike but that have similar attributes. The paragraph that developed the likeness between Dr. Henshaw and Mr. Johnson (p. 70) is a straight comparison: both belong to the same class. However, a comparison of death and sleep is an analogy; they are not similar states, but they have similar attributes—the cessation of activity and the appearance of repose.

Carefully used, the analogy can be instructive. Alexander Pope, an eighteenth-century English poet known for his wit, uses a brief analogy to emphasize a truth about human egoism:

'Tis with our judgments as our watches, none
Go just alike, yet each believes his own.

The analogy is especially helpful in explaining the unfamiliar in terms of the familiar. For example, a lecturer in physiology in a class of teenage boys might compare the heart with an automobile engine. Or a historian might compare the rise and fall of great civilizations with the life cycle of a human being. In the following paragraph Paul and Anne Ehrlich use an analogy between planet Earth and a spaceship, the rivets on the spaceship compared with the species of life that have inhabited the earth.

> Over most of the several billion years during which life has flourished on this planet, its ecological systems have been under what would be described by the airline industry as "progressive maintenance." Rivets have dropped out or gradually worn out, but they were continuously being replaced; in fact, over much of the time our spacecraft was being strengthened by the insertion of more rivets than were being lost. Only since about ten thousand years ago has there been any sign that that process might be more or less permanently reversed. That was when a single species, *Homo sapiens,* began its meteoric rise to planetary dominance. And only in about the last half-century has it become clear that humanity has been forcing species and populations to extinction at a rate greatly exceeding that of natural attrition and far beyond the rate at which natural processes can replace them. In the last twenty-five years or so, the disparity between the rate of loss and the rate of replacement has become alarming; in the next twenty-five years, unless something is done, it promises to become catastrophic for humanity. (From Paul and Anne Ehrlich, "The Rivet Poppers," *Extinction: The Causes and Consequences of the Disappearance of Species,* Random House, Inc., 1981.)

In the following passage Robert Penn Warren uses analogy to characterize the law.

> "I'm not a lawyer. I know some law. In fact, I know a lot of law. And I made some money out of the law. But I'm not a lawyer. That's why I can see what the law is like. It's like a single-bed blanket on a double bed and three folks in the bed and a cold night. There ain't never enough blanket to cover the case, no matter how much pulling and hauling, and somebody is always going to nigh catch pneumonia. Hell, the law is like the pants you bought last year for a growing boy, but it is always THIS year and the seams are popped and the shankbones to the breeze. The law is always too short and too tight for growing mankind. The best you can do is do something and

then make up some law to fit and by the time the law gets on the books you have done something different. . . ." [From Robert Penn Warren, *All the King's Men,* Harcourt Brace Jovanovich, 1946.]

A beast fable is a short narrative involving animals that act and talk like human beings from which a moral is drawn. A literary form that dates back hundreds of years, the beast fable is based on analogies between human beings and animals. Its primary purpose is to illustrate some human trait, to comment upon human behavior. The following beast fable, entitled "The Courtship of Arthur and Al," comments on workaholics, sometimes known as "eager beavers."

Once upon a time there was a young beaver named Al and an older beaver named Arthur. They were both in love with a pretty little female. She looked with disfavor upon the young beaver's suit because he was a harum-scarum and a ne'er-do-well. He had never done a single gnaw of work in his life, for he preferred to eat and sleep and to swim lazily in the streams and to play Now-I'll-Chase-You with the girls. The older beaver had never done anything but work from the time he got his first teeth. He had never played anything with anybody.

When the young beaver asked the female to marry him, she said she wouldn't think of it unless he amounted to something. She reminded him that Arthur had built thirty-two dams and was working on three others, whereas he, Al, had never even made a breadboard or a pin tray in his life. Al was very sorry, but he said he would never go to work just because a woman wanted him to. Thereupon she offered to be a sister to him, but he pointed out that he already had seventeen sisters. So he went back to eating and sleeping, swimming in the streams and playing Spider-in-the-Parlor with the girls. The female married Arthur one day at the lunch hour—he could never get away from work for more than an hour at a time. They had seven children and Arthur worked so hard supporting them he wore his teeth down to the gum line. His health broke in two before long, and he died without ever having had a vacation in his life. The young beaver continued to eat and sleep and swim in the streams and play Unbutton-Your-Shoe with the girls. He never Got Anywhere, but he had a long life and a Wonderful Time.

Moral: It is better to have loafed and lost, than never to have loafed at all. (From James Thurber, *Fables for Our Time,* Harper and Row, 1940.)

EXERCISE 8

Write a paragraph of 100 to 150 words on one of the following topics, and develop it by means of comparison or contrast. Decide on the bases of your comparison or contrast before you begin to write, and keep these bases in mind as you write. For example, if you plan to contrast two political leaders, you might contrast their origins, personalities, and political and philosophical attitudes. If you plan to compare two automobiles, you might want to compare their design, performance, economy, and comfort. If you are writing an essay of several paragraphs, you may want to include both similarities and differences, a more difficult process in a single paragraph because of limitations of space.

1. a comparison or contrast of two employers, two well-known athletes, two political leaders, two musical groups, men's and women's fashions in clothing, two automobiles, a fast food place with an expensive restaurant
2. a comparison or contrast between two attitudes, two conflicting points of view, on one of the following subjects: success, abortion, big-time college athletics, the role of women in society, gun control, motherhood, premarital cohabitation
3. a contrast of the teaching styles of two teachers, the personalities of two friends, a high school class with a college class, urban and rural living, the benefits of general and career education, the values of paying by cash and by installment
4. an analogy between a quarterback on a football team and a general commanding infantry, between an auto mechanic and a physician, the President of the United States and a ship's captain, a train ride and the process of getting an education
5. a contrast between a conservative and a liberal, a neurotic and a psychotic, a socialist and a communist, an enthusiast and a fanatic, a football fan and a tennis fan, a devout person and a pious person
6. a contrast between two qualities: fame and celebrity, wit and humor, intelligence and wisdom, courage and rashness, tolerance and cowardice
7. a contrast between the appearance of a neighborhood, a favorite recreational spot, hometown, and so on as you remember it from childhood and its appearance today

◉ ANALYSIS (DIVISION AND CLASSIFICATION)

Analysis is the process of dividing a whole into its parts to provide better understanding of the whole. It serves a variety of purposes: to inform, persuade, amuse, and entertain. Sometimes it combines two or more of these purposes. A director of marketing, for example, may be given the task of analyzing the potential market for a new product his or her company is thinking of producing. Such an analysis would be intended not only to inform but also, very likely, to persuade the executive officers of the company to proceed with or abandon the project.

Analysis involves both *division,* the separation of a single concept (the American West, for example) into its subunits (geographical regions—Northwest, Southwest, Pacific Coast), and *classification,* the placing of examples of a subject (teachers) into categories that share common characteristics (scholars, entertainers, friendly philosophers). The subjects to be analyzed may be *entities,* that is, structurally complete units; *classes,* collections of things; and *processes* or *sequences of action.*

The writer of the passage below analyzes an entity, the Pine Barrens, by showing us how the quadrants of this heavily wooded area relate to each other spatially.

> From the fire tower on Bear Swamp Hill, in Washington Township, Burlington County, New Jersey, the view extends about twelve miles. To the north, forest land reaches to the horizon. The trees are mainly oaks and pines, and the pines predominate. Occasionally, there are long, dark, serrated stands of Atlantic white cedars, so tall and so closely set that they seem to be spread against the sky on the ridges of hills, when in fact they grow along streams that flow through the forest. To the east, the view is similar, and few people who are not native to the region can discern essential differences from the high cabin of the fire tower, even though one difference is that huge areas out in this direction are covered with dwarf forests, where a man can stand among the trees and see for miles over their uppermost branches. To the south, the view is twice broken slightly—by a lake and by a cranberry bog—but otherwise it, too, goes to the horizon in forest. To the west, pines, oaks, and cedars continue all the way, and the western horizon includes the summit of another hill—Apple Pie Hill—and the outline of another fire tower, from which the view three hundred and sixty degrees around is virtually the same as the view from Bear Swamp Hill, where, in a moment's sweeping glance, a person can see hundreds of square miles of wilderness. The picture of New Jersey that most people hold in their minds is so different from this one that, considered beside it, the Pine Barrens, as they are called, become as incongruous as they are beautiful . . . . (From John McPhee, *The Pine Barrens,* Farrar, Straus and Giroux, Inc., 1967, 1968.)

In the following paragraph the writer analyzes a digital computer, a structural whole, by dividing it into its three parts, subdividing the parts, and providing a brief explanation of the operational process as well.

Most digital computers are structurally organized into three parts: input and output elements, storage elements, and arithmetic and control elements. The input element transfers information external to the computer to the storage element. This information—which may be a program, that is, a predefined sequence of instructions, or data on which the program operates—is fed into the storage unit by means of a card or paper tape reader, a magnetic unit, a disc, or a video terminal. The storage element holds the input information and the intermediate and final results produced during execution of the program. The control element carries out the program instructions and controls the flow of information. All arithmetic and logical operations dictated by the program are performed by the arithmetic element under the supervision of the control element. The final results of these operations are presented through an output device—which may be a card or paper tape punch, a magnetic tape unit, a disc, a printer, or a video terminal.

In this paragraph the writer analyzes a class, Americans, by dividing the class into its sub-classes—Top Out-of-Sight Class; Upper Class; Upper Middle Class; Middle Class; High-, Middle-, and Low-Proletarian; Destitute; and Bottom Out-of-Sight—on the bases of habits and attitudes.

Class is thus defined less by bare income than by constraints and insecurities. It is defined also by habits and attitudes. Take television watching. The Top Out-of-Sight Class doesn't watch at all. It owns the companies and pays others to monitor the thing. It is also entirely devoid of intellectual or even emotional curiosity: it *has* its ideas the way it has its money. The Upper Class does look at television but it prefers Camp offerings, like the films of Jean Harlow or Jon Hall. The Upper Middle Class regards TV as vulgar except for the highminded emissions of National Educational Television, which it watches avidly, especially when, like the Shakespeare series, they are the most incompetently directed and boring. Upper Middle makes a point of forbidding children to watch more than an hour a day and worry a lot about violence in society and sugar in cereal. The Middle Class watches, preferring the more "beautiful" kinds of

non-body-contact sports like tennis or gymnastics or figure-
skating (the music is a redeeming feature here). With High-,
Mid-, and Low-Proles we find heavy viewing of the soaps in the
daytime and rugged body-contact sports (football, hockey, boxing) in the evening. The lower one is located in the Prole classes
the more likely one is to watch "Bowling for Dollars" and
"Wonder Woman" and "The Hulk" and when choosing a game
show to prefer "Joker's Wild" to "The Family Feud," whose
jokes are sometimes incomprehensible. Destitutes and Bottom
Out-of-Sights have in common a problem involving choice. Destitutes usually "own" about three color sets, and the problem is
which three programs to run at once. Bottom Out-of-Sights exercise no choice at all, the decisions being made for them by cor-
rectional or institutional personnel. (From Paul Fussell, "Notes
on Class, *The Boy Scout Handbook and Other Observations,*
Oxford University Press, Inc., 1982.)

An analysis of a process or a sequence of actions divides on the basis
of time. A process is a series of actions repeated in chronological order
for the purpose of producing a product or a desired result, as in the
refining of crude oil to produce gasoline. Narrating the stages of a historical event or the incidents in a story involves an analysis of a sequence of actions. In the latter case the actions are not performed over
again and are not intended to produce any product or result. The following paragraph is a process analysis that explains the steps a British
student must follow in his quest for a university degree.

Earning a university degree in Great Britain is a rigorous,
competitive process. It commonly begins at the age of eleven, or
thereabouts, when elementary children take the "eleven plus"
examination to determine whether they will attend a secondary
modern school, which provides a more comprehensive curriculum, or one of the more select private or public schools, which
emphasize a more academic curriculum for those planning to
enter the university. Between fourteen and sixteen years of age,
students take another examination, a national, public, "O-level"
examination, to earn a certificate that represents the terminal
degree for most, since relatively few go on to the university.
Those intent on university training spend the two years following successful performance on the O-level preparing for the "A-
level" examination. Those passing this examination may enter
the university. At the university the student must pass an examination at the end of his second year to continue on to his third
year, at the end of which he takes a final examination to qualify

for the bachelor's degree. This final examination at Cambridge and Oxford universities is rigorous indeed. In the arts section it usually consists of nine three-hour written examinations plus an oral. The English system, with its examination-oriented tracking process, may seem a bit rigid when compared with the more flexible American system; but it does assure quality in the final product.

The following paragraph analyzes a sequence of actions, Germany's military progress in the first year of World War II.

During the first year of the Second World War, German military forces thrust first to the east, then to the north, and finally to the west. Successful in his attempt to regain the Sudetenland from Czechoslovakia, Hitler demanded that Poland give up the Polish Corridor and Danzig. When it became evident that Poland would not submit to his demand, German troops invaded Poland in September of 1939. German aircraft bombed and strafed Polish military formations and defenseless cities as well. Then mobile armored divisions drove through, encircled, and cut off enemy ground forces. After twenty-seven days Poland capitulated. In April of the following year, the German army occupied Denmark and Norway on the pretext that Britain and France were preparing to attack Russia, Germany's new ally, through the Scandinavian countries. On May 10, 1940, Germany's military juggernaut invaded the Netherlands and Belgium in its drive to conquer France. French defenses proved no match for Hitler's blitzkrieg tactics either, and on June 22, 1940, France was forced to sign an armistice with Germany.

These categories of analysis—the whole, the class, the process, and the sequence of actions—are not always exclusive. In some cases an analysis may involve more than one type of analysis, as in the analysis of the computer (p. 77), which involves both a structure and a process. When analyzing a class or group of things, however, you must make certain that your classification system is logical, that the categories do not overlap. Classifying college students under the headings of the *serious-minded,* the *moderately interested,* the *indifferent,* and the *athlete* is obviously illogical since a student could be classified as an athlete and as serious-minded as well.

Here are additional examples of paragraphs developed by analysis.

Francis Bacon—a famous English lawyer, philosopher, and essayist—won renown for emphasizing the need for verifiable experiment, rather than accepted "truths," as the basis of scientific investigation. He identified four species of "Idols," errors in thinking, which those seeking the truth about the world should avoid: (1) Idols of the Tribe, (2) Idols of the Den, (3) Idols of the Market, and (4) Idols of the Theater. Idols of the Tribe are those bad habits of mind inherent in human nature, the reliance on the senses, for example, as the arbiter of truth, rather than verifiable experimentation. Idols of the Den are the personal prejudices of the individual investigator—the product of his own disposition, education, background—that distort his search for truth. The third species of error, Idols of the Market, are caused by the subjectivity of language, the ambiguities in the meaning of words as well as their misuse. And, finally, Idols of the Theater refer to errors that have "crept into men's minds from the various dogmas of peculiar systems of philosophy. . . ." The most noteworthy examples in Bacon's view were the errors produced by a slavish adherence to the systems of thought of Aristotle and the scholastic philosophers. "For we regard all the systems of philosophy hitherto received or imagined," writes Bacon, "as so many plays brought out and performed, creating fictitious and theatrical worlds."

In this next paragraph the writer uses judgment, comparison, and contrast in her analysis of college students.

In terms of their general attitude toward politics and the world around them, many students can be placed in one of four basic groups: the contented, the rebels, the escapists, and the reformers. Those in the first group pretty much accept their lot. They don't seriously question the political, economic, social, and educational institutions that govern their lives. Of course, they may occasionally complain about the President, a boring part-time job, or a graduation requirement, but they don't worry about changing much. On the other end of the continuum are the rebels. They think the world's a hopeless mess and the only solution a radical restructuring of society. In their view politicians, business leaders, their teachers and parents—the establishment—conspire to prevent a free expression of humanity's inherent goodness; and the solution to all this is a big bonfire. Their motto is "Up against the wall for the oppressors." The third group includes students who want to escape the system. Though they may, and often do, agree with the rebels that the system is hopelessly corrupt, their reaction is flight, not fight—a retreat into an isolated and insulated world of their own pleasures. And, finally, there are those who are concerned about contemporary social issues, who seek

change, but who favor evolutionary rather than revolutionary solutions. They sense that civilized life is not assured, that human
beings and their institutions, though capable of change, are not
changed quickly nor painlessly.

EXERCISE 9

Write a paragraph of 100 to 150 words, or a three paragraph essay, developing by means of analysis one of the following topics. If you are analyzing a
class, remember to divide your subject into three or four subclasses; then
describe and differentiate each subclass from the others and, especially if
you're writing a multiparagraph essay, present vivid examples. One more
point: make certain your subclasses don't overlap.

1. a *process* analysis of any of the following: producing oil from shale; producing electricity from nuclear energy; diamond cutting; sky diving; making a good impression upon a boyfriend or girlfriend or his or her parents;
   operation of a jet engine or a laser beam; reading a textbook or a newspaper; scuba diving; tuning a motorcycle or automobile; making gasohol
2. a *class* analysis of any of the following: teachers, sports fans, wines,
   restaurants, recreational activities, women on the basis of their attitude
   toward the women's liberation movement, neighborhoods, drugs, college
   courses, cigarette smokers, bores, campus Romeos, rock singers, athletes,
   automobile drivers, comedians, parents, coaches, politicians
3. an analysis of a *whole,* a structure: a modern windmill; a diesel engine; a
   modern tank; a character sketch of a friend, describing briefly those characteristics that distinguish him/her as an individual; a limited geographical area—such as a stretch of beach, a mountain scene, a desert scene, a
   campsite, a boulevard scene (Select a specific scene and describe what you
   see from left to right, right to left, near to far, or far to near.)
4. an analysis of a *sequence of actions,* such as a narrative of something of
   interest or importance that happened to you, an important battle of the
   Revolutionary War, Civil War, World War I or II (In the latter consider
   El Alamein, Bastogne, Guadalcanal, the Coral Sea, the D-Day invasion.)

◨ DEFINITION

Definition serves a number of purposes. By identifying precisely the
special characteristics of an idea, an institution, or a group, you can
fix their meaning and significance more firmly in your mind as well
as communicate them to another person. Definition thus serves to
promote clear thinking and writing on the one hand and to facilitate

explanation and persuasion on the other. Many disagreements would never occur if disputants took care to define their terms adequately. Learning to define will also be of practical value to you, since you are likely to be asked to define terms from a variety of disciplines: *capitalism, naturalism, monetarism, osmosis, plasticity, symbolism,* and so forth.

You can define in a number of ways. One is to use *examples,* illustrative instances:

> An example of a crustacean is a lobster.

This method is useful when writers can assume that readers know something of the meaning of the term: the examples simply provide further clarification. But when the reader lacks this knowledge, this method is rather confusing.

A second method defines by means of a *synonym,* a word with a similar meaning:

> Pejorative means disparaging, derogatory.
> An efflux is an emanation.

This method is helpful if the synonym clarifies the original term, not if the synonym is likely to be more abstract or general.

> Flagitious means heinous.

A third method, the *historical* or *etymological* method of definition [*dictionary type definition*] clarifies the meaning of a word by revealing its origin and the changes in meaning it has undergone.

> The word *vulgar* derives from a Middle English word based on the medieval Latin word *vulgaris,* from *vulgus,* the common people. In the 15th century it denoted the common or usual language of a country, the vernacular. By the 16th century it referred to persons belonging to the ordinary or common class, especially the ignorant or uneducated. The term has continued its pejorative decline over the past two hundred years, and today it denotes a person with a common or offensively mean character, one who is rude, coarse, lacking refinement or good taste.

Another method, the *formal* definition, defines a term by placing its referent in a general class and then differentiating it from other members of the same class:

Term		Class	Differentiating Detail
A marsupial	*is*	an animal	that shelters its young in an external abdominal pouch containing mammary glands.
A hypothesis	*is*	an inference	that accounts, within the framework of a theory, for a set of facts and that can be used as the basis of action or further investigation.
Serendipity	*is*	the faculty	of stumbling upon fortunate, unexpected discoveries.

Defining formally is an exacting process. You must observe several precautions to avoid inadequate and fallacious definitions:

1. The term to be defined should be specially placed in a class. Statements that appear to be analytic definitions are sometimes simply descriptions of the object:

   A steel mill is a noisy, smoky place with tall chimneys.

   and sometimes they are interpretations of it:

   Home is where the heart is.

   In classifying an object, avoid using "is where" or "is when." *Where* signifies location, *when* signifies time, and neither represents a class of things:

   Original   Democracy is when the people rule themselves.
   Revision   Democracy is a form of government in which the people rule themselves.

2. The general class into which the term is placed should not be too extensive. Defining a telescope as something that helps the eye to see distant objects is not very helpful: the class of things is simply too broad. It could include, for example, binoculars, eyeglasses, magnifying glasses, and many others. In general, the narrower the

classification, the clearer the definition. A telescope would thus be more precisely defined as an optical instrument, consisting of parts that fit and slide one within another, that enlarges the image of a distant object.

3. The definition should not repeat the name of the thing to be defined or a derivative of it:

> Certified mail is mail that has been certified.

This definition still leaves the reader uninformed as to what "certified mail" means. Definitions that repeat the term to be defined, as in the example above, are called *circular* definitions, for they lead the reader back to where he started. A better definition would be:

> Certified mail is first class mail for which proof of delivery is secured but for which no indemnity value is claimed.

4. The differentiation should be sufficient to distinguish the term clearly from other members of the class:

> Buddhism is a religion of Asia.

This definition does not supply enough information to distinguish Buddhism from Mohammedanism, Hinduism, or Christianity, all religions of Asia. With the necessary information added, the meaning is clearer:

> Buddhism is a religion of central and eastern Asia derived from the teachings of Gautama Buddha, who taught that suffering is inherent in life and that one can escape from it into *nirvana*—a state of spiritual peace—through mental and moral self-purification.

5. The definition should not be expressed in highly technical, obscure language. Dr. Samuel Johnson's definition of *network* as "anything reticulated or decussated, at equal distances with interstices between the intersections" is accurate but complex. The definition of *network* as a fabric or structure of threads, cords, or wires that cross each other at regular intervals and are knotted or secured at the crossings, as defined in *Webster's Third International Dictionary,* is much simpler and clearer.

Observing these precautions will improve the clarity and precision of your formal definitions. There are times, however, when you will have to write more than a single sentence, a *minimum* definition, to define a term adequately. An explanation of Mohammedanism, freedom, or liberalism would obviously require more than one sentence. In developing a paragraph by means of definition, it is a good idea to start with a minimum definition as a basis and then use examples, comparisons, contrasts, historical information, and so forth, to support and extend your definition. Definitions that are developed in one or more paragraphs are called *extended* definitions.

The following paragraph offers a definition of a hypochondriac.

Minimum   A hypochondriac is a person who is preoccupied
Definition   with his imaginary ill health. He is constantly fearful of
                   developing some dreadful disease, or he is convinced he
                   already has one, though medical examination reveals
Differentiating his fears to be groundless. A typical hypochondriac
Detail   does not suffer from deep dejection, from melancholia.
                   He doesn't try to hide his concern. On the contrary, he
                   loves to talk about his diseases, his colds, the gory de-
                   tails of an operation, his close calls with death. My un-
Use of   cle Cedric is a perfect example. No conversation with
Example   him is complete without a detailed description of his
                   past illnesses, an analysis of some new pills he is taking,
                   and an update of his current condition. His physical
                   ailments are clearly very dear to his heart, his traumatic
                   experiences almost sacred. He derives his deepest
                   pleasure, however, when his listeners catch their breath
                   when he starts slumping in his easy chair and sliding to
                   the floor in an apparent physical collapse.

In the paragraph below Cardinal Newman defines a university. The opening sentence provides a minimum definition of the term, the body of the paragraph differentiating detail, and the conclusion a repeat of the minimum definition.

                   If I were asked to describe as briefly and popularly as
                   I could, what a University was, I should draw my answer
Minimum   from its ancient designation of a *Studium Generale*
Definition   or "School of Universal Learning." This description

Differentiating Detail implies the assemblage of strangers from all parts in one spot—*from all parts;* else, how will you find professors and students for every department of knowledge? and *in one spot;* else, how can there be any school at all? Accordingly, in its simple and rudimentary form, it is a school of knowledge of every kind, consisting of teachers and learners from every quarter. Many things are requisite to complete and satisfy the idea embodied in this description; but such as this a University seems to

Minimum Definition Repeated be in its essence, a place for the communication and circulation of thought, by means of personal intercourse, through a wide extent of country. (From John Henry Newman, "What Is a University," *The Rise and Progress of Universities.*)

A psychiatrist, Ian Stevenson, defines prejudice in this paragraph. A minimum definition of the term appears in the third sentence.

Differentiating Detail Prejudiced thinking is rarely, probably never, confined to any one subject. Those prejudiced against one group of people are nearly always prejudiced against

Minimum Definition others. Prejudice, then, could said to be a disorder of thinking: a prejudiced person makes faulty generalizations by applying to a whole group what he has learned

Differentiating Detail from one or a few of its members. Sometimes, he doesn't even draw on his own experiences but bases his attitudes on what he has heard from others. Then he behaves toward a whole group as if there were no indi-

Analogy vidual differences among its members. Few people would throw out a whole box of strawberries because they found one or two bad berries at the top—yet this is the way prejudiced people think and act. (From Ian Stevenson, "People Aren't Born Prejudiced," *Parents' Magazine,* February, 1960.)

In this paragraph the author defines *euphemism*. His first sentence provides a minimum definition, which he amplifies by historical reference, judgment, and example in the sentences that follow.

Minimum Definition From a Greek word meaning "to use words of good omen," euphemism is the substitution of a pleasant term for a blunt one—telling it like it isn't. Euphemism

Historical
Reference

Judgment

Example

has probably existed since the beginning of language. As long as there have been things of which men thought the less said the better, there have been better ways of saying less. In everyday conversation the euphemism is, at worst, a necessary evil; at its best, it is a handy verbal tool to avoid making enemies needlessly, or shocking friends. Language purists and the blunt-spoken may wince when a young woman at a party coyly asks for direction to "the powder room," but to most people this kind of familiar euphemism is probably no more harmful or annoying than, say, a split infinitive. [From "Euphemism," *Time, The Weekly Newsmagazine,* 1969.]

EXERCISE 10

A. In the blanks below indicate which of the following methods is used to define: (1) example, (2) synonym, (3) formal. Write the number of your answer in the blank to the right of the sentence.

1. *Ubiquitous* means omnipresent.   *2*

2. Kangaroos, wombats, opossums, koalas—all are examples of marsupials.   *1*

3. A debenture is an unsecured bond issued by a corporation or governmental agency backed only by the credit standing of the issuer and often convertible into common stock.   *3*

4. John Milton's *Paradise Lost* illustrates the literary epic.   *historical* *1*

5. The mistral is a cold, dry, northerly wind blowing down from the French Alps through the Rhone Valley and the southern regions of France toward the Mediterranean.   *3*

B. Some of the definitions given below violate the conditions necessary for a minimum formal definition. Mark the definition as follows: (1) if the term is not specifically placed in a class, (2) if the class is too large, (3) if the term is not sufficiently differentiated from other members of the class, (4) if the term to be defined, or a derivative of it, is repeated in the definition, (5) if the definition is expressed in highly technical language, (6) if the definition seems clear and sound.

1. Platonic love derives from the teachings of Plato.   *4*

2. Islam is a religion based on the teachings of the prophet Mohammed set forth in the Koran and the Sunna and which inculcates the belief in one God (Allah) and in Paradise and Hell.

3. A jackhammer is a thing which is used to dig up concrete and asphalt.

4. A *carpetbagger* went to the South after the Civil War to seek his own political or financial advantage.

5. A paranoiac has a persecution complex.   *1*

6. Louisiana Cajun is a unique American dialect.   *3*

7. The psychological novel is a work of prose fiction that places more than the usual amount of emphasis on interior characterization, on the mental states, motives, and circumstances

88

of characters, which result from and develop the external
action.

8. Criticism of a literary work may focus on the reader, the
work itself, or the writer.

9. A *raphe* is the part of the funiculus of an anatropous ovule
adnate to the integument, forming a ridge along the body of
the ovule that provides a diagnostic character in the various
seeds.

10. A Marxist is one who believes in and promulgates the ideas of
Karl Marx.

C. Rewrite each of the following definitions in one sentence making them
more precise or more informative. Be prepared to explain why the original version is inadequate.

1. *Chutzpah* is a Yiddish slang term with both positive and negative associations.

_____

_____

_____

2. *Connoisseur* derives from a French word meaning to know.

_____

_____

_____

3. An *altruist* is one who does good for others.

_____

_____

_____

D. Reread the three paragraphs defining the terms *hypochondriac, university,*
and *euphemism* (pp. 85–87). For each definition list (1) the *general class*
into which the referent of the term has been placed and (2) the *differentiating detail* that distinguishes the term from other members of the class.

89

Term	Class	Differentiating Detail
1. A hypochondriac	_____	_____
		_____
		_____
2. A university	_____	_____
		_____
		_____
3. Euphemism	_____	_____
		_____
		_____

E. Write a paragraph definition of any of the following terms. Begin with a minimum definition (term, class, differentiating detail) as your topic sentence and use whatever kind of support you wish—facts, analysis, illustration, analogy, judgment—to develop your definition.

1. a classic
2. a klutz, a mature person, a successful person
3. a particular breed of animal—Arabian horse, Hungarian puli dog, river otter, and so on
4. a neurotic, a psychotic, a paranoiac
5. a liberal, a conservative, a reactionary, a fundamentalist
6. prejudice, fanaticism, sentimentality
7. a gourmet, a gourmand, a glutton
8. an idealist, a pragmatist, a fatalist, a stoic, a cynic, an existentialist
9. a boor, a bore
10. a connoisseur, a dilettante
11. a male chauvinist, a *macho* man
12. a demagogue, a patriot, a racist, a fascist
13. wisdom, intelligence, wit, humor
14. civil disobedience, charity
15. a sportsperson, an amateur
16. a communist, a socialist
17. a liberated woman
18. a scholar, a swinger, an intellectual
19. chutzpah, pizzazz

90

20. a snob
21. a good or bad boss
22. a current slang term: e.g., *spacey, flaky, kinky, gross, letting it all hang out, winging it, bulletproof,* . . . (or any of your own choice)
23. a permissive parent

F. Write a paragraph definition of one of the following terms using the historical or etymological method: (Consult the *Oxford English Dictionary*)

1. villain	2. sinister	3. assassin	4. yahoo
5. limousine	6. boycott	7. mistress	8. maverick
9. liberal	10. serendipity		

or noun type word

G. Write a three-paragraph definition of one of the following words. In your opening paragraph provide a formal definition of the term and some mention of origin and historical background. In your second and third paragraphs use contrast (with a term similar in meaning), analysis, exemplification, or analogy to provide further development.

1. fanaticism	2. charity	3. liberal	4. agnostic
5. patriotism	6. puritanical	7. devout	8. charisma
9. success	10. classic	11. An English gentleman	

destr

◨ COMBINATION OF METHODS

A good many, if not most, of the paragraphs you write will use a combination of the methods of paragraph development that have been explained and illustrated in this chapter. If you are developing a paragraph by means of examples, then statistics and other factual detail may strengthen your point. If your controlling idea requires definition for support, you will probably find comparison and contrast useful in providing additional clarification.

Here are two selections that combine several methods in their development. In the first Marie Winn presents an opinion about the television addict. She uses illustration, comparison, judgment, analogy, and cause and effect patterns in support of her main idea.

Examples   The self-confessed television addict often feels he "ought" to do other things—but the fact that he doesn't read and doesn't plant his garden or sew or crochet or play games or have conversations means that those activities are no longer as desirable as television

Comparison   viewing. In a way a heavy viewer's life is as unbalanced by his television "habit" as a drug addict's or an alco-

Analogy   holic's. He is living in a holding pattern, as it were, passing up the activities that lead to growth or develop-

Judgment   ment or a sense of accomplishment. This is one reason people talk about their television viewing so ruefully,

Cause and   so apologetically. They are aware that it is an unpro-
Effect   ductive experience, that almost any other endeavor is more worthwhile by any human measure. (From Marie Winn, "TV Addiction," *The Plug-in Drug: Television, Children, and Family.* Viking Penguin, Penguin Books, USA, Inc.)

This next selection uses definition, exemplification, and anecdote:

Definition   Blue is the color of royalty and quality. A *blueblood* is a person of noble or aristocratic descent. A *blue chip* is the poker chip of highest value, the stock that is the safest investment. The *blue ribbon* is the prize given the winner of the horse race, the dog show, the pie-baking contest.

Example

In England, the blue ribbon is worn by members of the Order of the Garter, the highest order of knighthood. In France, it is worn by Knights of the Holy Ghost. In France, of course, a blue ribbon is not called a blue ribbon. It's a *cordon bleu,* which gets us, in a roundabout way, to a question posed by a reader: "Why is a great chef known as a *cordon bleu?*"

Anecdote

One story has it that in days gone by those Knights of the Holy Ghost were fellows who loved to eat. If they were served a wonderful meal, so the story goes, they told the chef that it was a blue-ribbon meal, *un repas de cordon bleu.* At any rate, *cordon bleu* eventually attached itself to chefs, first in a jocular way and later in quite a serious way. So today, a distinguished chef is known as a *cordon bleu* or a *cordon bleu* chef. . . . [From Michael Gartner, "Words' Worth," *Los Angeles Times,* May 10, 1981.]

EXERCISE 11

A. In the space provided indicate a suitable method, or methods, of developing the controlling idea in each of the following topic sentences.

1. One sees a variety of clothing fashions on a college campus.

   _____

2. Professional athletes in the United States are well paid.

   _____

3. Students who work while attending college realize several benefits.

   _____

4. Abraham Lincoln was a very effective President.

   _____

5. The epithets *racist* and *fascist* are often misused in political discussions today.

   _____

6. Cleaning up oil spills in the ocean is an expensive operation.

   _____

7. Politics and warfare are alike in some respects.

   _____

8. Albert Camus' *The Stranger* reveals the writer's existential principles.

   _____

9. Lexicographers follow a fixed process in determining the meaning of a word.

   _____

   _____

94

10. The structure of atoms is like a miniature solar system.

   _____

11. There are three kinds of bookworms.

   _____

12. Insanity is not always easy to define or identify.

   _____

13. Snorkeling in the Caribbean is an exhilarating experience.

   _____

14. The similarities between Saddam Hussein and Joseph Stalin are striking.

   _____

15. Carried to the extreme, tolerance becomes cowardice.

   _____

16. The "perched" villages of southeastern France usually have three distinct parts: at the top of the hill the old quarter, clustered around a modest chateau; down the slope the newer houses; and farther down still the newest houses spreading out into the valley.

   _____

17. The American wine industry has grown markedly within the past thirty years.

   _____

18. The modern American fighter plane is a very destructive weapon.

   _____

19. Gene Kelly and Fred Astaire were both excellent dancers, but their styles contrasted sharply.

   _____

95

20. Bull McCrunch and Nigel Fitzhugh differed in their approach to sports.

_____

B. For each of the topics listed below, write three topic sentences that could
   be used as the basis of a paragraph.

  1. safety features in the modern automobile

   _____

   _____

   _____

  2. a friend with an unusual trait

   _____

   _____

   _____

  3. solar-powered automobiles

   _____

   _____

   _____

  4. robotics in the manufacturing industry

   _____

   _____

   _____

  5. the range of styles among popular musical groups

   _____

   _____

   _____

96

C. Use the following sentences to compose a paragraph on gobbledygook. Do not begin with the topic sentence, but lead into it. (See pp. 37–38)

1. Governmental gobbledygook describes poor and ill-fed people as having "inadequate financial resources to purchase the products of agricultural communities and industrial establishments. . . ."
2. In simpler terms, you can charge your dental bills to the Public Health Service.
3. Those who wish to communicate with others should aim to express, not impress.
4. It seems to be especially difficult for Washington bureaucrats.
5. Interoffice memos, particularly in the defense industries, are loaded with phrases like "balanced logistical contingency," "integrated organizational mobility," and "parallel policy options."
6. Legal documents are larded with such phrases as "party of the first part," "cease and desist," "give and convey," "irrelevant, incompetent, and immaterial."
7. The following is fairly typical of insurance policy prose: "This policy is issued in consideration of the statements in the application of this policy and the payment in advance of the first premium stated in the schedule which includes premiums for attached riders, if any. . . ."
8. The ability to write clear, concise, uncluttered prose is not common.
9. Maury Maverick, a Congressman from Texas, invented a term, "gobbledygook," to describe the kind of pretentious, long-winded, poly-syllabic language found in government documents and memos.
10. Stuart Chase cites another instance, a government department announcement on dental bills: "Voucherable expenditures necessary to provide adequate dental treatment required as adjunct to medical treatment being rendered a pay patient in in-patient status may be incurred at the expense of the Public Health Service."[5]
11. Gobbledygook also flourishes in law, business, and industry.
12. Though gobbledygook is a pervasive disease of language, it can, fortunately, be eradicated by careful elimination of the excess baggage, the clutter, the pretense of long-winded prose.

D. Analyze the following paragraphs for fullness of development. Explain how those paragraphs you believe to be underdeveloped could be improved.

1. The college freshman faces a number of problems that he or she must solve to succeed in college. The first concerns study habits. He or she must be able to concentrate seriously on the material presented in class, take notes on important points in the lecture or discussion, and prepare

---

[5] *The Power of Words,* Harcourt Brace Jovanovich, 1953.

out-of-class assignments on time. He or she must budget time carefully so that he or she doesn't concentrate on one or two subjects to the detriment of the others. Another problem concerns extra-curricular activities. They must not be neglected either.

2. The rising divorce statistics of recent years have prompted the suggestion that the traditional lifetime marriage contract be replaced by a short-term, renewable contract. This solution would, however, aggravate, not improve the situation, for it would create serious complications in the lives of the children of such a marriage and undermine the emotional relationship of the husband and wife. Those who support renewable, short-term marriages claim that traditional marriage ties are unrealistic because they seek to bind a couple together for life, a chancy proposition in a fast-moving world. But loosening those ties through short-term marriages will simply increase marital instability. In a successful marriage there must be time for the partners to adjust to each other's temperament. A short-term marriage decreases the chance of a husband and wife's working out difficult problems by giving each partner an easy way out. Moreover, a happy marriage is not likely to result if one partner worries about whether the other will renew the contract.

3. The foreign aid program of the United States needs to be continued for pragmatic as well as moral reasons. American economic aid helps under-developed countries get on their feet, develop their manufacturing and agriculture bases, and develop foreign markets for their products. As they develop their economies, they will be in a position to reduce their debt to United States banks and import more American products, thus stimulating American industry as well. This reciprocal economic benefit will, moreover, help to maintain a peaceful, stable political environment in underdeveloped countries, which, in turn, further their economic development.

4. After years of neglect, the study of foreign languages is beginning to gain more attention again, and a good thing, too. To begin with, anyone wishing to work abroad for an American company should know more than a smattering of phrases if he hopes to communicate successfully with foreigners in a business or social context. German, Dutch, or French businessmen may speak English, but they are more responsive to Americans who can readily communicate with them in their own language. Travelers will also benefit from language study.

5. I have been observing cigarette smokers for some time now, and I have tried to classify the different types. First, there is the puffer. By holding the cigarette between the forefinger and the thumb, he avoids nicotine stains on his hands. His little finger is usually crooked, and the hand is held perfectly still to avoid dropping hot ashes on himself or the floor. Next is the dragon. This smoker is completely different from the puffer. He has no particular grip for holding the cigarette. He

98

takes large drags, one after another, which tend to form a rather long hot ash on the end of the cigarette. He then inhales deep into the lungs and exhales quietly and quickly through his nostrils, giving the impression of a fire-breathing dragon. Last, there is the whoosher. He has, essentially, the same characteristics as the dragon, except that the whoosher spews smoke out in all directions, the sound reminiscent of wind escaping from a wind tunnel. These three types, and others, should quit smoking before they impair their health. They would probably enjoy life more—and longer.

E. As a preliminary suggestion to help you develop a paragraph by means of examples (pp. 54–57), you were advised to work up an outline, transforming the topic into a specific topic sentence, jotting down details as they entered your mind, eliminating irrelevant items, and so forth. This procedure is helpful, for it demands that you think about your subject and get your thoughts in order before you begin to write, thus ensuring a more unified paragraph. Another useful technique, one proposed by Robert Louis Stevenson, involves imitation. Stevenson urged the young writer to imitate a variety of writing styles. Through such imitation, he argued, the writer would gradually begin to develop a richer style of his own. One advantage of this method is that it offers the writer a model, a standard for comparison—a decided asset to an inexperienced writer, who, though he may have a fairly good idea of what he wants to say, begins to flounder because he cannot find the right words, phrases, or sentences in which to express it.

After selecting a passage to imitate, Stevenson read the selection carefully, concentrating on its rhythm and structure. When he had fixed this movement and pattern in his mind, he selected an appropriate subject and tried to express his own thoughts in a similar style. Apply this procedure in this exercise. Read the model paragraph carefully, noting the placement of the topic sentence, the kinds of detail used to support the controlling idea, and the wording and sentence structure. Then choose one of the topics listed and compose your own paragraph, imitating the general pattern and style of the model.

The topic sentence in this paragraph is the second sentence, which asserts the value of studying the liberal arts and informs the reader that the primary detail will consist of reasons. (The first sentence is a lead-in sentence.) Sentences 3, 5, 7, and 10 supply these reasons. Sentences 4, 6, 8, 9, and 11 provide secondary support. You need not try to imitate exactly the structure or wording of each sentence, but copy the general plan of the paragraph and use expressions such as *in recent years, but reasons for, for one thing, another reason, a third value,* and *but perhaps the strongest argument* to introduce your reasons. Round off your paragraph with an appropriate quoted passage.

99

(1) *In recent years* increasing numbers of college students have abandoned the liberal arts to concentrate on the "useful" arts, on vocationally related subjects. (2) This preference for the utilitarian has strong support among those who believe the primary function of colleges and universities is to prepare students to earn a living in the "real world," *but reasons for* the study of the liberal arts are not hard to find. (3) *For one thing* the liberal arts—literature, languages, philosophy, history, and abstract science—widen students' range of intellectual interests. (4) They introduce students to the network of important philosophic and religious ideas, to significant historical events, and to the development and achievement in science that have shaped man's life and stimulated his mind for centuries. (5) *Another reason* is that liberal arts studies help students learn to see themselves in their proper perspective apart from purely personal concerns. (6) A narrow emphasis on the utilitarian, on technical subjects, on the other hand, ignores the need to train a person's purposes as well as his skills, to develop in him an understanding of and sympathy with other people's, other societies' struggles to achieve fulfillment in life. (7) *A third value* in the study of the liberal arts concerns leisure time. (8) Those whose mental horizons, whose intellectual interests have been broadened have a wider range of activities to choose from to entertain themselves away from work. (9) The enormous increase in leisure time has improved the quality of life for many, but it can be tedious for those without intelligent interests and activities, for those whose only recreation is passively watching others perform. (10) *But perhaps the strongest argument* for the liberal arts is that they promote a contemplative habit of mind that can help one achieve emotional and mental balance in a confusing, dangerous world. (11) As Bertrand Russell reminds us, "A habit of finding pleasure in thought rather than action is a safeguard against unwisdom . . . a means of preserving serenity in misfortune and peace of mind among worries."[6]

---

[6] "Useless Knowledge," *In Praise of Idleness and Other Essays,* George Allen and Unwin Hyman, Ltd., 1935.

100

TOPICS

1. one year of governmental service for 18-year-olds, bilingual education, the value of a college education, the virtues (or vices) of grading
2. population growth, drilling for oil in coastal waters
3. natural gas as an automotive fuel, building a "Star Wars" strategic defense capability against a missile attack
4. a favorite recreational activity: board surfing, wind surfing, hang gliding, skydiving, cycling, weight lifting, scuba diving, sailing, etc.
5. owning a van, motorcycle, bicycle, sports car, etc.; the value of owning a personal computer; motorcycle racing across the desert
6. prohibiting smoking in airplanes, public buildings, etc.; fighting pollution with a gasoline tax; toll roads as an alternative to tax-supported freeways
7. restricting imports of foreign steel, textiles, automobiles, etc., to force foreign countries to open their markets; economic assistance for the republics of the former Soviet Union
8. logging of old redwood forests, protecting whales (or any other endangered species), a political leader you admire
9. limiting terms of state and national legislators, the influence of lobbyists on legislators
10. identifying AIDS carriers, investing in the stock market, animal rights

Bear in mind that this assignment asks you to provide *reasons* to support your controlling idea. You must explain *why* drilling for oil in coastal waters is beneficial or harmful, *why* one should or should not own a computer, *why* the whale needs protection. Reasons are judgments, opinions. (See pp. 62–66.) Although you may already have opinions on the subject, investigate your subject by consulting a reference work. This research will strengthen your understanding of the subject, give additional supporting reasons for your controlling idea, and, of course, provide a quoted passage to reinforce your final reason. It will also provide relevant secondary detail.

In connection with your library research, fill in the reference sheet. It will serve as a rudimentary outline for your paragraph. The topic sentence on this sheet is the tentative topic sentence for the paragraph you will write. Make certain that each of the four items is a reason that directly supports the controlling idea. The fourth item should contain a quoted passage.

101

Reference Sheet for Exercise 11E

Author ————————————————————————————————

Title of magazine article or book chapter ——————————————————

——

Title of magazine or book ————————————————————————

Date of publication ———————— Volume ———————— Page numbers ————————

Tentative topic sentence: ————————————————————————

——

——

Reasons:

1. ———————————————————————————————————

——

2. ———————————————————————————————————

——

3. ———————————————————————————————————

——

4. (Include a quoted passage) ———————————————————————

——

102

◪ SUMMARY

Good paragraphs must be adequately developed. You should therefore take special care to see that your paragraphs contain sufficient supporting material to explain clearly and fully your topic statement. There are a number of ways to to this: (1) use *illustrative detail* — examples, illustrations, anecdotes—when you can clarify by pointing to a particular incident, a concrete phenomenon; (2) use *facts* and *statistics* when verifiable detail is required to substantiate your point; (3) use *comparison* and *contrast* when you can explain your subject best by noting how it is similar to or different from another object or situation; (4) use *analysis* when your subject lends itself naturally to subdivision; (5) use *definition* when your purpose requires the establishment of the meaning of a term; and (6) use a *combination* of any of these methods whenever you need or desire a variety of supporting material.

CHAPTER

Coherence

Clear, readable paragraphs must be coherent as well as unified and well developed. Their sentences must not only adequately develop a controlling idea but they also must link together smoothly. Each sentence should lead into the next so that the reader can easily follow the progression of thought. To achieve this orderly progression, you must arrange your material in some logical sequence and provide connecting links between sentences. + Paragraphs)

To help your reader understand your meaning quickly and easily, you must take special care with this first task, the proper ordering of ideas. In the following paragraph, for example, the lack of an orderly grouping of the sentences disrupts the continuity.

(1) The dramatic increase in violent crime in southern California in recent years—in particular the senseless, random killings that have occurred in broad daylight in affluent communities— has angered citizens and government officials alike. (2) Everyone wants the slaughter stopped, but before solutions can be found and implemented, the nature of the violence must be understood. (3) A recent California Department of Justice study provides this kind of information in its analysis of the victims, the perpetrators of violence, the weapons used, and the judicial treatment of criminal defendants.[1] (4) These facts do not by themselves point the way to a solution, but any proposed solution that ignores, for example, the prominence of the handgun or the violence from which minorities suffer, is bound to fail. (5) The perpetrators of the violence also are likely to come from minority communities: of those arrested for murder, 71 percent were from minority groups; 29 percent were white. (6) Though members of minorities are often thought to suffer most in the dispensation of criminal justice, the report reveals that race is not a significant factor. (7) Of those charged in court with murder, 77 percent of the whites charged were convicted, Blacks at a rate of 76 percent,

[1] John Van de Kamp, "The Slaughter Statistics: Working Together for a Better Tomorrow," *Los Angeles Times,* December 31, 1980.

Mexican-Americans at a rate of 74 percent. (8) The majority of the victims were from minority communities: 62 percent were Black, Mexican-American, or from other nonwhite minorities; 38 percent were white. (9) The most commonly used weapon in killings was the gun, the handgun in particular, which was used in about 75 percent of the murders committed by firearms.

This paragraph contains enough detail to support its controlling idea, but the sentences are not well ordered. The first sentence provides an introduction to the controlling idea, which is expressed in the next two sentences: the nature of criminal violence must be understood—in terms of its victims, the perpetrators, the weapons used, and the judicial treatment of those charged—before solutions can be implemented. The fourth sentence, however, is a conclusion, a summing up, and should be placed at the end of the paragraph. The fifth sentence begins the analysis, but it focuses on perpetrators rather than victims, as it should, because of the order of items in the topic sentence. The subjects of the succeeding sentences are also not presented in the order in which they were originally presented. The paragraph would have been more coherent if the detail had been discussed in the proper order. In particular, the judicial treatment of criminal defendants should be left to the end since it is the most emotionally charged of the four subjects and deserves such emphasis. As mentioned, the fourth sentence rounds out the paragraph and should appear last. Notice how the coherence of the paragraph is strengthened when the sentences are grouped more logically.

The dramatic increase in violent crime in southern California in recent years—in particular the senseless, random killings that have occurred in broad daylight in affluent communities—has angered citizens and government officials alike. Everyone wants the slaughter stopped, but before solutions can be found and implemented, the nature of the violence must be understood. A recent California Department of Justice study provides this kind of information in its analysis of the victims, the perpetrators of violence, the weapons used, and the judicial treatment of criminal defendants. The majority of the victims were from minority communities: 62 percent were Black, Mexican-American, or from other nonwhite minorities; 38 percent were white. The perpetrators of the violence also are likely to come from minority communities: of those arrested for murder, 71 percent were from minority groups; 29 percent were white. The most commonly used weapon in killings was the gun, the handgun in particular, which was used in about 75 percent of the murders committed by firearms. Though members of minorities are often thought to suffer most in the dispensation of criminal justice, the report reveals that race is not a significant factor. Of those charged in court with murder, 77 percent of the whites charged were convicted, blacks at a rate of 76 percent, Mexican-Americans at a rate of 74 percent. These facts do not by themselves point the way to a solution, but any proposed solution that ignores, for example, the prominence of the handgun or the violence from which minorities suffer is bound to fail.

◼ ORDERING DETAIL

If your paragraphs are to be coherent, you must first arrange your materials in a reasonable, consistent order. The kind of order you use will depend on your purpose and the nature of your materials. When you wish to narrate an experience, describe an event, or present the steps of a process, you should normally order your detail on the basis of time. When you wish to describe something other than a process or an event—a landscape, a person, the structure of an atom, for example—you should organize your detail in terms of its spatial relationships. And when you wish to explain an idea or defend an opinion, you should arrange your detail in a logical order that effectively presents the continuity of ideas from sentence to sentence. These three methods of ordering detail are somewhat arbitrary. The controlling idea of a paragraph explaining or defending an idea, for example, may employ a spatial or chronological analysis. A narrative paragraph may include a description of items in terms of their spatial relationships as well as their occurrence in time. Nonetheless, these methods do provide a convenient illustration of common patterns of ordering sentences in a paragraph. In the discussion that follows we shall explain and illustrate these methods in greater detail.

Time

Arranging the detail of a paragraph in chronological order is an effective method of describing historical events. The writer of the following paragraph groups his detail in this manner as he briefly reconstructs the history of the Donner Party.

> The Donner Party—to summarize briefly—was formed from family groups of other emigrant parties in July, 1846, and set out by themselves from Little Sandy Creek, in what is now Wyoming, to reach California by the so-called Hastings Route. They lost

much time, found the gateway to California blocked by snow, built cabins to winter it out, and ran short of food. Soon they were snowed in deeply, and began to die of starvation. A few escaped across the mountains on improvised snowshoes. Others were saved by the heroic work of rescue parties from the settlements in California. As the result of hardships the morale of the party degenerated to the point of inhumanity, cannibalism, and possibly murder. Of 89 people—men, women, and children—involved with the misfortunes of the party, 47 survived, and 42 perished. (From George Stewart, "The Smart Ones Got Through," *American Heritage,* June, 1955, p. 61.)

Space

The details of a paragraph describing an object are arranged spatially to give the reader a clear picture of the object described. In this paragraph Isak Dinesen describes a stretch of African landscape seen from the Ngong Hills, first to the south, then to the east and north, and finally to the west.

> From the Ngong Hills you have a unique view, you see to the South that vast plains of the great game-country that stretches all the way to Kilimanjaro; to the East and North the park-like country of the foot-hills with the forest behind them, and the undulating land of the Kikuyu-Reserve, which extends to Mount Kenya a hundred miles away—a mosaic of little square maize-fields, banana-groves and grass-land, with here and there the blue smoke from a native village, a small cluster of peaked mole-casts. But towards the West, deep down, lies the dry, moon-like landscape of the African low country. The brown desert is irregularly dotted with the little marks of the thorn-bushes, the winding river-beds are drawn up with crooked dark-green trails; those are the woods of the mighty, wide-branching Mimosa-trees, with thorns like spikes; the cactus grows here, and here is the home of the Giraffe and the Rhino. [From *Out of Africa,* Random House, 1937, 1952, pp. 5–6.]

Continuity of Idea

The details of a paragraph intended to explain or persuade can be grouped in a number of patterns. The most frequently used are the *inductive,* the *deductive,* and the *climactic.* Induction is a process of reasoning in which one proceeds from an examination of particular facts to the formulation of an inference to account for them. An inductive paragraph often ends with a topic sentence. When writers think their readers may resist the point they wish to make, they often use an inductive order to present their facts, illustrations, and definitions before their conclusion.

In the following paragraph Francis Parkman reserves his main point for the last sentence after he has presented the concrete detail that illustrates it.

> The face of the country was dotted far and wide with countless hundreds of buffalo. They trooped along in files and columns, bulls, cows, and calves, on the green faces of the declivities in front. They scrambled away over the hills to the right and left; and far off, the pale blue swells in the extreme distance were dotted with innumerable specks. Sometimes I surprised shaggy old bulls grazing alone, or sleeping behind the ridges I ascended. They would leap up at my approach, stare stupidly at me through their tangled manes, and then gallop heavily away. The antelope were very numerous; and as they are always bold when in the neighborhood of buffalo, they would approach to look at me, gaze intently with their great round eyes, then suddenly leap aside, and stretch lightly away over the prairie, as swiftly as a racehorse. Squalid, ruffian-like wolves sneaked through the hollows and sandy ravines. Several times I passed through villages of prairie dogs, who sat, each at the mouth of his burrow, holding his paws before him in a supplicating attitude, and yelping away most vehemently, whisking his little tail with every squeaking cry he uttered. Prairie dogs are not fastidious in their choice of companions; various long checkered snakes were sunning themselves in the midst of the village, and demure little gray owls, with a large white ring around each eye, were perched side by side with the rightful inhabitants. The prairie teemed with life.

Deduction is a process of reasoning that proceeds from a generalization to a conclusion derived from that generalization. A paragraph in which the materials have been arranged deductively thus begins with the topic statement followed by the detail in support of this statement. The following paragraph illustrates the deductive order of development:

> Expressing one's thoughts is one skill that the school can easily teach, especially to people born without natural writing or

speaking talent. Many other skills can be learned later—in this country there are literally thousands of places that offer training to adult people at work. But the foundations for skill in expression have to be laid early: an interest in and an ear for language; experience in organizing ideas and data, in brushing aside the irrelevant, in wedding outward form and inner content into one structure; and above all, the habit of verbal expression. If you do not lay those foundations during your school years, you may never have an opportunity again. [From Peter Drucker, "How to Be an Employee," *Fortune,* May 1952, p. 127.]

Readers are apt to remember best what they read last. Therefore, writers frequently organize their detail in an order of climax, beginning with the least important detail and closing with the most important. This pattern is effective when one of the facts, examples, or judgments used to develop a paragraph is especially relevant and impressive. In the following sentences the ideas are arranged in an order of climax.

1. In 1984 Antonia graduated from college, was accepted at Stanford law school, and married her childhood sweetheart.
2. Emily is witty, sophisticated, and beautiful, but much too imperious.
3. This past year has been a disaster for me: in April I had to pay $10,000 in back taxes to the IRS, in June I lost my job, and in September my wife divorced me.

The following paragraph is arranged in an order of climax:

Our primary focus has been on the launching of a new business, which is in many ways a most extraordinary kind of undertaking. When you go into business for yourself you trade off the familiar and the safe for the unknown and the risky. The business is the only source of support for you and your family. You take on long-term financial obligations with money that belongs to relatives, friends, strangers, and institutions. You have to work 14 hours a day, seven days a week, for the foreseeable future. And, after all that, the odds are you'll fail; although there are no reliable data, conventional wisdom says that two thirds of new businesses go under by the fifth year. [From Albert Shapero, "The Displaced, Uncomfortable Entrepreneur," *Psychology Today,* November 1975, p. 83.]

Three other possibilities for the ordering of detail in an expository paragraph are the orders of *familiarity, complexity,* and *cause and effect.* Writers attempting to explain a difficult subject frequently arrange detail in an order of familiarity, proceeding from the known to the unknown. For example, if a writer were explaining the principle of jet propulsion, he or she might begin with a reference to the flight of a balloon from which the air had suddenly been released. In the order of complexity, simpler details are presented first and are followed by more complicated ones. And in the order of cause and effect, the writer organizes the material to trace the relationship between a cause and its resulting effect. The cause-and-effect order is quite similar to the narrative order, but it has a causal rather than a chronological emphasis.

EXERCISE 12

A. The sentences in the following paragraphs have been scrambled so that they are improperly ordered. Rearrange the sentences to form a more coherent paragraph and indicate the new order by writing the numbers of the sentences in their proper sequence in the blanks following each paragraph. Indicate also the type of order each writer has used: *time, space,* or *continuity of idea.*

1. (1) It has been one of the great errors of our time to think that by think-ing about thinking, and then talking about it, we could possibly straighten out and tidy up our minds. (2) The human mind is not meant to be governed, certainly not by any book of rules yet written; it is supposed to run itself, and we are obliged to follow it along, trying to keep up with it as best we can. (3) It is all very well to be aware of your awareness, even proud of it, but never try to operate it. (4) There is no delusion more damaging than to get the idea in your head that you un-derstand the functioning of your own brain. (5) You are not up to the job. (6) Once you acquire such a notion, you run the danger of moving in to take charge, guiding your thoughts, shepherding your mind from place to place, *controlling* it, making lists of regulations. (From rear-ranged Lewis Thomas, "The Attic of the Brain," *Late Night Thoughts on Listening to Mahler's Ninth Symphony,* Viking Penguin, Inc., 1980.)

   Proper Sequence _____

   Type of Order _____

2. (1) His hair was silvery gray, and although it wasn't cut short, it usually looked like an overgrown "butch" haircut. (2) A pair of dark, horn-rimmed glasses, which usually rested on the tip of his nose, seemed too large for his narrow, wizened face. (3) I first met "Pop" Evans at a YMCA summer camp in 1975. (4) The loose-fitting trousers he wore also made his slight frame seem even slighter. (5) I secretly believe that the sus-penders he used to hold up those spacious pants must have been what bowed his shoulders, or perhaps it was the weight of the world.

   Proper Sequence _____

   Type of Order _____

3. (1) *Spinster,* according to dictionaries, originally and sensibly meant noth-ing more than a woman who spins. (2) Poor degenerate word! (3) By Eliza-bethan times it was restricted to refer to an unmarried woman of "gentle" birth. (4) Finally, perhaps in the patriarchal prime of the Victorian

112

period, it acquired its classic—to us—significance: unattractive, elderly, unmarried female. (5) In the seventeenth century it lost this aura of aristocracy and designated any unmarried woman. (6) Era by era it has been stripped linguistically of 1) occupation, 2) husband, 3) social status, 4) youth and beauty—and now of any viable meaning whatever. . . . [From (rearranged) Audrey C. Foote, "Notes on the Distaff Side," *The Atlantic Monthly,* January 1977.]

Proper Sequence _____

Type of Order _____

B. Leaf through a magazine, newspaper, or book to find an example of a paragraph organized in each of the following patterns: (1) chronological sequence, (2) spatial relationships, and (3) continuity of idea. Be prepared to explain which of the various types of patterns is used in the paragraph arranged on the basis of continuity of idea.

C. Using a climactic order, write a paragraph or a three-paragraph theme on one of the following subjects. (If you write the longer composition, review the procedure presented on pp. 58–61.)

1. things my parents never told me
2. what you like most (or least) about college, American life, the business world, etc.
3. the desirability of an army of volunteers or conscripts
4. dieting, an American fetish (styles, dangers, appeal, etc.)
5. a disastrous personal experience
6. gradations in taste (or levels of appeal) of television commercials
7. the value of maintaining greenbelts, wilderness areas, wetlands
8. ways of conserving energy in the United States (at least three)
9. ways of conserving water in the western United States
10. why marriages fail

◨ DEVICES FOR ENSURING COHERENCE

Coherence in a paragraph depends basically on an orderly arrangement of the ideas. If readers cannot follow the direction of thought, they are apt to become confused and puzzled, to feel that the parts of the paragraph do not cohere. But coherence is not solely a matter of logical sequence. It depends also on the use of explicit connecting links between sentences. Consider, for example, the following adaptation of a paragraph about the relevance of love in public affairs.

> Respectfully but firmly, I disagree. Love is a great force in private life; it is the greatest of all things; love in public affairs does not work. It has been tried again and again: by the Christian civilizations of the Middle Ages, and by the French Revolution, a secular movement which reasserted the Brotherhood of Man. It has always failed. The idea that nations should love one another, or that business concerns or marketing boards should love one another, or that a man in Portugal should love a man in Peru of whom he has never heard—it is absurd, unreal, dangerous. It leads us into perilous and vague sentimentalism. "Love is what is needed," we chant, and then sit back and the world goes on as before. We can only love what we know personally. We cannot know much. In public affairs, in the rebuilding of civilization, something much less dramatic and emotional is needed, tolerance. Tolerance is a very dull virtue. It is boring. Unlike love, it has always had a bad press. It is negative. It merely means putting up with people, being able to stand things. No one has ever written an ode to tolerance, or raised a statue to her. This is the quality which will be most needed after the war. This is the sound state of mind which we are looking for. This is the only force which will enable different races and classes and interests to settle down together to the work of reconstruction.

The continuity of thought in this paragraph is diminished by the lack of explicit connecting links between sentences. As a result, the writer's thought does not flow as smoothly from sentence to sentence. When the links (shown in italics) are provided, notice how much more coherent the paragraph becomes.

> Respectfully but firmly, I disagree. Love is a great force in private life; it is *indeed* the greatest of all things; *but* love in public affairs does not work. It has been tried again and again: by the Christian civilizations of the Middle Ages, and *also* by

the French Revolution, a secular movement which reasserted the Brotherhood of Man. *And* it has always failed. The idea that nations should love one another, or that business concerns or marketing boards should love one another, or that a man in Portugal should love a man in Peru of whom he has never heard—it is absurd, unreal, dangerous. It leads us into perilous and vague sentimentalism. "Love is what is needed," we chant, and then sit back and the world goes on as before. *The fact is,* we can only love what we know personally. *And* we cannot know much. In public affairs, in the rebuilding of civilization, something much less dramatic and emotional is needed, *namely* tolerance. Tolerance is a very dull virtue. It is boring. Unlike love, it has always had a bad press. It is negative. It merely means putting up with people, being able to stand things. No one has ever written an ode to tolerance, or raised a statue to her. *Yet* this is the quality which will be most needed after the war. This is the only force which will enable different races and classes and interests to settle down together to the work of reconstruction. (From E. M. Forster, "Tolerance," *Two Cheers for Democracy,* Harcourt Brace Jovanovich, Inc., 1951, 1979.)

Transitional Words and Phrases

The words and phrases italicized in the preceding paragraph act as bridges between the sentences. *For example, but, in the first place,* and similar expressions provide transitions between sentences to make it easier for the reader to follow the writer's thought. Although overuse of such expressions as *therefore, however,* and *in the last analysis* can make writing awkward and mechanical, used moderately and with variety they can improve paragraph coherence. Beginning writers should try to develop skill in the use of these expressions.

The following is a list of words and phrases commonly used to provide continuity between sentences or within the sentence itself.

Relationship	Expression
addition, sequence	and, also, in addition, moreover, furthermore, first, second, again
contrast	but, however, nevertheless, notwithstanding, on the other hand, yet, still

Relationship	Expression
similarity	similarly, likewise, in a like manner, in the same way, in a similar case
exemplification, illustration	for example, as an illustration, for instance, as an example
restatement, clarification	in other words, that is, in particular, in simpler terms
concession	though, although, even though, granted that, it may be true that, admittedly
emphasis	most important, indeed, in fact, I repeat, certainly, truly
conclusion, result	therefore, consequently, thus, as a consequence, hence, as a result
summation	to sum up, in conclusion, finally, in short, in sum, in summary

Repetition of Key Terms

The repetition of key words and phrases provides another way to connect sentences within a paragraph. The deliberate repetition of words that carry the basic meaning emphasizes them in the reader's mind and thus serves to weave together the sentences that contain them. Students are frequently advised to avoid repeating words, and such advice is often valid. The frequent recurrence of unimportant words can make writing mechanical and monotonous, thus dulling reader interest. A haphazard use of synonyms for the sake of variety may simply confuse your reader and defeat your purpose. But do not be afraid to repeat important words to explain your thought clearly.

The paragraph below provides a pattern of linkage through the repetition of such words as *chivalry, code,* and *knight.*

Of *chivalry,* the culture that nurtured him, much is known. More than a *code* of manners in war and love, *chivalry* was a moral system, governing the whole of noble life. That it was about four parts in five illusion made it no less governing for all that. It developed at the same time as the great crusades of the 12th century as a *code* intended to fuse the religious and martial spirits and somehow bring the fighting man into accord with Christian theory. Since a *knight's* usual activities were as much at odds with Christian theory as a merchant's, a moral gloss was needed that would allow the Church to tolerate the warriors in good conscience and the warriors to pursue their own values in spiritual comfort. With the help of Benedictine thinkers, a *code* evolved that put the *knight's* sword arm in the service, theoretically, of justice, right, piety, the Church, the widow, the orphan, and the oppressed. *Knighthood* was received in the name of the Trinity after a ceremony of purification, confession, communion. A saint's relic was usually embedded in the hilt of the *knight's* sword so that upon clasping it as he took his oath, he caused the vow to be registered in Heaven. *Chivalry's* famous celebrator Ramon Lull, a contemporary of St. Louis, could now state as his thesis that "God and *chivalry* are in concord." (From Barbara W. Tuchman, *A Distant Mirror,* Ballantine Books, New York, 1978, p. 62.)

In the following paragraph the writer ties his sentences together through a repetition of the words *thinking, thought, writing, written,* and *words,* which we have emphasized with italics.

It is surely no accident that greater lucidity and accuracy in *thinking* should result from the study of clarity and precision in *writing.* For *writing* necessarily uses *words,* and almost all *thinking* is done with *words.* One cannot even decide what to have for dinner, or whether to cross town by bus or taxi, without expressing the alternatives to oneself in *words.* My experience is, and the point of my whole course is, that the discipline of marshaling *words* into formal sentences, *writing* them down, and examining the *written* statement is bound to clarify *thought.* Once ideas have been *written* down, they can be analyzed critically and dispassionately; they can be examined at another time, in another mood, by another expert. *Thoughts* can therefore be developed, and if they are not precise at the first *written* formulation, they can be made so at a second attempt. [From F. Peter Woodford, "Sounder Thinking Through Clearer Writing," *Science,* Vol. 156, May 12, 1967, pp. 743–45.]

Parallelism

A third way to ensure continuity within a paragraph is to phrase important ideas in the same grammatical structures. The recurrence of similar grammatical forms and the consequent repetition of rhythmic patterns tends to make writing concise, emphatic, and easy to follow. Recurring patterns of expressions are effective in speech as well as writing, as the examples below illustrate. The parallel repetitions in each passage have been italicized.

1. It is a misunderstanding of the American retail store to think we go there necessarily to buy. Some of us shop. There's a difference. . . . *We shop to cheer* ourselves. *We shop to practice* decision making. *We shop to be* useful. . . . *We shop to remind* ourselves how much is available to us. . . . (From Phyllis Rose, "Shopping and Other Spiritual Adventures in America Today," *The New York Times,* April 12, 1984.)

2. The typical cowboy, if we may speak of such an animal, does not *carry* a pistol, *strum* a guitar, or *burst* into song at the end of the day. He has never rescued a maiden in distress or cleaned the outlaws out of a saloon. *He can ride* a bucking horse, *but he can also* get piled. *He can rope* a cow in the pasture, *but he can also* burn three loops before he makes the catch. . . . (From John Ericson, *The Modern Cowboy,* University of Nebraska Press, 1981.)

Robert Elliot Fitch uses parallel repetition to order his ideas and given them balance and emphasis.

However, the universal alibi of irresponsibility is centered in the family. The family can be regarded as a focal point for the forces of heredity and of environment. Moreover, everybody has had, one way or another, a father and a mother. The father alone is a sufficient excuse for almost any irregularity of conduct—be he *famous or infamous, or mediocre, or non-functional. If the poor child has* a famous father, *then* we know *he must spend his* life in a desperate effort *to measure up* to an impossible standard of excellence. *If the poor child has* an infamous father, *then he must spend his* life in a desperate effort *to overcome* the shameful heritage which is his own. *If the poor child has* an ordinary, average father, *then he is bound to rebel* against this example of mediocrity, and to strive for some kind of distinction whether by conventional or by unconventional means. *If the poor child's* father is out of the picture after the time of conception, *then we have another* set of complexes and fixations, all of which relate to the mother. (From Robert Elliot Fitch, "The Irresponsibles," *Odyssey of the Self-Centered Self,* Harcourt, Brace and World, Inc., 1960, 1961.)

Pronoun Reference

Another way to establish continuity between sentences is through the use of pronouns. Using a pronoun in one sentence to repeat a noun in the same or in a previous sentence provides an effective link between these sentences. In the following paragraph, lines have been drawn connecting pronouns with their antecedents to indicate graphically how the reader's attention is naturally directed back to the antecedent of a pronoun. This repetition of key words through the use of pronouns ties these sentences together.

> We might call this the right of curiosity, the right to ask whatever questions are most important to us. As adults, we assume that we have the right to decide what does or does not interest us, what we will look into and what we will leave alone. We take this right for granted, cannot imagine that it might be taken away from us. Indeed, as far as I know, it has never been written into any body of law. Even the writers of the Constitution did not mention it. They thought it was enough to guarantee citizens the freedom of speech and the freedom to spread their ideas as widely as they wished and could. It did not occur to them that even the most tyrannical government would try to control people's minds, what they thought and knew. That idea was to come later, under the benevolent guise of compulsory universal education. [From John Holt, "The Right to Control One's Learning," *Escape from Childhood*, E. P. Dutton, 1974.]

In the next example Mark Twain repeats *he, his,* and *him* to carry his thought throughout the paragraph.

> The higher animals engage in individual fights, but never in organized masses. Man is the only animal that deals in that atrocity of atrocities, War. *He* is the only one that gathers *his* brethren about *him* and goes forth in cold blood and with calm pulse to exterminate *his* kind. *He* is the only animal that for sordid wages will march out, as the Hessians did in our Revolution, and as the boyish Prince Napoleon did in the Zulu war,

and help to slaughter strangers of *his* own species who have done *him* ṇo harm and with whom *he* has no quarrel. (From Mark Twain, "The Damned Human Race," *Letters From the Earth,* Harper and Row, 1962.)

Beginning writers frequently have trouble in using the demonstrative pronouns *this* and *that* as a means of transition. When *this* or *that* is placed on the beginning of one sentence to refer to something in a previous sentence, ambiguity can result if the pronoun is not followed by a noun. Consider, for example, the following sentence:

> Father could get angry, all right, but he had a sense of humor, too. This used to upset Mother, however, for . . . .

It is not clear from reading this sentence whether *this* refers to Father's anger or to his sense of humor. This ambiguity is easily avoided by placing a noun immediately after *this,* specifying to what it refers.

> Father could get angry, all right, but he had a sense of humor, too. This sense of humor (or this anger) used to upset Mother, however, for . . . .

Ambiguity does not, however, always result when *this* appears by itself at the beginning of a sentence. So long as the writer's meaning is clear—an important "if"—there is no reason *this* or *that* may not refer to a larger element than a single antecedent, to a clause, or even to the general idea of a preceding sentence.

> Occasionally, of course, a senator or a congressman becomes involved in a dishonest business affair. This does not mean that politicians are crooks. On the contrary . . . .

EXERCISE 13

A. Underline the transitional expressions in the following paragraphs and indicate in the blanks at the end of each paragraph the relationship that each expression shows.

1. The term "Third World" has been frequently used to refer to the 130 or more underdeveloped nations of the world as if they were a cohesive entity sharing the same interests and ideologies. Actually, they do share certain attitudes such as an intense nationalism and a hypersensitivity to foreign criticism of their internal affairs, but they have not formed a tightly knit alliance by any means. For example, this group contains oil exporters and oil importers, nations with healthy growing economies and others whose economies are stagnating, and nations with centrally planned economies as well as those with market economies. Another myth is that achieving economic development in the Third World is almost impossible owing to the rigidity of the world economic order and the lack of concern of the capitalistic nations of the West. Achieving rapid development is, of course, not easy; but several Third World nations—Brazil, Korea, Taiwan, Singapore—have achieved solid growth rates above 8 percent in the last 15 years. Much of their economic success can be attributed to three conditions: a stable government, an economic climate hospitable to foreign investment, and a reasonably controlled rate of inflation. A third myth is that the most important objective of Third World [countries] is to modernize their economies. In fact, many, if not most, have other goals: achieving recognition and prestige in the international community, pursuing their own political aims, and acquiring modern military equipment. In short, if Third World leaders truly want to develop and modernize their economies, they are not doomed to failure. As Charles Wolf, Jr., of the Rand Corporation writes, "If development is accorded primary emphasis among national objectives, success seems to depend on imposing limits on the scope and character of government intervention. Few Third World leaders are willing to let go the reins of control and unleash the market forces that can help their economies grow."[2]

_____

_____

_____

_____

[2] "Third World—Myths and Realities," *Los Angeles Times,* January 27, 1981.

121

2. The slaughter of baby harp seals in Newfoundland, Canada, is arousing the anger of increasing numbers of people throughout the world, and for good reason, too; for it is a cruel waste of precious life. For example, in killing them, hunters club these one- to six-week-old pups over the head with a blunt or spiked bat, sometimes a dozen times. And the murder takes place right in front of the pup's helpless mother. Moreover, about fourteen percent of the seal pups are not completely dead when their furry white coats are stripped from their still warm bodies. Another argument frequently raised against the hunt is that stopping it would not seriously affect the economy of Newfoundland since only two percent of the province's income is derived from the seal skins and only one tenth of one percent of the population is actually employed in the hunt, and for only four to six weeks. But perhaps the most persuasive argument against killing the seal pups is that it may well lead to the extinction of the harp seal. Since 1960, for instance, the harp seal population has declined sixty percent to a current population of about one million. But in 1900, it is estimated, there were more than ten million harp seals, a decline in eighty years of ninety percent.

_____

_____

_____

B. What device or devices does the writer of the following paragraph use to provide coherence? Write your answers in the blanks following the paragraph.

The liberation of the immigrant from his mother tongue was something that only time and two generations of American schoolchildren would achieve. By, say, the Second World War, it had been done. But in the past ten years or so there has appeared a new strain of ethnic pride, almost an insistence on reverting to hyphenated Americanism. The blacks who, arguing that "black is beautiful," refused to be assimilated in the white man's world may have led the way, but a similar pride in national origin is now being flaunted by immigrants old and new. As early as the first decade of the century, there were protests and small riots outside burlesque and vaudeville theaters against the caricaturing of German and Italian and Jewish traits. In the 1930s the motion picture industry devised a code to eliminate the representations of Greeks as conniving merchants, Italians as gangsters, Negroes as shiftless clowns. This new pride springs, I think, partly from a desperate desire of the underdog in the faceless cities to claim an identity, partly from the pragmatic aim of new immigrants—the Puerto Ricans after the Second World War, the Cubans after Castro's coup, the Hungarians after the Soviet invasion—to

122

arrest at once their automatic consignment to the bottom of the labor market. They do not necessarily succeed, but at least they organize and agitate for the rights of equal pay and first-class citizenship. (From Alistair Cooke, "The Huddled Masses," *Alistair Cooke's America,* Alfred Knopf, Inc., 1973.)

———————————————————————————————————

———————————————————————————————————

———————————————————————————————————

C. In the following pairs of sentences the flow of thought between sentences is somewhat obstructed. Rewrite the sentences to make this connection smoother, using the specific devices indicated in the parentheses.

1. In the 1930s Winston Churchill was frequently dismissed as a warmonger. Had it not been for his steadfast campaign to warn and ultimately lead England against the Nazis, Western civilization would have suffered grievously. (transition word)

———————————————————————————————————

———————————————————————————————————

———————————————————————————————————

2. Great minds discuss ideas; average minds discuss events. People are the subject discussed by people with small minds. (parallel repetition)

———————————————————————————————————

———————————————————————————————————

———————————————————————————————————

3. According to Oscar Wilde, America was not discovered. America was detected. (pronoun reference)

———————————————————————————————————

———————————————————————————————————

———————————————————————————————————

123

4. Modern education, some critics contend, emphasizes relativism because certitude about values is thought to be arbitrary and arrogant. Education that teaches young people to pick up their values wherever they can from the smorgasbord of life produces "flat-souled" individuals. (transition word)

_____

_____

_____

5. To achieve a more efficient use of energy in this country, Americans will have to abandon some long-held attitudes. Americans increasingly reject any increase in taxes on gasoline in spite of the need to reduce air pollution and generate government funds to reduce the deficit. (repetition of key term—try "attitude")

_____

_____

_____

6. Joe Montana is a great professional quarterback. He is the dominant offensive threat for the San Francisco Forty-Niners: His ability to read defenses, pick up his team when they're losing, and generate scores when needed is uncanny. Many sportswriters consider him the greatest quarterback who ever played the game. (transition word)

_____

_____

_____

7. Terrorist groups that kidnap people for use as pawns to gain political concessions from hostile governments have created difficulties for law enforcement authorities. Protecting innocent lives and preventing further kidnappings presents police with a dilemma. (repetition of key word)

_____

_____

_____

124

8. American manufacturers have increasingly transferred assembly plants to foreign countries to take advantage of cheap foreign labor. Manufacturers defend the practice as a means of keeping American products competitive, though the resulting long-term loss in purchasing power among American workers will likely damage the American economy substantially. (pronoun reference)

_____

_____

_____

9. Breakfast cereal makers are trying hard to appeal to adults in the 18- to 45-year-old age bracket who want nutritional value. Kellogg Company, the number one cereal maker in the United States, spent over $50 million to market a new natural cereal called "Nutri-Grain." (transition word)

_____

_____

_____

10. Leon Trotsky was a difficult man to please. He didn't like the Czar, so he murdered him. He didn't like the Imperial Government, so he blew it up. His attitude toward the moderate views of Kerensky and Savinkov was negative, and they were removed from their positions in the Social Revolutionary Party. (parallel repetition)

_____

_____

_____

D. The transitional expressions in the following paragraphs have been omitted. Read the paragraph carefully. Determine the relationship between the ideas in the sentences to be connected and select an appropriate word or phrase that expresses this relationship.

1. Because of the development of new electronic machines for recording, duplicating, and transmitting the human voice and the written word, many students seem to think that there is no compelling need for them

125

to know how to write well. _____ this notion that only newspaper workers, novelists, scholars, researchers, and the like have to know how to write is foolish. Students majoring in business, _____, think their secretaries will do their writing for them, _____ this belief reveals a rather naive faith in the competency of secretaries. _____ young business men and women seldom have their own secretaries. Students going into science and engineering _____ believe that writing is something they will seldom have to do, _____ scientists and engineers say they spend almost half their time writing letters and reports. _____, those persons who can express themselves well in writing are sure to succeed more rapidly than those whose command of language is minimal.

2. Words in themselves are not dignified, or silly, or wise, or malicious. _____ they can be used in dignified, silly, wise, or malicious ways by dignified, silly, wise, or malicious people. *Egghead,* _____, is a perfectly legitimate word, as legitimate as *highbrow* or *long-haired.* _____ there is something very wrong and very undignified, by civilized standards, in a belligerent dislike for intelligence and education. *Yak* is an amusing word for persistent chatter. Anyone could say, "We were just yakking over a cup of coffee," with no harm to his dignity. _____ to call a Supreme Court decision *yakking* is to be vulgarly insulting and so, undignified. _____ there's nothing wrong with *confab* when it's appropriate. _____ the work of a great research project, employing hundreds of distinguished scholars over several decades and involving the honor of one of the greatest publishing houses in the world, is described as *confabbing* (as *The New York Times* editorially described the preparation of the Third International), the use of this particular word asserts that the lexicographers had merely sat around and talked idly. _____ the statement becomes undignified—if not _____ slanderous. (From Bergen Evans, "But What's a Dictionary For?" *The Atlantic Monthly,* May, 1962, p. 62.)

E. Construct a coherent paragraph using the following notes and any pertinent information you wish to add. Use at least two of the devices for ensuring continuity discussed in this chapter: transitional words, pronoun reference, parallelism, and repetition of key words and phrases. Underline whatever transition words you use. The notes are not now listed in a logical order.

1. Serious problems developing in Russia today
2. Production of consumer goods down, quality shoddy
3. Conservative communists still in positions of power in bureaucracy resisting movement toward democracy and free market economy
4. Three basic problems—political, economic, psychological
5. Ukraine's fear of Russian dominance souring economic cooperation between them and thus slowing Russian economic recovery
6. Yeltsin's political support weakening because of popular discontent with instability of economy
7. Lowered morale of people because of failure of socialist system
8. Growing problems with alcoholism, unemployment, crime increasing tensions among people
9. Failure on the farm—machinery breaking down, distribution network ineffectual, lack of storage plants
10. Inflation increasing, purchasing power of ruble falling
11. Military leadership restless because of breakup of Soviet Union and their diminishing influence and power

127

◨ POINT OF VIEW

Point of view defines the position, the point of focus a writer assumes in relation to the subject. It embraces matters of tone, person, tense, number, and voice. Maintaining a consistent point of view is essential to paragraph coherence. If, for example, you are discussing a subject in the third person, you should stay in the third person unless you have a good reason for shifting to first or second person. The same principle applies to tense, number, tone, and voice. A reader is likely to become confused if you change from the past to the present tense, from a singular to a plural noun, from an objective, matter-of-fact tone to a subjective one, or from the active to the passive voice of the verb.

Tone

Tone refers to the attitude a writer takes toward her subject and reader. It can vary widely, depending on her purpose, subject, audience, and interests. A student writing about her roommate might assume an informal, personal, even whimsical tone. If she were discussing the advisability of tax reform, however, her tone would probably be more serious and objective.

The problem of tone is complex, but a knowledge of the distinctive qualities of the formal and the informal tone should be helpful. Formal writing uses a more extensive and exact vocabulary. It may allude to historical and literary events; its sentences are usually longer and more carefully constructed than those used in informal writing; and it follows the traditional conventions of English grammar carefully, avoiding contractions, omissions, and abbreviations. Informal writing permits the use of colloquial words and phrases. Its vocabulary is less extensive and its sentences less elaborate, with a more conversational rhythm. Informal writing also permits the use of first- and second-person personal pronouns (I, you, we) and contractions (I'm, you're, he's).

The following student essay is written in an informal style. The tone is chatty, conversational, good-humored. The writer uses many colloquial words and phrases ("sandbagger," "pretty sly," "a lot of," "drops on you like a load of bricks"), the second-person pronoun *you,* and contractions ("should've," "he's," "don't"). The sentences and paragraphs are also not very long. The style and tone are appropriate here because the writer is addressing his fellow students on a topic of common, lively interest; and he wants to convey his feelings and attitudes in a friendly, lively manner.

Pals, Preachers, and Mr. Sly

My adviser told me that to succeed in any class, you had to study your teacher first. She was right. But she should've added, "Be especially careful if you get a sandbagger, a friendly philosopher, or a true believer." The first type, the sandbagger, is pretty sly. At the beginning of the semester, he's nice and easy—reasonable assignments, a lot of smiles, a few jokes, all sweetness and light. But after the withdrawal deadline, look out! He drops on you like a load of bricks, with lots of homework, weekly quizzes, and a term paper he neglected to tell you about. He figures you're committed to the course now, and he lets you have it.

By contrast, the friendly philosopher is a pussycat. He loves to rap with students, whom he calls by their first name, to share experiences with them, to meet them on their own level. Unfortunately, his class discussions often degenerate into free-wheeling bull sessions on the lawn in the quad. Students often like him, for he's a nice guy and an easy grader, but by the end of the semester they haven't learned much.

Unlike the friendly philosopher, the true believer doesn't want pals. She wants converts, followers, apostles. Serious and intent, she prefers preaching to teaching. She may be a very stimulating lecturer—she often is—but don't cross her if you're looking for a good grade. For there is but one truth, and she has it. The sandbagger, the friendly philosopher, and the true believer do make college life more interesting. But pray to the gods you don't get all three in the same semester.

This next paragraph is more formal. It is excerpted from an essay on the uses of philosophy that appeared in a magazine whose readers are typically intelligent, well-educated, and seriously interested in ideas. Its tone is, appropriately, more serious, its sentences are longer, its diction ("an activity of logical analysis," "scrutinizes the premises," "methodological sophistication") is more formal.

This suggests the third use of philosophy. Awareness and self-consciousness do not come about by revelation. For the revelations—"the moments of truth," as the phrase goes—which overtake us are themselves in need of understanding. This can be reliably achieved only by the activity of logical analysis. A person may utter statements that are true or false and yet not be clear about their meaning or their justification or relevance.

Whatever else philosophy is, it is an activity of logical analysis which seeks to locate issues in dispute and to help clarify them. When properly pursued, philosophy gives a methodological sophistication that can be achieved by no other discipline. It is not a mere matter of reasoning from premises to conclusions, as in mathematics or chess, because it scrutinizes the premises and basic terms which all subjects take for granted. It enables us to distinguish between statements of fact and disguised definitions, between hypotheses which may be true or false and resolutions which are adequate or inadequate. It is always prepared to consider alternatives to the familiar. William James actually defines philosophy as a quest for alternatives and their investigation. In summary, then, philosophy consists of an analysis of concepts and ideas in an attempt to cut through slogans to genuine issues and problems. (From Sidney Hook, "Does Philosophy Have a Future?" *Saturday Review,* Nov. 11, 1967, Saturday Review Inc.)

The style and tone of your writing should, as mentioned earlier, be appropriate to your subject and audience. While you are in college, your audience will usually be your teacher or your fellow students; and unless, like the student who wrote the essay on professors, you wish to assume a light-hearted tone for the purpose of humor, you will need to master the more formal style and tone used in the discussion of serious issues. But whatever tone you adopt, be careful not to shift from an impersonal, serious treatment of your subject to a breezy, colloquial tone, and vice versa, unless there is good reason for doing so and your reader has been adequately prepared for the shift.

Inconsistent

The patient's pathetic amatory history had traumatized him severely, and the therapist figured he might go round the bend.

Rocko McNally was a gutty fighter. He could take it as well as dish it out. His capacity for absorbing punishment was, however, exceeded during a match with Kid McGruff. In that contest, he was rendered unconscious in the sixth round by his opponent's right fist.

Consistent

The patient's unsuccessful love life had seriously affected his self-esteem, and the therapist worried that he might lose touch with reality.

Rocko McNally was a gutty fighter. He could take it as well as dish it out. His ability to take a punch was, however, exceeded in his match with Kid McGruff, who flattened him with a right in the sixth round.

Person

Pronouns and verbs can be classified according to person, a form whose change indicates whether a person is speaking (first person), is being spoken to (second person), or is being spoken about (third person). A shift in person, as indicated earlier, disrupts continuity. Be careful, therefore, not to change person carelessly from sentence to sentence as you develop your paragraph. Whether you decide to use the informal first or second person (*I, we, you*) or the more formal third person (*he, she, they*), maintain a consistent point of view throughout.

Inconsistent	Consistent
One who succeeds in life takes the credit himself. Those who fail blame others.	Those who succeed in life take the credit themselves. Those who fail blame others.

Tense

A verb undergoes changes in form to show the time of its action or state of being—the past, present, or future. These changes in verb forms are called tenses. Once you have determined the tense you will use in developing your topic, avoid shifting this tense unless you have prepared your reader for the change.

Inconsistent	Consistent
After a delay of thirty minutes, the curtain came down, and the orchestra begins to play. Then the house lights dim, and the audience grows quiet.	After a delay of thirty minutes, the curtain came down, and the orchestra began to play. Then the house lights dimmed, and the audience grew quiet.

As noted above, if tense changes occur, the reader must be prepared for them. When he or she is, they do not violate the principle of consistency. In the following passage the writer maintains a consistent point of view with regard to time even though she changes tense.

> The original settlement of Paris *was founded* by a Gallic tribe in the first century B.C. Paris *is* thus about 2000 years old. During these years it *has become* perhaps the most beautiful and cultured city in Europe. In fact, in the opinion of many travelers, it *is* the most beautiful city in the world.

The writer begins in the past tense to establish a point of reference for her remarks. In the second sentence she moves into the present tense to state a fact about Paris at the present time. In the third sentence she shifts to the present perfect tense with *has become,* but this shift does not violate consistency of tense either, for the verb reports a condition—the beauty and sophistication of Paris—that began in the past and continues into the present. And in the last sentence the writer returns to the present tense, again to express a current opinion about her subject.

Number

Number refers to the changes in a word that indicate whether its meaning is singular or plural. As you read over your writing, make certain that you have not shifted number needlessly. In particular, make certain that your pronouns agree in number, as well as in person, with their antecedents, the things or persons to which they refer.

Inconsistent	Consistent
The student who wants to improve her writing can, in the majority of cases, do so if she puts her mind seriously to it. If they are not willing to make this effort, however, the results will be minimal.	The student who wants to improve her writing can, in the majority of cases, do so if she puts her mind seriously to it. If she is not willing to make this effort, however, the results will be minimal.

Voice

Voice refers to the form of the verb that indicates whether its subject acts or is acted upon. If the subject of the verb acts, the verb is said to be in the *active* voice:

> Guillermo won the election.

If the subject is acted upon, the verb is said to be in the *passive* voice:

> The election was won by Guillermo.

The active voice is used more often than the passive voice, the latter being reserved for occasions when the doer of the action is either unknown or unimportant or when the writer wishes to stress the importance of the receiver of the action. Examine your sentences carefully to make certain that you have used the appropriate voice.

Inconsistent	Consistent
In September of his freshman year, Harvey decided to work thirty hours a week in order to buy a car. After conferring with his counselor about his program, however, the plan was abandoned by him.	In September of his freshman year, Harvey decided to work thirty hours a week in order to buy a car. After conferring with his counselor about his program, however, he abandoned the plan.

EXERCISE 14

A. Read each of these paragraphs carefully, and in the blanks provided describe (1) the writer's tone, (2) the linguistic elements (vocabulary, sentence length, allusions, grammatical conventions) that create the tone, and (3) the audience for whom the passage was likely intended. (Review pp. 128–130 on tone.)

1. Men are not gentle creatures who want to be loved, and who at the most can defend themselves if they are attacked; they are, on the contrary, creatures among whose instinctual endowments is to be reckoned a powerful share of aggressiveness. As a result, their neighbor is for them not only a potential helper or sexual object, but also someone who tempts them to satisfy their aggressiveness on him, to exploit his capacity for work without compensation, to use him sexually without his consent, to seize his possessions, to humiliate him, to cause him pain, to torture and to kill him. *Homo homini lupus.* Who, in the face of all his experience of life and of history, will have the courage to dispute this assertion? As a rule this cruel aggressiveness waits for some provocation or puts itself at the service of some other purpose, whose goal might also have been reached by milder measures. In circumstances that are favorable to it, when the mental counterforces which ordinarily inhibit it are out of action, it also manifests itself spontaneously and reveals man as a savage beast to whom consideration toward his own kind is something alien. Anyone who calls to mind the atrocities committed during the racial migrations or the invasions of the Huns, or by the people known as Mongols under Jenghiz Khan and Tamerlane, or at the capture of Jerusalem by the pious Crusaders, or even, indeed, the horrors of the recent World War—anyone who calls these things to mind will have to bow humbly before the truth of this view. (From Sigmund Freud, *Civilization and Its Discontents,* W. W. Norton and Company, Inc., The Hogarth Press Ltd., 1961, by James Strachey.)

   Tone _____

   Linguistic Elements _____

   _____

   Audience _____

2. Some professional athletes really give their sport a bad name, and they give me a pain in the neck, too. Take tennis, for instance. The way some topflight players chew out line judges, shout at the referee, and badger the fans you'd think the game owes them a living—a very good one at that—

134

and that spectators are privileged to see them play. And, of course, base-ball has its egomaniacs, too, guys who hit .265 and demand a long-term, no-cut contract in the millions of dollars or they'll quit. I suppose if base-ball club owners want to shell out millions of bucks to some players, that's their business. Paying such players more than four or five times as much as the President earns in a year may make economic sense, but I wish these superstars would quit bellyaching about their contract dis-putes to sports reporters. And, finally, what about ice hockey! It's always been a tough game involving a lot of body contact; but what was only a part of the game, the violence, is now the main point. The stick-swinging goons, the flying elbows and fists, the brawls—they make me sick.

Tone ＿＿＿＿＿＿＿＿＿＿＿＿＿＿＿＿＿＿＿＿＿＿

Linguistic Elements ＿＿＿＿＿＿＿＿＿＿＿＿＿＿＿

＿＿＿＿＿＿＿＿＿＿＿＿＿＿＿＿＿＿＿＿＿＿＿＿

Audience ＿＿＿＿＿＿＿＿＿＿＿＿＿＿＿＿＿＿＿

B. In the following paragraph underline the words and phrases that reveal an inconsistency in point of view. In the blanks following the paragraph identify the error more specifically as an inconsistency of tone, person, number, tense, or voice.

One of the most enduring myths of popular psychology is that admitting and expressing anger are necessary to mental health and stability. The no-tion that releasing one's anger is beneficial was traced to Sigmund Freud, who believed that an aggressive pool of energy existed in the body and when blocked in one direction simply flowed out in another. Venting one's anger was, thus, cathartic. Today, however, many psychologists argue that ventilat-ing anger when one is frustrated is kind of stupid. Apparently, you don't just let it all hang out when you get ticked off. According to recent studies when a person gets angry, they don't really clear the air by expressing it. Actually, such behavior creates more problems than it solves by increasing hostility and anxiety. It has also been thought by psychologists that talking about his anger can make one feel better, but those who fume to a neutral party in an effort to legitimize their rage only increases their anger by rehearsing the emotion. A third commonly held assumption is that participating in violent sports like football, boxing, ice hockey provides a means of releasing anger. Instead of punching out his boss, players attack opponents and so release their frustrations harmlessly. But such activity only removes the anger for a time; it doesn't dissolve it. Moreover, a peaceful game of chess will dissolve anger equally well. To sum up, dealing with anger is not easy, a cake walk; holding in a black rage is not worse for you than letting it hit the ceiling,

135

though neither is the answer. Common sense is still the best advice. Says John Carey, "When your heart races, your blood boils, and you want to strangle someone, stop . . . decide if rage is the best response."[3] It often is not.

_____

_____

_____

_____

C. In each of the following passages the point of view is inconsistent because of a shift in *tone, tense, number, person,* or *voice.* Indicate the particular error in each passage and correct it in the blanks provided.

1. To convey a sense of reality in her depiction of character, description of setting, and construction of plot, a novelist must have a good eye for specific detail. If they lack this, they will fail to attract the interest of an intelligent reader.

   Error _____

   _____

   _____

   _____

2. One who wants to maintain friendly relations with others should not speak the truth unseasonably. If you do, you're apt to hurt people's feeling and find yourself *persona non grata.*

   Error _____

   _____ _____

   _____

   _____

3. The fundamental requirement of any successful democratic society is tolerance, a willingness to allow divergent political, social, religious beliefs. This forbearance applies especially to political leaders and

[3] "Better Temper That Temper," *Newsweek,* January 3, 1983.

136

their relations with the press. Presidents, for example, who lose their cool when journalists and political commentators get their goat with dumb questions need to be reminded of this by their cronies in the Oval Office.

Error _____

_____

_____

_____

4. A good military commander needs courage and self-assurance in the face of hostile fire. Imagination and an intuitive grasp of strategy and tactics are also needed by him.

Error _____

_____

_____

_____

5. "Everyone is born a king," said Oscar Wilde, and most people died in exile.

Error _____

_____

_____

_____

6. Succeeding in professional sports requires talent, concentration, self-confidence. Anyone who comes up short in any of these categories hasn't got a prayer in professional sports.

Error _____

_____

_____

_____

137

7. If you want to persuade others of the soundness of your arguments, listen to theirs carefully, attentively. An attitude of contempt for their point of view should be avoided.

   Error _____

   _____

   _____

   _____

8. They laughed when I sat down to play the concerto. Their laughter subsided, however, when they discover that I could tickle those ivories sweetly.

   Errors _____

   _____

   _____

   _____

9. A first-class chef needs training, experience, imagination. They must have style, flair, personality.

   Error _____

   _____

   _____

   _____

10. To get the most from a lecture, a student must listen carefully and take precise notes. You should not, however, try to record everything your instructors say.

   Error _____

   _____

   _____

   _____

138

◪ SUMMARY

Coherence is a third quality of good writing. To make your writing coherent, be sure that your material is organized in some logical order, that your sentences are tied together smoothly, and that your point of view is consistent throughout. The most important quality is the first, for if your thought is developed in an orderly way, you have the basis of a coherent paragraph. Continuity between sentences and point of view are then less of a problem. If your thought lacks logical progression, the addition of transitional expressions and the maintenance of a consistent point of view cannot by themselves supply coherence.

Coherence is the result of careful planning and organization. Therefore, think through what you want to say before you begin to write, and keep your reader in mind as you write. If you build your paragraph as a unit of thought and help your reader to move smoothly from sentence to sentence as you develop that thought, your reader will have no trouble grasping the meaning of your paragraph.

CHAPTER

The Expository Theme

The general process of writing the longer theme has been presented in Chapter One. In this chapter we will review and elaborate upon that discussion, developing in greater detail many of the suggestions.

◼ GETTING STARTED— SELECTING A SUBJECT

Selecting a topic for a theme is directly related to your purpose in writing. At times a specific subject will be assigned, as, for example, on an essay examination, and your response, the essay you write, will be governed by the terms of the question. In this instance, your purpose will be to demonstrate your knowledge of the subject in an essay that is well focused; supported with facts, judgments, and examples; and clear and coherent. At other times you will have greater latitude, often a choice among a number of topics, or perhaps complete freedom. When you have a measure of choice take time to think about your subject, to talk to yourself and explore your thoughts and feelings about it: Does the subject interest you? Would your readers find it interesting? Is it significant? What would you try to accomplish in a paper on the subject? Fixing upon a purpose is not necessary at this time. In fact, many times your purpose will gradually evolve as you work up your material.

For example, if your subject is a public issue, a current controversy, you may simply want to inform your reader about an important aspect of the subject that has been neglected or take a stand on the issue or refute an opinion you think wrongheaded. With this kind of subject, you will want to investigate what others have to say about the issue in books, journals, magazines, and newspapers to buttress your own ideas on the subject. If, on the other hand, your subject is more personal, one derived from your own experience, your basic source of material will be your memory bank, as well as your current observations, feelings, attitudes, and opinions. As mentioned earlier, you may

141

underrate the value of your own experience, but a personal experience that clarified something for you, changed the way you thought or acted, can make an interesting subject for an essay. It need not be an earthshaking event, one that illuminated a profound idea, but simply an experience that had meaning for you and that you would like to share with a reader.

Freewriting

Selecting a subject and getting started can be exasperating. Many writers, professionals as well as beginners, have trouble getting out of the starting blocks. They steam and fret, pace the room, scribble words on a sheet and then throw it away. If you have experienced writer's block, you might want to try freewriting to help you choose a subject. Simply sit down and begin writing whatever comes into your head. Don't worry about punctuation, perfect sentences, unity, coherence, spelling—just write for ten or fifteen minutes without stopping. Focus on one topic or shift back and forth among several. The important thing is to get on with it. The activity of putting ideas on paper in a free association process, forgetting your critical sense for the moment, will help relieve tensions and fears and release creative energy to help focus your thoughts. After you have written for a while, look over what you have written. Very likely your will discover a topic that can be developed into a theme. Of course, much will be confused, repetitive, and incoherent; that's not important here. If you find a topic, you can use whatever ideas seem relevant and discard the rest.

Here is a sample of a student's freewriting exercise.

"Seems like a waste of time . . . putting down what's in my head. That's the problem, I guess, nothing in my head. Depressing . . . a beautiful day out there, and I'm in here racking my brain for something to say on this stupid theme. Maybe I ought to write on why I can't write. Yeah, that'd be great. Kind of funny. Probably come up with something lively . . . some pizzazz. Don't bore us to death. I wonder how he is, old Jonesy, a nice guy. Wanted to be a writer, he said . . . good class that senior English class. I'm getting nowhere. Remember how his eyes sparkled when he read a favorite passage from Hemingway. *The Sun Also Rises* and the lost generation. I'm getting lost . . . and depressed. Wonder what it's like to face a bull, two tons of pot roast coming at you . . . only a piece of cloth between you and death in the afternoon. Hemingway was depressed. Couldn't lick it. Depressed. Many people depressed these days . . . hot lines, drugs, liquor. Wonder why. I suppose the fast pace of twentieth century. Travel . . . Pamplona, Paris, Serengetti Plain, Africa. Maybe I should learn to box. Old Jonesy would chuckle at that."

This bit of rambling freewriting may seem unpromising at first glance, but a closer reading suggests at least two topics: Mr. Jones, his high school English teacher or, perhaps, depression, the blues, and what to do about them.

EXERCISE 15

A. List five topics of current public interest that have generated lively controversy. Select subjects you'd like to learn more about or ones you already know something about and on which you have an opinion to express.

1. _____

2. _____

3. _____

4. _____

5. _____

B. The following subjects should bring to mind specific experiences that taught you something worth sharing with a reader. For each area provide a more specific subject.

Example   School—My Favorite High School Teacher

1. Family _____

2. Friends _____

3. Work _____

4. Disappointments _____

5. School _____

6. Happy times _____

7. First love _____

8. Cars _____

9. Vacations _____

10. Hopes, fears _____

C. In the space on page 145 or on a separate sheet, try your hand at freewriting. For ten or fifteen minutes write down anything that comes into your

144

mind. Don't worry about perfect sentences, spelling, and so on; just keep writing uninterruptedly. Then look over what you've written, and list one or more topics that suggest themselves as possible subjects for a theme.

Topics _____

_____

_____

EXERCISE 16

A. Select a subject from the following list, and split it up into four or five more specific subjects:

1. Modern weapons of war
2. Combatting the drought in the West
3. Popular music
4. New sources of energy
5. Technology and modern life
6. Physical fitness
7. Men's or women's clothing fashions or fads
8. The drug war
9. Owning a sports car
10. Population growth

General Subject _____

Specific Subjects _____

_____

_____

_____

B. Select one of the general categories of Exercise 15B, narrow it down, and then divide that less general subject into four specific subjects.

> Example *General Category*—Disappointments
> *Less General*—Learning from Mistakes
> *Specific*—Dating My Best Friend's Gal
> Lending My Car to Crazy Al
> Taking Boxing Lessons
> Backpacking in the Sierras in Late Fall

General Category _____

Less General _____

Specific _____

_____

_____

_____

146

◨ LIMITING YOUR SUBJECT

Limiting your subject is not so crucial if you have been assigned a specific topic to begin with. If you are allowed to choose your topic, or if the assigned topic is rather broad, restrict it to one you can deal with effectively within the length of the paper you intend to write. The subject of a 300-word theme to be written in class needs to be more narrowly restricted than a 700-word paper written out of class. This stipulation of length is not designed to make you produce an exact number of words: it is meant to define the scope of your subject. The shorter your paper, the more you will have to restrict your focus.

The degree to which a large, general subject is to be narrowed depends, as we said above, on the length of the paper to be written. A subject such as Sports in America can be restricted to yield subjects for a medium-sized paper, 500–700 words, or a shorter paper, 300–500 words:

General Subject	Sports in America
Medium-Sized Paper	Salaries of Professional Athletes
	Upgrading Intercollegiate Sports for Women
	Banning Professional Boxing
	Steroids and Sports
	Violence in Professional Sports
Short Paper	Football Fans
	Synthetic versus Natural Turf
	Jaguar versus Porsche
	Hang Gliding

Like these subjects of public concern, topics drawn from personal experience must also be limited. For example, should you decide to write about Mr. Jones, your high school English teacher, you would be wise to concentrate on a few dominant traits or qualities rather than attempt a comprehensive treatment covering many aspects of his character and personality, a paper that would likely be more superficial and therefore less convincing.

General Subject	Mr. Jones and Senior English
Restricted Focus	Mr. Jones: Teacher, Philosopher, Ham
	Ol' Jonesy: Humor, Humanity, and Homework
	Mr. Jones: Firm, Fair, and Friendly
	Mr. Jones: No Pal, But a Fine Friend

Again, keep your audience in mind when selecting and narrowing your subject. You can expect an audience of your classmates to understand and respond to a lively discussion of some topic of current public interest or an account of a personal experience. But they would not likely respond to a technical explanation of some complicated engineering process. A paper on the possibilities of solar energy would be more suitable than a technical, detailed discussion of a particular solar heating device.

◼ GENERATING IDEAS ABOUT A TOPIC

Having chosen your topic and limited it, you must now generate ideas about it. Sometimes, as we've noted earlier, you will have a fairly definite idea of what you want to do in a paper—for example, to inform your audience on some aspect of a general subject that is not commonly known or understood, or to persuade your audience to follow a course of action. In this case you can explore your subject systematically. At other times your subject will require you to probe your memory for ideas, and, usually, you will not be able to formulate your purpose until you have generated and organized your material in some detail. A good method of generating ideas about a subject based upon personal experience is to brainstorm it.

Brainstorming: Probing Your Memory

Brainstorming is like freewriting: both strategies are designed to help you overcome inertia and get moving. Both involve a free association of ideas and feelings in which you write down quickly what comes into your head without regard to order, precision of thought, punctuation, and so on. There is a slight difference in that when freewriting you write out your thoughts and feelings in longer phrases and in full sentences. When brainstorming you simply jot down these ideas and feelings in single words, phrases, bits of sentences. Brainstorming about Mr. Jones, a high school English teacher mentioned earlier, might look something like this:

Ol' Jonesy

1. heavy-rimmed glasses, blue eyes
2. tall, slender, slight roll to walk

3. gray hair, thinning on top
4. pacing behind lectern, eyes on floor, lost in thought at times
5. cardigan sweaters, windbreaker jackets, always a tie
6. friendly, courteous, somewhat formal, the old school
7. frequent jokes to lighten mood
8. laughed at his own jokes, sometimes subtle
9. everpresent tie, usually solid color
10. loafers, slacks, never jeans
11. not serious about self, but serious about subject
12. mid-forties, maybe older, laugh wrinkles
13. tough-minded about good work, tender-minded in personal contacts
14. a good listener
15. firm, fair, friendly—his code
16. lots of homework, too much
17. Socratic method—lots of questions—no place to hide
18. nailed you for lack of preparation, goofing off
19. pop quizzes, essays
20. simplicity, clarity, write to express, not to impress
21. eyes sparkled, laughed at his own jokes
22. occasional stories, family, friends
23. loved his subject . . . cummings, Hemingway, Fitzgerald . . . literature
24. liked students, attended games, dances, senior picnic
25. somewhat formal with students, Mr. this, Miss that, friendly, but no pal
26. praised good work, smiled, a wink for excellence
27. popular with students, but no nonsense
28. tough but fair
29. an existentialist of sorts
30. brought in books, loaned his own, always reading and recommending books
31. some teacher, knew his subject, loved it, shared it
32. open-minded about politics, religion

The Impersonal Paper

Material for papers on the more impersonal public issue topic, like the one on college athletics presented in Chapter One, is derived from a variety of sources: your own observations of the current scene—people, ideas, events; lecture notes; class discussions, conversations with friends; investigations of the opinions of authorities in books, magazines, newspapers; your own research on the subject—public records, documents, and so on. Working with this kind of subject, you may have a tentative idea of what you want to accomplish in the paper, the point you want to make, before you begin collecting your data and going over your notes. It's wiser, however, not to decide upon a purpose and thesis until you've assembled your material, thought about it, and put it in some sort of order since your preliminary ideas may change as you proceed.

Let's assume that you've decided to write on American economic competitiveness among the world's trading nations in a paper of 500 words. You would want to know the answers to such questions as the following: Is the United States in danger of economic decline? If so, why? If not, what are the reasons for optimism? What information will my reader have to have to understand the problem, causes, and possible solutions?

Such questions do not exhaust the possibilities. Others may suggest themselves as you proceed. After you have done some reading and thinking on your subject, jot down the ideas that come to mind. Your list will contain irrelevant and awkwardly phrased items, but, like the process of brainstorming a personal subject, the important thing is to get your ideas down on paper so that they don't get away from you. A preliminary listing on America's economic competitiveness might develop in this manner:

1. much talk in media about decline of American power and influence because of alleged decline in economic competitiveness
2. why the fear—domestic economic weaknesses
3. dire predictions of America's future . . . world's largest debtor nation
4. increasing federal and trade deficits
5. increasing foreign competition, another cause of fear
6. low rate of savings by Americans
7. decline in supply of educated workers
8. fears real but exaggerated . . . reasons for optimism in an American resurgence
9. emergence of European Community as a formidable trading bloc led by Germany
10. cheaper dollar another reason of reduced costs of American exports
11. fall in dollar tied to decreasing interest rates in U.S. and increasing rates in Europe and Japan

12. Japanese investors reducing purchases of American securities and government bonds
13. dramatic growth of Japan as economic superpower, hence more competition
14. American manufacturing regaining competitiveness because of increased efficiency
15. increasing efficiency owing to increased investment in new technology . . . computers, robots
16. American research and inventions often adopted and applied by Japanese
17. increased efficiency, fall in dollar produce U.S. cost advantage over trading partners
18. growth in exports a second reason for optimism
19. U.S. merchandise exports $394 billion in 1990, up from $250 billion in 1987, 50 percent increase while growth in imports slowing
20. U.S. exporting brainpower also
21. American industry—highest output per employee in world
22. and productivity growing in manufacturing
23. Pacific Telesis servicing telecommunications in Germany
24. Fluor and Bechtel overseas construction projects in Middle East
25. American economic resurgence a plus but changes for Americans
26. fewer goods available for American consumers as exports emphasized
27. drop in dollar, cost of imports up, more inflation
28. U.S. unit labor costs 15 percent below those of major industrial countries
29. foreign companies setting up operations in U.S. to benefit from lower costs and large market
30. some decline likely in numbers of American travellers abroad
31. America to remain largest trading nation and maintain power and influence
32. Japanese refusal to buy more American goods and services—a problem
33. failure of international trade talks also ominous

EXERCISE 17

A. Select a subject from one of the exercises indicated below, and provide additional details—facts, judgments, examples—about the subject to serve as the basis of an essay of 300 to 500 words. Choose your subject from one of the following exercises: 6A; 6B; 8; 9; 10E, F, G; 11E; 15A; 16A, B.

Topic _____

Detail   1. _____

2. _____

3. _____

4. _____

5. _____

6. _____

7. _____

8. _____

9. _____

10. _____

11. _____

12. _____

13. _____

14. _____

15. _____

152

B. Select one of the subjects dealing with a personal experience in Exercise 15B, limit it, and, in the spaces provided on the following page, list details that can be organized and developed into a theme.

General Topic ———————————————————————————————

Specific Topic ———————————————————————————————

Detail   1. ———————————————————————————————

2. ———————————————————————————————

3. ———————————————————————————————

4. ———————————————————————————————

5. ———————————————————————————————

6. ———————————————————————————————

7. ———————————————————————————————

8. ———————————————————————————————

9. ———————————————————————————————

10. ———————————————————————————————

11. ———————————————————————————————

12. ———————————————————————————————

13. ———————————————————————————————

14. ———————————————————————————————

15. ———————————————————————————————

153

◼ PURPOSE AND AUDIENCE

The process of generating ideas about your subject, the mental activity involved in writing down ideas, will help to clarify your subject as well as your purpose. Looking over your list of items, you will begin to see more clearly what your subject is and what you want to accomplish in your paper, what effect you want to have on your reader. It is important at this stage to think more precisely about your purpose because your purpose will determine the kind of information you'll want to include and exclude, your strategies for organizing and developing the ideas, as well as matters of tone, style, and length.

In deciding upon a purpose, you must also give serious thought to your audience, for your readers' knowledge of your subject, their attitudes and biases, interests, and level of sophistication will affect the choices you make about detail, strategies of organization and development, tone, style, and so on. For the papers you write in college, your audience will usually be your classmates and instructor, and, to be sure, yourself as well.

As you read over what you've written, ask yourself, as a representative of your audience, whether what you've written is clear, informative, timely, and persuasive to you. You can't give it a completely objective reading because of your own bias, the effort and time you've invested, and your natural desire to succeed in achieving your purpose. But you can pretty well determine if what you've written is not working. If your paper seems vague, poorly focused, and dull, your readers are likely to have the same reaction. After you have considered your own response, think about your fellow students, or the general reader. How much do they know about the subject? What ideas and images do they have in their heads about the subject? Do they have special interests you can appeal to? If their ideas about the subject differ from yours, you must consider your tone, style, and supporting detail carefully so that you can change their ideas and images to those you want them to have. Speaking of tone and style, the kinds of words you use, the length of your sentences and paragraphs, and similar matters will be affected by your audience. If that audience is your fellow students and your subject not too serious, you would want to adopt a lighter tone, a more informal style. If your audience is your instructor and your subject more serious, you would want to adopt a more serious, objective tone and a more formal style.

How a consideration of purpose and audience affects, and is affected by, the shaping of material for an essay can be illustrated by reviewing the detail about Mr. Jones (pp. 148–149) and the American economy (pp. 150–151). The items about Mr. Jones, for example, focus on his appearance, his personality, his relations with students, and his teaching methods. Though his teaching methods are described, the primary emphasis here is on Mr. Jones as a person—a friendly, sensitive, concerned human being, enthusiastic about his subject and eager to share his knowledge and enthusiasm with his students. A paper concentrating on his personal qualities would very likely appeal to an audience of college students, most of whom probably remember a favorite high school teacher and whose remembered impressions are likely to be about the person who taught the class rather than about the subject matter. A personal emphasis would warrant a lighter tone, a less formal style, and the writer's purpose would be to amuse and entertain as well as to inform and persuade.

A paper on American economic competitiveness generated from the details listed on pp. 150–151 presupposes a reasonably informed audience interested in and concerned about the state of the economy. Though such a discussion could be technical and complex, the facts and judgments presented here are not abstruse; but they must be intelligently ordered and sifted. The items deal with (1) fears about the decline of the economy, (2) reasons for optimism about it, (3) the effects on consumers as emphasis on exports grows, and (4) a deepening recession if exports fail to lift the economy. Since not all these matters could be dealt with in a paper of 500 words and since the preponderance of the detail focus on the first three, it makes sense to eliminate the fourth.

■ FORMULATING A THESIS STATEMENT

Your thesis is the one major point you want to drive home, the controlling idea of the essay. An examination of the ideas you have jotted down about your subject will give you a clearer idea of your thesis as well as your purpose. It is important in this stage to formulate your main point in a thesis statement, for it will provide a point of reference for organizing and unifying the materials you have developed. The thesis statement for an essay thus performs the same function as the controlling idea of a paragraph—to keep out irrelevant ideas.

A thesis statement, as we have mentioned earlier, is not a statement of purpose: "In this paper I want to inform and persuade my reader of the admirable human qualities of Mr. Jones, my senior English teacher," nor is it a statement of the topic: "In this paper I want to talk about Mr. Jones, my senior English teacher." A thesis statement *neither states an intention nor announces a topic.* It *expresses an attitude* toward the topic in a complete sentence. It makes a *judgment* about it: "Mr. Jones, my senior English teacher in high school, is a friendly, sensitive, concerned human being; enthusiastic about his subject; and eager and able to share his enthusiasm and knowledge."

One other point, a corollary of the one just made (see also pp. 17–19, Chapter Two): if the thesis statement is to be judgmental, *it should not be a factual statement.*

> John Steinbeck was born in Salinas, California.
> Banks now charge 10 percent on home loans.

These statements would not work as thesis statements because they lead nowhere. They're self-contained. They could serve as supporting detail but not as unifying generalizations that other sentences could support because they need no support. The fact that John Steinbeck was born in Salinas, California, could be used to support the thesis that John Steinbeck's work reflects his California roots, but it would not work as the thesis itself.

What was said about the controlling idea of a paragraph also applies to thesis statements: they need to be *limited, specific.* A broad, general thesis statement simply covers too much territory; it justifies the inclusion of such a range and variety of detail that any essay based on it would be superficial, vague, poorly focused.

General	Better
A well-educated person is a combination of many qualities.	A well-educated person is a harmonious blend of intellectual, moral, and emotional capacities.
A checking account is a good idea.	A checking account is useful because it provides convenience, safety, and a record of payment.
Emily Brett is a great girl.	Because of her wit, charm, and sophistication, Emily Brett is very popular.
The Bugliachi straight-eight roadster is a fine car.	The Bugliachi straight-eight roadster has beautiful lines, superior workmanship, and durability.

EXERCISE 18

A. Choose two of the subjects listed in Exercise 15B and make up a purpose and a thesis statement for each.

> EXAMPLE
> *Subject* My First Date with Alex
>
> PURPOSE STATEMENT I want to describe my first date with Alex, to make my reader understand the anticipation and anxiety I felt, the pleasure, and the panic and pain of that rainy evening.
>
> THESIS STATEMENT An experience that begins in eager anticipation and proceeds smoothly may still end in disaster but nonetheless teach you something useful about human beings and human relationships.

1. *Subject* _____

   PURPOSE STATEMENT _____

   _____

   _____

   THESIS STATEMENT _____

   _____

   _____

2. *Subject* _____

   PURPOSE STATEMENT _____

   _____

   _____

   THESIS STATEMENT _____

   _____

   _____

157

B. Choose two of the specific topics you split off from a general subject in Exercise 16A and provide a thesis statement about each. Your thesis sentence, remember, should be a full sentence, not a phrase. It should be limited and specific, not general and vague.

> EXAMPLE
> *Subject* Running for political office
>
> THESIS STATEMENT Running for political office is physically exhausting, emotionally depleting, and, at times, spiritually demoralizing.

1. *Subject* _____

THESIS STATEMENT _____

_____

_____

2. *Subject* _____

THESIS STATEMENT _____

_____

_____

C. Using the detail in the following groups of sentences, phrase a concise, comprehensive thesis statement for an outline on the subject. Write your thesis statement in the blanks provided.

1. A very common type is simple plagiarism. Lazy, unmotivated students copy the work of other students. Some buy term papers and turn them in as their own work. Sometimes code signals are used during examinations when a well-prepared student transmits information by hand signals to one or more students taking the same examination. Another way is to write notes and formula on the cuffs of shirts, palms of hands, on the covers of books. And, finally, a student may leave the examination room, on the excuse of going to a restroom, to reach a previously hidden bit of information.

THESIS STATEMENT _____

_____

158

2. Throughout history several groups who have been discriminated against have, nonetheless, substantially outperformed those who have practiced the discrimination. All over Southeast Asia, the Chinese have often been denied the same rights and treatment as native peoples, but their earned income in these countries has been much higher than that of the natives. This disparity in income and performance has produced envy, exampled in the exclusion of the Chinese after the war in Vietnam in the 1970s. The history of the Jews in many countries of Europe, North Africa, and the Middle East reveals a similar story; and the Ibos in Nigeria have had a similar history as have the Armenians in Turkey and the Italians in Argentina. The Japanese in California, though victims of discrimination until relatively recently, have achieved financial and professional success well above that of the more favored WASPs.

THESIS STATEMENT _____

_____

_____

3. Central Valley farmers will have to pay more for water from the state and federal governments. Acreage planted in crops requiring abundant water, such as alfalfa and rice, will have to be reduced. Coastal cities—San Diego, Santa Barbara, Monterey, and others—are building desalinization plants to provide water for households. Southern California water pumped down from northern California will be reduced and cut off at times. New suburban housing developments will also be scaled back because of the drought. Much greater use will be made of recycled water and drip-irrigation systems.

THESIS STATEMENT _____

_____

_____

4. In New York State each year there are some 130,000 felony arrests; approximately 8,000 people go to prison. There are 94,000 felony arrests in New York City; 5,000 to 6,000 serve time. A 1974 study of the District of Columbia came up with a similar picture. Of those arrested for armed robbery, less than one-quarter went to prison. More than 6,000 aggravated assaults were reported; 116 people were put away. A 1977 study of such cities as Detroit, Indianapolis, and New Orleans produced slightly better numbers, but nothing to counteract the exasperation of New York Police Commissioner Robert McGlire: "The criminal justice

159

system almost creates incentives for street criminals." (Rearranged from Roger Rosenblatt, "Why the Justice System Fails," *Time,* 1981.)

THESIS STATEMENT _____

_____

_____

5. Over the eighty years of its history, winners of the Nobel Prize have been recognized as international leaders in their fields. (2) The Nobel award amounts to about $710,000 for the winner, or winners if more than one is chosen in a field. (3) Award winners receive additional honors and rewards: honorary degrees, higher salaries, large lecture fees, consulting fees, and membership on boards of corporations. (4) These extras can amount to several times the amount of the award itself. (5) There is a prestige connected with the award that can elevate an unknown researcher into prominence overnight.

THESIS STATEMENT _____

_____

_____

160

◨ ORGANIZING DETAIL

The Scratch Outline

The ideas and impressions you have generated in support of a limited topic in the preceding pre-writing activities must now be organized and developed to carry out your purpose and support your thesis. They must be transformed into the sentences and paragraphs of a first draft of your theme. A scratch outline is an effective tool to help you sort through the material you have accumulated—ideas from brainstorming and freewriting, notes from readings and lectures, remembered experiences, conversations, and so on—to see if you can discover some pattern in your detail and establish relationships among the items. Consider, for example, the detail developed about Mr. Jones (pp. 148–149). Sorting through the detail, we can see that it can be organized into three main groups: those items dealing with his appearance, others with his personality and attitude toward students, and a third group with his teaching techniques. Grouping related items under these three headings produces this preliminary outline. Note that items #24 and #29 on the original list have been omitted: #24 because it has been included under #25 and #27 below, #29 because it introduces a digression.

1. appearance
   - #1   heavy-rimmed glasses, sparkling blue eyes
   - #2   tall, slender, slight roll to walk
   - #3   gray hair, thinning on top
   - #5   cardigan sweaters, windbreaker jackets, always a tie
   - #10   loafers, slacks, never jeans
   - #12   mid-forties, maybe older, laugh wrinkles
2. personality
   - #6   friendly, courteous, somewhat formal in class
   - #7   jokes to lighten the mood
   - #8   laughed at his own jokes—make sure we knew it was a joke, he said
   - #11   not serious about self, but serious about subject
   - #13   tough-minded about good work, tender-minded in personal contacts
   - #14   a good listener
   - #15   firm, fair, friendly—his code

    #25 somewhat formal with students, Mr. this, Miss that, friendly, but no pal

    #27 popular with students, but no nonsense

    #28 tough but fair

3. teaching methods

    #4   pacing behind lectern, eyes on floor, lost in thought at times

    #16 lots of homework, too much

    #17 Socratic method—lots of questions, no place to hide

    #18 nailed you for lack of preparation, goofing off

    #19 pop quizzes, essays

    #20 simplicity, clarity, write to express, not to impress

    #22 occasional stories, family, friends

    #23 loved his subject . . . cummings, Hemingway, Fitzgerald . . . literature

    #30 brought in books, loaned his own, always reading and recommending books

As you look over your groupings, you may discover that one heading contains more items than any other. The second and third groupings of this outline contain about twice as many items as the first. When this occurs, you may decide to change your subject to one of the main headings. Shifting your attention to your new subject, you could then supply additional detail and organize it in the same manner as you did the original topic. With a few more details a short theme of 300 words could be developed on Mr. Jones' personality. This possibility illustrates an important fact about a scratch outline: it is simply a tool, a means to an end. It's not inviolable. When you modify your purpose, modify your outline accordingly.

The initial grouping completed, you must now arrange your major and minor ideas in some effective order. The order you use will depend on the nature of your material and on your purpose. The order of detail about Mr. Jones focuses first on his appearance, then on his personality, then on his teaching methods. This order is reasonable since the first impression students usually form of instructors is of their general appearance. If readers get a strong image of Mr. Jones in their minds at the outset, they are more likely to understand more clearly and visualize more precisely his personality and teaching methods as they are presented.

Here is a revised version of the first outline. The order of the minor items under the main headings has been rearranged a bit to put closely related items together, and some new items have been added. Note also that a thesis statement has been added to serve as a visible guide to minimize the possibility of irrelevant material creeping in.

Ol' Jonesy: Firm, Fair, and Friendly

1. appearance
   tall, slender, with a roll to his walk
   mid-forties or so
   gray hair, thinning on top
   great smile: face lights up, eyes sparkle
   cardigan sweaters, windbreaker jackets, slacks
   always a tie—solid color
   loafers
2. personality—relations with others
   friendly but a bit formal in class, courteous
   addressed students as Mr. or Miss
   jokes to lighten mood
   laughed at his own jokes—to make sure we knew it was a joke, he said
   not serious about self, but serious about subject
   tough-minded about good work, tender-minded in personal contacts
   liked students, a good listener, generous with time in office
   popular with students—attended games, dances, senior picnic
   respected, popular with faculty
3. teaching methods
   lots of homework—too much
   Socratic method—questions, lots of questions, no place to hide
   pop quizzes, essays, seldom objective tests
   paced behind lectern at times, eyes on floor, lost in thought
   occasional stories about family, friends, college days
   loved his subject . . . cummings, Hemingway, Fitzgerald . . . literature, slides of Paris, Montparnasse
   brought in books, loaned his own, always reading and recommending books
   tough but fair
   praised good work, smiled at a good response, a wink for excellence
   nailed you for lack of preparation, goofing off, slipshod work

With this rough outline as a framework for your theme, you can begin the first draft. You may still want to supply additional clarifying and supporting detail, but this plan will provide sufficient direction for a theme of 500 words.

Before moving on to the formal outline, we should mention one other use of the scratch outline. Besides helping you discover the pattern in a list of details, a scratch outline is useful for organizing ideas on essays and examinations written in class. In this instance, begin with the major ideas, the ideas that will serve as the topic sentences of your paragraphs, and then jot down a few supporting details under each of the main ideas. The time it takes to develop a brief outline is time well spent, for your essay will be more unified and coherent than it would otherwise be. A scratch outline on the advantages or urban life might look like the following:

nearness of essential services
    grocery and drug stores, shopping malls
    hospitals
    police substation, post office
convenience and economy of public transportation
    good bus system
    no need to fight freeway traffic
    less dependence upon automobile, less expense for car
variety of recreational and cultural activities
    movie theaters, stage plays, museums
    nearby parks, musicals in summer
    little cafes and restaurants

EXERCISE 19

A. Work up a scratch outline of the detail you listed on a subject for Exercise 17A or B. Present three or four main headings and arrange your minor detail under the appropriate heading. Compose a purpose statement and a thesis statement and write them in the blanks provided.

Title _____

PURPOSE STATEMENT _____

_____

_____

THESIS STATEMENT _____

_____

_____

1. _____

_____

_____

_____

2. _____

_____

_____

_____

3. _____

_____

_____

_____

165

B. In each of the following groups, one idea could serve as a major heading for the other ideas. Identify the heading, and write it in the blank space provided.

1. he could be wasteful, uncouth, indifferent to the social amenities; virtues included a sturdy independence, the ability to look every man in the eye and tell him to go to hell; could express opinions forcefully; opinions frequently deplorable, his acts crude and peremptory; but true to himself; pioneer no "yes" man; could vote for candidates he liked and refuse to do jobs he considered demeaning.

Main Heading _____

2. Hegel, famous German speculative philosopher, considered deficient in philosophy when he graduated from university at Tubingen; F. H. Bradley, distinguished 19th century logician, almost failed Oxford University's entrance exams in mathematics; A. E. Housman, perhaps finest Latin scholar in the world, failed degree examination; many of world's famous men experienced early lack of success; George Bernard Shaw's early writings consistently rejected by publishers; Somerset Maugham's first ten years as a writer unsuccessful.

Main Heading _____

3. Bison meat eaten fresh or dried, pounded, mixed with berries to make pemmican; hides made into moccasins, leggings, dresses, shirts; hides also used to cover teepees; nothing wasted; hoofs boiled to make glue; tail used as a fly swatter or whip; thick, woolly bison hair stuffed medicine balls; rib bones formed sled runners; sinews made into bowstrings.

Main Heading _____

4. the world not running out of mineral resources; production of chromite, essential to metals industry, increased 248 percent in last decade; 200 years worth of land-reserve supply of manganese on hand at current use levels; American industry not threatened by lack of mineral resources; embargoes of vital mineral imports not likely; U.S. has large, untapped reserves and stockpiles of most minerals; U.S. imports 20 percent of minerals needed—much less than other industrial nations; large reserves of cobalt and manganese in seabed nodules

Main Heading _____

166

5. waste products include strontium 90 and plutonium 239, both deadly; strontium is carcinogenic and plutonium can poison all vegetation; plutonium 239 needs to be isolated for more than 250,000 years, strontium for 600 years; no container yet devised is foolproof even for decades, let alone for thousands of years; dumping nuclear wastes in the ocean creates problems because containers corrode; serious weakness of nuclear power is disposal of wastes; problem of corrosion and cracking in underground salt bed storage sites; by 2000 A.D. millions of gallons of wastes will have to be disposed of

Main Heading _____

C. Arrange the following items under three main headings. One of the items will serve as a title, another as a thesis statement (the statement that expresses the main point). Place the number of the item in the appropriate blank.

1. Continued dependence on oil as a primary source of energy presents two serious problems.
2. Solar energy is still in its infancy, and it will not reach its potential for several decades.
3. America has abundant supplies of coal, but it is dangerous to mine and burn.
4. The Israeli-Palestinian conflict exacerbates the volatility of the region.
5. Thousands of miners have died digging coal.
6. Nuclear power is relatively pollution-free.
7. Though not risk-free, nuclear power should not be abandoned at this time.
8. Rivalries among Muslim sects, particularly between the Shiites and Sunnis, are another source of instability with the potential of endangering access to Middle Eastern oil.
9. Coal plants emit dangerous pollutants into the air, some of them radioactive.
10. Nuclear power demands constant scrutiny of its operation, but it is a reasonably safe, assured, efficient means of providing energy.
11. To date no one has been killed by a nuclear power failure in the United States, whereas coal mines and oil fields have killed thousands.
12. Wind power will never be more than a minor source of energy.
13. Converting tidal power into electrical energy is practicable only in certain coastal regions.
14. The United States must import increasing amounts of oil, putting the American economy at risk should foreign supplies of oil be cut off.
15. The Middle East, for example, supplies over 30 percent of the oil the United States imports, and that area is a potentially explosive region.

167

16. The United States has adequate supplies of nuclear fuel within its borders, supplies that are not apt to be disrupted by unfriendly foreign powers.
17. The cost of converting oil shale into oil is high and the environmental problems are complicated.
18. Other sources of energy are not capable, at present, of supplanting nuclear power.
19. One problem concerns supply.
20. Another problem is that burning fossil fuel in power plants and automobiles produces pollution.
21. Nuclear power, an indispensable resource.

Title _____

THESIS STATEMENT _____

1. First main heading _____

   a. _____

   _____

   _____

   _____

   _____

   b. _____

2. Second main heading _____

   a. _____

   _____

   _____

   b. _____

   c. _____

168

     d. _____

     e. _____

3. Third main heading _____

     a. _____

     b. _____

     c. _____

169

The Formal Outline

The kind of scratch outline described in the preceding section is usually sufficient for a theme of 300 to 500 words. For a longer, more intricate writing assignment, however, you will find it helpful to make a more detailed, formal outline. The longer paper requires more careful preparation; it requires you to work out the relationships and the development of your thought more thoroughly. And a formal outline forces you to do just this. Beginning writers sometimes neglect the outline because of the time required to prepare it. But, as you will discover, the more time you spend in carefully preparing your outline, the less time you will waste when you begin to write. With a clearly detailed plan of your theme before you, you will not have to grope for ideas to clarify and develop your thesis. Properly used, an outline will give your writing a sense of proportion and direction. It should not, however, be thought of as a sacred covenant, an inflexible contract that must be adhered to at all costs. You should depart from it by adding an idea or illustration whenever you can move your thought forward more smoothly.

An outline has three parts: the *title,* the *thesis statement,* and the *body.* The body consists of the major and minor ideas that develop the main idea of the outline expressed in the thesis statement. The main ideas are represented by Roman numerals, minor ideas by capital letters, Arabic numerals, and lowercase letters, as illustrated in the following system:

   I.
      A.
         1.
           a.
             (1)
               (a)

Each main heading (I, II, and so on) need not be developed in as much detail as this illustration. An outline for a theme of 300 to 500 words usually does not require subdivision beyond the first Arabic numerals.

   I.
      A.
         1.
         2.
      B.
   II.

Capitalize the first word of each heading, and if the heading is a sentence place a period at the end. Occasionally the entries on a sentence outline may extend to two or three lines. When they do, make certain that your left-hand margin does not extend to the left of the period after the topic symbol, as illustrated below.

I. _____

   A. _____

      _____

      _____

The thesis statement appears between the title and the first Roman numeral.

Title

THESIS STATEMENT _____

_____

I. _____

The most frequently used forms of the outline are the *topic outline* and the *sentence outline.* The entries on a topic outline are made up of short phrases or single words. The following exemplifies a topic outline:

Violence in School: A Growing Problem in the United States

THESIS STATEMENT The increase in violence in American schools is creating serious financial and educational problems for school districts.

    I. Nature of problem
       A. Abuse of students
          1. Physical assaults
             a. Beatings
             b. Rape
             c. Murder
          2. Mental and emotional harassment
       B. Attacks on teachers and school board members
       C. Vandalism of school property

II. Response by school authorities
   A. Increased use of armed guards
      1. Off-duty police officers in Chicago
      2. District-employed patrols in Los Angeles
   B. Increased use of hardware
      1. Laser-beam alarm signals
      2. Walkie-talkies for teachers
      3. Police helicopters
III. Consequences of increasing violence
   A. Depletion of school budgets
      1. Less money for supplies and facilities
      2. Less money for maintenance
      3. Less money for teaching staff
   B. Adverse effect on student learning
   C. Community anger at lack of safety in schools
      1. Attacks on school board members
      2. Lack of financial support for school bonds
IV. Solutions to problem
   A. Hard-line approach
      1. Increased use of armed guards and police
      2. Swift apprehension of offenders
      3. Jail and prison sentences for juveniles
   B. Long-term approach
      1. Reduction of violence in mass media
      2. Improvement in lives of underprivileged
      3. Restructuring of schools to ease competition and tensions
   C. Other approaches
      1. More vocational education
      2. Reductions in class size
      3. Release of unmotivated students
      4. Alternative of community service instead of jail for offenders
      5. New rights and responsibilities for students to aid in control of violence

In a sentence outline each entry is a sentence.

The Ecological Importance of Open Space

THESIS STATEMENT Open space is essential to the maintenance of a healthful, life-supporting environment.

   I. Open space plays a vital role in maintaining breathable air.
      A. Open space vegetation filters particles from the air.
      B. It produces oxygen through the process of photosynthesis.
      C. Automobiles and factories in urban areas produce smog.
  II. Intelligent use of open space can help to maintain a healthful
      climate.
      A. Open space dissipates islands of heat produced in urban
         areas.
         1. Covered surfaces, such as asphalt, absorb heat.
         2. Urban areas produce heat through combustion.
      B. Native vegetation of open space helps to reduce humidity
         produced by evaporation of water used to irrigate exotic
         plants in cities and suburbs.
 III. Invasion of open space by urban and suburban sprawl im-
      pairs its recreational use.
      A. Open space surrounding cities is often used by city-
         dwelling hikers and cyclists.
      B. Housing tracts and shopping centers occupy space that
         could be better used for public parks and campgrounds
         near densely populated cities.
      C. Empty beach land should be purchased by a state or the
         federal government and preserved for recreational use.
  IV. Wildlife, essential to a healthful ecological system, is threat-
      ened by the elimination of open space.

Of the two forms, the topic outline is generally easier to manage,
but because the theme itself will be composed of sentences, the sentence outline provides a more convenient basis than the topic outline
for the translation of thought from outline to theme.

If you are to do an effective job of outlining, you must know something of the principles that govern the construction of an outline,
as well as its format. These concern (1) logic subordination of ideas,
(2) parallel structure, (3) single subdivisions, and (4) specific, meaningful headings. The most important of these principles is the first, for
the main purpose of your outline is to give you a logical, well-
organized structure for your composition. Examine your outline first
to be sure that your main headings are logical divisions of the subject
expressed in the title and thesis statement. Make certain that the subheadings are logical divisions of the headings under which they are
listed. In the outlines on school violence and open space presented
above, the main and subheadings are logically subordinate to the thesis and main headings respectively.

The principle of parallelism, which requires that ideas of equal importance in a sentence be expressed in the same grammatical form, applies to the construction of outlines. An outline is parallel when the headings designated by the same kind of letter or numeral are phrased in parallel form. That is, if Roman numeral I is a prepositional phrase, the other Roman numerals should be prepositional phrases also. If A and B under I are nouns, so must be the other capital letters under II, III, and so on. A sentence outline is automatically parallel, for each entry is a sentence and hence parallel. In the topic outline on school violence, each main heading—"Nature of problems," "Response by school authorities." and so on—is a noun followed by a prepositional phrase.

The third and fourth criteria—single subdivisions and specific, meaningful headings—follow logically from the process and purpose of outlining. The basis of outlining, as we have seen, is the division of larger topics into smaller ones. When you divide a topic into its parts, you must, logically, have at least two parts. In constructing an outline, therefore, avoid the single subdivision. If you divide a Roman numeral heading, you must have at least an A and a B under it. If you divide a capital letter heading, you must provide at least a 1 and a 2 under it, and so on through each successive stage of the outline.

Since the purpose of an outline is to provide a framework, a concise structure of the thought of a composition, make certain your headings convey specific, meaningful ideas. General headings such as "Introduction," "Body," "Conclusion," or "Examples," "Functions," "Types," and the like do not represent the subject matter of an outline very clearly and therefore provide little guidance when you translate the ideas from your outline to the essay itself.

After you have completed your outline, examine it carefully to see that its format is correct and that the organization of its ideas is logical and consistent. Be sure that you have included a title and a thesis statement and that you have used symbols correctly and consistently. As you check the body of the outline, make certain that you have avoided single subdivisions and vague, meaningless headings and that entries of the same rank are expressed in parallel structure. If your outline meets these tests, you are ready to begin your first draft.

EXERCISE 20

A. Compose a formal sentence outline on the American economy using the detail presented on pages 150–151. Arrange the detail under three main headings, and provide a title and thesis statement. Eliminate any items that don't belong under any of the three headings, and make certain minor items are placed under the appropriate heading.

Title _____

THESIS STATEMENT _____

_____

_____

   I. _____

_____

      A. _____

_____

         1. _____

_____

         2. _____

_____

         3. _____

_____

      B. _____

_____

         1. _____

_____

         2. _____

_____

175

II. _____

_____

A. _____

_____

1. _____

_____

a. _____

_____

b. _____

_____

2. _____

_____

a. _____

_____

b. _____

_____

B. _____

_____

1. _____

_____

2. _____

_____

a. _____

_____

176

      b. _____

         _____

III. _____

         _____

      A. _____

         _____

      B. _____

         _____

      C. _____

         _____

      D. _____

         _____

B. List below the numbers of the items you omitted from the original list of detail on the American economy, pages 150–151, in making up your outline for 20A above and briefly explain why.

          Detail Omitted   Reason

        1. _____   _____

        2. _____   _____

        3. _____   _____

        4. _____   _____

        5. _____   _____

177

■ THE FIRST DRAFT   *Need Theses complete*

The scratch or formal outline completed, you are now ready to write the first draft of your paper. Your outline provides the framework; now you must transform this plan into the sentences and paragraphs of your theme.

The major headings of your outline will become the topic sentences of your paragraphs, though the correspondence is not always exact. That is, a major heading may occasionally require more than one paragraph to develop it, depending upon the amount of supporting material it encompasses. The first main heading of the outline "Violence in School: A Growing Problem in the United States" (pp. 171–172):

    I. Nature of problem
        A. Abuse of students
        B. Attacks on teachers and school board members
        C. Vandalism of school property

would require at least a paragraph and possible two or three for full development. Conversely, in a short composition, two Roman numeral headings might be included in one paragraph.

Plan your time so that you can revise your first draft carefully. Concentrate on the body of your paper, the major points of your outline. You can work on your opening and closing later. Once you begin, move steadily forward. Do not worry about perfection at this stage. The important thing is to get your ideas on paper. You can correct errors in spelling, punctuation, and grammar; make improvements in wording; and add, delete, or reorder material later when you revise this draft. If you stop to check these items now, you may lose your train of thought.

Here is a first draft of a theme developed from the scratch outline on Mr. Jones, pp. 148–149.

Firm, Fair, and Friendly

In my senior year in high school, I had Mr. Jones for English, one of the best teachers I've ever had. He was a tall, slender man in his late forties with gray, thinning hair. Heavy rimmed glasses perched precariously on his nose, which he was always taking off and polishing or sticking in his mouth while he mulled over a response to a student's question. When he walked into class, he always carried two or three books under his arm with strips of paper dangling from them, marking passages he planned to read. I remember, too, the cardigan sweaters—he must have had a dozen of them—neatly pressed slacks, Oxford loafers, and a tie, always a tie. On rainy days he wore a navy blue windbreaker jacket, but that was the only time he was without a sweater. He was always carefully dressed, but he was no dandy. But perhaps the thing I remember best was his smile. When he smiled, his blue eyes sparkled and crinkled at the corners. His smile made you feel good, at ease, somehow reassured.

But though he was friendly and naturally at ease in company with others, he was a bit formal in class. He never called us by our first names. It was always Mr. Weaver or Miss Powers, never Brad nor Marie. He obviously loved his work and liked his students, but he kept his distance somehow. Yet though he never deliberately embarrassed a student in front of the class with a sarcastic remark, he could communicate his displeasure all right. He'd look steadily at the offending student for a few seconds, his lips firming slightly shut. That was usually enough, but if it didn't work, he'd say something in a lowered tone of voice. He didn't have to do this often because students liked and respected him and wanted to please him. I suppose because he liked and respected us and was so obviously serious about his subject and intent on our learning it and sharing his enthusiasm. He was serious about his subject, his teaching, but not about himself. He always had a witty comment or a joke to lighten the mood when necessary. He'd laugh harder than anyone else, to make sure we knew it was a joke he said. His friendliness, his enthusiasm, his wit attracted students wherever he was. Students were always waiting to talk to him in his office, to ask advice about college, for a letter of recommendation, or just to chat a bit. I don't think he ever missed a football game or the senior dance or picnic, for that matter.

Jonesy had personality, integrity, vitality—all of which made him popular, as I said; but what I liked most about him was that he was a fine teacher. Yes, he cared about students, but he cared more about teaching them his subject. And that meant homework, lots of it, and pop quizzes now and then to keep them current on the reading. He lectured occasionally, to provide background information whenever we moved on to a new period in American literature. After a brief glance at his notes, he'd begin to move around—to the blackboard, to the windows, back to the lectern—as he talked; but he preferred discussion, a Socratic dialogue. He'd write several questions on the board for the next day's discussion, and he'd expect you to be prepared to discuss them. He directed the discussion, but he didn't dominate it; for he was a good listener and made sure every student had a chance to respond, whether he or she wanted to or not. If he were pleased with a response, he'd nod his head and smile. Occasionally he'd also read a good essay from a student, praising its good points and then winking at the writer when he handed it back. But he was tough-minded, too. He really nailed you for sloppy work or inattention. When you got an A from him, you really felt good, for he wasn't an easy grader. We used to moan about his grading standards, usually to no avail, though he would change a grade if after rereading a student's paper he thought he had been unfair.

We had many interesting discussions on Twain, Crane, and Dreiser, as I recall, but his favorite period was the 1920s. He loved the expatriates: Anderson, cummings, Hemingway, Fitzgerald. He was always bringing in books for us to read, as I said; but when he got to this period, he was a walking library. I think he'd read every book written by or about Hemingway and Fitzgerald, or about Paris in the twenties. He must have seen the films and slides he showed us about the expatriates and Paris dozens of times, but his enthusiasm never flagged when he discussed them. I can still see him, and hear him, reading and chuckling over some passage from *The Sun Also Rises* or *A Moveable Feast.* Yes, I can still see him.

EXERCISE 21

Write a first draft of a theme based on the outline you prepared for 17A or B.

◼ REVISING THE FIRST DRAFT

Revision is the final stage in the process of composition, and it is an important one. Revision means to see again, and that's what you must do now: look again at what you've written to see what changes need to be made in the content and organization and how you might polish and refine the writing itself. Actually, you have been revising at every stage along the way—selecting and revising your subject, revising your scratch outline, rethinking your purpose and thesis, and so on. This final revision, is, however, more than just a brief last look to correct some spelling or grammatical errors. It requires a serious re-examination of your first draft to make sure it does what you want it to do.

As we have suggested earlier, don't begin to revise your first draft immediately after you have completed it. Don't think about it for at least a day or two. When you look at it again, you will be able to view it more objectively, to discover more clearly what you must do to give it its final shape.

First Stage

In the first stage of your revision, re-examine the *content* and *organization* of your paper. Put yourself in the mind of your reader as you take a fresh, objective look at your paper. Have you ordered your paragraphs in an effective sequence so that your reader can easily follow the progress of your thought? Do your paragraphs support your thesis and advance the thought logically, compellingly? Have you provided enough detail, enough evidence and illustration of your ideas? Do any parts need to be rewritten to add or delete material? Have you defined important terms and concepts? Is your tone appropriate, consistent?

After you have looked at the structure of the whole paper, concentrate on your paragraphs. Read them carefully to see that they are unified, well developed, and coherent.

Unity   The controlling idea of each paragraph should be clearly and concisely stated in a topic statement. Each sentence of the paragraph should support this idea.

Development   Each paragraph should contain enough detail—enough facts, illustrations, comparisons, judgments—to explain the controlling idea adequately. The supporting detail should be concrete and specific. Every generalization should be supported by sufficient evidence to persuade a fair-minded reader.

Coherence   The ideas in each paragraph should be arranged in a logical sequence and the sentences linked together smoothly with transitional expressions, repetition of key terms, parallel structure, and pronoun reference. *for the benefit of the audience*

The last suggestion regarding coherence needs further comment. Our previous discussion of coherence concentrated on coherence *within* the paragraph. When you write a longer composition, you must make certain that the thought flows smoothly *between* paragraphs as well as between sentences. If you have organized your paper carefully, there should be a steady development of thought from paragraph to paragraph, but you can accentuate this continuity through judicious use of transitional expressions and through repetition of key words. In the following passage, for example, the writer uses both these devices to ensure continuity between paragraphs.

> Even the shift in the kind of curriculum is upsetting. The students are used to having the day arranged for them from, say, nine to three, high-school fashion. They now find themselves attending classes for only fifteen hours or so a week. The concentration in depth on a few subjects is a new idea to them. The requisite self-discipline is often something they learn only after painful experience.
>
> Furthermore, college is the students' first encounter with live intellectuals. They meet individual members of the faculty who have written important books or completed important pieces of research. The various intellectual fields become matters of personal experience. The students learn that work does not just happen to get done. They find that the productive intellectual is not a superman but an everyday figure. They will also make the discovery that there are those who consider intellectual pursuits reason enough for an entire life. Students are nearly always surprised to find such pursuits valued so highly.
>
> Students are surprised, too, at their first meeting with really violent political opinion. . . . [From James K. Feibleman, "What Happens in College," *Saturday Review,* October 20, 1962.]

Furthermore, the first word of the second paragraph, informs us that the writer is adding another illustration of the idea he has been developing in the preceding paragraph. The transition between the second and third paragraphs is especially smooth.

> . . . Students are nearly always surprised to find such pursuits valued so highly.
>
> Students are surprised, too, at their first meeting . . .

The repetition of the word *students* in the latter sentence plus the use of the transitional *too,* which signals an additional illustration of the author's point in the preceding two paragraphs, provides an uninterrupted bridge of thought as we move from one paragraph to the next. The repetition of key words such as *students* and its pronoun *they* throughout the passage also ties the paragraphs together.

Emphasis

After you have tested your paper for unity, development, and coherence, examine it once more to make certain you have given your most important ideas the proper emphasis. To make your reader receptive to the effect you wish to create, you must communicate your thoughts clearly and forcefully. The most emphatic positions in a composition are the beginning and the end. Reread your opening and closing sentences. Now is the time to revise and polish these sentences. What you say in the opening sentence often determines the kind of reading your paper will receive. If your first sentence successfully arouses the interest and curiosity of your readers, they will probably give your paper a sympathetic reading. If it is rather dull and colorless, their reading will probably be more perfunctory. The first few sentences are especially important if the purpose of your paper is to argue a point. In this case you must establish yourself as a reasonable individual, not a fanatic. If your introduction makes the readers suspicious or uneasy about your motives, it will be difficult to persuade them of anything.

What you say in the closing sentence is even more important. You can regain your readers' interest after an uninspiring introduction with lively material in the body of the paper, but you have no second chance after they have finished reading. What your readers read last, they usually remember best. If your last sentence is vague and inconclusive, their final impression is not apt to be favorable. Read over your first draft carefully, therefore, and revise your opening and closing sentences to make them as effective as possible. The following discussion will provide some specific suggestions for opening and closing sentences.

Beginning the Paper

The beginning of an essay must do three things: it must engage the reader's attention, introduce the subject, and set an appropriate tone for the essay. We have considered tone in a previous chapter. Tone, we said, defines your attitude toward your subject, the stance you take toward your readers. If your purpose is humor or autobiography, a light, playful tone is in order. But if you are dealing with a serious subject, as you will be in much of your college writing, you should adopt a more straightforward, serious tone. Above all, you should establish yourself as a reasonable, trustworthy person. If your readers conclude at the outset that you are a hothead or a bigot, they will simply tune you out.

A paper of 500 words or longer may require an introductory paragraph, but for most short themes of 300 words or less the first paragraph can introduce the subject, set the tone, and begin the first main idea. Whether your introduction is a single sentence or a whole paragraph, however, begin with a sentence that is interesting and says something important about the subject.

You may use a number of ways to gain your reader's attention at the beginning of an essay:

1. An *unusual comparison* may stimulate reader interest:

> Prime Minister Trudeau has observed that, for Canada, coexisting with the United States is like sleeping with an elephant. No matter how friendly the animal, every grunt and twitch shakes the smaller partner. (From Henry C. Wallich, "The Elephant in Bed," *Newsweek,* September 22, 1969, p. 94.)

2. Or a slightly barbed, *provocative statement:*

> Ah, spring. The sap is rising and so is what passes for idealism on campuses where love of justice is expressed by shouting down conservative speakers. (From George F. Will, "Ah, Idealism," *The Morning After,* The Free Press, 1986.)

3. A *simple, direct statement* of the main idea can be effective:

> The time has come for some truly dramatic solutions to the problems plaguing so many of our urban schools. (From Franklyn G. Jennifer, "For Children at Risk, a Sanctuary," *Los Angeles Times,* 1991.)

> When we speak of "equal justice under the law," we simply mean applying the same rules to everybody. That has nothing to do with whether everyone performs equally. A good umpire calls balls and strikes by the same rules for everyone, but one batter may get twice as many hits as another. (From Thomas Sowell, "We're Not Really Equal," *Newsweek,* September 3, 1981.)

4. An *appropriate quoted passage* may attract reader attention:

> Being well informed may not be the mark of a progressive mentality it's commonly thought to be. "The mind of a thoroughly

well-informed man," says Oscar Wilde, "is a dreadful thing. It is like a bric-a-brac shop, all monsters and dust, with everything priced above its proper value."

Courage and fear are often thought of as mutually exclusive states of mind, one admirable, the other shameful. Mark Twain knew better. "Courage," he said, "is resistance to fear, mastery of fear—not absence of fear. Except a creature be part coward it is not a compliment to say it is brave; it is merely a loose misapplication of the word. Consider the flea!—incomparably the bravest of all the creatures of God, if ignorance of fear were courage." (From *Pudd'nhead Wilson.*)

5. The writer may use a *startling statistic:*

Harry is one of 5,000 young Americans a year who commit suicide—a near epidemic average of thirteen a day. Suicide is now the third leading cause of death for 15- to 24-year-olds, after accidents and homicides. [From "Teen-Age Suicide," *Newsweek,* August 28, 1978, p. 74.]

6. A *personal experience* can be effective in catching reader interest, particularly when you are writing about yourself:

I'll never forget one Saturday night when I was a junior in high school and my pals decided to take me to my first burlesque show in downtown Los Angeles. They were all older and taller than I, and I had always felt a bit self-conscious with them, as if I somehow had to prove my manhood to be worthy of their friendship. I wanted to go, but I was a bit nervous for fear I'd reveal my naiveté, my innocence. On the way they decided to stop for a beer, and of course I had to drink one, too. As a matter of fact, I drank two, to fortify myself, I suppose. . . .

These suggestions do not exhaust the possibilities, of course. As you gain experience, you will discover other effective ways to introduce your subject and to elicit reader interest at the same time. As you experiment with various openers, keep the following points in mind.

First, limit your introduction to one or two sentences and get directly into your subject unless you are writing a paper of 400 words or longer. Wandering, irrelevant introductions like the following are deadening:

Why I Want to Be a Doctor

I guess I've always wanted to be a doctor. My grandfather on my mother's side was a doctor, and I was very fond of Granddad. He used to take me with him on his house calls. . . .

Next, avoid apologizing. A theme that begins "I am not an expert on politics, but . . ." is not likely to arouse much interest.

Third, avoid the kind of provocative, intimidating statement that forces a response from your reader. "We've had enough of politicians who promise fiscal responsibility and then saddle hardworking Americans with backbreaking taxes." Such a beginning suggests anger and narrow-mindedness. It will cause a thoughtful reader to lose interest quickly.

Be wary also of the broad generalization as an opener. Statements like "Americans have always envied the Europeans' cultural sophistication" are simply too comprehensive to be supportable. They will not impress an intelligent reader.

Finally, make certain that your first sentence is easily understood without reference to the title. For a theme entitled "Tobacco and the Teen-ager," the following beginning sentence would only confuse the reader: "I guess everybody has tried it at least once by the time he or she is seventeen."

Ending the Paper  (*Conclusions*)

For the short theme of 300 to 400 words a special summarizing paragraph is not necessary. A sentence or two is usually sufficient. If your paper is well organized and coherent,

1. A *final detail* will often provide a satisfactory conclusion:

> To sum up, unchecked population growth is not merely an annoying problem exaggerated by pessimists who always worry about the future. It is, on the contrary, the most serious problem humanity faces today. Hunger and starvation, environmental destruction, and increasing human tensions and irritability—these are the certain results if we are not able to solve it.

2. An *apt quotation* may conclude as well as begin an essay:

> Many Americans seem to be reluctant to express emphatic moral judgments on crime, criminals . . . on evil. They stress socioeconomic factors as the source of criminal acts, not

the character, the behavior of the criminal. But as George Will reminds us, "A society that flinches from the fact of evil will flinch from the act of punishment. It should not wonder why it does not feel safe."

3. If you have focused on a problem in your essay, you may conclude with a *call for action.*

> A large number of Americans favor government subsidies for day-care centers, but the cost would be horrendous and divert scarce funds from the truly needy, working parents with low incomes. Instead of granting a federal tax credit for child care that benefits, for the most part, middle class families, the government should grant greater tax relief to the working poor.

4. A conclusion that *repeats an idea expressed in the opening paragraph* may provide an effective finishing touch. Henry Wallich provides an illustration as he summarizes his thesis about American economic relations with foreign countries (see p. 184, number 1, "The Elephant in Bed"):

> It is good to know that, in a pinch, we could go it alone. It adds to our bargaining power. But we must remember that the final result of isolationism is isolation. If the U.S. cannot be a comfortable sleeping partner, at least it can try to be a considerate one.

5. And you may refresh your reader's mind by *enumerating the main points* of your paper:

> The United States needs a more coherent, efficient mass transit system in order to 1) reduce its dependence on imported oil, 2) reduce traffic congestion in urban areas, 3) reduce air pollution, and 4) ensure a satisfactory means of transportation for all citizens lacking access to automobiles.

Study the final paragraph of your first draft. If you think a special concluding sentence would give emphasis to your paper, add one. But do not tack on unneeded sentences after you have completed your thought, especially if they contain apology. An apology at the end of your paper is just as ineffectual as one at the beginning. And do not inject a new idea into your final sentences. A paper that concludes

> Increased pollution, rapid depletion of vital natural resources, increased world hunger and starvation—all these await

us if world population continues its rapid expansion. And yet one wonders if such dire predictions will really come to pass, for if human beings can split the atom and land a man on the moon, surely they can defuse the population bomb.

makes a reader wonder whether the writer had second thoughts about the validity of his own conclusions.

Proportion

The preceding discussion has stressed the importance of *position* in achieving emphasis. Of equal importance is *proportion,* or balance. In a well-proportioned essay the more important points are given more space; they are developed at greater length. Minor ideas and illustrative detail are not allowed to overshadow or obscure the central thesis. The following essay, based on the outline in Exercise 20A, illustrates this principle.

A Fading Superpower?

Introduction   The condition of the American economy and its impact upon American influence and power throughout the world have been much in the news recently. Many observers—economists, members of Congress, columnists, scholars—have predicted a decline in the American standard of living and power because of a loss of economic competitiveness in international trade. This *First Topic* fear is not illusory. For one thing, increasing federal *Sentence* and trade deficits as well as increasing numbers of foreign purchasers of American assets, have made the United States the world's largest debtor nation. Not too long ago the United States was the leading creditor nation in the world. Economists also worry about Americans' low rate of savings, a rate which impedes the formation of capital needed for continuing the modernizing of American industry. Prominent business leaders and industrialists lament the decreasing supply of educated, trained workers. The emergence of the European Community as a formidable trading bloc led by the powerful German economy as well as the dramatic rise of Japan as an economic superpower provide additional evidence for the purveyors of gloom.

Second Topic Sentence

But though fears of American economic decline are not groundless, they are exaggerated. In fact, optimists detect hopeful signs of a resurgence of American economic power and influence. For example, American manufacturing is not losing its competitiveness. Owing to increased investment in new technology, especially computerized processes and the increasing use of robots, American industry now boasts the highest output per employee in the world. And productivity in the manufacturing sector is growing. This increased efficiency, as well as the fall in the dollar against foreign currencies, have given American industry a cost advantage over its trading partners. Currently, United States labor costs are 15 percent below those of the other major industrialized countries. As a result, more and more foreign manufacturers, particularly Japanese automobile manufacturers, are setting up operations in the United States to take advantage of these lowered costs.

Growth in American exports provides a second reason for optimism. In 1990, for instance, the United States exported $394 billion worth of goods, up from $250 billion in 1987—a 50 percent increase. Imports grew at half this rate during this period. The United States exports brainpower as well. Pacific Telesis is currently providing expertise to improve German telecommunications. Fluor and Bechtel corporations are heavily involved in construction projects in the Middle East. And in 1989 foreign tourists spent $1.2 billion more in this country than Americans spent abroad. In 1991 more than 40 million foreign tourists are expected to visit the United States.

Third Topic Sentence

This new emphasis upon exports, though beneficial, will effect some changes in the American economy and lifestyle. An increasing number of Americans will earn their living selling to foreigners, and the economy will become more firmly global in scope, the American worker less parochial in his thinking. But as more goods are produced for export, fewer goods will be available for consumers. Moreover, a weak dollar, though it helps exports, makes imports more expensive; and consumer spending will probably not grow at fast in the '90s as it did in the '80s. More expensive imports also means

Conclusion
higher inflation, a drop in the purchasing power of the consumer, and, consequently, a slightly lower standard of living. American tourists will find foreign travel more costly as well. In short, Americans will be less self-indulgent in the '90s than they were in the '80s; but these changes certainly do not mean that the United States is a mortally weakened, waning power among its trading partners. The long-term trend emphasing exports will reshape the American economy, but it will be a boon. And the United States will be for some time to come the world's largest trading nation.

Second Stage

In the second stage of your revision, you must edit the writing itself: the sentence structure, diction, mechanics, and punctuation.

Sentence Structure, Diction, Mechanics, and Punctuation

If your ideas are to have force and significance, to arouse the interest of your reader, they must be expressed in sentences that are clear, grammatical, and forceful. Clarity is primary. If your sentences are vague, awkward, or imprecise, you will not communicate your ideas effectively. Reread your essays carefully, then, to make certain that

1. each sentence is clear, without dangling or misplaced modifiers, ambiguous pronoun reference, or shifts in point of view;
2. each sentence is grammatically complete, not a fragment;
3. you have avoided fused sentences and comma splices.

The *sentence fragment,* the *fused sentence,* and the *comma splice* need special attention since they confuse readers about the beginnings and endings of sentences. The *sentence fragment,* as its name implies, is not a complete sentence. Though it begins with a capital letter and ends with a period, the group of words does not form an independent clause that makes sense by itself. Sometimes the group lacks a subject and/or a predicate:

A night on the town.
My favorite singer.

Sometimes a dependent clause is punctuated as if it were a complete sentence:

> Even though the doctor had explained in great detail the seriousness of his illness.

In the fragment above the subordinating conjunction *even though* renders the clause that follows it subordinate, and so incomplete as a sentence. Without the conjunction, the clause would be independent and able to stand as a full sentence:

> The doctor had explained in great detail the seriousness of his illness.

To qualify as a complete sentence, a group of words must have a subject and a predicate, and the subject-predicate construction must not be preceded by a subordinating conjunction.

Fragments also occur when *verbals* are confused with verbs. A verbal is a word (or words), derived from a verb, but which does not function as a verb. Instead, verbals function as modifiers or nouns. One type of verbal, the *participle,* commonly ends in *ing, ed, t,* or *en.* It is used as an adjective to modify (or describe) nouns and pronouns:

> The wave *pounding* the shore damaged the beach houses.
> The runner, *exhausted* by the race, fell to the ground.

The participle *pounding* in the first sentence modifies the noun *waves;* in the second the participle *exhausted* modifies the noun *runner.*

Another type of verbal, the *infinitive,* consists of the word *to* plus a verb form: *to read, to write, to sleep.* The infinitive functions as a noun or modifier:

> To *ski* well requires concentration, patience, and courage.
> Don has the desire to *succeed.*
> Dorothy plays *to win.*

In the first sentence above, the infinitive *to ski* functions as a noun, as the subject of the verb *requires;* in the second, *to succeed* functions as a modifier of the noun *desire;* in the third, *to win* functions as a modifier of the verb *plays.*

A third type of verbal is the *gerund.* Like one form of the participle, the gerund ends in *ing,* but it functions as a noun, frequently as the subject or object of the verb, and as the object of a preposition:

Living well is the best revenge.
Coaches discourage *smoking.*
The fireman died from *inhaling* smoke.

In the first sentence, the gerund *living* is the subject of the verb *is;* in the second sentence, *smoking* is the object of the verb *discourage;* and in the third sentence, *inhaling* is the object of the preposition *from.*

To reiterate, *verbals are not verbs.* If the only verb form in a sentence is a verbal, the sentence is a fragment.

Fragments sometimes result from a lack of understanding of the fundamentals of sentence construction, sometimes from carelessness and haste. Though permissible in certain circumstances, as will be explained below, you should avoid them, for they are confusing and indicative of sloppy thought. As you read over your sentences, keep in mind what you have learned about verbals, subordinate or dependent clauses, and independent clauses.

In other words, never punctuate as complete sentences any of the following:

1. a group of words lacking a subject and/or a predicate, like "Along the beach near the jetty"
2. a dependent clause preceded by a relative pronoun, like "Who turned out to be my best friend"
3. a dependent clause preceded by a subordinating conjunction, like "Although I had learned a good deal"
4. an infinitive construction, like "To ensure the success of our venture"
5. a gerund construction, like "From a love of swimming"
6. a participial construction, like "Believing he had won the race"

The simplest way to eliminate fragments like these is to tie them to independent clauses: "Believing he had won the race, Leonard raised his arms and waved to the crowd." Or, as illustrated earlier, simply add a subject and/or a predicate to complete the thought of a phrase: "Dave jogged along the beach near the jetty." It is also helpful to read your sentences aloud, for the pitch of your voice drops more sharply at the end of a sentence than it does at the end of a phrase or subordinate clause. If your ear does not detect such a drop at the end of a word group you have punctuated as a sentence, your sentence may be a fragment.

The warning against the use of fragments is important advice, but since you will occasionally find them used by experienced writers, we should explain the circumstances that permit them. A nonsentence, for example, may be used for emphasis:

> Young writers are advised to be true to themselves, to be honest. They are told to respect their readers, to be clear. And they are told to be brief, not to waste their readers' time. *All good advice, but hard to follow.*

Or it may be used to present a number of separate, distinct impressions in a passage of description:

> The road curved to the left around the hill. The desert heat beat down on us after we abandoned the car and started walking north. *Nothing but cactus and sand. Drifting tumbleweed. Swirls of dust.*

And it is often used in dialogue or in answers in questions:

> Where did you go with Karen? *To the dance.*

> Should we be persuaded on such flimsy evidence as the testimony of a convicted perjurer? *Certainly not.*

A *fused sentence* results when two independent clauses come together with no punctuation between them.

> Many edible fish have unappetizing names the ratfish, the dogfish, the gagfish, and the grunt are among them.

The lack of punctuation or a conjunction after *names* produces a confusing sentence. You should be able to detect fused sentences like this one by simply listening to your voice as you read your sentences aloud. When reading this one aloud, you will observe the pause and drop in voice after *names,* evidence of the end of one independent clause and so requiring a period, a semicolon, or a comma with a coordinating conjunction before the beginning of the next independent clause.

> Many edible fish have unappetizing names; the ratfish, the dogfish, the gagfish, and the grunt are among them.

A *comma splice* results when two independent clauses are joined by only a comma:

> Parents who indulge their children's every whim don't help them, children need to know how to handle disappointment.

The comma after *them* does not clearly reveal the relationship between the two ideas, that each is a self-contained thought. A period, a semicolon, or a coordinating conjunction is needed:

> Parents who indulge their children's every whim don't help them. Children need to know how to handle disappointment.

> Parents who indulge their children's every whim don't help them; children need to know how to handle disappointment.

> Parents who indulge their children's every whim don't help them, for children need to know how to handle disappointment.

When you are satisfied with the content and clarity of your sentences, examine them for *variety of length and pattern.* The length of your sentences should vary. A continuous use of short sentences will make your writing choppy and prevent a smooth flow of thought. On the other hand, a succession of long sentences often weakens the interest and tires the patience of readers as they seek to keep important ideas in mind and distinguish major from minor points.

Remember to vary the order of your sentences as well. Normally, the subject precedes the verb in a sentence.

> The English coffeehouse was a meeting place for men with similar interests in the eighteenth century.

But an essay composed entirely of sentences that begin with the subject is less interesting, and therefore less effective, than one that contains variety in sentence order. Experienced writers put something before the subject in almost half of their sentences.

One of the simplest ways to vary sentence order is to place a *prepositional phrase* before the subject. *Prepositions* are words like *in, on, around, above, below,* that connect a following noun or pronoun to the rest of the sentence. A preposition plus the following noun or pronoun is called a prepositional phrase: *over the river, through the woods, to Grandmother's house.* The sentence about the English coffeehouse would be more emphatic if the prepositional phrase ending the sentence were placed at the beginning.

> In the eighteenth century the English coffeehouse was a meeting place for men with similar interests.

Adverbs modify the meaning of verbs, adjectives, or other adverbs. They commonly answer such questions as how, when, where, or why:

> The soldier strode *energetically* up the street.
> She seemed *somewhat* frightened.
> They scampered *very* quickly across the field.

An *adverb clause* is simply a dependent clause that functions as an adverb:

> Vivian worked on her needlepoint *while her husband dozed in his chair.*

Though they commonly appear after the subject, adverbs and adverbial clauses may also be placed before the subject for purposes of variety and emphasis:

> *Eventually,* Mother Nature punishes those who do not learn her lessons.
>
> *Again and again* we learn that human desires are infinite and insatiable.
>
> *Although he is irascible and moody,* he is a good public administrator.

And you may begin a sentence with a *verbal phrase:*

> *To increase circulation,* some newspapers focus on crime, scandal, and corruption on the front page.
>
> *After winning his tennis match,* Jim shook hands with his opponent.
>
> *Pushing her way through the crowd,* Marilyn approached the speaker's platform.

The methods of altering sentence order described above are those most commonly used, but occasionally you may also want to begin with the *object of the verb* or with one or more *adjectives*. In most sentences the object comes after the verb, as in the sentence "Frank detests self-pity." Placing the object before the subject makes the sentence more emphatic: "Self-pity Frank detests." Adjectives frequently occur between *a, an,* and *the* and a following noun or nouns:

The *beautiful, airy* patio provided a cool retreat from the heat of the sun.

Placing them at the very beginning of a sentence or between the subject and the verb, as in the following instances, often makes for a more interesting, graceful sentence.

Beautiful and *airy,* the patio provided a cool retreat from the heat of the sun.

The patio, *beautiful* and *airy,* provided a cool retreat from the heat of the sun.

To recapitulate, look over your sentences to make sure

1. that you have used at least some of the grammatical elements described above—prepositional phrase, verbal phrase, adjective, adverb, adverbial clause, direct object—to vary sentence order;
2. that you have also varied the length of your sentences.

Diction   As you read over your sentences, make certain also that the words and phrases you have used are accurate, specific, and vigorous. In particular, limit the use of *passive verbs* and eliminate *clichés* and *deadwood.*   avoid   avoid

Passive verbs, those which act upon the subject, often produce wordy sentences and colorless writing:

The assault on the fortress was considered risky by the general.

This sentence is more concise and pointed without the passive verb construction *was considered:*

The general considered the assault on the fortress risky.

Clichés are expressions so overused that they have lost whatever vigor and freshness they originally possessed. Instead of communicating thought they block it, for the reader becomes bored and irritated by the writer's inability or unwillingness to suit word to thought. Here is a brief list:

trials and tribulations   few and far between
in the last analysis   footloose and fancy-free
        in this day and age

last but not least   in the same boat
sight for sore eyes   light as a feather
in this point of time

Deadwood is superfluous language. It is a roundabout language that blurs rather than focuses meaning, diffuses rather than concentrates thought. It often occurs in short phrases involving direct duplication: *the modern woman of today, a mistaken fallacy, in close proximity, utmost peak, a total of ten, an extra added attraction, a miserly attitude toward money.* The expressions *there is* and *there are* often produce wordy sentences. They can often be removed with a resultant gain in conciseness and emphasis.

> There are many historians who believe that Lincoln was America's greatest President.

> There is one thing that I know.

Revised:

> Many historians believe that Lincoln was America's greatest President.

> One thing I know.

And a final suggestion: check your spelling carefully, especially with a word that has the same sound as another word but a different spelling and meaning. Their differing meanings may provide a bit of unintended humor for your reader and embarrassment for you.

> American military forces were stymied by the stealth of the Vietnamese gorillas.

> In the 1930s Britain's Lord Keynes was hailed as the profit of a new era of responsible capitalism.

> Harvey asked his boss to except his apologies for being late.

Mechanics, Spelling, Punctuation Look over your mechanics, spelling, and punctuation to see to it that

1. sentences are correctly punctuated and paragraphs properly indented
2. words are correctly spelled, apostrophes are in the right place
3. verbs agree with their subjects and pronouns with their antecedents

Here is a revision of the first draft of the theme on Mr. Jones presented on pages 178–180. Note the changes that have been made in organization as well as language.

Firm, Fair, and Friendly

I liked most of my teachers in high school. They were, for the most part, friendly and competent, willing to help students who showed the faintest flicker of interest in their subjects. I liked them—but I don't remember them very well, except for Mr. Jones, my senior English teacher. He was a friendly, enthusiastic, sensitive man, who knew his subject and was determined that we would learn it and love it, too.

Mr. Jones was a tall, slender man in his mid forties with gray, thinning hair and sparkling blue eyes. Perched precariously on his nose, his glasses gave him a serious, studious look. But they didn't remain there long, for he was always taking them off and polishing them and putting them in his mouth while he mulled over a response to a student's question. When he walked into class, he was always carrying two or three books with strips of paper sticking out of them, marking passages he planned to read. I remember, too, the cardigan sweaters—he must have had a dozen of them—the neatly pressed slacks, Oxford loafers, the tie, always a tie. On rainy days he substituted a navy blue windbreaker for the sweater. He was no dandy, but he was always carefully dressed. He was definitely not the Levis-and-tennis-shoes type. But what I remember best was his smile. When he smiled, his whole face lit up; his eyes sparkled. His smile made you feel good, at ease, somehow reassured.

Yet though he was friendly and naturally at ease with people, he was a bit formal in class, and he could be stern on occasion. He never called us by our first names. It was always "Mr. Weaver" or "Miss Powers," never "Brad" nor "Marie." He obviously loved his work and liked his students, but he kept his distance. He never deliberately embarrassed a student in front of the class with a sarcastic remark, but he could communicate his displeasure all right. He'd look steadily at the offending student for a few seconds, his lips firming slightly shut. That was usually enough, but if it didn't work, he'd say something to the student in a lowered tone of voice. He didn't do this often. He didn't have to, because we liked and respected him and wanted to please him. And the reason was that he respected us and was serious about his subject and intent on our learning it and sharing his enthusiasm.

He *was* serious about his subject, his teaching, but not about himself. He could always come up with a witty comment or a joke to lighten the mood when necessary. He'd laugh harder than anyone else, to make sure we knew it was a joke, he said. His friendliness, his enthusiasm, his wit attracted students wherever he was. Students were always waiting to talk to him in his office, to ask his advice about college, to request a letter of recommendation, or just to chat a bit. I don't think he ever missed a football game, or the senior dance or picnic, for that matter. And wherever he was, in the stands or on the dance floor, students gathered around him.

Jonesy had personality, integrity, vitality—all of which made him popular, as I said; but what I liked most about him was that he was a fine teacher. Yes, he cared about students, but he cared more about teaching them his subject. And that meant homework, lots of it, and pop quizzes now and then to keep them current on the reading. He lectured occasionally, to provide background information whenever we moved on to a new literary period. After a brief glance at his notes, he'd begin to move around as he talked—to the blackboard, to the window, back to the lectern. But he preferred discussion, a Socratic dialogue. He'd write several questions on the board for the next day's discussion, and he'd expect you to be prepared to discuss them. He directed the discussion, but he didn't dominate it; for he was a good listener and made sure we all had a chance to respond, whether we wanted to or not. If he were pleased with a response, he'd nod his head and smile. Occasionally he'd read a student's essay, praising its good points and then winking at the writer as he passed it back. But he was tough-minded, too, as I suggested before. He really nailed you for sloppy work or inattention. When you got an A from him, you really felt good, for he wasn't an easy grader. We used to moan about his grading standards, usually to no avail, though he would change a grade if he thought he had been unfair.

We had many interesting discussions on Twain, Crane, and Dreiser, as I recall, but his favorite period was the 1920s. He loved the expatriates: Anderson, cummings, Hemingway, Fitzgerald. He was always bringing in books for us to read, but when he got to this period, he was a walking library. I think he'd read every book written by or about Hemingway and Fitzgerald, or about Paris in the twenties. He must have seen the films and slides he showed us about Paris and the expatriates dozens of times, but his enthusiasm never flagged when he discussed them. I can still see him, and hear him, reading and chuckling over some passage from *The Sun Also Rises* or *A Moveable Feast*. Yes, Jonesy was a fine teacher all right; he knew his subject, and he could teach it. But more than that, he made us love it, too. He made us want to continue to read it and study it on our own.

The first paragraph has been divided into two paragraphs. The original paragraph is rather long for an opening paragraph, and it provides no unifying idea for the essay. The last sentence of the revised opening paragraph, "He was a friendly, enthusiastic man . . . too," supplies a thesis. It introduces the reader to the traits of character and personality—friendliness, enthusiasm, sensitivity, forcefulness—that will be described in the essay. The introduction has also been changed: the original one-sentence lead-in is a bit prosaic, lackluster. The revised opening is sharper, shorter, more direct. And the friendly tone ("I liked most of my teachers in high school. . . .") is appropriate. It suggests an amiable, fair-minded individual whose impressions and judgments would not be biased. The second paragraph of the revised version includes all the details of the original first paragraph that concern the subject's appearance, focusing first on his head and eyes, then clothing, then back to his eyes, the feature the writer remembers most vividly and therefore logically placed at the end of this paragraph. The sentence "He was definitely not the Levis-and-tennis-shoes type" has been added after "He was no dandy" for emphasis.

The second paragraph of the first draft has also been divided into two paragraphs. It is a long paragraph, fifteen sentences; but, more important, it presents two ideas: his formal manner in class and his friendliness and wit. In the revised draft a paragraph is devoted to each idea. And the topic sentence of the paragraph dealing with his formality has been altered to mention his sternness since the paragraph discusses the latter idea as well as formality.

The last two paragraphs have not been changed. They describe Mr. Jones's classroom teaching and make up about half of the essay. This proportion is reasonable since the writer admired most this aspect of his subject. The conclusion has been changed: the final sentence "I can still see him" has been enlarged upon to reinforce the ideas mentioned in the thesis in the first paragraph and provide an effective conclusion to the theme.

Some changes have been made in word choice, but the diction remains essentially the same. And a few sentences have been reconstructed to begin with something other than the subject. In the first draft fifteen sentences vary the normal subject-verb pattern, in the second draft nineteen.

EXERCISE 22

A. The following essay by William F. Buckley, Jr., is about national service. The author's tone is serious, but not solemn. Read the essay twice, and on the second reading note the devices the author uses to connect his paragraphs, particularly transitional words, pronouns, and the repetition of key terms. Are the opening and closing paragraphs effective? If so, why? What idea in the opening paragraph is developed in the body of the essay? What is the author's principal justification for establishing a national service program?

National Debt, National Service

New York—The points of light of George Bush, those little oases of civic-mindedness and philanthropy he spoke of during his presidential campaign, have ended in comedy routines ("Mister, can you spare a point of light?")

Yet in 1988, 23 million Americans gave five hours per week or more in volunteer social work. Assuming that the labor of those who engage in such activity is worth only the minimum wage, we are talking about $25 billion worth of time already given to serve concerns other than one's own, or one's family's.

All this suggests the spirit is there; but it coexists with a strange and unhealthy failure by many Americans to manifest any sense of obligation to the patrimony, a phenomenon noted long ago by the Spanish philosopher Ortega y Gasset, except of course that he was speaking about Modern Man, not Americans.

My thesis is that Americans need a national service. There are proposals sitting around in Congress, which I have evaluated elsewhere. Here the focus is on the spirit that prompts the proposal: the search for an institutional vehicle through which we Americans could give expression to the debt we feel, or should feel, to the patrimony. Here are the distinctive aspects of the program I have elaborated.

1. The program should be voluntary, both because voluntary activity is presumptively to be preferred to obligatory activity, and because although we are thinking in terms of requital (what can we do for our country, in return for what it has done for us?), man, lest he become unrecognizable, should be left free to be ungrateful.

2. That does not mean society should not use incentives, the positive and negative reinforcements the behaviorist B. F. Skinner wrote about, to press the point that those citizens who appreciate the Bill of Rights and the legacies of the Bible, of Aristotle, Shakespeare, and Bach, and who document that appreciation by

201

devoting a year of their lives to civic-minded activity, are to be distinguished from those who do not.

Distributive justice never hesitates to treat unequally unequal people, in respect of rewards and esteem. There is such a thing as a first-class and a second-class citizen, and although commutative justice is owed to them equally, that is the end of it.

The person who devotes 40 hours a week to community service is a better citizen than his ungrateful counterpart, and society shouldn't funk acknowledging that. Those who fear a class system should ponder the offsetting effects of shared experience, shoulder to shoulder.

3. The objective of national service should not be considered in the tender of Good Deeds. Tending to the sick, teaching illiterates to read, and preserving libraries are desireable ends.

But the guiding purpose here is the spiritual animation of the giver, not the alms he dispenses. The person who has given a year in behalf of someone or something else is better for the experience. National service is not about reducing poverty, it is about inducing gratitude.

There is not any way in which we can tangibly return to our society what we have got from it: liberty and order, access to the poetry of the West, the devotion of our parents and teachers. The point needs to be made that tokenism is not to be dismissed because, in other contexts, it is scorned.

Because the dead of the Civil War cannot be revived doesn't mean, as Lincoln told us, that they can be forgotten. And the search for the practical way in which to hold them in esteem should go beyond national holidays we spend on the beach. The cultivation of the rite of passage, from passive to active citizenship, is the challenge of national service.

We will always be short of Americans who can add to the Bill of Rights, or compose another "Don Giovanni." But there is the unmistakable means of giving witness to the gratitude we feel, or ought to feel, when we compare our lot with that of so many others who know America only in their dreams. (From William F. Buckley, Jr., "National Debt, National Service," *The New York Times,* October 18, 1990, p. A25.)

B. The following paragraph communicates the writer's idea clearly and forcefully. Examine the opening and closing sentences in particular. What devices does he use to arouse reader interest and to stress his main idea?

Is the sport of hunting, simply as such, a man-worthy thing or isn't it? Let it be supposed that all hunters obey all regulations. Let it be supposed that no whiskey bottle is dropped to pollute any glen or dingle, no fence is broken, no fawn is shot, no forest is set afire, no robins are massacred in mistake for

202

pheasants and no deer-hunters in mistake for porcupines (or possible chip-munks), and no meditative philosopher, out to enjoy the loveliness of autumn, is ever plugged through the pericardium. The question persists: Is it a spectacle of manhood (which is to say of our distinctive humanness), when on a bracing morning we look out upon the autumn, draw an exhilarating breath, and cry "What a glorious day! How golden is the light of the sun, how merry the caperings of creatures; *Gloria in excelsis Deo!* I will go out and kill something"? [From Alan Devoe, "On Hunting," *American Mercury,* February 1951.]

C. Construct three effective opening sentences for each of the following topics. Use any of the methods illustrated on pages 184–185 or any of your own invention.

  1. a remembered pet

    a. _____

    _____

    b. _____

    _____

    c. _____

    _____

  2. what you like most, or least, about Americans

    a. _____

    _____

    b. _____

    _____

    c. _____

    _____

  3. styles of driving

    a. _____

    _____

b. _____

_____

c. _____

_____

D. Find three examples of good concluding sentences in recent magazine or newspaper articles, and write them in the appropriate spaces below. Be prepared to explain why you think the conclusion is effective.

1. SUBJECT MATTER _____

   Concluding Sentence _____

   _____

   _____

2. SUBJECT MATTER _____

   _____

   _____

3. SUBJECT MATTER _____

   _____

   _____

E. The paragraph below illustrates a monotony of sentence patterns, an excess of deadwood, and an occasional misuse of words. Revise it by (1) varying the pattern of the sentences (most are subject-verb pattern), (2) eliminating deadwood and any irrelevant sentences, (3) improving word choice where warranted, and (4) joining some sentences to provide smoother transition of thought.

Teachers perform a vital function in American culture. Teachers perform an essential sociopathic function. Teachers help children move from the self-contained world of their mothers and fathers and brothers and sisters to the wider world of their school and community outside of their own world. Children must learn to work and play harmoniously and happily in the larger group, adjusting to the environment of a wider social circle if they are to

204

acquire the foundation of a happy, useful life in a democracy. The teacher is largely responsible for transmuting the cultural heritage, the essential facts and values of their country's history—its political, social, cultural institutions. Teachers should not attempt to indoctrinate, intimidate, or manipulate their students into accepting their own political views and agenda. A teacher helps a child to develop a healthy, recessive attitude toward intellectual pursuits as well as social activities, to respect and respond to the life of the mind as the child matures. They help students to discover and develop their own special talents, to acquire vocational skills. Teachers can strongly influence the moral life of students when they are dedicated to their profession of teaching. A teacher can help them develop a sound, useful philosophy of life. The future of this nation, its place in the international community of nations, as well as the happiness, contentment, and well-being of its citizens, is in no small way dependent upon how well teachers perform their function.

F. Revise the draft of the paper you prepared for Exercise 21.

◨ PREPARING THE FINAL COPY

Before you prepare your final copy, read your essay aloud to yourself (or to a friend) to test once more its clarity, unity, and coherence, and to catch any omission of words or punctuation errors. Examine your title in this reading also. Is it brief, accurate, and consistent with the tone of the paper? Will it catch the reader's attention and stimulate interest? Remember that the title is not part of the composition itself. As mentioned earlier, the first sentence of the essay should not depend on the title for its meaning.

If possible, type your final copy on 8½ × 11-inch unlined white paper. Double space so that your instructor can insert comments between the lines when necessary. Double spacing also makes for easier reading. If you must write your final copy, use ink and write on only one side of the paper. The other side may be required for later revisions when your theme is returned to you. Next, space the body of your composition evenly on the page with suitable margins on each side and at the top and bottom. Center your title and place it a few spaces above the first sentence of your text. Capitalize the first word and all other words in the title except articles, conjunctions, and short prepositions. Number your pages and endorse your paper in the manner prescribed by your instructor. The endorsement usually includes your name, the title of your paper, and the date.

EXERCISE 23

Turn in a final copy of the theme you revised for Exercise 22F.

◨ SUMMARY

Like the paragraph, the theme requires careful attention to unity, development, coherence, and emphasis. Because of its increased length and complexity, however, you must plan its construction in greater detail. To help you with this planning, we have suggested the following steps:

1. Limit your topic in accordance with the length of your paper and the interests and background of your reader.
2. Think through your subject.

3. Gather and organize your material; group major and minor ideas, and arrange them in a logical sequence to effect your purpose.
4. Outline your theme. For a short paper, especially one written in class, a rough outline will suffice. For a longer paper the formal outline is almost essential.
5. Write your first draft as rapidly as possible, using your outline as a guide. Put the first draft aside for a few hours, and do not think about it.
6. After you have been away from your first draft for a while, revise it, giving close scrutiny to content and organization as well as to mechanics. In particular, check opening and closing sentences and the continuity of thought between paragraphs.
7. Prepare a final copy, observing the conventions for preparing a manuscript prescribed by your instructor.

Argumentation

The preceding chapters have concentrated on exposition, the kind of writing that explains and clarifies. At times, however, you will want to persuade your reader of the soundness of a judgment, to convince him or her of the appropriateness of a course of action. On such occasions you will have need of the skills of *argumentation.* Exposition and argumentation are not, to be sure, mutually exclusive categories. Writers of expository essays hope to persuade the reader that their explanations are informative and reasonable. The characteristics of good exposition—unity, adequate development, coherence—apply as well to argumentation. But in writing devoted to argument, writers make clear the logic behind the positions they take. They spell out the logical steps that led them to their conclusions. Specific knowledge of the processes of logical reasoning will help you to think more clearly, to construct logical arguments, and to follow and analyze arguments of other writers and speakers. Combined with facility in the arts of persuasion, it will make your writing more thoughtful and convincing.

Simply defined, argumentation is a process of reasoning in which a coherent series of facts and judgments is arranged to establish a conclusion. A discussion of argumentation can be complex, for there are many ways of arranging these facts and judgments. However, the discussion that follows will be a simple one, for what is important here is not that you gain a precise knowledge of the variety and complexity of argumentation, but rather that you understand the basic pattern of all arguments and, more important, that you learn to use sound, logical arguments in your own writing.

Any argument, however complex, expresses a relationship between one assertion and another. The first assertion serves as the reason for the second. For example, if you say "Professor Sanderson's exams are difficult. Therefore, I'll have to study hard this weekend," you are making an argument. The second statement is a conclusion based on the first statement.

The first part of an argument may consist of a series of statements:

> In the presidential election of 1976, 56.5 percent of those Americans eligible to vote actually voted. In the election of 1980, the percentage was 54. And in 1984 it was 53. As these statistics reveal, a sizable segment of the American electorate does not take its voting privilege seriously.

In this example, the *conclusion,* the last sentence, follows a series of factual statements. This kind of argument, which proceeds from a study of particulars to the making of a generalization or hypothesis based on those particulars, is called an *inductive argument;* and the supporting particulars that precede the conclusion are called the *evidence.*

The other basic form of argument is called *deduction.* The *deductive argument* has more than one form. A common type, the *categorical syllogism,* begins with a general statement and closes with a particular statement. The supporting reasons in this type of argument are called the *premises.* In the following categorical syllogism the premises provide the basis for the conclusion:

Premises	All Americans are freedom-loving.
	George is an American.
Conclusion	George is freedom-loving.

◼ THE INDUCTIVE ARGUMENT

As mentioned above, the inductive argument has two forms: one concluding with a *generalization,* the other with a *hypothesis.* In an inductive argument ending in a generalization, the generalization makes a statement about a class or group of things or people, and the evidence consists of statements about individual members of that class. The inductive argument about American voters (see above) is of this type. The evidence consists of three statements, each one a particular factual observation about members of the same class, American voters. And the conclusion, ". . . the American electorate does not take its voting privilege seriously," is a more general statement, covering more ground than any of the particular facts that preceded it. This conclusion is an inference about American voters' attitude toward voting; the evidence consists of observations about their behavior at the polls in 1976, 1980, and 1984.

Here is another example:

Evidence	1. Professor Rodriguez is witty and perceptive.
	2. Professor Armstrong is witty and perceptive.
	3. Professor Weiss is witty and perceptive.
Conclusion	All professors are witty and perceptive.

The conclusion of an inductive argument is a hypothesis when it deals not with a class but with an individual object or situation. In this case the hypothesis attempts to account for the set of facts that preceded it.

Evidence	1. The Hawkins' front lawn across the street is getting long.
	2. It is getting brown in spots.
	3. Newspapers have been accumulating on the front porch.
	4. The drapes have been pulled across the living room windows.
	5. Today is August 15.
Conclusion	The Hawkins are on vacation.

The conclusion of this argument does not concern a class of things, but rather one particular situation. It is not a generalization, but an inference that attempts to account for the five preceding observations. Each item of the evidence is not a member of a class or group mentioned in the conclusion, as is true of the previous arguments about professors and American voters, but is a description of a different aspect of the appearance of a house on a summer day.

An inductive argument thus begins with a look at the evidence and ends with a conclusion based on that evidence. It moves from the particular to the general, from fact to conclusion. The distinguishing quality of the inductive argument, however, the characteristic that differentiates it from the deductive argument, is not this movement, but the degree of certainty of the conclusion. The conclusion of an inductive argument *does not necessarily follow* from the evidence. The concluding hypothesis or generalization is only a probability: other conclusions are possible. The conclusion that American voters do not take their voting seriously, because of their failure to turn out in great numbers on three consecutive national elections, may be erroneous. The voters may have been essentially satisfied with the candidates running for election at the time and did not vote because of general contentment rather than indifference. And another hypothesis is possible to explain the appearance of the Hawkins' house—the family could be away on an emergency visit to a disabled relative.

Evaluating the Evidence of an Inductive Argument

The conclusion of an inductive argument will be sound if there is a logical connection between the evidence and the conclusion. If the connection is missing, the conclusion will not be valid even though it may satisfy the person making the argument. In the following discussion we will examine several general principles that will help you to determine whether the arguments you construct or encounter are sound.

Supporting a Generalization

The conclusion that any researcher draws from the study of specific cases is necessarily tentative. As you would expect, a generalization based on many samples is more reliable than one based on few. A large sampling, however, does not guarantee a sound generalization. The sampling must be representative as well. For example, to ensure the reliability of his conclusions regarding the popularity of political figures, Dr. Gallup, as well as other professional pollsters, makes certain to poll a sufficient number of voters from a broad cross section of American life. To ensure the soundness of the generalizations you use, follow this important principle:

> 1. Support your generalizations firmly with an *adequate, repre-sentative,* and *relevant* sampling of evidence.

The generalization on page 211 that all professors are witty and perceptive is clearly not justified by the evidence presented. More than three professors must be observed before a valid generalization about the wit and perceptivity of all professors can be made. A more accurate generalization would result if a more specific poll of student opinion of professorial wit and perceptivity were conducted. A professional pollster such as Dr. Gallup would have to poll at least several hundred students on campuses throughout the country before reaching a conclusion. But even this kind of poll would not support the original conclusion that *all* professors are witty and perceptive. It might reveal, however, that 34.6 percent, or 41.3 percent, or 61.7 percent, or some other proportion of the group, are witty and perceptive.

But the point here is not that you should generalize about a group of people or any group of objects only if you have made a scientific study of the subject. We all live and work by generalizations, and common-sense generalizations based on previous experience are ordinarily trustworthy in everyday life. Persons who have enjoyed reliable service from automobiles manufactured by one company will likely consider the same make of automobile when they are ready to purchase a new one. Investors consistently disappointed by the performance of stock they have purchased on the advice of a broker are not likely to continue following that advice. Nonetheless, though scientific precision is not essential in formulating useful generalizations, a generalization based on many samples is obviously more dependable than one based on just a few.

The following paragraph is interesting and lively. The evidence is relevant, but there is not enough of it, and what there is, is not sufficiently representative to justify the sweeping generalization in the opening sentence.

> You can't trust politicians. Whenever I receive a progress report in the mail from Assemblyman Parker, I wince. During his campaign he lambasted his incumbent opponent for refusing to support legislation restricting campaign contributions. Yet he is now under investigation for diverting money from his campaign funds to redecorate his summer cottage at Blue Lake. It's just as bad at City Hall. Councilman Bertoli has been extolled for years as the pride of our fair city, the symbol of clean, honest, responsible government. But according to yesterday's paper he has been indicted by the Grand Jury for soliciting a bribe from a builder whose proposal to construct a condominium at Third and Fairhaven had been rejected by the Council. And then, of course, there is the ongoing cozy, profitable relationship between congressmen, senators, and lobbyists for big corporations seeking preferential treatment from the federal government.

Inexperienced writers who base their conclusions on atypical evidence frequently do so through ignorance of the complexity of their subjects. However, well-informed, experienced writers who select only those facts that support their positions and ignore others that do not are guilty of *stacking the cards*. Writers who stack the cards may cite an impressive body of facts and maintain a fairly objective tone, yet create a false impression of their subjects in the reader's mind because of the facts that they have omitted. Consider, for instance, this argument concerning the desirability of eliminating compulsory school attendance laws.

Public elementary and secondary schools in the United States are not doing an effective job of educating American youth. In fact, the situation is deplorable; and the main reason is that many children and teenagers simply don't care about school and don't want to be there. The solution is to abolish compulsory attendance. Students who are forced to attend school don't care about learning, and they don't learn. Not only do they not learn much, they are often antagonistic to the process—to their teachers, school administrators, fellow students—and, as a consequence, disrupt the attempts of others who want to learn. Private schools do a better job than public schools because they can dismiss reluctant, recalcitrant students. Furthermore, enforcing laws that require uninterested and disruptive students to attend school is expensive. The money spent on keeping track of absentees could better be used on educating those who care about school, especially in a time of shrinking education budgets.

Abolishing compulsory attendance would produce several benefits. It would allow teachers to concentrate on teaching rather than on disciplining disorderly students. It would also improve the climate for learning and encourage a seriousness of purpose among students, for they would know they would be expelled if they didn't produce. A third benefit concerns the public's perception of public schools. As teachers and students became more productive, successful, public support for education would dramatically increase, an extremely important factor in maintaining the prosperity and well-being of the United States. Public schools shouldn't be day-care centers, disciplinary institutions. They should be educational centers. Eliminating mandatory school attendance would do much to bring this about.

Although the writer presents relevant facts and judgments in support of his contention that compulsory school attendance should be abolished, his presentation is one-sided. He doesn't, for example, consider the problem of what to do about those who would leave school. They may not be learning much in school, but they would learn less in the streets. The current high school dropout rate among some minorities approaches 50 percent. It is difficult to understand how increasing this rate would help in "maintaining the prosperity and well-being of the United States." The writer is also guilty of a sweeping generalization when he brands public schools as failures and private schools as successes. Many public schools throughout the country have enviable reputations, and not all private schools are roaring successes. And, finally, though removing disruptive, antagonistic students would improve the learning atmosphere of those who remain in school voluntarily, the writer ignores the fact that the most important influence in a child's learning is family cohesion, support, parental encouragement. If that is lacking, the child's mere presence in school will not ensure success in learning. A more objective, persuasive assessment of the desirability of eliminating compulsory school attendance would consider facts and judgments on both sides of the question. In your own attempts at persuasive writing, be sure that you have not omitted important facts that do not support your argument. If you have, revise your paper to present a more balanced view. A balanced view may not be as bold or dramatic as a one-sided view, but it is more effective with informed readers.

> 2. Back up your generalizations with *accurate, verifiable* evidence.

The following paragraph illustrates a common failing in the writing of persons who feel so strongly about an issue that they fail to provide any factual detail to anchor their generalizations.

> Americans need not worry about the gloomy predictions of pessimists that disaster awaits us because of population growth and pollution. For example, (reports indicate) that city air is getting cleaner, not dirtier. One hundred years ago the air over large eastern cities was filled with smoke so thick it could be cut with a knife. Yet today coal smoke has been largely eliminated. Our rivers, lakes, and oceans may not be as pure as they once were, but the amount of water pollution has been grossly exaggerated. Alarmists point to mercury contamination of fish caused by industrial wastes as proof of contamination; yet, as (scientists know,) the amount of mercury in the oceans today is not significantly higher than it was fifty years ago. Doomsayers predict that world population growth represents a time bomb that will explode and destroy us if population is not curtailed. But (according to government reports,) the birth rate in the United States has been dropping since 1955. Moreover, demographic experts believe) that if the trend is not reversed, the United States will be faced with a serious shortage of people. An objective assessment of these facts invalidates the assumption that pollution and population growth pose a serious threat to the American people.

This paragraph appears to contain a good deal of factual information to support its thesis, but a careful reading reveals that the evidence is tenuous and vague, incapable of justifying the assertion made in the first sentence. Such phrases as "reports indicate," "as scientists know," "according to government reports," and "demographic experts believe" purport to introduce concrete, factual detail. But what specific reports contain information of the quality of city air? What scientists say that mercury contamination of the oceans has not increased? And what demographic experts believe that population growth is not a serious problem? Unless such particulars are supplied, thoughtful readers are justified in withholding their assent to the writer's conclusion.

> 3. Make certain that the *opinions* or *testimony* of authorities you use to buttress your arguments are those of a qualified observer.

A "qualified observer" is one who is competent in his or her field and able to report observations accurately and objectively. We all tend to believe in those who share our opinions and to seek out evidence that confirms these opinions, but it is a tendency that can be fatal to persuasive writing—and to truth. The president of a tobacco company is hardly an unbiased source of information on the health hazards of cigarettes. A chief of police may not be qualified to determine satisfactorily the difference between pornography and literary art. And a retired physicist, however famous for research done in the past, may not be able to speak authoritatively on recent scientific developments.

The preceding discussion has emphasized the need to supply sufficient evidence for generalizations. We have said that the evidence must not be one-sided, that it should be grounded in fact, and that if "experts" are quoted, they must be legitimate authorities. When evidence supporting generalizations meets these tests, a thoughtful reader is likely to consider them carefully.

Common Inductive Fallacies

A *fallacy* is an error in reasoning. It refers to an argument that violates a principle of logical inference. In the following discussion we will examine briefly a few common types of faulty induction.

A writer who makes a *hasty generalization* fails to supply enough evidence to support the generalization. The writer "jumps to a conclusion." The author of the paragraph on politicians (p. 213) is guilty of this error.

A *sweeping generalization* results when the writer provides no evidence at all to support an assertion: "Economists know that government spending simply produces inflation." Modified, this statement is much more defensible: "Many economists fear that continued high levels of deficit government spending will produce a dangerous increase in inflation." The point is not to avoid generalizations for fear they might be exaggerated, but to make certain your generalizations are justified by the supporting evidence. Reread your papers carefully, therefore, and avoid extravagant, unsupported statements.

No one can say precisely how much evidence is needed to produce a reliable generalization, but common sense would suggest these simple precautions:

1. Do not generalize too quickly.
2. Modify sweeping generalizations, the generalization that covers all the members of a class. Use such words as *all, every, no one, always, never, average, typical,* and the like, cautiously.
3. Consult the judgments of recognized authorities when you are uncertain about the adequacy or accuracy of your own data and opinions.
4. To measure the soundness of your evidence supporting a generalization, ask yourself whether that generalization has proven a reliable basis for action over a period of time. Students entering college soon discover that success in their studies demands hard work, self-discipline, and perseverance. Such a generalization is clearly dependable. It has been proven true, painfully true, for many generations of students in the past.

A second common fallacy is the generalization based on *deceptive statistics*. Generalizations drawn from statistical data need to be examined carefully because statistics can be manipulated to yield a variety of interpretations. For example, if a man increases his contribution to a charitable organization from five dollars to ten dollars a year, he can legitimately claim to have increased his contribution 100 percent, an impressive figure to one not aware of the actual amount involved. Or suppose that a report of the income of individuals working in a small business firm indicates that the average annual salary of the employees is $22,000. This information by itself might lead you to the conclusion that these employees were well paid and that the owners of the firm were justified in refusing to consider salary increases. Upon closer examination, however, you discover that, of the ten persons working in the firm, five earn $10,000 annually, three $15,000, one $25,000, and one $100,000. The average annual salary of this group is in fact $22,000, but for most people *average* connotes *typical;* yet only two of the ten persons actually earns $22,000 or more in a year. The typical salary in this case would be closer to $12,000 than $22,000. Be careful, then, when you use statistics to establish or reinforce a generalization. If one figure in a set of figures is considerably larger or smaller than the others (for example, the $100,000 salary in the case cited above), taking an average of them will distort their relationship. In such cases it would be more informative to report the *median* value (the middle figure in an odd number of figures) or the *mode* value (the figure that appears most frequently). In short, use statistics as honestly and informatively as you can, lest your reader suspect that you have manipulated them to suit your purpose.

The *post hoc fallacy,* a third type of faulty induction, occurs when we assert that one event caused another because it preceded it. If one thing occurs before another, it does not *necessarily* cause the latter. This kind of inference is known technically as the *post hoc, ergo propter hoc fallacy* ("after this, therefore because of this"), or more simply, the post hoc fallacy. That one political administration was in office when war broke out, for example, does not mean that that administration brought on the war. The fact that the number of capital crimes committed in a state decreased the year after capital punishment was abolished does not prove that the change in punishment caused this decrease.

It frequently happens, of course, that one event *is* the cause of another. When a person collapses after being struck a blow on the head, it is fairly clear that the first event, the blow, caused the second, the collapse. But establishing a causal relation between two events is often more difficult. It is especially difficult in the field of economics. Here is an example:

> The recent tax cut passed by Congress was obviously warranted. The American economy was given the shot in the arm it needed. Retail sales and business profits have gone up, the rate of unemployment has gone down, and our foreign trade has expanded.

To prove that the tax cut specifically caused the improvement in retail sales, business profits, and foreign trade would necessitate the examination of a considerable body of facts. An economist, or an experienced reader, would want to know, for example, the effect of seasonal variation in consumer and government spending, the business community's confidence in the economy, and the actions of foreign governments in reducing tariffs before accepting such an explanation.

One of the methods of paragraph development presented in Chapter Two was the *analogy,* a comparison of two things that are unlike but that have similar attributes. Analogy is frequently used as evidence to support an argument.

> Recently *The New York Times* reported an address by Supreme Court Justice Powell in which he deplored the deterioration of the nation's moral fiber and cited, as an example, the open selling of student themes and term papers to college and university undergraduates.
>
> It seemed to me a rather feeble for instance, and one which a politician (and let's not pretend the Supreme Court isn't a political as well as a judicial body) might well eschew. If it's all right for the President of the United States to hire people to write his speeches on which the fate of nations may rest, why isn't it equally acceptable for a college student to hire someone to write his term papers, on which nobody's fate rests but his own! [From Ed Zern, "Exit Laughing," *Field and Stream,* December 1972, p. 160.]

The argument contained in this passage is a *false analogy,* another common inductive fallacy. Its comparison of the selling of term papers to college students with the President's hiring of speech writers overlooks an important difference between these two practices. The awesome responsibilities and complex, time-consuming duties that burden a President of the United States make it impossible for him to write every speech he gives and, therefore, justify the employment of speech writers. The public understands and accepts the practice. A college student is not so burdened. Moreover, the obvious fraudulence of falsifying the authorship of term papers and the prohibition against it are clearly understood and accepted by most college students.

This example illustrates an important weakness in arguing by analogy; an analogy frequently breaks down by ignoring basic differences in the two things being compared. When you use analogy to buttress an argument, therefore, keep its limitations in mind. It can clarify a point made in an argument, but it cannot settle the argument.

EXERCISE 24

A. Factual information and the testimony of experts could be used to support the following generalizations. In the blanks below each statement list the kinds of factual information you could use and an authority you might consult.

> Example   Americans have become more health conscious.
>
> 1. statistics on increase in number of health food stores, joggers, purchases of physical fitness equipment and clothing; on decrease of smokers; popularity of diet books, and so on
> 2. emphasis on physical fitness of executives in American business and industry today as contrasted with situation in the past
> 3. opinions of leaders of American Medical Association, physical fitness experts, book publishers

1. The American banking system has suffered serious setbacks in the past few years.

_____

_____

_____

2. Terrorism remains a serious problem for governments and law enforcement agencies throughout the world.

_____

_____

_____

3. Communism has proven to be an economic disaster in Eastern Europe.

_____

_____

_____

220

4. The Japanese have invested heavily in the United States in recent years.

_____

_____

_____

5. Iraq paid heavily for its brutal attack on Kuwait in 1990.

_____

_____

_____

B. Classify the following arguments as inductive or deductive.

1. Giovanni Gigglio is amorous, demonstrative, and fanatic about soccer and opera. Such attitudes are not surprising; Giovanni is Italian.

_____

2. Winston Churchill served his country as a soldier in India, the Sudan, Belgium, and France. He devoted more than 50 years to his country as a member of Parliament and in the Cabinet as a minister of several governmental departments. In the Second World War he was Prime Minister and Minister of Defense. To support himself and his family, he worked as a journalist, writing 56 books and hundreds of articles for newspapers and magazines. It is not difficult to understand why many historians consider him to be the greatest of Britain's famous political leaders.

_____

3. Oil company stocks have lost value on the New York Stock Exchange lately. The price of gasoline in the United States has held steady or dropped slightly for the past year. The number of service stations has declined dramatically throughout the United States in recent years. And the OPEC nations have had to cut back oil production because of a drop in world demand. It is clear that the oil industry is not flourishing as well as it did a decade ago.

_____

221

4. Madeline Shadbolt is financially independent. She has a house on Balboa Island and spends her summers in Europe. Moreover, she wears designer clothes, dines at the best French restaurants, and drives a new BMW 735. She is, obviously, a financially successful woman.

_____

5. The American Civil Liberties Union opposes school prayer. They must be atheists.

_____

C. Scale down the following sweeping generalizations.

   Example   Young people today have abandoned morality.
   Revised   A higher percentage of young people today are living to-
             gether before, or instead of, getting married than was true
             a generation ago.

1. The Israelis and the Arabs will never make peace in the Middle East.

_____

_____

2. Americans are too self-indulgent and undisciplined to conserve energy.

_____

_____

3. The American banking system is headed for collapse.

_____

_____

4. Intercollegiate athletics programs have no educational value and should be abolished.

_____

_____

222

5. American newspapers sensationalize the news to make money for their publishers.

_____

_____

D. Weaknesses in inductive arguments discussed in the preceding pages include the following:

1. sampling of evidence too selective
2. lack of sufficient evidence
3. incompetent or biased authority
4. generalization based on deceptive statistics
5. hasty or sweeping generalization
6. post hoc fallacy
7. false analogy

Each of the following arguments demonstrates one or more of these weaknesses, though usually one type predominates. Identify these weaknesses by placing one or more of the numbers in this list after the argument.

1. The school board's plan to scale down interscholastic athletic programs to cope with reduced tax income was opposed by all ten speakers at the board meeting last night. The speakers, all members of the Sunday Morning Quarterback Club, vociferously opposed any reduction in financial support. It is clear that interscholastic athletic programs are very popular in River City.

2. Wesley Wainright—a successful, highly respected attorney—met Daphne Sodbury in the fall of 1978 at an alumni party. He began to date her thereafter and continued to do so for the next five years. In January 1984, she inherited $630,000 from her favorite aunt. In June 1984, Wesley and Daphne were married. Apparently Wesley could no longer resist Daphne's charms when they were reinforced by $630,000.

3. I don't see why Professor Moriarity won't let us use our books on her history exams. Doctors examine x-rays of their patients before they operate, and lawyers read over their notes before they address the jury.

4. Who says skiing is a healthful, exciting sport? The last two times I've skied I broke my skis each time after hitting a tree. The second time I also banged my head on a rock and was hospitalized for ten days.

223

5. Carter Ravenal, the owner of Holiday Travel Tours, returned from a two-week trip to the Far East. Accompanied by an interpreter, he spoke with several Japanese businessmen and enjoyed his trip immensely. He was particularly impressed with the Japanese culture. In his monthly newsletter he spoke highly of the Japanese and stated that, in his opinion, Japanese automobile exports represent no real threat to the American automobile industry.

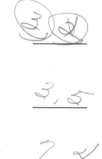

6. According to Samuel Johnson, English lexicographer and writer, "A woman preaching is like a dog walking on its hind legs. It is not done well, but you are surprised to find it done at all."

7. Uncle Schuyler is more generous than my Uncle Dudley. In 1980 Uncle Schuyler increased his contributions to charity by 50 percent, whereas Uncle Dudley didn't increase his at all.

8. Montgomery Fitzgerald, director of a local bank in Arroyo Seco, has been accused of laundering drug money for the Mafia. Mr. Fitzgerald, however, is clearly innocent of such charges. Two of his associates at the bank testified without reservation about his honesty and good character.

9. The news media were definitely biased in their coverage of the 1980 presidential campaign. Slanted television reporting, distorted newspaper reporting, and prejudicial radio news commentary caused President Carter's defeat.

10. In 1938 Leslie Harper was elected mayor of the city of Mesa Grande, Nevada. In his campaign speeches he promised to reduce unemployment, which at that time was running about 17 percent. He won the election. In 1942 he ran for a second term. In the latter campaign he argued that he should be re-elected because he had reduced unemployment to 3 percent since his election in 1938. Obviously, he deserved another term as mayor.

E. Provide at least two hypotheses to explain the set of circumstances narrated below. What additional facts would make one of them more credible?

Monty Sayers, basketball coach of Western State University, had two very successful seasons in his first two years as coach. His star guards, Mike Garcia and Larry Harper, were selected as the two best guards in their league. Because of his coaching success, he urged the student athletic council to approve an emergency request for funds so that he could attend a coaching seminar at Northeastern University. The council approved his request, though the

224

vice president of the council, Sydney Walton, objected. That spring Sayers attended the seminar at Northeastern, his alma mater, where he was an All-American basketball player. On returning to Western, Sayers informed the athletic director and the president of the college that he would be leaving Western to become head basketball coach at Northeastern University in the fall. In his sports column in the college paper, the sports page editor revealed that Garcia and Harper had applied for admission to Northeastern University four weeks before Sayers had appeared before the student athletic council.

F. Read the following selections carefully and evaluate the logic used in each. Identify the main weaknesses in the arguments advanced.

1. American military leaders have praised the armed forces of the United States for their unselfish action in defeating the Iraqi army and forcing Saddam Hussein out of Kuwait. But this praise is simply a smokescreen put up by American militarists, egged on by their political stooges, who simply want to re-assert their influence on American foreign policy. The truly peace-loving leaders of Cuba, Jordan, Iran, and Yemen, who know the truth about the United States, agree that the American action in the Middle East was simply another example of insidious American meddling in other people's affairs across the face of the earth. Power-hungry American generals, incompetent ambassadors, unintelligent intelligence agents are making the world's flesh creep. American participation in the organizing and implementing a system for ensuring stability and peace in the Middle East is not needed, for it would simply increase tensions in that area. It would be like throwing a lighted match into a keg of gunpowder. Moreover, if American soldiers, sailors, and airmen are stationed in the Persian Gulf, they won't want to leave.

2. The most deadly war the United States faces is occurring on the streets of American cities and towns. In 1990 over 23,000 persons were murdered. The causes of this devastating increase in crime are not hard to find. It is really not surprising that homicide is the primary cause of death among Black males between the ages of 17 and 25; that illicit drug use threatens inner-city neighborhoods; and that muggings, robberies, and vandalism have made city streets unsafe, day or night. What can you expect when parents have simply abdicated their responsibility in disciplining their children? Yes, I know that sociologists and liberal politicians attribute crime to poverty, but that's an evasion, an unwillingness to admit that the potential for evil lurks in the hearts of all youth and needs to be sternly repressed in the home and school. Another cause is soft judges, "humanitarians," who refuse to sentence youthful offenders for fear of damaging their psyches. The other day I read about a young punk who had admitted to taking part in a robbery but who was released from custody because the judge took pity on the boy's mother, who claimed

225

her son was a good boy who needed love not punishment. And, finally, there's the violence on TV. Allowing TV networks to show films depicting sadistic cops and handsome, successful criminals is like throwing gasoline on a fire.

G. Write a short paper, one or two paragraphs, on one of the following topics, using an inductive process. That is, investigate the subject firsthand, record your observations in note form, consult relevant experts, and then write up the results of your investigation. Present your data first and your conclusion near or at the end of your paper.

1. student attitudes toward success, their teachers, or marriage
2. part-time work done by students
3. political preference or affiliation of students or faculty
4. educational objectives of students, motivation for attending college
5. student conceptions of the ideal job
6. student preferences regarding entertainment

226

◘ THE DEDUCTIVE ARGUMENT

In the preceding pages we have studied the relation between inductive reasoning and writing, but, as we mentioned there, writing uses both induction and deduction. In induction you examine a number of particulars and formulate a conclusion to account for them. If the conclusion is a generalization, you can then, by means of a deductive process, apply the generalization to a particular case. For example, if you learn through personal experience that salespeople are extroverts, you can apply this information to the salesperson sitting beside you on a train and anticipate a lively conversation. Your reasoning process could be patterned as follows:

Inductive Process

1. Salesperson 1 is an extrovert.
2. Salesperson 2 is an extrovert.
3. Salesperson 3 is an extrovert.
Conclusion   All salespeople are extroverts.

Deductive Process

1. All salespeople are extroverts.
2. The person sitting beside me is a salesperson.
Conclusion   The person sitting beside me is an extrovert.

This argument is an example of the *categorical syllogism* described earlier. It has three parts: two premises followed by a conclusion. The *major premise* makes a general statement about something—an object, an idea, a circumstance. In the example above, "All salespeople are extroverts" is the major premise. The *minor premise* contains further information about one of the terms in the major premise. "The person sitting beside me is a salesperson" is the minor premise of the example. And the *conclusion* is a logical inference to be derived from the premises. The last sentence in our syllogism is its conclusion.

The movement of this kind of syllogism is from the general to the specific, from a statement about a larger group to a statement about an individual member of that group. The categorical syllogism simply classifies an individual, object, or idea as a member of a group and assumes that the object so classified will have qualities of that group.

Unlike the inductive argument ending in a generalization, which moves from the specific to the general, the categorical syllogism moves from the general to the specific. But the essential difference between a deductive and an inductive argument is not this direction of movement but the fact that the conclusion of a deductive argument can be proven to follow necessarily from the premises, whereas, as explained earlier, the conclusion of an inductive argument is always somewhat uncertain.

Here is a syllogism with its premises and conclusion indicated:

1. Major Premise   All human beings are mortal beings.
   Minor Premise   Socrates is a human being.
   Conclusion   Socrates is a mortal being.

The major premise commonly precedes the minor premise, but it need not:

2. Minor Premise   Tippy is a cocker spaniel.
   Major Premise   Cocker spaniels are dogs.
   Conclusion   Tippy is a dog.

The Valid Conclusion

If the conclusion of a syllogism logically follows from the ideas contained in the premises, as in the syllogisms above, the conclusion is said to be *valid*. A conclusion that doesn't follow, an invalid conclusion, is called a *non sequitur*. It is possible to determine the validity of the conclusion of the kind of basic syllogism illustrated in these pages by learning and applying a few simple rules:

1. The syllogism must have three, and only three, terms.
2. The middle term must be "distributed" in one of the premises.
3. The middle term must not shift its meaning.

A *term* is the subject or predicate of a statement. In a syllogism with a valid conclusion, each term will appear twice in the three statements.

3. Major Premise   All children are curious.
   Minor Premise   Stephen is a child.
   Conclusion   Stephen is curious.

The three terms of this syllogism are *children, curious,* and *Stephen.* The *middle term* is the term that appears in both the major and minor premise (but not in the conclusion), in this case *child. Child* and *children* are considered just one term since they both refer to the same thing.

The second rule, that the middle term be "distributed," simply means that the middle term must appear in a premise that includes or excludes all the members of its class. For example, the term *chemists* is distributed in each of these statements: "All chemists are intelligent." "No chemists are intelligent." In syllogism (3) the term *children* is distributed in the major premise. But in this next syllogism

4. Major Premise   All Italians are music lovers.
   Minor Premise   Gilbert is a music lover.
   Conclusion   Gilbert is an Italian.

the middle term, *music lover,* is not distributed in either premise. Neither premise includes or excludes all music lovers. The term *Italian* is distributed in the major premise, but it is not the middle term; and the conclusion is a non sequitur.

A syllogism in which the meaning of the middle term changes from major to minor premise also produces an invalid conclusion because the term signifies a different thing in each premise, and hence there are four terms. In the following syllogism the meaning of *democratic* differs in the two premises, and the conclusion therefore doesn't follow.

5. Major Premise   All political leaders having democratic sympathies are popular.
   Minor Premise   Governor Fagin has Democratic sympathies.
   Conclusion   Governor Fagin is popular.

The pattern of valid and invalid deductions is usually clarified by the use of diagrams. For example, in syllogism (3) the major premise states "All children are curious." If we draw a small circle to represent children and a larger one to represent individuals who are curious and then place the small circle within the larger (p. 230), we can diagram the relationship between children and curiosity contained in the major premise.

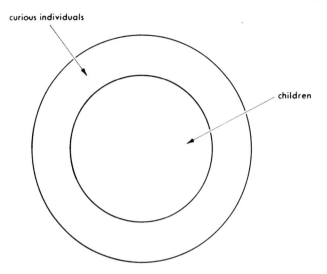

By drawing a still smaller circle to represent Stephen and placing it within the circle marked "children" we can diagram the minor premise, "Stephen is a child."

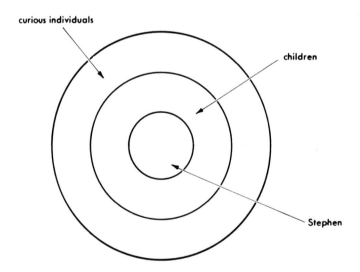

As the diagram now shows, the smallest circle is necessarily included in the largest circle, and the conclusion is thus valid: Stephen *is* curious.

Using the same system of circles to diagram syllogism (4), we can clearly see that its conclusion does not follow. The major premise, "All Italians are music lovers," can be represented thus:

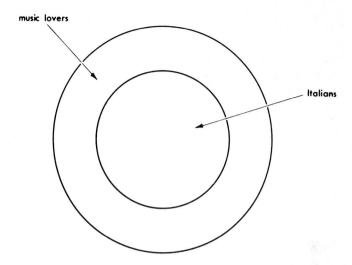

The minor premise, "Gilbert is a music lover," allows us to place the circle representing Gilbert any place within the larger circle: it does not have to be placed within the circle marked "Italians."

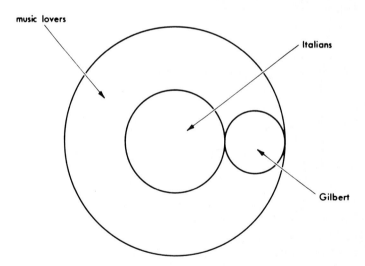

Therefore, the conclusion "Gilbert is an Italian" is a non sequitur—it does not follow.

The True Conclusion and the Probable Conclusion

We have defined a valid conclusion as a conclusion that follows from the ideas expressed in the premises, but a valid conclusion is not necessarily a *true conclusion*. The premises must be true before the argument can produce a true conclusion. The more firmly rooted in accurate observation the major premise is—the more thorough the process of induction that produced it—the sounder it is. "All human beings are mortal beings" is an accurate premise: it is a generalization born of universal human experience. Any syllogism based on it may yield a true conclusion. Few premises, however, are so demonstrably accurate. Arguments based on such sweeping, faulty premises as "Americans are crass materialists" or "Blondes have more fun" will not produce true conclusions.

Though arguments based on universally accepted generalizations do produce true conclusions when the rules governing syllogisms are followed, most of the generalizations you will use as major premises will not be absolutely accurate, unquestionably accepted. Most of them will be qualified; they might apply to many or most of the members of a class, but not to all of them. A major premise such as "All Democrats favor welfare programs supported and administered by the federal government" is likely to encounter resistance from an informed, intelligent audience. Modified, it becomes the basis of a more acceptable argument:

Major Premise	Most Democrats favor welfare programs supported and administered by the federal government.
Minor Premise	Harvey Ritter is a Democrat.
Conclusion	Harvey Ritter is likely to favor welfare programs supported and administered by the federal government.

This type of syllogism, a modification of the categorical syllogism since the middle term, Democrat, is not distributed, produces a *probable conclusion*. The greater the percentage of Democrats who favor welfare programs supported and administered by the federal government, the stronger the probability that Harvey Ritter does so too.

The criteria for the valid conclusion and the true conclusion mentioned above do not cover all syllogisms, but they are sufficient for our purposes here. In the section that follows we will consider several fallacies that are a blend of inductive, deductive, and emotional fallacies; but before we leave the syllogism, let us focus briefly on the problem of the *concealed premise*.

The Concealed Premise

A writer or speaker frequently omits one of the premises of a syllogism. Such a syllogism is not necessarily unreliable, but it presents a problem for an inexperienced writer or listener, who may accept an argument without realizing it is an argument and that its implied premises must be tested. The statement "Realtors make good school-board members; therefore, Hannah Babbit should be elected to the school board" is a syllogism with its minor premise, "Hannah Babbit is a realtor," missing. In such cases the minor premise is easily supplied and tested. Greater care, however, needs to be taken when the major premise is missing. The statement "The current tax bill before Congress should be passed: the United States Chamber of Commerce favors it" contains the concealed premise that the kind of tax legislation promoted by this organization is good for all Americans and should be enacted. The truth of this assumption is open to serious question—many economists would certainly oppose it—and because it is so central to the argument, the writer cannot ignore it without weakening her case.

Examine your own arguments, then, to see that they are not based on hidden, untenable premises. And when reading or discussing an issue with others, analyze the arguments proposed for the same purpose. If any contain concealed premises, supply the missing premises and test them for accuracy.

▣ MISCELLANEOUS FALLACIES

Begging the Question

An argument that begs the question assumes that the point the argument ought to be establishing is proven. This fallacy is also known as the circular argument, for the conclusion of the argument is merely a restatement in the same words or synonyms of the basic premises, leaving readers no wiser at the end of the argument than they were at the beginning. The following arguments illustrate this fallacy:

1. Man will never be able to control the weather because it is impossible.
2. Genuine tax reform will be a Herculean task because it is so difficult.

3. People who favor gun control are really hopeless because they can't be very bright.

Frequently a circular argument extends over several sentences:

> I am adamantly opposed to the appointment of James Virdon as head of the committee to investigate charges of rent gouging in the city. The chairman of such a committee should not be a controversial figure. Since I am opposed to him, he is a controversial figure; and he should be removed from the chairmanship of this committee.

The core of this argument is (1) I object to James Virdon because he is controversial, and (2) he is controversial because I object to him. The argument runs in circles with the conclusion simply repeating the original assertion. The writer should either give reasons for his opposition to Virdon or provide another reason why he is controversial. As it stands, it is no argument at all since the conclusion of an argument requires some basis in fact or judgment. As this example illustrates, the lack of logic and supporting evidence makes the circular argument a poor risk with careful readers.

Oversimplification

Oversimplification is a common fallacy in argumentation. Persons who are frustrated with the complexity of modern life and who desire simple, direct solutions for its problems commonly indulge in oversimplification. The rabid segregationist who regards civil rights legislation as indicative of the federal government's desire to tyrannize the South, the radical reactionary who believes that abolishing the income tax would solve the unemployment problem, and the military leader who feels that American security can be ensured by simply brandishing nuclear weapons—all these views are oversimplifications of complex problems.

A characteristic tendency of people who oversimplify is to divide people, ideas, and things into two or three sharply contrasting groups. There is a right way and a wrong way to do things, a moral way and an immoral way. Democrats are good, Republicans are bad; the federal government is bad, local government is good; economic systems are socialistic or capitalistic. The weakness of such conclusions is that they omit the possibility of other alternatives: they reject any middle ground between these polar positions. Few economic systems in the world, for example, are either purely capitalistic or purely socialistic. When revising your papers, therefore, re-examine your statements to see that you have not oversimplified issues. An intelligent reader will not be persuaded by simple answers to difficult questions.

Evading the Issue

The evidence used to prove an argument not only must be sufficient and representative, as explained earlier; it must be pertinent as well. When a writer or speaker engaged in a dispute presents evidence that does not relate to the point of his or her opponent's argument, he or she commits the error of evading the issue. An arguer who evades the issue often uses one of the following techniques: (1) the "smear" technique, (2) the "transfer" technique, and (3) the "bandwagon" technique. In the first of these, the arguer attacks the person instead of dealing with the issues he or she introduces. The following arguments illustrate the smear technique:

1. I can't imagine why Jeanette Crosley is such a popular actress. Her militant support of left-wing causes is disgraceful.
2. We should ignore the warnings of the president of the Auto Workers' Union on the increase of Japanese automobile imports. He simply wants to get more money for his union and bolster his image as a protector of the working man and woman.
3. Lord Harry, Senator Richardson is one brick short of a load. His opposition to handgun control is psychopathic. He seems to be indifferent to the ever-increasing carnage in American cities caused by the proliferation of the "Saturday Night Special."

In each of these examples, the writer uses abuse rather than relevant evidence to support her argument. Jeanette Crosley's militant support of left-wing causes, for example, is not a relevant consideration in an evaluation of her acting ability.

The transfer technique involves an appeal to authority—to a famous name or universally sanctioned idea—to validate an argument. Advertisers, newspaper editors, and politicians frequently attempt to gain acceptance for a product or a point of view by using this technique.

1. Olympic skier Claude Savant drives an Alpine Roadster. He says . . . .
2. Rock star Michele Donovan brushes her teeth with Lustrous toothpaste.
3. Benjamin Franklin would never have approved of such a huge federal debt.
4. Henry Kissinger, discussing recent developments in modern art, said . . . .

All these statements illustrate the fallacy of the simple appeal to authority. What Benjamin Franklin said may no longer be relevant in today's world. Nor can one accept Henry Kissinger's opinion on art simply because he is widely known. Of course, if these individuals were quoted on subjects within their competence, this fallacy would not apply. Skier Savant's knowledge might be relevant in a discussion of the winter Olympics and Henry Kissinger's in one about international relations.

Speakers or writers who ignore the issue through an appeal to the passions and prejudices of the crowd use the bandwagon approach. For example, a political campaigner frequently modifies his approach to accommodate his audience. In Harlem he appeals to his listeners as blacks; in Arkansas he appeals to them as farmers. The following passage illustrates this emotional appeal:

> I know that the people of this great nation will not reject a man who has throughout his entire public life worked and fought for the good of America. I know that they will not reject a man of the people, a man dedicated to the preservation of American freedoms against the threat of godless communism.

Advertisers also use this device:

> Don't be left behind. Join the crowd and switch to Blitz beer.

The weakness of the bandwagon approach is that in its appeal to the emotions of the audience it submits little or no factual or logical evidence for consideration.

The Loaded Question

The fallacy of the loaded question, like that of begging the question, assumes the truth of something that has not been proved, but it also implies wrongdoing on the part of the person to whom the question is directed. One cannot answer such a question without incriminating himself or committing himself to something he doesn't believe. The question "Why does the government permit big unions to seriously disrupt the economy of this country?" assumes two things, that big unions do seriously disrupt the economy of the country and that the federal government permits it, both of which have not been established. One really cannot reply to such a question. The best one can do is to point out that the question is faulty because it contains unproven assumptions.

EXERCISE 25

A. Place a V after each of the following syllogisms that has a valid conclusion and an I after each one that has an invalid conclusion. (Diagram each syllogism on a piece of scratch paper to help you determine its validity.) Indicate the cause of an invalid argument by writing one of the following numbers next to an I: (1) undistributed middle term, (2) more than three terms used, (3) shift in meaning of middle term.

    Example   All dogs drool.
                 Hugo drools.
                 Hugo is a dog.   __I,1__

1. All geniuses are eccentric.
   Professor Hudson is a genius.
   Professor Hudson is eccentric.   _____
2. The monsoon is a powerful wind.
   This wind is powerful.
   This wind is a monsoon.   _____
3. Designing women are manipulative.
   Madeline Foster is a designer.
   Madeline Foster is manipulative.   _____
4. All vegetarians avoid beef.
   Roger is a fastidious eater.
   Roger is a vegetarian.   _____
5. All laws that promote personal savings are good.
   This law promotes personal savings.
   This law is good.   _____

B. In the following syllogisms some conclusions are true, some are valid, and some are invalid. If the conclusion is true, place a T in the blank after it. If it is valid, place a V in the blank, and if it is invalid, place an I in the blank. (Remember that a true conclusion and a valid conclusion follow logically from the premises, but only a true conclusion follows from sound, accurate premises.)

1. The search for truth must govern all scientific research.
   Dr. Irma Perez is engaged in AIDS research.
   Dr. Perez must seek the truth about an AIDS vaccine.   _____
2. Randy Morris is a drunk.
   All drunks are dangerous.
   Randy Morris is dangerous.   _____
3. Successful persons are those who have acquired financial independence.
   My stockbroker is a successful person.
   My stockbroker has acquired financial independence.   _____

238

4. All persons who deliberately misreport their income on their income tax forms are unethical.
Some Americans deliberately misreport their income on their income tax forms.
Some Americans are unethical. _____

5. People who obey laws they don't like deserve praise.
Jim Ratlin, a trucker, doesn't like the 55 mph speed limit, but he obeys it.
Jim Ratlin deserves praise. _____

C. The following items are deductive arguments with hidden premises. Supply the missing premise of each argument.

> Example   Of course Clampson Dental Cream is good; it's advertised in *Peek* magazine.
> *Missing Premise*   Products advertised in *Peek* magazine are good.

1. Professor Walker is obviously an excellent teacher. Her students rave about her sense of humor.

Missing Premise _____

_____

2. Cyril Percy is an Englishman, so he probably believes in strict gun control.

Missing Premise _____

_____

3. *The Bountiful Boudoir* is obviously a good book; it sold more than two million copies the first year of its publication.

Missing Premise _____

_____

4. A sports columnist in the *Los Angeles Times* criticized the exorbitant salaries paid to basketball players. Very likely he doesn't like basketball.

Missing Premise _____

_____

239

5. Of course Japanese cars sell well in the United States. They are reasonably priced, fuel efficient, and durable.

Missing Premise _____

_____

D. Identify the fallacies in the following arguments. In some instances there will be more than one.

1. Governor Guile will never accept no-fault insurance legislation. Prior to his election he was president of the state's trial lawyers association, and he's obviously not going to support legislation so strongly opposed by lawyers whose income depends on automobile accident litigation.

_____

2. I'm curious as to why Senator Brewster continues to bash the Japanese on the free-trade issue.

_____

3. Conservation groups have been battling the lumber companies in the West over their desire to clear-cut stands of giant redwood trees. What enrages environmentalists is the fear that lumber companies are putting profits above long-term benefits to the American people. Spokesmen for the industry, however, discount these fears. They have promised not to cut trees vital to the preservation of the forests. Moreover, this country needs the wood for home construction, and the lumber companies have paid for the right to log the trees. To deny them this right would be to deny citizens the right to use their property as they see fit. This right is fundamental to the American way of life. The evidence clearly supports the lumber companies. They should be permitted to log the trees.

_____

_____

_____

4. Increasing taxes to reduce budget deficits would be foolish. Americans are not going to approve of higher taxes because they are not fools.

_____

240

5. *Modern Times* is an up-to-date, thoughtful, influential journal of opinion. You should subscribe to it today. Seventy-five percent of its readers are college graduates with incomes above $60,000 per year.

---

6. The clamor from doctors about rising costs of malpractice insurance is nothing but a convenient ruse to hide medical incompetence, as well as a ploy to increase their fees. The American public pays doctors handsomely and deserves competent treatment. Doctors lay much of the blame for the increased costs on lawyers, who, they claim, often receive exorbitant fees when they win a judgment for their clients. I've talked to three of my friends who are lawyers, and they say that idea is nonsense. They say the problem is simply the failure of the medical profession to weed out incompetents, and I agree. For all the money they make doctors ought to be able to assure their patients of expert care. With all the modern equipment at their disposal, doctors shouldn't make mistakes. If this country can put up a space rocket to orbit the earth, our doctors should be able to cure human ailments.

241

◼ THE SYLLOGISM AS THE BASIS OF ARGUMENTATIVE WRITING

The syllogism can form the basis of an argumentative paragraph or essay. If, for example, you want to argue that working while attending college is beneficial, your first step would be to construct a syllogism with your proposition as the conclusion of your argument. Then devise a minor premise to connect your conclusion to a major premise.

Major Premise	Experience that helps students to become more self-reliant, purposeful, and responsible helps them in their studies.
Minor Premise	Working while attending college helps students to become more self-reliant, purposeful, and responsible.
Conclusion	Working while attending college helps students in their studies.

In developing your paragraph or essay from this syllogism, you would first support your major premise, then the minor premise, and end with your conclusion. The major premise in this pattern is extremely important. It should be one your reader will accept as probably true, as is the case in the example above. If your major premise is reasonable and your minor premise well supported and logically linked to the major premise, your conclusion should be convincing.

A syllogism forms the organizing principle of the following brief essay on senior citizens. It can be formulated approximately as follows:

Major Premise	Any population group whose members on the whole receive a reasonable yearly income, whose expenses have been stabilized, and who are given special reductions in the prices of goods and services should not be homogenously lumped together as poor.
Minor Premise	America's senior citizens on the whole receive a reasonable yearly income, have stabilized incomes, and receive special reductions in the prices of goods and services.
Conclusion	America's senior citizens should not be homogenously lumped together as poor.

Old and Needy?

It is not surprising that Americans, particularly younger Americans, believe that older people deserve special attention and consideration. Newspaper and magazine articles and television commentaries have, in recent years, focused on the plight of the aged neglected by their families and ignored by a penurious, indifferent government. Stories and films about old people rotting away in convalescent homes, standing in lines at soup kitchens, and staggering under a heavy burden of medical expense have been in the news and on the minds of millions of Americans. To many of these Americans, old means poor, deprived, neglected. But just how needy are America's senior citizens? Does "old" necessarily mean "poor"?

Any humane society should be concerned about the welfare of its citizens, about their income and expenses, their ability to maintain themselves in a reasonable *Major Premise* standard of living. Any population group that enjoys a reasonable yearly income, stabilized expenses, and special perquisites and benefits is not really poor. And by these standards, senior citizens are not, as a whole, poor. For example, recent census figures indicate that people over sixty-five have a per capita annual income after taxes of $6,299, $335 more than the national average, and a poverty rate of 14 percent, about that of the general population. Their per capita income is twice that of families headed by a single woman. Moreover, their Social Security payments have been adjusted upward annually to protect them against inflation, an advantage not enjoyed by millions of young factory workers in recent years. And speaking of Social Security benefits, the typical retired person gets back more than four times as much money from Social Security as he or she has contributed to the system. According to *U.S. News and World Report,* a married man who began contributing to Social Security in 1937, retired in 1982, and whose wife did not work would have got back all of his payroll contributions in just fourteen months.[1]

[1] Teresa Anderson, "The Best Years of Their Lives," *Newsweek,* January 7, 1985, p. 7.

Minor   Senior citizens not only receive reasonable incomes,
Premise   they also have more stabilized expenses than other
                 groups; and they get special benefits as well. Propo-
                 nents of increased governmental assistance for the el-
                 derly frequently refer to their fixed incomes in arguing
                 their case, but older people's expenses are more stabi-
                 lized than those of other groups. Their medical ex-
                 penses, though substantial, are mitigated by Medicare,
                 and supplemental coverage can be obtained through
                 private insurance companies at a nonprohibitive cost.
                 About 70 percent of them own their own homes; others
                 have sold theirs for a tidy, untaxed profit. They also
                 receive an extra deduction on their income taxes. Pub-
                 lic transportation is cheap: in Portland, Oregon, for in-
                 stance, senior citizens can ride anywhere in the city for
                 a quarter, in Minneapolis for a dime. And they are
                 given reduced prices for a host of services and amuse-
                 ments, from haircuts to hotel rooms to European pack-
                 age tours. To be sure, we must treat senior citizens with
                 kindness and consideration, with respect for their expe-
                 rience and wisdom. We must meet their real needs. But
Conclusion   if we are to do this effectively, we must not lump them
                 all together as poor, as a "homogenous blob of senile
                 men and women eating cat food in lonely rooms."[2]

EXERCISE 26

A. Construct a syllogism for each of the following propositions. As in the
   preceding essay, use the proposition as the conclusion of your argument
   and construct a minor premise to link your conclusion to a major
   premise that would probably be accepted.

1. Oil consumption in the United States needs to be reduced to protect the
   environment as well as the economy.
2. Public financed day-care centers are (are not) needed in the United
   States.
3. Worldwide population growth represents (or does not represent) a serious
   problem.

B. Use the syllogism you developed for one of the items above as the basis
   of a paragraph or essay.

___
[2] Anderson, p. 7.

◙ TRACING CAUSE AND EFFECT RELATIONSHIPS

Another method of structuring an argument is to trace cause and effect relationships, as, for example, when you wish to explain the cause of a problem as a means of convincing your reader to approve of a solution you propose. Causal analysis is similar to sequence or process analysis discussed in Chapter Three (pp. 78–79), for each involves actions that occur in chronological order. They are not the same, however, for a sequence or process analysis simply tells *how* actions or steps are related, not *why.* In a report on the bombing of Pearl Harbor in 1941, for instance, you could simply relate the sequence of events that took place or attempt a more ambitious analysis of the cause and effect of the attack.

Cause and effect writing is a common ingredient in much writing today because it attempts to get at the reasons that underlie events and human behavior, and people want and need to know the causes and effects of forces that influence or govern their lives. Tracing cause and effect is common in systematic, scientific investigation and in the writing of political scientists, historians, and economists; but it is not limited to such formal, argumentative uses. It may be used in expository writing where its purpose is simply to inform, clarify, or perhaps to amuse, rather than to argue a case.

Causal analysis may be used in a number of ways. You may describe an event and emphasize the consequences that followed from it. In a paragraph or paper about a change in graduation requirements—adding a test on writing ability for graduating seniors, let's say—you might briefly mention the substance of the change and the faculty action that produced it and then devote more space to the effects of the change. A second approach would be to describe the event, this time focusing on the causes that produced it. Using this approach, you would proceed as above in describing the new writing requirement and then focus your attention on why the change was enacted. A third strategy would be to deal with both cause and effect after presenting the action. This approach would likely require more than a single paragraph, particularly if your causal analysis formed the basis of an argument.

Whether you write a single paragraph or a longer essay will depend on how thoroughly you wish to explore your subject. In a short paper you would commonly limit yourself to *immediate* causes and effects, those close in time to the event. In a longer paper you could explore *ultimate* causes and effects, those more remote in time from the event. In the case of the graduation requirement referred to above, the immediate cause of the change might simply be the faculty action and the immediate effect the necessity of students to make arrangements to take the test. Dealing with the ultimate causes, you might uncover the following: faculty displeasure with general student writing ability, pressure from the public, and perhaps pressure from state legislators as well. An investigation of ultimate effects would likely turn up these: an increase in student demand for tutorial assistance, changes in students' schedules, the addition of composition classes to the curriculum, delays in graduation, and added student frustration.

A final word. As you're making your investigation and writing your analysis, keep in mind what you've learned about reasoning in this chapter:

1. Avoid oversimplification. Investigate your subject carefully and objectively, and don't claim too much for your analysis.
2. Avoid the *post hoc* fallacy. Don't assume that something that happens before or after something else is a cause or effect of it.
3. Let your reader see the evidence or the reasoning that supports your attribution of cause and effect relationships.

The two paragraphs below are developed by causal analysis, the first focusing on cause, the second on effect.

But perhaps other societal factors have caused children to give up play. Children's greater exposure to adult realities, their knowledge of adult sexuality, for instance, might make them more sophisticated, less likely to play like children. Evidence from the counterculture communes of the sixties and seventies adds weight to the argument that it is television above all that has eliminated children's play. Studies of children raised in a variety of such communes, all television-free, showed the little communards continuing to fill their time with those forms of play that have all but vanished from the lives of conventionally reared American children. And yet these counterculture kids were casually exposed to all sorts of adult matters—drug taking, sexual intercourse. Indeed, they sometimes incorporated these matters into their play: "We're mating," a pair of six-year-olds told a reporter to explain their curious bumps and grinds. Nevertheless, to all observers the commune children preserved a distinctly childlike and even innocent demeanor, an impression that was produced mainly by the fact that they spent most of their time playing. Their play defined them as belonging to a special world of childhood. [From Marie Winn, "The End of Play," *Children Without Childhood,* Pantheon Books, a division of Random House, 1981.]

Cardiologists, physical therapists, trainers, athletes—all tout the beneficial effects of vigorous exercise, but what precisely are these effects? According to recent studies vigorous physical exercise benefits the cardiovascular system, bone and muscle tissue, and the general health and emotional well-being of the participant. The more physically active person, for example, is less apt to suffer a heart attack because exercise strengthens the heart, increases the network of blood vessels feeding the heart, and keeps the arteries open, all of which improve the capacity of the physically fit person to distribute oxygen throughout the body tissues. Regular physical exercise also helps to reduce the loss of calcium in the bodies of people over fifty. Osteoporosis, a loss of calcium in aging people, especially women, produces brittle bones and more fractures. Continued exercise lessens the risk of this condition. Another effect of exercise is to burn calories, helping to reduce obesity, and tone the muscles, giving one a trimmer look. Because muscle tissue consumes more calories in sustaining itself than fatty tissue, trim, well-muscled persons are less likely to put on excess weight. And, finally, regular exercise programs have been found to reduce anxiety and depression among people whose jobs and lives are filled with stress.

EXERCISE 27

A. In a paragraph of 100 to 150 words describe the effects of one of the following situations. In the first two or three sentences present your topic sentence and a brief description of the event; then move on to effects.

1. the invention of the automobile, computer, pocket calculator, nuclear power, jet engine, laser beam, telephone
2. the availability of contraceptive devices
3. the continuation of a weakened dollar in international trade, the high cost of new homes, the effects of high or low taxes on the welfare of the United States
4. the AIDS epidemic
5. students dropping out of high school, the continuing drought in California

B. In a paragraph of 100 to 150 words speculate about the causes of one of the following. Follow the same procedure in structuring your paragraph as explained in A above.

1. the increasing interest in physical fitness in the United States
2. the high divorce rate, the high cost of medical care in the United States
3. the increasing incidence and violence of crime among American youth
4. the popularity of diet books, soap operas, jogging, horror or catastrophe movies, mystery novels
5. the particular behavior pattern or eccentricity of a friend

C. Select one of the following topics, or one listed in A or B above, and write a 300-word (three-paragraph) essay treating both cause and effect. Either one of the following strategies will help you to organize your paper: (1) In the first paragraph focus on effects, in the second on causes, and in the third on a solution, your recommendation for a course of action; or (2) in the first paragraph describe the problem at some length, in the second deal with causes, and in the third deal with effects. This assignment will require library research to provide you with relevant evidence to substantiate your ideas and arguments.

1. the increasing congestion of American airports, highways
2. American youth's love affair with the automobile
3. the continuing intense interest among foreigners in emigrating to the United States
4. Americans' continuing high consumption of imported oil
5. the dramatic increase in the number of working women in the past fifty years

◙ PERSUASION

Persuasive writing is not solely a matter of logic: it is also a matter of language, attitude, and character. We persuade others by an appeal to their emotions as well as to their reason, and by the strength of our personality and character, too. To convince your reader, you must attend to the clarity, honesty, and emotional impact of your arguments as well as to their logical construction. You must present yourself as a person of good sense, integrity, and good will.

Analyzing Your Audience

Persuasive writing, like expository writing, is directed to an audience. In school you will be writing for your instructors and classmates for the most part. Out of school your reader may be a prospective employer, a newspaper editor, a legislator, or a personal friend. In any case you should analyze your audience before you plan your arguments since their interests, educational and social background, knowledge, loyalties, and motives will affect their receptivity to your arguments. What persuades one audience will not necessarily persuade another, as you have undoubtedly learned in arguing the same subject with a number of friends, or with friends and your parents. The *tone* you assume, the *words and sentence patterns* you use, the *length of your paragraphs,* the *arguments* you select—all will vary to accord with your audience. In the essays and reports you write in college, for example, your tone will probably be more serious, your diction more formal, and your sentences and paragraphs longer than would be the case in articles you write for student magazines or in letters you write to friends. The following arguments could be used to support the proposition that living away from home in apartments is beneficial to college students: (1) promotes self-reliance, (2) reduces parental control over choice of friends, (3) helps the student learn to manage a budget, (4) permits a less inhibited life style, (5) reduces household chores, and (6) promotes self-discovery and creativity in human relationships. If you were arguing this proposition with your parents, you would stress arguments 1, 3, and 6. If you were attempting to convince a potential roommate, you would stress 2, 4, and 5.

If you keep your audience in mind, you will keep your arguments more specific, more relevant. By adjusting your tone to the sensitivities of your readers, you will make them more receptive to what you say, less inclined to tune you out. And a knowledge of your audience will often save you needless effort in explaining terms and concepts that are already known and understood.

Defining Important Terms

An awareness of the intellectual level and knowledge of your audience does limit the need of defining familiar terms. But accurate, precise definition of terms is, nonetheless, important, especially when they are subject to varied interpretation. Words like *liberty, freedom, truth, justice, liberal, conservative, radical,* and *propaganda* need to be pinned down. Consider the following passage:

> The American people have been deceived about the nature of their government. They have been taught that the United States is a democracy, when actually it is a republic. Consequently, proposals to modify the system of electing a president to make it more democratic are irrelevant.

This passage is vague because of the writer's failure to tell us what she means by *democracy* and *republic*. Since both terms can be used to describe forms of government in which the power resides in the voters who elect representatives to decide public issues, the writer should specify the sense in which she is using these terms if she is to convince rather than confuse us. The revision below eliminates this confusion, although one may still not agree with the conclusions.

> A republic is commonly defined as a form of government in which the voters elect representatives to meet and decide public issues. A pure democracy is a form of government in which the voters themselves assemble in one place to decide these issues. Accepting this distinction, we can describe the United States as a republic rather than a democracy. Hence, proposals to modify the system of electing a president to make it *more* democratic are irrelevant.

Vague

It is time Americans recognized the danger of extremist groups. The subversives should be controlled before they do real damage to the American way of life.

Improved

Political groups and organizations that advocate radical measures to meet the problems of our time threaten the stability of American life. What constitutes a "radical" measure is, of course, open to dispute, but most Americans would probably agree that the term could be applied to such actions as bombing federal buildings to express opposition to governmental policies; advocating elimination of welfare programs, Medicare, and the Social Security system; and establishing local guerrilla "armies." Although radical groups have a right to express their opinions and gain adherents to their cause, they should be watched carefully to see that they do not break any laws.

Appealing to the Emotions

An appeal to the emotions of an audience can be very persuasive, a fact long recognized by writers, propagandists, political leaders. All of us at one time or another are moved to action or to change our opinions through our emotions. Sound, carefully reasoned arguments should be the foundation of your attempts to persuade, but on occasion you will want to couple logic with an appeal to your reader's feelings, loyalties, and aspirations. Martin Luther King, Jr., used an emotional appeal to great effect in persuading Americans of the justice of the civil rights movement:

> We have waited for more than 340 years for our constitutional and God-given rights. The nations of Asia and Africa are moving with jetlike speed toward gaining political independence, but we still creep at horse-and-buggy pace toward gaining a cup of coffee at a lunch counter. Perhaps it is easy for those who have never felt the stinging darts of segregation to say, "Wait." But when you have seen vicious mobs lynch your mothers and fathers at will and drown your sisters and brothers at whim; when you have seen hate-filled policemen curse, kick and even kill your black brothers and sisters; when you see the vast majority of your twenty million Negro brothers smothering in an airtight cage of poverty in the midst of an affluent society; when you suddenly find your tongue twisted and your speech stammering as you seek to explain to your six-year-old daughter why she can't go to the public amusement park that has just been advertised on television, and see tears welling up in her eyes when she is told that Funtown is closed to colored children, and see ominous clouds of inferiority beginning to form in her little mental sky, and see her beginning to distort her personality by developing an unconscious bitterness toward white people . . . [From Martin Luther King, Jr., "Letter from Birmingham Jail," April 16, 1963, *Why We Can't Wait,* Harper & Row, 1963.]

An emotional appeal is a legitimate weapon in any writer's arsenal, but it needs to be used honestly and carefully, for it can backfire if it becomes obvious to readers, particularly well-informed and thoughtful readers, that the writer is simply pandering to their biases to further his or her own interests. Advertisers, editorial writers, lawyers, politicians, extremists in favor of one cause or another have on occasion deviated from the truth with emotional appeals; but those who continually use such appeals for unscrupulous purposes ultimately damage whatever cause they serve. In your own efforts at persuasion avoid routine exaggeration and highly charged language or the abuse of those whose opinions you do not share. In the paragraph below the writer's anger clearly gets the best of his judgment.

> The welfare mess in this country can be laid to the door of those muddle-headed, fuzzy-minded liberals who for the past four decades have bemoaned the sad fate of the chiseling, ignorant misfits among us who are too lazy to get off their duffs and get a job. If Americans ever hope to eliminate this something-for-nothing boondoggle, they will simply have to put their feet down and demand that the paper-shuffling bureaucrats in Washington stop squandering taxpayers' money on socialistic schemes that perpetuate sloth and irresponsibility. [From William F. Smith and Robert G. Wicks, *Communicating Through Word and Image,* Winthrop Publishers, 1975.]

Such phrases as "chiseling, ignorant misfits," "paper-shuffling bureaucrats," and "socialistic schemes" tell us more about the writer's state of mind than about his subject. Here are examples of exaggerated statements with suggested revisions:

Exaggerated	Revised
The foreign aid program succeeds in doing nothing but pouring money down a rat hole. It is a vast giveaway program that aids no one.	Our foreign aid program needs to be examined carefully to see if we can eliminate some of the waste and mismanagement in its operation.
The lessons of history are unmistakable. Either we reduce our tax rate, or the U.S. faces imminent economic chaos and disaster.	Reducing tax rates in the countries of Western Europe after the Second World War provided a needed stimulus to their economies. In all likelihood, lower taxes in the U.S. would produce a similar expansion.

Emotive Language

As noted earlier, an emotional appeal may involve loaded or slanted words, words that reveal the user's feelings and attitudes, approval or disapproval. Loaded words are rather commonly used in situations in which people's feelings are aroused—political discussions, for example. In the opinion of one person, Senator Jones is intelligent, fair, compassionate in his regard for the underdog. To another he is opinionated, rigid, a maudlin do-gooder. In the course of a conversation between these two persons, people working in Washington, D.C., might be referred to as intellectuals or eggheads, public servants or bureaucrats, faithful employees or time-servers.

The following passage provides further illustration of the use of loaded words. The opinions are those of a Mississippi circuit judge on the subject of Mississippi whiskey.

> If when you say whiskey you mean the devil's brew, the poison scourge, the bloody monster, that defiles innocence, dethrones reason, destroys the home, creates misery and poverty, yea, literally takes the bread from the mouths of little children; if you mean the evil drink that topples the Christian man and woman from the pinnacle of righteous, gracious living into the bottomless pit of degradation and despair, and shame, and helplessness, and hopelessness, then certainly I am against it.
>
> But if when you say whiskey you mean the oil of conversation, the philosophic wine, the ale that puts a song in their hearts and laughter on their lips, and the warm glow of contentment in their eyes; if you mean Christmas cheer; if you mean the stimulating drink that puts the spring into the old gentleman's step on a frosty, crispy morning; if you mean the drink which enables a man to magnify his joy, and his happiness, and to forget, if only for a little while, life's great tragedies, and heartaches, and sorrows; if you mean that drink, the sale of which pours into our treasuries untold millions of dollars, which are used to provide tender care for our little crippled children, our blind, our deaf, our dumb, our pitiful aged and infirm; to build highways and hospitals and schools, then certainly I am for it.
>
> This is my stand, I will not retreat from it. I will not compromise. [From Kenneth Vinson, "Prohibition's Last Stand," *The New Republic,* October 16, 1965, p. 11.]

As these differences of opinion about Senator Jones and about whiskey reveal, special feelings and associations attach to words. The person who approves of Senator Jones describes him in words that arouse favorable feelings—*intelligent, fair, compassionate.* The person who disapproves of the senator uses words that arouse unfavorable feelings—*opinionated, rigid, do-gooder.* Similarly, one who refers to whiskey as the *oil of conversation,* the *philosophic wine, Christmas cheer* clearly approves of it; one who regards it as the *devil's brew,* the *poison scourge,* the *bloody monster* rather clearly disapproves of it. The suggestions and associations that cluster about a word make up its *connotative* meaning. The connotations of *firm,* for instance, are positive: the word suggests determination, courage, solidity—all attractive qualities. The connotations of *rigid,* however, are negative: it suggests stubbornness, inflexibility, a narrowminded unwillingness to compromise—all unattractive qualities. The tendency to use words with favorable connotations, honorific words, in referring to what we like can be seen in a common practice today, the substitution of a word with more pleasant associations for one that conveys a less pleasant reality. These sugar-coated words and phrases are called *euphemisms.*

Words have *denotative* meanings as well as connotative meanings. The denotative meaning of a word signifies its literal, explicit meaning—the object or idea it stands for. The denotation of "firm" and "rigid" is the same—unyielding, difficult to move. The distinction, then, between the connotative and denotative meaning of a word is that its connotation includes the feelings and attitudes associated with it; its denotation does not. And, as illustrated, the connotation of a word may be positive or negative.

Emotive words, words with strong connotations, vary in their power to arouse feeling. *Political nonconformist, reactionary, fascist*—all evoke feelings of anger in many people's minds. But *fascist* evokes a stronger reaction than does *political nonconformist.* Because emotive words can powerfully influence people's opinions, some writers employ them frequently to condemn persons and ideas they do not like. By using loaded words, such as *traitor, subversive, demagogue,* and the like, they hope to lead their readers into forming unfavorable opinions of their subjects without examining the supporting evidence.

Although emotive language is customarily used by those who distort and exaggerate, it need not be avoided absolutely. Persuasive writing deliberately and legitimately appeals to the emotions of the reader. Many respected writers and speakers employ emotion successfully to persuade others of the truth of their ideas. But it must be used with care. If your readers believe that you are substituting emotion for credible evidence, that you are trying to browbeat them into agreement, they are apt to dismiss your arguments as biased and unreliable. In short, deal honestly with your readers. If you use an emotional appeal, let them see the evidence that justifies it.

Countering the Opposition

To achieve the results you want in a persuasive paper, you will often have to do more than make a strong case for your own point of view, especially when your reader is well informed and thoughtful. You will have to consider and counter important opposition arguments. Countering opposing arguments makes sense for several reasons. First, if you do not, your reader may conclude that you are ignorant of the complexities of your subject and reject your arguments as one-sided and simplistic. Second, even if your reader is unaware of opposing arguments, he or she will be impressed with your fairness; and as we mentioned earlier, a writer's integrity is an important element in persuasion. And, finally, countering opposition arguments is strategically wise: once you have demolished the primary arguments of the opposition, your own arguments will stand more securely.

Note how clearly and judiciously the student writer of the following editorial considers and counters opposition arguments:

Opposition Argument	When the dean of men used his veto power last week to squash a Student Commission proposal to pay part of the costs of a radio station on campus, he was well within his rights. As policy now stands, the adviser's veto on the Student Commission measures is meant to prevent unwise action on the part of student leaders.
Counter Argument	Though ostensibly sound, however, this procedure actually renders commissioners impotent before the dean of men.
Opposition Argument	The dean's suggestion that the Board of Trustees be requested to put up the $10,000 in question seemed to make sense. However, the commission had hoped to allocate funds while the money was available, as it presently is in the Associated Student Body reserve fund, and not allocated for other less worthy projects.
Counter Argument	Commission members also feel that the board may not come through with the funds. Although Dr. Robert Winslow, chancellor of the college district, is reportedly highly enthusiastic about the radio station, he vacates his post in June. Since the student government does not operate during the summer months, the board may not get around to considering the radio funds requested

until September. Then, with a new chancellor, the $10,000 may be hard to get.

Counter
Argument
When presented with the facts, student commissioners can be presumed to have as sound a judgment as one administration adviser. The adviser's function is to spell out to commissioners the implications of their proposals, not to block them because of personal preference. The commission, of course, should weigh carefully every suggestion of the adviser, and the adviser should be allowed to veto commissioners' proposals when he disagrees with the conclusions commissioners have drawn. After the veto, however, the commissioners, if they are convinced of the rightness of their decisions, should be allowed to override that veto with, say, a two-thirds vote. Commission members would not be inclined to abuse their veto-overriding power since measures that have hurdled the veto still must be approved by the President's Council. This change in policy would therefore not imperil college stability. Because those proposals having unanimous or near unanimous support of the Student Commission would have direct access to the president, actions strongly desired by the students would be more seriously considered, and student government would become more efficient and meaningful.

This next essay is a longer essay using the same strategy of countering the opposition. In it the writer presents her case against the growing tendency of school boards and other groups to censor books considered obscene or subversive. Because of the length and amplitude of the essay, the writer is justified in devoting a full paragraph to the introduction and to the conclusion. In the first paragraph she introduces her subject broadly and narrows to her thesis at the end of the paragraph. In developing her case, she follows the strategy suggested on page 255 and illustrated on pages 255–256, introducing and countering important opposition arguments. Note that, in the second and fourth paragraphs, the writer begins by presenting an opposition argument and then counters it with her own. In the fifth and sixth paragraphs, having previously disposed of the opposition, she now concentrates on her own strongest arguments.

Surveying the theme as a whole, we can see how she has achieved emphasis through position and proportion. The opening paragraph leads into the subject. The more fully developed middle paragraphs carry the main burden of her case. And the final paragraph, reminding the reader of an important point made in the opening paragraph, the protection of intellectual freedom guaranteed by the First Amendment, forcefully concludes the essay with a quoted passage.

A Deadly Virus

Freedom of speech has long been considered the foundation of American democracy, a principle that antedates and engenders all the other freedoms guaranteed in the Bill of Rights. Because of the First Amendment, Americans have been relatively free of governmental interference in expressing their ideas and opinions in speech and writing. But this restraint has been less characteristic of volunteer censors, of private groups that have wanted to control or curtail free expression to protect people from religious heresy, moral corruption, or unwelcome political ideas. At one time or another, *Huckleberry Finn, The Canterbury Tales, The Merchant of Venice, Grapes of Wrath* and many other classics have felt the hot breath of the censor. In recent years efforts to remove books from public libraries and schoolrooms have increased significantly, due, in part at least, to a resurgent fundamentalist spirit of the Moral Majority, though liberal groups have also on occasion favored suppression of books and films they considered *Thesis* bigoted or reactionary. Whether censorship originates from the right or left, however, from governmental agencies or private groups, it must be opposed.

Opposition Argument Those who favor book banning, or even burning, frequently argue that "dirty" books corrupt the morals and pervert the psychological orientation of the young toward love and sex. They deplore the "degrading" sexual behavior, the coarse language, the disreputable characters in books their children are exposed to; and they want them suppressed. One need only scan the offerings of a typical newsstand or note the aggressive vulgarity of much prime time television to be aware that the reading and viewing tastes of the American public are not burdened by a Victorian prudery. It is also true that parents and teachers need to exercise care and judgment in guiding the reading of elementary school children and adolescents to protect immature minds and sensibilities unable to understand or emotionally cope with the harsh reality of immoral behavior depicted in adult fiction. But when sensible precaution is *Counter* carried to the point of banning books in high schools *Argument* and removing them from public libraries, it is misguided, harmful, and, at times, ludicrous.

The primary purpose of serious literature is to communicate human experience, and since illicit sex and immoral behavior are a part of human experience, it follows that serious writers will deal with sex and human depravity on occasion. The candid representation of such matters may be shocking and offensive to some readers, but the writer's purpose in depicting sinful acts is not to dwell on salacious details for their own sake nor to arouse an interest in evil, but to reveal aspects of his vision of reality. Hiding such situations from students will not help them to understand and deal with such problems as adults. Moreover, the books that have been proscribed for their vivid descriptions of sexuality and alleged obscenity include many written by famous authors: Shakespeare, Chaucer, Hawthorne, Hemingway, Steinbeck, Faulkner, Huxley, Vonnegut, and Salinger, to name but a few. And passages from the Bible have not escaped the wrath of some purists.

Opposition Censors also want to prohibit the expression of ideas *Argument* they regard as pernicious, subversive, or un-American. The conflicts and violent ideologies of the twentieth century, in particular the growth of communism and its attendant evils, account for much of the drive of reactionary political groups to rid America of "alien" ideas by banning books and other printed matter that seem communist inspired or directed. The works of Karl Marx have often been denounced and their study by college students deplored. But there are censors on the left as well, who speak on behalf of minorities. *Mary Poppins* was banned from the San Francisco Public Library because it reflected racist attitudes, *The Merchant of Venice* has been condemned because of its alleged anti-Semitism, and a homosexual organization in New York City attempted to persuade the city to

Counter Argument withdraw its cooperation from the production of a film in which homosexuals were depicted unfavorably. But whatever their motives and however sincere their beliefs, censors are misguided and dangerous. They are misguided, for they assume the wisdom and authority to decide which ideas are safe and which not, not only for members of their own groups but for others as well. Ironically, they demand freedom of expression for the ideas they support and suppression of those they oppose. And censors are dangerous because of the constrictive, chilling effect they can have on the free and open discussion of ideas, which is the lifeblood of American political and cultural life.

Counter Argument The argument against censorship does not mean that books may not have negative as well as positive effects on readers. It does not mean that pornography doesn't exist, that printed matter is never, under any circumstance, truly subversive. But it does mean that outright censorship and suppression of books, or films, is seldom justified. Admittedly, the reading and viewing of children should be prudently supervised in accordance with their level of maturity. Older youths, however, should not be subject to such close supervision and adults not at all, except in the case of a work "utterly without redeeming social importance" and therefore subject to legal restriction by the courts. As mentioned earlier, many books proscribed by school boards and religious groups in recent years have been regarded as classics. Moreover, banning books because of their alleged obscenity is often self-defeating, for it simply stimulates students to want to read them. Removing books from libraries because they offend the political or social beliefs of some group would just about empty our libraries.

Counter Argument The urge to censor written words has existed in every society since man learned to write. Modern tyrannies, in particular, seek to control their subjects and keep them contented by rigorously preventing their exposure to troubling ideas in books and periodicals. But this attempt at mind control—and censorship is just that— runs counter to important American values. If successful it would place Americans, young and old, in intellectual and spiritual bondage. Censors and book banners surfacing in school districts across the nation imply that ideas must be made safe for students, whereas, in truth, students must be made safe for ideas. And to be made safe, they must be given the opportunity to develop the capacity to examine books and ideas and to judge their merit for themselves. This process is not always a soothing experience for adults, but then neither is democracy in action. As Professor Bishin of the University of Southern California College of Law reminds us, ". . . the literature and art which the First Amendment protects does not consist of only that which makes us comfortable or happy. The reason why speech and press must be protected from the majority by a constitutional amendment is precisely because humanity is endowed with the stubborn, blind tendency to strike down the new and unconventional, to view it as a threat which must be put down, rather than a possibility to be studied and criticized."[3]

---

[3] William R. Bishin, "The Supreme Court vs. Obscenity," *Los Angeles Times,* October 30, 1968, Part II, p. 9.

EXERCISE 28

A. Read the following passage carefully. Underline the emotive terms, list
   them below, and indicate their connotations.

In the old days when you wanted something you worked and saved. Today
spoiled young kids belly-ache to their spineless, permissive parents who give
it to them so they won't be deprived. If your father lost his job, he took
whatever work he could find even if he had to move the family to another
town. Nowadays hordes of lazy loafers line up for welfare rather than take an
honest job. The immigrants who built this country would have scorned the
"something for nothing" attitude of these welfare whiners. The sturdy immigrants believed in hard work, scrimping, and saving to support themselves.
Now liberal patsies demand that "developing nations" be given American
taxpayers' money to save them from their own inept, wasteful ways and
corrupt, sleazy governments. Throughout the world "minority groups" rant
and rave about racism in the industrialized nations as the cause of their
plight, whereas their real problem is a lack of willingness to work, of ambi-
tion. In the United States, too, the vicious destructiveness of minority gangs
require higher taxes for decent, law-abiding citizens to pay more for police
protection. Those who are really a deprived minority are the self-reliant,
hard-working, long-suffering American taxpayers who have pampered evil
too long.

Emotive Words   Connotations

_____   _____

_____   _____

_____   _____

_____   _____

_____   _____

_____   _____

_____   _____

_____   _____

261

B. Opposite each of the words or phrases in the following list, place a word or phrase with roughly the same denotation as the word in the left-hand column but with a different connotation as directed.

    Example   tax loophole (more favorable)—tax incentive

1. an elderly spinster (less favorable) __old maid__

2. flexible (less favorable) __spineless)__

3. taxpayers' money (more favorable) __public funds__

4. law officer (less favorable) __Cop__

5. soldier of fortune (less favorable) __mercinary__

6. crammed hard but flunked the test (more favorable) __Studied diligently__

7. courageous (less favorable) _____

8. maid (more favorable) _____

9. made a pile of dough on slick real estate deals (more favorable)

_____

_____

10. used car (more favorable) __pre-owned__

C. The words in the following lists have about the same denotation, but their connotations vary markedly. Rank them in order of the favorability of their connotations, beginning with the word with the most favorable associations.

1. ignorant, innocent, naive, uninformed

_____

2. obese, fat, portly, stout, pudgy

_____

3. playboy, swinger, *bon vivant,* hedonist, lecher

_____

4. eccentric, odd, nonconformist, weird, individualistic

_____

5. devout, godly, sanctimonious, religious, pious

_____

D. The following list contains ten euphemisms (sugar-coated words or phrases substituted for words and phrases with less favorable connotations). For each euphemism select the word or phrase for which it is a substitute.

1. recycling station or refuse station _____

2. antisocial act _____

3. memorial garden _____

4. substandard housing _____

5. career apparel _____

6. petrochemical dispenser _____

7. maximizing profit _____

8. language facilitator _____

9. high yield bonds _____

10. horse mackerel sandwich _____

E. The following "speech," which appeared in Brown University's *The Daily Herald,* presents a distinguished scholar's opinions of or advice to graduating seniors.[4] Read the composition carefully, and in a brief essay evaluate its persuasiveness. Does the writer support his judgments with facts? Does he select his facts to slant his article? Does he use emotive terms, loaded language? Is he fair with the opposition? Support your judgments with specific examples.

[4] Jacob Neusner, Brown University's *The Daily Herald,* June 12, 1983.

263

The Speech the Graduates Didn't Hear[5]

We the faculty take no pride in our educational achievements with you. We have prepared you for a world that does not exist, indeed, that cannot exist. You have spent four years supposing that failure leaves no record. You have learned at Brown that when your work goes poorly, the painless solution is to drop out. But starting now, in the world to which you go, failure marks you. Confronting difficulty by quitting leaves you changed. Outside Brown, quitters are no heroes.

With us you could argue about why your errors were not errors, why mediocre work really was excellent, why you could take pride in routine and slipshod presentation. Most of you, after all, can look back on honor grades for most of what you have done. So, here grades can have meant little in distinguishing the excellent from the ordinary. But tomorrow, in the world to which you go, you had best not defend errors but learn from them. You will be ill-advised to demand praise for what does not deserve it, and abuse those who do not give it.

For four years we created an altogether forgiving world, in which whatever slight effort you gave was all that was demanded. When you did not keep appointments, we made new ones. When your work came in beyond the deadline, we pretended not to care.

Worse still, when you were boring, we acted as if you were saying something important. When you were garrulous and talked to hear yourself talk, we listened as if it mattered. When you tossed on our desks writing upon which you had not labored, we read it and even responded, as though you earned a response. When you were dull, we pretended you were smart. When you were predictable, unimaginative, and routine, we listened as if to new and wonderful things. When you demanded free lunch, we served it. And all this why?

Despite your fantasies, it was not even that we wanted to be liked by you. It was that we did not want to be bothered, and the easy way out was pretense: smiles and easy Bs.

It is conventional to quote in addresses such as these. Let me quote someone you've never heard of: Prof. Carter A. Daniel, Rutgers University (*Chronicle of Higher Education,* May 7, 1979):

"College has spoiled you by reading papers that don't deserve to be read, listening to comments that don't deserve a hearing, paying attention even to the lazy, ill-informed, and rude. We had to do it, for the sake of education. But nobody will ever do it again. College has deprived you of adequate preparation for the last 50 years. It has failed you by being easy, free, forgiving, attentive, comfortable, interesting, unchallenging fun. Good luck tomorrow."

That is why, on this commencement day, we have nothing in which to take pride.

---

[5] Jacob Neusner, Brown University's *The Daily Herald,* June 12, 1983.

264

Oh, yes, there is one more thing. Try not to act toward your co-workers and bosses as you have acted toward us. I mean, when they give you what you want but have not earned, don't abuse them, insult them, act out with them your parlous relationships with your parents. This too we have tolerated. It was, as I said, not to be liked. Few professors actually care whether or not they are liked by peer-paralyzed adolescents, fools so shallow as to imagine professors care not about education but about popularity. It was, again, to be rid of you. So go, unlearn what lies we taught you. To Life!

F. The following excerpt from *The Adventures of Sherlock Holmes* by Sir Arthur Conan Doyle reveals Holmes' ability to make unerring hypotheses to account for the details he observes. Dr. Watson, Holmes' friend and fellow adventurer, narrates.

I did not gain very much, however, by my inspection. Our visitor bore every mark of being an average commonplace British tradesman, obese, pompous, and slow. He wore rather baggy grey shepherds' check trousers, a not over-clean black frock-coat, unbuttoned in the front, and a drab waistcoat with a heavy brassy Albert chain, and a square pierced bit of metal dangling down as an ornament. A frayed top-hat, and a faded brown overcoat with a wrinkled velvet collar lay upon a chair beside him. Altogether, look as I would, there was nothing remarkable about the man save his blazing red head, and the expression of extreme chagrin and discontent upon his features.

Sherlock Holmes' quick eye took in my occupation and he shook his head with a smile as he noticed my questioning glances. "Beyond the obvious facts that he has at some time done manual labour, that he takes snuff, that he is a Freemason, that he has been in China, and that he has done a considerable amount of writing lately, I can deduce nothing else."

Mr. Jabez Wilson started up in his chair, with his forefinger upon the paper, but his eyes upon my companion.

"How, in the name of good fortune, did you know all that, Mr. Holmes?" he asked. "How did you know, for example, that I did manual labour? It's as true as gospel, and I began as a ship's carpenter."

"Your hands, my dear sir. Your right hand is quite a size larger than your left. You have worked with it, and the muscles are more developed."

"Well, the snuff, then, and the Freemasonry?"

"I won't insult your intelligence by telling you how I read that, especially as, rather against the strict rules of your order, you use an arc-and-compass breastpin."

"Oh, of course, I forgot that. But the writing?"

"What else can be indicated by that right cuff so very shiny for five inches, and the left one with the smooth patch near the elbow where you rest it upon the desk."

"Well, but China?"

"The fish which you have tattooed immediately above your right wrist could only have been done in China. I have made a small study of tattoo

265

marks, and have even contributed to the literature of the subject. That trick of staining the fishes' scales of a delicate pink is quite peculiar to China. When, in addition, I see a Chinese coin hanging from your watch-chain, the matter becomes even more simple." [From "The Red-Headed League," *The Adventures of Sherlock Holmes,* The Heritage Press, New York, 1950, pp. 266–267.]

> Using this excerpt as a model, construct a brief scene in which a character of your invention, a brilliant detective, forms one or more hypotheses to explain a number of details he observes.

G. Using the essay on pp. 257–260 as a model, write a five-paragraph essay on one of the topics listed below. In your first paragraph introduce your subject, beginning broadly and narrowing down to a thesis at the end of the paragraph. In the next two paragraphs begin with an opposition argument and then counter that argument. In the fourth and fifth paragraphs focus solely on your own arguments and provide a strong conclusion in your last paragraph. In working up a scratch outline for your paper, jot down the two or three strongest arguments you can think of against your position and provide a counter to each. Then list two or three final arguments of your own. Your sheet might look something like this:

Opposition Arguments	Counter Arguments
1. _____	1. _____
2. _____	2. _____

Final Arguments Supporting Your Own Position

1. _____

2. _____

Topics

1. You had planned to study medicine and become a doctor. At the end of your sophomore year, you decide to change your major to business administration. Your father and mother, who are doctors, strongly oppose your decision. They provide full support for your education and threaten to cut off your support if you make the change.

266

2. You have been going steady with the same person for three years. You are both twenty-two and juniors in college. You plan to marry when you graduate. You inform your parents that you are going to move in together until you marry. Your parents strongly object.

3. You are a college sophomore whose parents have continually urged you to go to college so that you can find a profession and meet someone who also will be financially successful and share a comfortable life with you. Your parents were very happy when you were dating a medical student but are totally opposed to your present plan to drop out of school and marry a sales clerk whom you began to date when you broke up with the medical student.

4. You are finishing your second year in college but getting tired of school. You are uncertain about your future, your course of study, and you want to drop out of college for a year to rethink your goals and renew your energy and enthusiasm. Your parents oppose your plan. Neither went to college. They fear that you won't want to return to college after a year off.

◙ SUMMARY

Effective argumentative writing requires the ability to think logically—to reason correctly from the evidence or premises—and to persuade others to accept your reasoning. In this chapter we have briefly investigated the basic processes of reasoning, induction and deduction, and examined some common fallacies in reasoning. We have said that generalizations resulting from induction must be adequately supported; that is, there must be sufficient, relevant evidence to justify the generalization, and the evidence must be representative, accurate, and verifiable. And if testimony is used, the authority quoted must be qualified and objective. A deductive argument produces a sound conclusion when the premises are accurate and the conclusion follows logically from the premises.

Persuasive writing requires that you analyze your audience and use an appropriate tone, diction, sentence and paragraph pattern, and choice of argument in appealing to their legitimate interests. Persuasive writing, though directed primarily to your readers' reasoning powers, also uses an emotional and ethical appeal. Appealing to the emotions of your readers is a legitimate, honorable tactic, but it needs to be used with care, for if your readers believe that you are substituting emotion for credible evidence, that you are trying to bully them, they will dismiss your arguments as biased and unreliable. You must convince your readers of your integrity, so deal honestly with them by avoiding fallacies and highly charged language, unless the latter is clearly justified by the evidence you present.

PART

READER

Narration

GARY SOTO

Like Mexicans

A a teenager growing up in Fresno, California, Gary Soto expected to follow his grandmother's "good advice" and "marry a Mexican girl." At the age of 20, he fell in love not with a Mexican but with a Japanese. In the following essay from his collection, Small Faces, *Soto recalls that advice and his own expectations before falling in love. He then takes us to the young woman's home, where he discovers something fundamental that both families have in common.*

After reading the essay, review it to see how the author selects and organizes key events and details to arrive at the insight which concludes it.

1   **M**y grandmother gave me bad advice and good advice when I was in my early teens. For the bad advice, she said that I should become a barber because they made good money and listened to the radio all day. "Honey, they don't work como burros," she would say every time I visited her. She made the sound of donkeys braying. "Like that, honey!" For the good advice, she said that I should marry a Mexican girl. "No Okies, hijo"—she would say—"Look my son. He marry one and they fight every day about I don't know what and I don't know what." For her, everyone who wasn't Mexican, black, or Asian were Okies. The French were Okies, the Italians in suits were Okies. When I asked about Jews, whom I had read about, she asked for a picture. I rode home on my bicycle and returned with a calendar depicting the important races of the world. "Pues si, son Okies tambien!" she said, nodding her head. She waved the calendar away and we went to the living room where she lectured me on the virtues of the Mexican girl: first, she could cook and, second, she acted like a woman, not a man,

in her husband's home. She said she would tell me about a third when I got a little older.

2   I asked my mother about it—becoming a barber and marrying Mexican. She was in the kitchen. Steam curled from a pot of boiling beans, the radio was on, looking as squat as a loaf of bread. "Well, if you want to be a barber—they say they make good money." She slapped a round steak with a knife, her glasses slipping down with each strike. She stopped and looked up. "If you find a good Mexican girl, marry her of course." She returned to slapping the meat and I went to the backyard where my brother and David King were sitting on the lawn feeling the inside of their cheeks.

3   "This is what girls feel like," my brother said, rubbing the inside of his cheek. David put three fingers inside his mouth and scratched. I ignored them and climbed the back fence to see my best friend, Scott, a second-generation Okie. I called him and his mother pointed to the side of the house where his bedroom was a small aluminum trailer, the kind you gawk at when they're flipped over on the freeway, wheels spinning in the air. I went around to find Scott pitching horseshoes.

4   I picked up a set of rusty ones and joined him. While we played, we talked about school and friends and record albums. The horseshoes scuffed up dirt, sometimes ringing the iron that threw out a meager shadow like a sundial. After three argued-over games, we pulled two oranges apiece from his tree and started down the alley still talking school and friends and record albums. We pulled more oranges from the alley and talked about who we would marry. "No offense, Scott," I said with an orange slice in my mouth, "but I would never marry an Okie." We walked in step, almost touching, with a sled of shadows dragging behind us. "No offense, Gary," Scott said, "but I would *never* marry a Mexican." I looked at him: a fang of orange slice showed from his munching mouth. I didn't think anything of it. He had his girl and I had mine. But our seventh-grade vision was the same: to marry, get jobs, buy cars and maybe a house if we had money left over.

5   We talked about our future lives until, to our surprise, we were on the downtown mall, two miles from home. We bought a bag of popcorn at Penneys and sat on a bench near the fountain watching Mexican and Okie girls pass. "That one's mine," I pointed with my chin when a girl with eyebrows arched into black rainbows ambled by. "She's cute," Scott said about a girl with yellow hair and a mouthful of gum. We dreamed aloud, our chins busy pointing out girls. We agreed that we couldn't wait to become men and lift them onto our laps.

6   But the woman I married was not Mexican but Japanese. It was a surprise to me. For years, I went about wide-eyed in my search for the brown girl in a white dress at a dance. I searched the playground at the baseball diamond. When the girls raced for grounders, their hair bounced like something that couldn't be caught. When they sat together in the lunchroom, heads pressed together, I knew they were talking about us Mexican guys. I saw them and dreamed them. I threw my face into my pillow, making up sentences that were good as in the movies.

7   But when I was twenty, I fell in love with this other girl who worried my mother, who had my grandmother asking once again to see the calendar of the Important Races of the World. I told her I had thrown it away years before. I took a much-glanced-at snapshot from my wallet. We looked at it together, in silence. Then grandma reclined in her chair, lit a cigarette, and said, "Es pretty." She blew and asked with all her worry pushed up to her forehead: "Chinese?"

8   I was in love and there was no looking back. She was the one. I told my mother who was slapping hamburger into patties. "Well, sure if you want to marry her," she said. But the more I talked, the more concerned she became. Later I began to worry. Was it all a mistake? "Marry a Mexican girl," I heard my mother say in my mind. I heard it at breakfast. I heard it over math problems, between Western Civilization and cultural geography. But then one afternoon while I was hitchhiking home from school, it struck me like a baseball in the back: my mother wanted me to marry someone of my own social class—a poor girl. I considered my fiancee, Carolyn, and she didn't look poor, though I knew she came from a family of farm workers and pull-yourself-up-by-your-bootstraps ranchers. I asked my brother, who was marrying Mexican poor that fall, if I should marry a poor girl. He screamed "Yeah" above his terrible guitar playing in his bedroom. I considered my sister who had married Mexican. Cousins were dating Mexican. Uncles were remarrying poor women. I asked Scott, who was still my best friend, and he said, "She's too good for you, so you better not."

9   I worried about it until Carolyn took me home to meet her parents. We drove in her Plymouth until the houses gave way to farms and ranches and finally her house fifty feet from the highway. When we pulled into the drive, I panicked and begged Carolyn to make a U-turn and go back so we could talk about it over a soda. She pinched my cheek, calling me a "silly boy." I felt better, though, when I got out of the car and saw the house: the chipped paint, a cracked window,

boards for a walk to the back door. There were rusting cars near the barn. A tractor with a net of spiderwebs under a mulberry. A field. A bale of barbed wire like children's scribbling leaning against an empty chicken coop. Carolyn took my hand and pulled me to my future mother-in-law who was coming out to greet us.

10   We had lunch: sandwiches, potato chips, and iced tea. Carolyn and her mother talked mostly about neighbors and the congregation at the Japanese Methodist Church in West Fresno. Her father, who was in khaki work clothes, excused himself with a wave that was almost a salute and went outside. I heard a truck start, a dog bark, and then the truck rattle away.

11   Carolyn's mother offered another sandwich, but I declined with a shake of my head and a smile. I looked around when I could, when I was not saying over and over that I was a college student, hinting that I could take care of their daughter. I shifted my chair. I saw newspapers piled in corners, dusty cereal boxes and vinegar bottles in corners. The wallpaper was bubbled from rain that had come in from a bad roof. Dust. Dust lay on lamp shades and window sills. These people are just like Mexicans, I thought. Poor people.

12   Carolyn's mother asked me through Carolyn if I would like a *sushi*. A plate of black and white things were held in front of me. I took one, wide-eyed, and turned it over like a foreign coin. I was biting into one when I saw a kitten crawl up the window screen over the sink. I chewed and the kitten opened its mouth of terror as she crawled higher, wanting in to paw the leftovers from our plates. I looked at Carolyn who said that the cat was just showing off. I looked up in time to see it fall. It crawled up, then fell again.

13   We talked for an hour and had apple pie and coffee, slowly. Finally, we got up with Carolyn taking my hand. Slightly embarrassed, I tried to pull away but her grip held me. I let her have her way as she led me down the hallway with her mother right behind me. When I opened the door, I was startled by a kitten clinging to the screen door, its mouth screaming "cat food, dog biscuits, *sushi*. . . ." I opened the door and the kitten, still holding on, whined in the language of hungry animals. When I got into Carolyn's car, I looked back: the cat was still clinging. I asked Carolyn if it were possibly hungry, but she said the cat was being silly. She started the car, waved to her mother, and bounced us over the rain-poked drive, patting my thigh for being her lover baby. Carolyn waved again. I looked back, waving, then gawking at a window screen where there were now three kittens clawing and screaming to get in. Like Mexicans, I thought. I remembered the Molinas and how the cats clung to their screens—cats they shot down with

squirt guns. On the highway, I felt happy, pleased by it all. I patted Carolyn's thigh. Her people were like Mexicans, only different.

QUESTIONS AND EXERCISES

VOCABULARY
1. meager (paragraph 4)
2. bale (9)
3. khaki (10)
4. sushi (12)

LANGUAGE AND RHETORIC
1. This selection is organized into three parts. Paragraphs 1 through 5 form the first part, 6–8 the second, and 9–13 complete the structure. Review each of the parts. How do they relate to one another? How do they relate to the author's thesis?
2. Note the specific details of paragraphs 9 through 11. Why are these details essential to the author's thesis? How important is his reference to the kittens? Explain your answer.
3. The author anticipates his thesis in the title of this selection. He sets it up in paragraph 8, and he states it explicitly in the last paragraph. Identify the key lines in each paragraph. State the thesis in your own words.

DISCUSSION AND WRITING
1. The author says that his grandmother's good advice was "that he should marry a Mexican girl." Why does he consider it good advice? Why doesn't he follow it? What is his point?
2. Do *you* think the grandmother gave him good advice? Why do you think as you do? Write a paper explaining the basis for your views.
3. For the grandmother, "Everyone who wasn't Mexican, black, or Asian were Okies." What does this statement tell you about her perspective on race? How common is this kind of perspective? What are your own views on this subject? Write a paper in which you explain those views, focusing on a single race and explaining your reasons for feeling as you do.
4. Consider your own childhood. Have you changed your attitude toward any race? If so, what motivated the change? Write a paper in which you explain how your attitude changed and why.
5. If you know a married couple with different racial or cultural backgrounds, write a paper about that situation, focusing on what you see as the specific reasons for its success or failure.
6. As a prospective parent or a parent yourself, what advice would you give to a child of yours who wanted to marry someone with a different racial or cultural background? Write a paper in which you present not only your advice to your child but your reasons for it.

RICHARD RODRIGUEZ

Complexion

Richard Rodriguez opens this selection from his book, Hunger of Memory, *with an incident that anticipates "the shame and sexual inferiority [he] was to feel in later years because of [his] dark complexion." After reflecting on that incident, he recounts his adolescent efforts to cope with this condition in the larger context of family, friends, and the outside world, including the Mexican field hands that he "resembled in one way and, in another way, didn't resemble at all." Denying himself any kind of physically active life, he turns to books to satisfy his unfulfilled longings.*

The author uses a loose narrative form along with personal reflections to build his basic structure, but his use of specific detail is what leads the reader from incident to insight.

1 Complexion. My first conscious experience of sexual excitement concerns my complexion. One summer weekend, when I was around seven years old, I was at a public swimming pool with the whole family. I remember sitting on the damp pavement next to the pool and seeing my mother, in the spectators' bleachers, holding my younger sister on her lap. My mother, I noted, was watching my father as he stood on a diving board, waving to her. I watched her wave back. Then saw her radiant, bashful, astonishing smile. In that second, I sensed that my mother and father had a relationship I knew nothing about. A nervous excitement encircled my stomach as I saw my mother's eyes follow my father's figure curving into the water. A second or two later, he emerged. I heard him call out. Smiling, his voice sounded, buoyant, calling me to swim to him. But turning to see him, I caught my mother's eye. I heard her shout over to me. In Spanish she called through the crowd: "Put a towel on over your shoulders." In public, she didn't want to say why. I knew.

2 That incident anticipates the shame and sexual inferiority I was to feel in later years because of my dark complexion. I was to grow up an ugly child. Or one who thought himself ugly. (*Feo.*) One night when I was eleven or twelve years old, I locked myself in the bathroom and carefully regarded my reflection in the mirror over the sink. Without any pleasure I studied my skin. I turned on the faucet. (In my mind I heard the swirling voices of aunts, and even my mother's voice, whispering, whispering incessantly about lemon juice solutions and dark, *feo* children.) With a bar of soap, I fashioned a thick ball of lather. I

began soaping my arms. I took my father's straight razor out of the medicine cabinet. Slowly, with steady deliberateness, I put the blade against my flesh, pressed it as close as I could without cutting, and moved it up and down across my skin to see if I could get out, somehow lessen, the dark. All I succeeded in doing, however, was in shaving my arms bare of their hair. For as I noted with disappointment, the dark would not come out. I remained. Trapped. Deep in the cells of my skin.

3   Throughout adolescence, I felt myself mysteriously marked. Nothing else about my appearance would concern me so much as the fact that my complexion was dark. My mother would say how sorry she was that there was not money enough to get braces to straighten my teeth. But I never bothered about my teeth. In three-way mirrors at department stores, I'd see my profile dramatically defined by a long nose, but it was really only the color of my skin that caught my attention.

4   I wasn't afraid that I would become a menial laborer because of my skin. Nor did my complexion make me feel especially vulnerable to racial abuse. (I didn't really consider my dark skin to be a racial characteristic. I would have been only too happy to look as Mexican as my light-skinned older brother.) Simply I judged myself ugly. And, since the women in my family had been the ones who discussed it in such worried tones, I felt my dark skin made me unattractive to women.

5   Thirteen years old. Fourteen. In a grammar school art class, when the assignment was to draw a self-portrait, I tried and I tried but could not bring myself to shade in the face on the paper to anything like my actual tone. With disgust then I would come face to face with myself in mirrors. With disappointment I located myself in class photographs—my dark face undefined by the camera which had clearly described the white faces of classmates. Or I'd see my dark wrist against my long-sleeved white shirt.

6   I grew divorced from my body. Insecure, overweight, listless. On hot summer days when my rubber-soled shoes soaked up the heat from the sidewalk, I kept my head down. Or walked in the shade. My mother didn't need anymore to tell me to watch out for the sun. I denied myself a sensational life. The normal, extraordinary, animal excitement of feeling my body alive—riding shirtless on a bicycle in the warm wind created by furious self-propelled motion—the sensations that first had excited in me a sense of my maleness, I denied. I was too ashamed of my body. I wanted to forget that I had a body because I had a brown body. I was grateful that none of my classmates ever mentioned the fact.

7   I continued to see the *braceros,* those men I resembled in one way and, in another way, didn't resemble at all. On the watery horizon of a Valley afternoon, I'd see them. And though I feared looking like them, it was with silent envy that I regarded them still. I envied them their physical lives, their freedom to violate the taboo of the sun. Closer to home I would notice the shirtless construction workers, the roofers, the sweating men tarring the street in front of the house. And I'd see the Mexican gardeners. I was unwilling to admit the attraction of their lives. I tried to deny it by looking away. But what was denied became strongly desired.

8   In high school physical education classes, I withdrew, in the regular company of five or six classmates, to a distant corner of a football field where we smoked and talked. Our company was composed of bodies too short or too tall, all graceless and all—except mine—pale. Our conversation was usually witty. (In fact we were intelligent.) If we referred to the athletic contests around us, it was with sarcasm. With savage scorn I'd refer to the "animals" playing football or baseball. It would have been important for me to have joined them. Or for me to have taken off my shirt, to have let the sun burn dark on my skin, and to have run barefoot on the warm wet grass. It would have been very important. Too important. It would have been too telling a gesture—to admit the desire for sensation, the body, my body.

9   Fifteen, sixteen. I was a teenager shy in the presence of girls. Never dated. Barely could talk to a girl without stammering. In high school I went to several dances, but I never managed to ask a girl to dance. So I stopped going. I cannot remember high school years now with the parade of typical images: bright drive-ins or gliding blue shadows of a Junior Prom. At home most weekend nights, I would pass evenings reading. Like those hidden, precocious adolescents who have no real-life sexual experiences, I read a great deal of romantic fiction. "You won't find it in your books," my brother would playfully taunt me as he prepared to go to a party by freezing the crest of the wave in his hair with sticky pomade. Through my reading, however, I developed a fabulous and sophisticated sexual imagination. At seventeen, I may not have known how to engage a girl in small talk, but I had read *Lady Chatterley's Lover.*

QUESTIONS AND EXERCISES

VOCABULARY
1. buoyant (paragraph 1)
2. menial (4)

3. vulnerable (4)
4. braceros (7)
5. precocious (9)

LANGUAGE AND RHETORIC

1. As close as the author comes to an explicit thesis statement is the opening of paragraph 2. Review the sequence of events in the essay to see how they relate to one another and what total effect they have. Now see if you can state the author's thesis in a single sentence of your own.
2. This selection is cast basically in a loose narrative form interspersed with personal reflection. Note how the author also uses specific examples to illustrate his insights. He also works with a particular pattern—cause and effect—to develop his thesis. Point out where and how he uses it.
3. The author uses a number of obviously intentional incomplete sentences or fragments. (See the first word of the selection, the end of paragraph 2, the opening of paragraphs 5 and 9; paragraph 6, sentence 3; paragraph 8, sentence 10; and the opening of paragraph 9.) Select one or two examples and recast them as complete sentences. What is the difference in effect?
4. As with any piece of writing, this one reveals the author's tone, his attitude toward his subject and audience. What words would you use to describe that tone? What specific elements of the essay do you base them on?
5. An examination of the author's tone in the previous selection, "Like Mexicans," is relevant here. Go over it in the same manner as outlined above, then compare and contrast the tone of the two essays.

DISCUSSION AND WRITING

1. When did you first become aware of your own physical appearance in some significant way? What called it to your attention and how did you react to it? Write a paper recounting the details of your experience.
2. What was your first conscious experience of yourself as seen by someone of the opposite sex? How did you become aware of it, and what was your reaction? Write a paper describing or recounting that experience.
3. Have you ever felt any sense of shame, embarrassment, or inferiority over your physical appearance? Or, on the other hand, have you ever felt any sense of great pride or superiority in your appearance? In either case, write a paper in which you describe your feelings in specific detail and explain the reasons for them.
4. Have you ever tried to change your physical appearance? (A change might include something as seemingly insignificant as dieting.) What were the reasons for it, and what were the results? Write a paper about your change.
5. This selection is not only about the author's efforts to come to terms with his personal appearance but to do so in relation to his sexuality. Write a paper in which you recall or describe efforts to cope with your own developing awareness of sex.

GORDON PARKS

My Mother's Dream for Me

This essay by Gordon Parks recalls several important experiences in his early life and their continuing impact on his later years. His recollections of family relationships, of violence and death, and of the constant undercurrent of prejudice around them go well beyond the personal narrative to make a subtle but powerful social statement.

Note how Parks ties the different dimensions of his subject together to present a unified, coherent whole.

1 The full meaning of my mother's death had settled over me before they lowered her into the grave. They buried her at two-thirty in the afternoon; now, at nightfall, our big family was starting to break up. Once there had been fifteen of us and, at sixteen, I was the youngest. There was never much money, so now my older brothers and sisters were scraping up enough for my coach ticket north. I would live in St. Paul, Minnesota, with my sister Maggie Lee, as my mother had requested a few minutes before she died.

2 Poppa, a good quiet man, spent the last hours before our parting moving aimlessly about the yard, keeping to himself and avoiding me. A sigh now and then belied his outer calm. Several times I wanted to say that I was sorry to be going, and that I would miss him very much. But the silence that had always lain between us prevented this. Now I realized that probably he hadn't spoken more than a few thousand words to me during my entire childhood. It was always: "Mornin', boy"; "Git your chores done, boy"; "Goodnight, boy." If I asked for a dime or nickel, he would look beyond me for a moment, grunt, then dig through the nuts and bolts in his blue jeans and hand me the money. I loved him in spite of his silence.

3 For his own reasons Poppa didn't go to the depot, but as my sister and I were leaving he came up, a cob pipe jutting from his mouth, and stood sideways, looking over the misty Kansas countryside. I stood awkwardly waiting for him to say something. He just grunted—three short grunts. "Well," Maggie Lee said nervously, "won't you be kissin' your poppa goodbye?" I picked up my cardboard suitcase, turned and kissed his stubbly cheek and started climbing into the taxicab. I was halfway in when his hand touched my shoulder. "Boy, remember your momma's teachin'. You'll be all

right. Just you remember her teachin'." I promised, then sat back in the Model T taxi. As we rounded the corner, Poppa was already headed for the hog pens. It was feeding time.

4   Our parents had filled us with love and a staunch Methodist religion. We were poor, though I did not know it at the time; the rich soil surrounding our clapboard house had yielded the food for the family. And the love of this family had eased the burden of being black. But there were segregated schools and warnings to avoid white neighborhoods after dark. I always had to sit in the peanut gallery (the Negro section) at the movies. We weren't allowed to drink a soda in the drugstore in town. I was stoned and beaten and called "nigger," "Black boy," "darky," "shine." These indignities came so often I began to accept them as normal. Yet I always fought back. Now I considered myself lucky to be alive; three of my close friends had already died of senseless brutality, and I was lucky that I hadn't killed someone myself. Until the very day that I left Fort Scott on that train for the North, there had been a fair chance of being shot or perhaps beaten to death. I could easily have been the victim of mistaken identity, of a sudden act of terror by hate-filled white men, or, for that matter, I could have been murdered by some violent member of my own race. There had been a lot of killing in the border states of Kansas, Oklahoma and Missouri, more than I cared to remember.

5   I was nine years old when the Tulsa riots took place in 1921. Whites had invaded the Negro neighborhood, which turned out to be an armed camp. Many White Tulsans were killed, and rumors had it that the fight would spread into Kansas and beyond. About this time, a grown cousin of mine decided to go south to work in a mill. My mother, knowing his hot temper, pleaded with him not to go, but he caught a freight going south. Months passed and we had no word of him. Then one day his name flashed across the nation as one of the most-wanted men in the country. He had killed a White millhand who spat in his face and called him "nigger." He killed another man while fleeing the scene and shot another on the viaduct between Kansas City, Missouri, and Kansas City, Kansas.

6   I asked Momma questions she couldn't possibly answer. Would they catch him? Would he be lynched? Where did she think he was hiding? How long did she think he could hold out? She knew what all the rest of us knew, that he would come back to our house if it was possible.

7   He came one night. It was storming, and I lay in the dark of my room, listening to the rain pound the roof. Suddenly, the window next to my bed slid up, and my cousin, wet and cautious, scrambled through the opening. I started to yell as he landed on my bed, but he

quickly covered my mouth with his hand, whispered his name, and cautioned me into silence. I got out of bed and followed him. He went straight to Momma's room, kneeled down and shook her awake. "Momma Parks," he whispered, "it's me, it's me. Wake up." And she awoke easily and put her hand on his head. "My Lord, son," she said, "you're in such bad trouble." Then she sat up on the side of the bed and began to pray over him. After she had finished, she tried to persuade him to give himself up. "They'll kill you, son. You can't run forever." But he refused. Then, going to our old icebox, he filled a sack with food and went back out my window into the cornfield.

8   None of us ever saw or heard of him again. And I would lie awake nights wondering if the whites had killed my cousin, praying that they hadn't. I remember the huge sacks of peanut brittle he used to bring me and the rides he gave me on the back of his battered motorcycle. And my days were full of fantasies in which I helped him escape imaginary white mobs.

9   When I was eleven, I became possessed of an exaggerated fear of death. It started one quiet summer afternoon with an explosion in the alley behind our house. I jumped up from under a shade tree and tailed Poppa toward the scene. Black smoke billowed skyward, a large hole gaped in the wall of our barn and several maimed chickens and a headless turkey flopped about on the ground. Then Poppa stopped and muttered, "Good Lord." I clutched his overalls and looked. A man, or what was left of him, was strewn about in three parts. A gas main he had been repairing had somehow ignited and blown everything around it to bits.

10   Then once, with two friends, I had swum along the bottom of the muddy Marmaton River, trying to locate the body of a Negro man. We had been promised fifty cents apiece by the same white policeman who had shot him while he was in the water trying to escape arrest. The dead man had been in a crap game with several others who had managed to get away. My buddy, Johnny Young, was swimming beside me; we swam with ice hooks which we were to use for grappling. The two of us touched the corpse at the same instant. Fear streaked through me and the memory of his bloated body haunted my dreams for nights.

11   One night at the Empress Theater, I sat alone in the peanut gallery watching a motion picture, *The Phantom of the Opera*. When the curious heroine, against Lon Chaney's warning, snatched away his mask, and the skull of death filled the screen, I screamed out loud and ran out of the theater. I didn't stop until I reached home, crying to Momma, "I'm going to die! I'm going to die."

12   Momma, after several months of cajoling, had all but destroyed this fear when another cruel thing happened. A Negro gambler called Captain Tuck was mysteriously killed on the Frisco tracks. Elmer Kinard, a buddy, and I had gone to the Cheney Mortuary out of youthful, and perhaps morbid, curiosity. Two white men, standing at the back door where bodies were received, smiled mischievously and beckoned to us. Elmer was wise and ran, but they caught me. "Come on in, boy. You want to see Captain Tuck, don't you?"

13   "No, no," I pleaded. "No, no let me go."

14   The two men lifted me through the door and shoved me into a dark room. "Cap'n Tuck's in here, boy. You can say hello to him." The stench of embalming fluid mixed with fright. I started vomiting, screaming and pounding the door. Then a smeared light bulb flicked on and, there before me, his broken body covering the slab, was Captain Tuck. My body froze and I collapsed beside the door.

15   After they revived me and put me on the street, I ran home with the old fear again running the distance beside me. My brother Clem evened the score with his fists the next day, but from then on Poppa proclaimed that no Parks would ever be caught dead in Cheney's. "The Koonantz boys will do all our burying from now on," he told Orlando Cheney.

16   Another time, I saw a woman cut another woman to death. There were men around, but they didn't stop it. They all stood there as if they were watching a horror movie. Months later, I would shudder at the sight of Johnny Young, one of my closest buddies, lying, shot to death, at the feet of his father and the girl he loved. His murderer had been in love with the same girl. And not long after, Emphry Hawkins, who had helped us bear Johnny's coffin, was also shot to death.

17   As the train whistled through the evening. I realized that only hours before, during what seemed like a bottomless night, I had left my bed to sleep on the floor beside my mother's coffin. It was, I knew now, a final attempt to destroy this fear of death.

18   But in spite of the memories I would miss this Kansas land that I was leaving. The great prairies filled with green and cornstalks; the flowering apple trees, the tall elms and oaks bordering the streams that gurgled and the rivers that rolled quiet. The summers of long, sleepy days for fishing, swimming and snatching crawdads from beneath the rocks. The endless tufts of high clouds billowing across the heavens. The butterflies to chase through grass high as the chin. The swallowtails, bobolinks and robins. Nights filled with soft laughter, with fireflies and restless stars, and the winding sound of the cricket rubbing dampness from its wing. The silver of September rain, the

orange-red-brown Octobers and Novembers, and the white Decembers with the hungry smells of hams and pork butts curing in the smoke-houses. Yet, as the train sped along, the telegraph poles whizzing toward and past us, I had a feeling that I was escaping a doom which had already trapped the relatives and friends I was leaving behind. For, although I was departing from this beautiful land, it would be impossible ever to forget the fear, hatred and violence that Negroes had suffered upon it.

19   It was all behind me now. By the next day, there would be what my mother had called "another kind of world, one with more hope and promising things." She had said, "Make a man of yourself up there. Put something into it, and you'll get something out of it." It was her dream for me. When I stepped onto the chilly streets of St. Paul, Minnesota, two days later, I was determined to fulfill that dream.

QUESTIONS AND EXERCISES

VOCABULARY
1. belied (paragraph 2)
2. staunch (4)
3. viaduct (5)
4. cajoling (12)
5. morbid (12)

LANGUAGE AND RHETORIC
1. How does Parks use his opening lines to establish the tone and purpose of what is to follow? What is the relationship between his opening and concluding paragraphs?
2. This essay deals with several important aspects of the author's early life. What are they, and how does he tie them together?
3. The author uses a personal narrative to make some points about prejudice. What are some of the advantages and disadvantages of Parks' approach?

DISCUSSION AND WRITING
1. Parks records several incidents in the increasing awareness of his own mortality. If you have had such an experience yourself, write a personal narrative recounting that experience and its effect on you.
2. Fear of death is, of course, common. If you have experienced this emotion, write an essay dealing with the fear and how it was—or might be—overcome.
3. There are several examples of prejudice in this essay, both obvious and subtle. Have you ever been involved in a situation where you were either

the victim or the source of prejudice? If so, write an essay recalling that situation and your role in it.

MAYA ANGELOU

Champion of the World

1   The last inch of space was filled, yet people continued to wedge themselves along the walls of the Store. Uncle Willie had turned the radio up to its last notch so that youngsters on the porch wouldn't miss a word. Women sat on kitchen chairs, dining-room chairs, stools, and upturned wooden boxes. Small children and babies perched on every lap available and men leaned on the shelves or on each other.

2   The apprehensive mood was shot through with shafts of gaiety, as a black sky is streaked with lightning.

3   "I ain't worried 'bout this fight. Joe's gonna whip that cracker like it's open season."

4   "He gone whip him till that white boy call him Momma."

5   At last the talking was finished and the string-along songs about razor blades were over and the fight began.

6   "A quick jab to the head." In the Store the crowd grunted. "A left to the head and a right and another left." One of the listeners cackled like a hen and was quieted.

7   "They're in a clench, Louis is trying to fight his way out."

8   Some bitter comedian on the porch said, "That white man don't mind hugging that niggah now, I betcha."

9   "The referee is moving in to break them up, but Louis finally pushed the contender away and it's an uppercut to the chin. The contender is hanging on, now he's backing away. Louis catches him with a short left to the jaw."

10   A tide of murmuring assent poured out the doors and into the yard.

11   "Another left and another left. Louis is saving that mighty right . . ." The mutter in the Store had grown into a baby roar and it was pierced by the clang of a bell and the announcer's "That's the bell for round three, ladies and gentlemen."

12   As I pushed my way into the Store I wondered if the announcer gave any thought to the fact that he was addressing as "ladies and gentle-men" all the Negroes around the world who sat sweating and praying, glued to their "master's voice."

13   There were only a few calls for R. C. Colas, Dr. Peppers, and Hire's root beer. The real festivities would begin after the fight. Then even the old Christian ladies who taught their children and tried themselves to practice turning the other cheek would buy soft drinks, and if the Brown Bomber's victory was a particularly bloody one they would order peanut patties and Baby Ruths also.

14   Bailey and I lay the coins on top of the cash register. Uncle Willie didn't allow us to ring up sales during a fight. It was too noisy and might shake up the atmosphere. When the gong rang for the next round we pushed through the near-sacred quiet to the herd of children outside.

15   "He's got Louis against the ropes and now it's a left to the body and a right to the ribs. Another right to the body, it looks like it was low . . . Yes, ladies and gentlemen, the referee is signaling but the contender keeps raining the blows on Louis. It's another to the body, and it looks like Louis is going down."

16   My race groaned. It was our people falling. It was another lynching, yet another Black man hanging on a tree. One more woman ambushed and raped. A Black boy whipped and maimed. It was hounds on the trail of a man running through slimy swamps. It was a white woman slapping her maid for being forgetful.

17   The men in the Store stood away from the walls and at attention. Women greedily clutched the babes on their laps while on the porch the shufflings and smiles, flirtings and pinching of a few minutes be-fore were gone. This might be the end of the world. If Joe lost we were back in slavery and beyond help. It would all be true, the accusations that we were lower types of human beings. Only a little higher than the apes. True that we were stupid and ugly and lazy and dirty and, unlucky and worst of all, that God himself hated us and ordained us to be hewers of woods and drawers of water, forever and ever, world without end.

18   We didn't breathe. We didn't hope. We waited.

19   "He's off the ropes, ladies and gentlemen. He's moving towards the center of the ring." There was no time to be relieved. The worst still might happen.

20   "And now it looks like Joe is mad. He's caught Carnera with a left hook to the head and a right to the head. It's a left jab to the body and another left to the head. There's a left cross and a right to the head.

The contender's right eye is bleeding and he can't seem to keep his block up. Louis is penetrating every block. The referee is moving in, but Louis sends a left to the body and it's the uppercut to the chin and the contender is dropping. He's on the canvas, ladies and gentlemen."

21 Babies slid to the floor as women stood up and men leaned toward the radio.

22 "Here's the referee. He's counting. One, two, three, four, five, six, seven . . . Is the contender trying to get up again?"

23 All the men in the store shouted, "NO."

24 "—eight, nine, ten." There were a few sounds from the audience, but they seemed to be holding themselves in against tremendous pressure.

25 "The fight is all over, ladies and gentlemen. Let's get the microphone over to the referee . . . Here he is. He's got the Brown Bomber's hand, he's holding it up . . . Here he is . . ."

26 Then the voice, husky and familiar, came to wash over us—"The winnah, and still heavyweight champeen of the world . . . Joe Louis."

27 Champion of the world. A Black boy. Some Black mother's son. He was the strongest man in the world. People drank Coca-Colas like ambrosia and ate candy bars like Christmas. Some of the men went behind the Store and poured white lightning in their soft-drink bottles, and a few of the bigger boys followed them. Those who were not chased away came back blowing their breath in front of themselves like proud smokers.

28 It would take an hour or more before the people would leave the Store and head for home. Those who lived too far had made arrangements to stay in town. It wouldn't do for a Black man and his family to be caught on a lonely country road on a night when Joe Louis had proved that we were the strongest people in the world.

CHAPTER

Description

MAXINE HONG KINGSTON
My Mother Cooked for Us

This selection from her book, The Woman Warrior, *shows how Maxine Hong Kingston recalls one aspect of family life from her early years: mealtime. Starting with a mixture of dietary items, several of which are unlikely to appear on family menus in other cultures, she moves to her mother's story of an unusual kind of feast—one you are not likely to forget. The author's reaction, like that of most readers, is obvious; and in very few words she says much about the difficulty of dealing with some aspects of one's own cultural heritage.*

As with most authors who write forcefully, the author relies on specific details, including some rather distasteful ones, to reach her reader.

1   My mother has cooked for us: raccoons, skunks, hawks, city pigeons, wild ducks, wild geese, black-skinned bantams, snakes, garden snails, turtles that crawled about the pantry floor and sometimes escaped under refrigerator or stove, catfish that swam in the bathtub. "The emperors used to eat the peaked hump of purple dromedaries," she would say. "They used chopsticks made from rhinoceros horn, and they ate ducks' tongues and monkeys' lips." She boiled the weeds we pulled up in the yard. There was a tender plant with flowers like white stars hiding under the leaves, which were like the flower petals but green. I've not been able to find it since growing up. It had no taste. When I was as tall as the washing machine, I stepped out on the back porch one night, and some heavy, ruffling, windy, clawed thing dived at me. Even after getting chanted back to sensibility, I shook when I recalled that perched everywhere there were owls with great hunched shoulders and yellow scowls. They were a surprise for my mother from my father. We children used to hide under the beds with our fingers in our ears to shut out the bird screams and the thud, thud of the turtles

swimming in the boiling water, their shells hitting the sides of the pot. Once the third aunt who worked at the laundry ran out and bought us bags of candy to hold over our noses; my mother was dismembering skunk on the chopping block. I could smell the rubbery odor through the candy.

2   In a glass jar on a shelf my mother kept a big brown hand with pointed claws stewing in alcohol and herbs. She must have brought it from China because I do not remember a time when I did not have the hand to look at. She said it was a bear's claw, and for many years I thought bears were hairless. My mother used the tobacco, leeks, and grasses swimming about the hand to rub our sprains and bruises.

3   Just as I would climb up to the shelf to take one look after another at the hand, I would hear my mother's monkey story. I'd take my fingers out of my ears and let her monkey words enter my brain. I did not always listen voluntarily, though. She would begin telling the story, perhaps repeating it to a homesick villager, and I'd overhear before I had a chance to protect myself. Then the monkey words would unsettle me; a curtain flapped loose inside my brain. I have wanted to say, "Stop it. Stop it," but not once did I say, "Stop it."

4   "Do you know what people in China eat when they have the money?" my mother began. "They buy into a monkey feast. The eaters sit around a thick wood table with a hole in the middle. Boys bring in the monkey at the end of a pole. Its neck is in a collar at the end of the pole, and it is screaming. Its hands are tied behind it. They clamp the monkey into the table; the whole table fits like another collar around its neck. Using a surgeon's saw, the cooks cut a clean line in a circle at the top of its head. To loosen the bone, they tap with a tiny hammer and wedge here and there with a silver pick. Then an old woman reaches out her hand to the monkey's face and up to its scalp, where she tufts some hairs and lifts off the lid of the skull. The eaters spoon out the brains."

5   Did she say, "You should have seen the faces the monkey made"? Did she say, "The people laughed at the monkey screaming"? It was alive? The curtain flaps closed like merciful black wings.

6   "Eat! Eat!" my mother would shout at our heads bent over bowls, the blood pudding awobble in the middle of the table.

7   She had one rule to keep us safe from toadstools and such: "If it tastes good, it's bad for you," she said. "If it tastes bad, it's good for you."

8   We'd have to face four- and five-day-old leftovers until we ate it all. The squid eye would keep appearing at breakfast and dinner until eaten. Sometimes brown masses sat on every dish. I have seen revulsion on the faces of visitors who've caught us at meals.

9   "Have you eaten yet?" the Chinese greet one another.

10   "Yes, I have," they answer whether they have or not. "And you?"

11   I would live on plastic.

QUESTIONS AND EXERCISES

VOCABULARY
1. dromedaries (paragraph 1)
2. sensibility (1)
3. dismembering (1)
4. leeks (2)
5. revulsion (7)

LANGUAGE AND RHETORIC
1. Without referring to the text, what specific detail(s) from this piece can you most readily recall? After responding to this question, go back to the book and see if you can determine what makes it/them so memorable.
2. How does the author use these details to contribute to an overall impression? What is that impression and how does it relate to her purpose in writing?
3. A writer may have one or more purposes: to entertain, to inform, to argue a point, to move the reader to agreement and/or action. What do you believe the author's purpose to be in this selection? How well has she fulfilled it? Support your answer.
4. Titles serve several purposes. They identify the subject or topic to be addressed; they attract the reader's attention; and they often suggest—or even state—the author's thesis. The title of this selection was provided by the editors of your textbook. How well does this title perform its functions? Review the selection and come up with at least one alternative title, then explain your choice.

DISCUSSION AND WRITING
1. Each culture—indeed, each family—tends to establish its own patterns of food selection and preparation. What did your mother or father cook for you? How were your foods and/or meals different from those of your friends? Describe in detail a typical meal in your home, either from your childhood or at the present time, focusing on those specific features that made or make it different from meals served by others.
2. What is your favorite food? Why is it your favorite? When and where did you develop your taste for it? Write a paper describing in detail your favorite food or meal and explaining how it came to be your favorite.
3. What food(s) do you dislike most? How did you develop your dislike for it/them? Write a paper explaining your specific reasons for disliking a particular food.
4. How did your eating habits (what and how you eat) develop? What part did your family play in those habits? Were you forced to eat things you

disliked, or denied an opportunity to eat those that you did like? What is the effect of those efforts on you today?

5. As a potential parent or as one yourself, how will or how do you contribute to the development of positive eating habits for your children? Write a paper explaining your plan or practice and its intended results.

M. F. K. FISHER

From Young Hunger

One of America's most respected writers on food, cooking, and eating, M. F. K. Fisher finds it impossible not to delight in these subjects, and she brings to her readers the great pleasure she has always taken in them. In this, the first half of her essay on young hunger, she recalls the frustrations associated with food and mealtime in the home of her "comparatively aged godparents." In doing so, she reminds all of us, whatever our age, not to forget how it feels to be young and hungry.

After reading the essay, review it to see how the author combines a narrative structure with the use of descriptive detail.

1 It is very hard for people who have passed the age of, say, fifty to remember with any charity the hunger of their own puberty and adolescence when they are dealing with the young human animals who may be frolicking about them. Too often I have seen good people helpless with exasperation and real anger upon finding in the morning that cupboards and iceboxes have been stripped of their supplies by two or three youths—or even *one*—who apparently could have eaten four times their planned share at the dinner table the night before.

2 Such avidity is revolting, once past. But I can recall its intensity still; I am not yet too far from it to understand its ferocious demands when I see a fifteen-year-old boy wince and whiten at the prospect of waiting politely a few more hours for food, when his guts are howling for meat-bread-candy-fruit-cheese-milkmilkmilk—ANYTHING IN THE WORLD TO EAT.

3 I can still remember my almost insane desperation when I was about eighteen and was staying overnight with my comparatively aged godparents. I had come home alone from France in a bad

continuous storm and was literally concave with solitude and hunger. The one night on the train seemed even rougher than those on board ship, and by the time I reached my godparents' home I was almost light-headed.

4   I got there just in time for lunch. It is clear as ice in my mind: a little cup of very weak chicken broth, one salted cracker, one-half piece of thinly sliced toast, and then, ah then, a whole waffle, crisp and brown and with a piece of beautiful butter melting in its middle—which the maid deftly cut into four sections! One section she put on my god-mother's plate. The next *two*, after a nod of approval from her mistress, she put on mine. My godfather ate the fourth.

5   There was a tiny pot of honey, and I dutifully put a dab of it on my piggish portion, and we all nibbled away and drank one cup apiece of tea with lemon. Both my godparents left part of their waffles.

6   It was simply that they were old and sedentary and quite out of the habit of eating amply with younger people: a good thing for them, but pure hell for me. I did not have the sense to explain to them how starved I was—which I would not hesitate to do now. Instead I prowled around my bedroom while the house slumbered through its afternoon siesta, wondering if I dared sneak to the strange kitchen for something, anything, to eat, and knowing I would rather die than meet the silent, stern maid or my nice, gentle little hostess.

7   Later we walked slowly down to the village, and I was thinking sensuously of double malted ice-cream sodas at the corner drugstore, but there was no possibility of such heaven. When we got back to the quiet house, the maid brought my godfather a tall glass of exquisitely rich milk, with a handful of dried fruit on the saucer under it, because he had been ill; but as we sat and watched him unwillingly down it, his wife said softly that it was such a short time until dinner that she was sure I did not want to spoil my appetite, and I agreed with her because I was young and shy.

8   When I dressed, I noticed that the front of my pelvic basin jutted out like two bricks under my skirt: I looked like a scarecrow.

9   Dinner was very long, but all I can remember is that it had, as *pièce de résistance*, half of the tiny chicken previously boiled for broth at luncheon, which my godmother carved carefully so that we should each have a bit of the breast and I, as guest, should have the leg, after a snippet had been sliced from it for her husband, who liked dark meat too.

10   There were hot biscuits, yes, the smallest I have ever seen, two apiece under a napkin on a silver dish. Because of them we had no dessert: it would be too rich, my godmother said.

11   We drank little cups of decaffeinized coffee on the screened porch in the hot Midwestern night, and when I went up to my room I saw that the maid had left a large glass of rich malted milk beside my poor godfather's bed.

12   My train would leave before five in the morning, and I slept little and unhappily, dreaming of the breakfast I would order on it. Of course when I finally saw it all before me, twinkling on the Pullman silver dishes, I could eat very little, from too much hunger and a sense of outrage.

13   I felt that my hosts had been indescribably rude to me, and selfish and conceited and stupid. Now I know that they were none of these things. They had simply forgotten about any but their own dwindling and cautious needs for nourishment. They had forgotten about being hungry, being young, being . . .

QUESTIONS AND EXERCISES

VOCABULARY
1. puberty (paragraph 1)
2. frolicking (1)
3. exasperation (1)
4. avidity (2)
5. concave (3)
6. sedentary (6)
7. sensuously (7)
8. exquisitely (7)
9. *pièce de résistance* (9)
10. snippet (9)

LANGUAGE AND RHETORIC
1. This selection combines a narrative structure with effective use of descriptive detail. Review it to see how the author handles these two aspects of her essay in relation to one another. Consider her purpose in writing, then see if you can justify including the essay as an example of description rather than narration.
2. What function do the first two paragraphs serve in relation to the rest of this selection?
3. The author spends little time recounting either of the two meals shared with her godparents, even though she tells us dinner was "very long." Review the pertinent paragraphs to see how she makes them effective despite this brevity.
4. In paragraph 11, the author refers to "a large glass of rich malted milk [left] beside my poor godfather's bed." How is she using the word "poor" in this context and for what purpose?

5. The last sentence of the selection concludes with the ellipsis, three spaced dots that seem to suggest something left unsaid. What does it say to you?

DISCUSSION AND WRITING
1. Select a time when you were feeling especially hungry and try to recapture those feelings in a paper. Describe in detail how you felt and what you wanted or needed to satisfy your hunger.
2. Think back to a particularly memorable meal that you have had. It might be memorable because it was so limited as in the author's case or because it was so abundant, pleasurable, or satisfying. Describe that meal, focusing on the specific details that made it memorable.
3. Have your attitudes toward food and/or eating changed in any significant way over the years? If so, write a paper in which you focus on the specific reasons for, and results of, that change.
4. On occasion some of us have been known to overeat. Indeed, in an extension of this same essay, the author describes an adolescent indulgence in chocolate bars. If you have "overindulged," describe one experience and its effect(s) on you.

ANNIE DILLARD
In My Own Way

In this essay from her book, An American Childhood, *Annie Dillard describes a coming of age that struck her before she knew what it was. The pains and pleasures of adolescence are presented here in a series of physical, intellectual, and emotional developments that move toward not only a description but a definition of those years that leave such lasting impressions on us as adults. Once having arrived at this state with the author, we can understand her reluctance to embrace it and to leave her childhood behind.*

In describing her condition, the author focuses more on inner feelings than on outer actions. Consider the reasons for her choice and how they relate to her purpose in writing.

1   When I was fifteen, I felt it coming; now I was sixteen, and it hit.
2   My feet had imperceptibly been set on a new path, a fast path into a long tunnel like those many turnpike tunnels near Pittsburgh, turnpike tunnels whose entrances bear on brass plaques a roll call of those men

who died blasting them. I wandered witlessly forward and found myself going down, and saw the light dimming; I adjusted to the slant and dimness, traveled further down, adjusted to greater dimness, and so on. There wasn't a whole lot I could do about it, or about anything. I was going to hell on a handcart, that was all, and I knew it and everyone around me knew it, and there it was.

3   I was growing and thinning, as if pulled. I was getting angry, as if pushed. I morally disapproved most things in North America, and blamed my innocent parents for them. My feelings deepened and lingered. The swift moods of early childhood—each formed by and suited to its occasion—vanished. Now feelings lasted so long they left stains. They arose from nowhere, like winds or waves, and battered at me or engulfed me.

4   When I was angry, I felt myself coiled and longing to kill someone or bomb something big. Trying to appease myself, during one winter I whipped my bed every afternoon with my uniform belt. I despised the spectacle I made in my own eyes—whipping the bed with a belt, like a creature demented!—and I often began halfheartedly, but I did it daily after school as a desperate discipline, trying to rid myself and the innocent world of my wildness. It was like trying to beat back the ocean.

5   Sometimes in class I couldn't stop laughing; things were too funny to be borne. It began then, my surprise that no one else saw what was so funny.

6   I read some few books with such reverence I didn't close them at the finish, but only moved the pile of pages back to the start, without breathing, and began again. I read one such book, an enormous novel, six times that way—closing the binding between sessions, but not between readings.

7   On the piano in the basement I played the maniacal "Poet and Peasant Overture" so loudly, for so many hours, night after night, I damaged the piano's keys and strings. When I wasn't playing this crashing overture, I played boogie-woogie, or something else, anything else, in octaves—otherwise, it wasn't loud enough. My fingers were so strong I could do push-ups with them. I played one piece with my fists. I banged on a steel-stringed guitar till I bled, and once on a particularly piercing rock-and-roll downbeat I broke straight through one of Father's snare drums.

8   I loved my boyfriend so tenderly, I thought I must transmogrify into vapor. It would take spectroscopic analysis to locate my molecules in thin air. No possible way of holding him was close enough. Nothing could cure this bad case of gentleness except, perhaps, violence: maybe if he swung me by the legs and split my skull on a tree? Would

that ease this insane wish to kiss too much his eyelids' outer corners and his temples, as if I could love up his brain?

9   I envied people in books who swooned. For two years I felt myself continuously swooning and continuously unable to swoon; the blood drained from my face and eyes and flooded my heart; my hands emptied, my knees unstrung, I bit at the air for something worth breathing—but I failed to fall, and I couldn't find the way to black out. I had to live on the lip of a waterfall, exhausted.

10   When I was bored I was first hungry, then nauseated, then furious and weak. "Calm yourself," people had been saying to me all my life. Since early childhood I had tried one thing and then another to calm myself, on those few occasions when I truly wanted to. Eating helped; singing helped. Now sometimes I truly wanted to calm myself. I couldn't lower my shoulders; they seemed to wrap around my ears. I couldn't lower my voice although I could see the people around me flinch. I waved my arm in class till the very teachers wanted to kill me.

11   I was what they called a live wire. I was shooting out sparks that were digging a pit around me, and I was sinking into that pit. Laughing with Ellin at school recess, or driving around after school with Judy in her jeep, exultant, or dancing with my boyfriend to Louis Armstrong across a polished dining-room floor, I got so excited I looked around wildly for aid; I didn't know where I should go or what I should do with myself. People in books split wood.

12   When rage or boredom reappeared, each seemed never to have left. Each so filled me with so many years' intolerable accumulation it jammed the space behind my eyes, so I couldn't see. There was no room left even on my surface to live. My rib cage was so taut I couldn't breathe. Every cubic centimeter of atmosphere above my shoulders and head was heaped with last straws. Black hatred clogged my very blood. I couldn't peep, I couldn't wiggle or blink; my blood was too mad to flow.

13   For as long as I could remember, I had been transparent to myself, unselfconscious, learning, doing, most of every day. Now I was in my own way; I myself was a dark object I could not ignore. I couldn't remember how to forget myself. I didn't want to think about myself, to reckon myself in, to deal with myself every livelong minute on top of everything else—but swerve as I might, I couldn't avoid it. I was a boulder blocking my own path. I was a dog barking between my own ears, a barking dog who wouldn't hush.

14   So this was adolescence. Is this how the people around me had died on their feet—inevitably, helplessly? Perhaps their own selves eclipsed the sun for so many years the world shriveled around them, and when

at last their inescapable orbits had passed through these dark egoistic years it was too late, they had adjusted.

15   Must I then lose the world forever, that I had so loved? Was it all, the whole bright and various planet, where I had been so ardent about finding myself alive, only a passion peculiar to children, that I would outgrow even against my will?

QUESTIONS AND EXERCISES

VOCABULARY
1. imperceptibly (paragraph 2)
2. turnpike (2)
3. appease (4)
4. demented (4)
5. maniacal (7)
6. transmogrify (8)
7. spectroscopic (8)
8. exultant (11)
9. egoistic (14)
10. ardent (15)

LANGUAGE AND RHETORIC
1. Where do you first learn what the "it" is that is referred to in the opening sentence? Why does the author wait so long to reveal it, and what is the effect of her doing so?
2. In describing her condition, the author focuses more on inner feelings than on outer actions. Why does she make the one choice rather than the other? How does it fit her purpose in writing?
3. A quick review of the essay reveals that the opening paragraphs (1 and 2) are set apart from the body of the essay as are the concluding paragraphs (13 through 15). How is the author using these five paragraphs to serve her purposes?
4. Re-read the final three paragraphs. What point is the author making? State it in your own words.
5. The title of this selection has been provided by the editors of your textbook. Why do you think it was chosen? Present at least one alternative title and state why you believe it to be appropriate and effective.
6. Examine the author's use of language in two of her key passages, paragraphs 3 and 13 through 15. What words, phrases, and sentences seem especially effective to you and why?

DISCUSSION AND WRITING
1. When did you first become self-consciously aware of your own adolescence or adulthood? What created the awareness on your part? How did

you react to it? Write a paper recounting that experience, focusing on the specific things that brought it to your attention and the specifics of your reaction.

2. What makes *you* angry? How do you cope with your anger? Write a paper identifying one source of the feeling in you and explaining the specific manner in which you deal with it.

3. What are some of the things that make you laugh or feel good or that give you great pleasure? Select one of them and write a paper explaining why you feel as you do and describing how you express those feelings.

4. What bores you? Choose something that bores you and explain what makes it boring to you. Then present one or more ways of either avoiding or overcoming your boredom.

BARRY LOPEZ
Apologia

1   A few miles east of home in the Cascades I slow down and pull over for two raccoons, sprawled still as stones in the road. I carry them to the side and lay them in sun-shot, windblown grass in the barrow pit. In eastern Oregon, along U.S. 20, black-tailed jackrabbits lie like welts of sod—three, four, then a fifth. By the bridge over Jordan Creek, just shy of the Idaho border, in the drainage of the Owyhee River, a crumpled adolescent porcupine leers up almost maniacally over its blood-flecked teeth. I carry each one away from the tarmac into a cover of grass or brush out of decency, I think. And worry. Who are these animals, their lights gone out? What journeys have fallen apart here?

2   I do not stop to remove each dark blister from the road. I wince before the recently dead, feel my lips tighten, see something else, a fence post, in the spontaneous aversion of my eyes, and pull over. I imagine white silk threads of life still vibrating inside them, even if the body's husk is stretched out for years, stuck like oiled muslin to the road. The energy that held them erect leaves like a bullet; but the memory of that energy fades slowly from the wrinkled cornea, the bloodless fur.

3   The raccoons and, later, a red fox carry like sacks of wet gravel and sand. Each animal is like a solitary child's shoe in the road.

4   Once a man asked, Why do you bother? You never know, I said. The ones you give some semblance of burial, to whom you offer an apology, may have been like seers in a parallel culture. It is an act of respect, a technique of awareness.

5   In Idaho I hit a young sage sparrow—*thwack* against the right fender in the very split second I see it. Its companion rises a foot higher from the same spot, slow as smoke, and sails off clean into the desert. I rest the walloped bird in my left hand, my right thumb pressed to its chest. I feel for the wail of the heart. Its eyes glisten like rain on crystal. Nothing but warmth. I shut the tiny eyelids and lay it beside a clump of bunch-grass. Beyond a barbed-wire fence the over-grazed range is littered with cow flops. The road curves away to the south. I nod before I go, a ridiculous gesture, out of simple grief.

6   I pass four spotted skunks. The swirling air is acrid with the rupture of each life.

7   Darkness rises in the valleys of Idaho. East of Grand View, south of the Snake River, nighthawks swoop the road for gnats, silent on the wing as owls. On a descending curve I see two of them lying soft as clouds in the road. I turn around and come back. The sudden slowing down and my K-turn at the bottom of the hill draw the attention of a man who steps away from a tractor, a dozen yards from where the birds lie. I can tell by his step, the suspicious tilt of his head, that he is wary, vaguely proprietary. Offended, or irritated, he may throw the birds back into the road when I leave. So I wait, subdued like a peni-tent, a body in each hand.

8   He speaks first, a low voice, a deep murmur weighted with awe. He has been watching these flocks feeding just above the road for several evenings. He calls them whippoorwills. He gestures for a carcass. How odd, yes, the way they concentrate their hunting right on the road, I say. He runs a finger down the smooth arc of the belly and remarks on the small whiskered bill. He pulls one long wing out straight, but not roughly. He marvels. He glances at my car, baffled by this out-of-state courtesy. Two dozen nighthawks career past, back and forth at arm's length, feeding at our height and lower. He asks if I would mind—as though I owned it—if he took the bird up to the house to show his wife. "She's never seen anything like this." He's fascinated. "Not close."

9   I trust, later, he will put it in the fields, not throw the body in the trash, a whirligig.

10   North of Pinedale in western Wyoming on U.S. 189, below the Gros Ventre Range, I see a big doe from a great distance, the low rays of

first light gleaming in her tawny reddish hair. She rests askew, like a crushed tree. I drag her to the shoulder, then down a long slope by the petals of her ears. A gunnysack of plaster mud, ears cold as rain gutters. All of her doesn't come. I climb back up for the missing leg. The stain of her is darker than the black asphalt. The stains go north and off to the south as far as I can see.

11   On an afternoon trafficless, quiet as a cloister, headed across South Pass in the Wind River Range, I swerve violently but hit an animal, and then try to wrestle the gravel-spewing skid in a straight line along the lip of an embankment. I know even as I struggle for control the irony of this: I could pitch off here to my own death, easily. The bird is dead somewhere in the road behind me. Only a few seconds and I am safely back on the road, nauseous, light-headed.

12   It is hard to distinguish among younger gulls. I turn this one around slowly in my hands. It could be a western gull, a mew gull, a California gull. I do not remember well enough the bill markings, the color of the legs. I have no doubt about the vertebrae shattered beneath the seamless white of its ropy neck.

13   East of Lusk, Wyoming, in Nebraska, I stop for a badger. I squat on the macadam to admire the long claws, the perfect set of its teeth in the broken jaw, the ramulose shading of its fur—how it differs slightly, as does every badger's, from the drawings and pictures in the field guides. A car drifts toward us over the prairie, coming on in the other lane, a white 1962 Chevrolet station wagon. The driver slows to pass. In the bright sunlight I can't see his face, only an arm and the gesture of his thick left hand. It opens in a kind of shrug, hangs briefly in limp sadness, then extends itself in supplication. Gone past, it curls into itself against the car door and is still.

14   Farther on in western Nebraska I pick up the small bodies of mice and birds. While I wait to retrieve these creatures I do not meet the eyes of passing drivers. Whoever they are, I feel anger toward them, in spite of the sparrow and the gull I myself have killed. We treat the attrition of lives on the road like the attrition of lives in war: horrifying, unavoidable, justified. Accepting the slaughter leaves people momentarily fractious, embarrassed. South of Broken Bow, at dawn, I cannot avoid an immature barn swallow. It hangs by its head, motionless in the slats of the grill.

15   I stop for a rabbit on Nebraska 806 and find, only a few feet away, a garter snake. What else have I missed, too small, too narrow? What has gone under or past me while I stared at mountains, hay meadows, fencerows, the beryl surface of rivers? In Wyoming I could not help but see pronghorn antelope swollen big as barrels by the side of the

road, their legs splayed rigidly aloft. For animals that large people will stop. But how many have this habit of clearing the road of smaller creatures, people who would remove the ones I miss? I do not imagine I am alone. As much sorrow as the man's hand conveyed in Nebraska, it meant gratitude too for burying the dead.

16   Still, I do not wish to meet anyone's eyes.

17   In southwestern Iowa, outside Clarinda, I haul a deer into high grass out of sight of the road and begin to examine it. It is still whole, but the destruction is breathtaking. The skull, I soon discover, is fractured in four places; the jaw, hanging by shreds of mandibular muscle, is broken at the symphysis, beneath the incisors. The pelvis is crushed, the left hind leg unsocketed. All but two ribs are dislocated along the vertebral column, which is complexly fractured. The intestines have been driven forward into the chest. The heart and lungs have ruptured the chest wall at the base of the neck. The signature of a tractor-trailer truck: 78,000 pounds at 65 mph.

18   In front of a motel room in Ottumwa I finger-scrape the dry stiff carcasses of bumblebees, wasps, and butterflies from the grill and headlight mountings, and I scrub with a wet cloth to soften and wipe away the nap of crumbles, the insects, the aerial plankton of spiders and mites. I am uneasy carrying so many of the dead. The carnage is so obvious.

19   In Illinois, west of Kankakee, two raccoons as young as the ones in Oregon. In Indiana another raccoon, a gray squirrel. When I make the left turn into the driveway at the house of a friend outside South Bend, it is evening, hot and muggy. I can hear cicadas in a lone elm. I'm glad to be here.

20   From the driveway entrance I look back down Indiana 23, toward Indiana 8, remembering the farm roads of Illinois and Iowa. I remember how beautiful it was in the limpid air to drive Nebraska 2 through the Sand Hills, to see how far at dusk the land was etched east and west of Wyoming 28. I remember the imposition of the Wind River Mountains in a hard, blue sky beneath white ranks of buttonhook clouds, windy hayfields on the Snake River Plain, the welcome of Russian olive trees and willows in creek bottoms. The transformation of the heart such beauty engenders is not enough tonight to let me shed the heavier memory, a catalogue too morbid to write out, too vivid to ignore.

21   I stand in the driveway now, listening to the cicadas whirring in the dark tree. My hands grip the sill of the open window at the driver's side, and I lean down as if to speak to someone still sitting there. The

weight I wish to fall I cannot fathom, a sorrow over the world's dark hunger.

22   A light comes on over the porch. I hear a dead bolt thrown, the shiver of a door pulled free. The words of atonement I pronounce are too inept to offer me release. Or forgiveness. My friend is floating across the tree-shadowed lawn. What is to be done with the desire for exculpation?

23   "Later than we thought you'd be," he says.

24   I do not want the lavabo. I wish to make amends.

25   "I made more stops than I thought I would," I answer.

26   "Well, bring this in. And whatever I can take," he says.

27   I anticipate, in the powerful antidote of our conversation, the reassurance of a human enterprise, the forgiving embrace of the rational. It waits within, beyond the slow tail-wagging of two dogs standing at the screen door.

Illustration

ROBERT SANTIAGO

Black *and* Latino

Robert Santiago is, as his title indicates, both Black and Latino. A Puerto Rican with a blend of his mother's "rich, dark skin tone and his father's White complexion," he tells us his life has been shaped by both heritages. It is ironic that he not only has to deal with the pressures of the "White" world but those of the "Black" world as well. In this essay, he explains his situation and its cost to him.

The author uses personal experience to illustrate his thesis. As you read, consider the advantages and disadvantages of this approach.

1 There is no way that you can be Black and Puerto Rican at the same time." What? Despite the many times I've heard this over the years, that statement still perplexes me. I *am* both and always have been. My color is a blend of my mother's rich, dark skin tone and my father's White complexion. As they were both Puerto Rican, I spoke Spanish before English, but I am totally bilingual. My life has been shaped by my Black and Latino heritages, and despite other people's confusion, I don't feel I have to choose one or the other. To do so would be to deny a part of myself.

2 There has not been a moment in my life when I did not know that I looked Black—and I never thought that others did not see it, too. But growing up in East Harlem, I was also aware that I did not "act Black," according to the African-American boys on the block.

3 My lighter-skinned Puerto Rican friends were less of a help in this department. "You're not Black," they would whine, shaking their heads. "You're a *boriqua* [slang for Puerto Rican], you ain't no *moreno* [Black]." If that was true, why did my mirror defy the rules of logic?

305

And most of all, why did I feel that there was some unknown force trying to make me choose sides?

4   *Acting Black. Looking Black. Being a real Black.* This debate among us is almost a parody. The fact is that I am Black, so why do I need to prove it?

5   The island of Puerto Rico is only a stone's throw away from Haiti, and, no fooling, if you climb a palm tree, you can see Jamaica bobbing on the Atlantic. The slave trade ran through the Caribbean Basin, and virtually all Puerto Rican citizens have some African blood in their veins. My grandparents on my mother's side were the classic *negro como carbon* (Black as carbon) people, but despite the fact that they were as dark as can be, they are officially not considered Black.

6   There is an explanation for this, but not one that makes much sense, or difference, to a working-class kid from Harlem. Puerto Ricans identify themselves as Hispanics—part of a worldwide race that originated from eons of white Spanish conquests—a mixture of white, African and *Indio* blood, which, categorically, is apart from Black. In other words, the culture is the predominant and determinant factor. But there are frustrations in being caught in a duo-culture, where your skin color does not necessarily dictate what you are. When I read Piri Thomas' searing autobiography, *Down These Mean Streets,* in my early teens, I saw that he couldn't figure out other people's attitudes toward his Blackness, either.

7   My first encounter with this attitude about the race thing rode on horseback. I had just turned 6 years old and ran toward the bridle path in Central Park as I saw two horses about to trot past. "Yea! Horsie! Yea!" I yelled. Then I noticed one figure on horseback. She was White, and she shouted, "Shut up, you f——-g nigger! Shut up!" She pulled back on the reins and twisted the horse in my direction. I can still feel the spray of gravel that the horse kicked at my chest. And suddenly she was gone. I looked back and, in the distance, saw my parents playing Whiffle Ball with my sister. They seemed miles away.

8   They still don't know about this incident. But I told my Aunt Aurelia almost immediately. She explained what the words meant and why they were said. Ever since then I have been able to express my anger appropriately through words or action in similar situations. Self-preservation, ego and pride forbid me from ever ignoring, much less forgetting, a slur.

9   Aunt Aurelia became, unintentionally, my source for the answers I needed about color and race. I never sought her out. She just seemed to appear at my home during the points in my childhood when I most needed her for solace. "Puerto Ricans are different from American

Blacks," she told me once. "There is no racism between what you call White and Black. Nobody even considers the marriages interracial." She then pointed out the difference in color between my father and mother. "You never noticed that," she said, "because you were not raised with that hang-up."

10   Aunt Aurelia passed away before I could follow up on her observation. But she had made an important point. It's why I never liked the attitude that says I should be exclusive to one race.

11   My behavior toward this race thing pegged me as an iconoclast of sorts. Children from mixed marriages, from my experience, also share this attitude. If I have to bear the label of iconoclast because the world wants people to be in set categories and I don't want to, then I will.

12   A month before Aunt Aurelia died, she saw I was a little down about the whole race thing, and she said, "Roberto, don't worry. Even if—no matter what you do—Black people in this country don't, you can always depend on White people to treat you like a Black."

QUESTIONS AND EXERCISES

VOCABULARY
1. perplexes (paragraph 1)
2. bilingual (1)
3. eons (6)
4. categorically (6)
5. predominant (6)
6. determinant (6)
7. duo-culture(6)
8. iconoclast (11)

LANGUAGE AND RHETORIC
1. What is the author's thesis? State it in your own words.
2. The author uses personal experience to illustrate his thesis. What are the advantages and disadvantages of his choice?
3. Although this selection is included in our group of four readings to demonstrate the use of illustration as a developmental pattern, the author also uses cause and effect to achieve his ends. Point out how he does so.
4. Identify the author's intended audience for this essay. Look for clues in paragraphs 1, 4, and 12. What changes could you make to direct it to a different audience?

DISCUSSION AND WRITING
1. In paragraph 2 the author tells us "There has not been a moment in my life when I did not know that I looked Black—and I never thought that others

did not see it, too." Compare and contrast Santiago's experience in this regard with that of Richard Rodriguez in "Complexion" (p. 276). Write a paper in which you point out the similarities and differences.

2. The author refers to "acting Black, looking Black, and being a real Black." What is a "real" Black? Write a paper in which you explain what a "real Black" is from your perspective.

3. Can someone be both Black and Puerto Rican (or any other nationality) by your definition? Why or why not? Is Santiago a Black by your definition? Write a paper explaining your response to either or both of these questions.

4. What does it mean to be "Latino" or "Hispanic"? What *is* Latino or "Hispanic"? Write a paper in answer to these questions. Or substitute any other race, color, or nationality for Latino or Hispanic, including White or Caucasian and write a paper in which you develop your answer to the question.

5. How do you see yourself? How do you identify or classify yourself with regard to race, color, or national background? Write a paper explaining your response.

6. The author refers to interracial or mixed marriages. Since this is also the subject of Gary Soto's essay, "Like Mexicans" (p. 271), write a paper comparing and contrasting the two authors' attitudes toward it.

7. The author quotes his aunt as saying "Even if . . . Black people in this country don't, you can always depend on White people to treat you like a Black." In your own words, what does she mean? Do you agree or disagree? Support your answer in a paper of your own.

JEWELL PARKER RHODES

The Double Whammy

Most people in recent years have been willing to grant, if not accept, the fact that at best it is tough to be a woman in a world dominated by men. If you are willing to accept that premise, try adding to it a condition of color; and imagine how doubly difficult that same world is likely to be for a woman who is Black as well. Jewell Parker Rhodes establishes her identity along with her thesis in the first two sentences of this essay, and in doing so immediately illuminates the meaning of "double whammy." Having briefly noted the source of her problem as sexism and racism, she provides a series of examples to illustrate the effects, and concludes with her own strategies for dealing with the situation.

While the framework of this essay is provided by a cause and effect relationship, notice how Rhodes uses her examples to illustrate it.

1   **B**usiness travel can be treacherous when you're female and Black. Sooner or later, in neon script, the double whammy of racism and sexism hits.

2   One morning in Saratoga, I was nibbling a cantaloupe for breakfast when a White colleague cracked a watermelon joke. "I thought y'all preferred to pick seeds," he said. A White couple at an Ivy League Club in New York mistook me for a maid and asked me to clean their room—despite the fact that my hair was neatly pinned, I carried a briefcase, and wore my "intellectual" glasses and my three-piece pin-stripe suit. A fellow professor at a convention in Detroit assumed I was a local Black hooker. Why? I wasn't near a bar. On one excursion South, I eschewed a conference cafeteria lunch in favor of a hamburger diner; over relish and onions, an ancient White man offered me five dollars if I took a trip to his house: "Just for an hour." (He must have been recalling preinflation days.) Needless to say, my professional performance lacked luster when I delivered my paper during the after-noon conference session.

3   Like an innocent or a fool, I began each trip with optimism, still determined that race and sex not impede my performance and accept-ance. My pretensions get depressed.

4   How potent is the subliminal irritation of being the only woman on the businessman's shuttle between New York and Washington? Of be-ing the only minority at a professional meeting? Each trip represents for me a lesson in alienation. Yet because I'm conducting business, "networking," and trying to promote a career, I can't afford feeling alien since it engenders mistrust and withdrawal. So each trip I'm vul-nerable anew.

5   Why *can't* business travel be pleasurable? I've read all the books and articles on "how to dress for success." Wind me up and I conduct my-self with adequate charm. But after following all the advice, I find myself still belittled—*and* rendered less effective—due to the emo-tional and psychological assaults.

6   Articles and books don't tell you how to deal with the loneliness of being the only visible minority in a Midwestern town, or in an airport, or at a meeting. Once I walked through a community for hours and never saw another face with the slightest hint of brown. I did, however, spend my evenings being interrogated by "well-intentioned" liberals who wanted my opinion on every civil rights issue since the Civil War. Willy-nilly, I am a spokesperson for my race.

7   Articles and books also don't tell you how to deal with sexual as-saults beyond "carry a book to dinner." My rage gets dissipated only in a Howard Johnson's hotel room, alone, with room service.

8   It becomes doubly hard to ward off sexual invitation when you feel intense loneliness because nowhere else in the conference, the hotel, or the lounge, is there anyone who in the least resembles your sex or color. One loneliness begets another. Yet ward off sexual invitations you must—since the macho, conquering male abounds at professional meetings and since men compound their sexism with racist awe regarding your color. Any non-White characteristics can be viewed as exotic plumes.

9   Once, in the District of Columbia following a conference dinner, my White male colleague and escort was nearly attacked by three Black youths. Only a police officer delayed their action. Do you honestly believe I was at my professional peak the next day? And there also have been predominantly Black conferences where sexist attitudes angered me so intensely I could barely function. I recall the time in Ohio when an African colleague called me in my hotel room at 1:30 in the morning so we could "discuss" improved relations between his country and mine. The rest of the night I didn't sleep.

10   In Atlanta, I spent a whole day shunning a Black male's advances. The bathroom provided my sole measure of peace. At dinner, I was enjoying my conversation with an author on my right when my ego-bruised pursuer shouted, "I'm a man too!" I groaned. I wanted to hide beneath the table. I'd forgotten that public conversation between a male and female is seen as sexual.

11   What are the strategies for negotiating the sexist and racist trials of professional meetings? I honestly don't know. A business suit doesn't necessarily serve as armor. A book doesn't shield one from all sexual encounters. I've tried wearing makeup and no makeup. I've tried dressing up and dressing down. I've tried the schoolmarm's bun and also the thick-rimmed glasses. Still sexism abounds. Superficial transformations don't negate discrimination. About my color, I can do nothing (nor would I want to if I could).

12   The best one can do is try to prevail with dignity. When I've been the only woman at a conference, I search for minority colleagues— shared interests and shared culture sometimes bind. When I've been the only Black, I search for women—women hug you when you're down and encourage you in your work. When I've been the only Black *and* the only woman, I call long distance to reach out and touch a friend.

13   Sometimes humor helps. One year I dressed severely to compensate for my baby face. I wore high heels to compensate for my lack of height. I felt every inch the professional. Yet at the academic

convention registration, I was brusquely pulled aside. "Can't you read the signs? Student registration is to the right."

14   If they don't get you for race and sex, they get you for something else.

QUESTIONS AND EXERCISES

VOCABULARY
1. eschewed (paragraph 2)
2. impede (3)
3. engenders (4)
4. interrogated (6)

LANGUAGE AND RHETORIC
1. What kind of audience does this author have in mind? Point out specific evidence of your conclusion.
2. This selection originally was published with the title "When Your Sense of Humor Is Your Best Traveling Companion." Which title do you prefer and why?
3. Although there are many brief paragraphs in this essay, the writer rarely introduces a new one without having a justification. Review her practice to see if you can identify any exceptions.
4. Examine the author's use of cause and effect to develop her thesis. Show how she combines that method with examples.
5. How would you characterize the tone of this piece? What specific passages can you cite to illustrate it?

DISCUSSION AND WRITING
1. If you have ever been the object of either the racism or the sexism that the author writes about here, develop an essay of your own in which you recall such an experience and the effect that it had on you.
2. What other kinds of "whammies" are there in addition to racism and sexism? Develop a list of them and select one that is particularly important to you. Then write an essay in which you review the cause and effect relationship.
3. Much has been written about sexual harassment aside from the matter of racial prejudice. Review some of the resources on this subject in your campus library and write a paper based on your findings.

N. SCOTT MOMADAY

A Vision Beyond Time and Space

The life of N. Scott Momaday bridges two cultures. As a Kiowa Indian, he recalls—and responds to—the heritage of his people, a heritage that he perpetuates as a writer of both fiction and nonfiction. As a Professor of English at Stanford University, he is part of a contemporary culture of quite another kind. This selection deals with the contrast between these two cultures by focusing on the world view of the Kiowa, "a vision beyond time and place" that, according to the author, makes the Indian "perhaps the most culturally secure of all Americans."

This selection is an excellent example of how a writer effectively combines methods of development. Framing his subject with the example of "old man Cheney" at both beginning and end, Momaday focuses on the contrast between cultures and shows its significance for our time.

When my father was a boy, an old man used to come to [my grandfather] Mammedaty's house and pay his respects. He was a lean old man in braids and was impressive in his age and bearing. His name was Cheney, and he was an arrowmaker. Every morning, my father tells me, Cheney would paint his wrinkled face, go out, and pray aloud to the rising sun. In my mind I can see that man as if he were there now. I like to watch him as he makes his prayer. I know where he stands and where his voice goes on the rolling grasses and where the sun comes up on the land. There, at dawn, you can feel the silence. It is cold and clear and deep like water. It takes hold of you and will not let you go. (From *The Way to Rainy Mountain.* The University of New Mexico Press.)

1   I often think of old man Cheney, and of his daily devotion to the sun. He died before I was born, and I never knew where he came from or what of good and bad entered into his life. But I think I know who he was, essentially, and what his view of the world meant to him and to me. He was a man who saw very deeply into the distance, I believe, one whose vision extended far beyond the physical boundaries of his time and place. He perceived the wonder and meaning of Creation itself. In his mind's eye he could integrate all the realities and illusions of the earth and sky; they became for him profoundly intelligible and whole.

2   Once, in the first light, I stood where Cheney has stood, next to the house which my grandfather Mammedaty had built on a rise of land

near Rainy Mountain Creek, and watched the sun come out of the black horizon of the world. It was an irresistible and awesome emergence, as waters gather to the flood, of weather and of light. I could not have been more sensitive to the cold, nor than to the heat which came upon it. And I could not have *foreseen* the break of day. The shadows on the rolling plains became large and luminous in a moment, impalpable, then faceted, dark and distinct again as they were run through with splinters of light. And the sun itself, when it appeared, was pale and immense, original in the deepest sense of the word. It is no wonder, I thought, that an old man should pray to it. It is no wonder . . . and yet, of course, wonder is the principal part of such a vision. Cheney's prayer was an affirmation of his wonder and regard, a testament to the realization of a quest for vision.

3   This native vision, this gift of seeing truly, with wonder and delight, into the natural world, is informed by a certain attitude of reverence and self-respect. It is a matter of extrasensory as well as sensory perception, I believe. In addition to the eye, it involves the intelligence, the instinct, and the imagination. It is the perception not only of objects and forms but also of essences and ideals, as in this Chippewa song:

> as my eyes
> search
> the prairie
> I feel the summer
> in the spring

Even as the singer sees into the immediate landscape, he perceives a now and future dimension that is altogether remote, yet nonetheless real and inherent within it, a quality of evanescence and evolution, a state at once of being and of becoming. He beholds what is there; nothing of the scene is lost upon him. In the integrity of his vision he is wholly in possession of himself and of the world around him; he is quintessentially alive.

4   Most Indian people are able to see in these terms. Their view of the world is peculiarly native and distinct, and it determines who and what they are to a great extent. It is indeed the basis upon which they identify themselves as individuals and as a race. There is something of genetic significance in such a thing, perhaps, an element of being which resides in the blood and which is, after all, the very nucleus of the self. When old man Cheney looked into the sunrise, he saw as far into himself, I suspect, as he saw into the distance. He knew certainly of his existence and of his place in the scheme of things.

5   In contrast, most of us in this society are afflicted with a kind of cultural nearsightedness. Our eyes, it may be, have been trained too long upon the superficial, and *artificial,* aspects of our environment; we do not see beyond the buildings and billboards that seem at times to be the monuments of our civilization, and consequently we fail to see into the nature and meaning of our own humanity. Now, more than ever, we might do well to enter upon a vision quest of our own, that is, a quest after vision itself. And in this the Indian stands to lead by his example. For with respect to such things as a sense of heritage, of a vital continuity in terms of origin and of destiny, a profound investment of the mind and spirit in the oral traditions of literature, philosophy, and religion—those things, in short, which constitute his vision of the world—the Indian is perhaps the most culturally secure of all Americans.

6   As I see him, that old man, he walks very slowly to the place where he will make his prayer, and it is always the same place, a small mound where the grass is sparse and the hard red earth shows through. He limps a little, with age, but when he plants his feet he is tall and straight and hard. The bones are fine and prominent in his face and hands. And his face is painted. There are red and yellow bars under his eyes, neither bright nor sharply defined on the dark, furrowed skin, but soft and organic, the colors of sandstone and of pollen. His long braids are wrapped with blood-red cloth. His eyes are deep and open to the wide world. At sunrise, precisely, they catch fire and close, having seen. The low light descends upon him. And when he lifts his voice, it enters upon the silence and carries there, like the call of a bird.

QUESTIONS AND EXERCISES

VOCABULARY
1. perceived (paragraph 1)
2. intelligible (1)
3. impalpable (2)
4. faceted (2)
5. extrasensory (3)
6. evanescence (3)
7. quintessentially (3)

LANGUAGE AND RHETORIC
1. What kind of audience does the author seem to have in mind for this selection? How can you tell?
2. What is his point of view in relation to that audience; that is, where does he stand in this matter? What clues helped you to determine your answer?

3. The author uses the example of "old many Cheney" to open and close his essay. Could he have achieved the same results if he had placed that example in the middle? Why or why not?

DISCUSSION AND WRITING
1. Sift through your memory to identify some of the friends, family, and associates who have particularly influenced you regarding the kinds of things dealt with in this essay: time, nature, the outdoors; a sense of place, heritage, or culture. Select a likely person and write an essay showing how he or she influenced you.
2. If you have ever had the experience of feeling intensely alive in a natural setting, write a paper describing or recounting that experience and its effect on you.
3. How do you respond to Momaday's comments on the "cultural nearsightedness" that afflicts most of us in the non-Indian culture? Is there a basis in fact for his generalization about not seeing beyond the superficial and artificial aspects of our environment? Support your conclusions in an essay.
4. Momaday says that the Indian is "perhaps the most culturally secure of all Americans." Others have argued to the contrary: that the Indian is caught between two cultures, that of the Native American heritage and that of the contemporary "Anglo." Advocates of this position maintain that the American Indian totally lacks a sense of personal identity. Investigate this subject in your campus library and explore some possible topics for writing.

JOE ESZTERHAS

The Beasts and the Children

1   When I was a little kid, some of the big kids had this thing they did in the alleys. They would glide around a cat, cans of lighter fluid in hand, squirting, and then one of them would drop the match and they'd leap away.

2   The cat would turn into a howling fireball and try to beat itself to death against the red-brick walls of the potato-chip factory.

3   I'm horrified now, and I wish I could say I was horrified then, but the truth is that I wasn't. I was awed, yes, and scared, too, but I watched the big kids, with big eyes, as they tripped down the alley on

humid summer nights, prowling for action . . . working-class heroes on the come . . . and if you didn't have a zip gun or a blade tied to the back of your wrist, well, lighter fluid was cheap.

4   I remember, too, a few years later, a bigger kid now, I cried when our own cat—found in a trash can in that same alley, so small she fit into my palm—sliced her face trying to come in through a window. But I somehow never put her pain together with those fireballs I'd seen bouncing off the red-brick walls.

5   My daughter is fourteen years old. She doesn't know anything about alleys, thankfully, although she knows many (but not all) of the things I saw in them. If she saw a cat going through that kind of horror, she would not watch big-eyed, she would not talk (tritely) about working-class heroes. She would risk her life to put a stop to it.

6   I don't know why it is exactly that my generation doesn't really care about animals. We reduce them to toys and furniture, indulging in cutesy oohing and ahhing, relating to them as in the past—on occasions when some trite screenwriter turned them human. Thinking dogs and talking mules and mind-reading dolphins . . . we'd watch and allow ourselves a few superior laughs and forget about it.

7   It is my suspicion that my daughter, Suzi, and her friends will not forget about it, that they will make it one of their tasks in life to deal with animals on the animals' own terms, to allow them dignity and protect them from insensitivity and ignorance. To say that they will make it a better world in the process is trite (again), but I *am* a screenwriter: research screenings have told me that within triteness there is sometimes truth.

8   I don't quite know where the depth and conviction of Suzi's concerns originated. We've always had household pets, of course, and we like to consider ourselves the kind of enlightened people who race our pets off to the vet at the slightest sign of *anything,* only to be told that it's a *nothing* that will cost $100. And, of course, we made the requisite rounds of zoos, in the days when Suzi was still willing to visit them.

9   But at some point, when she was eight or nine, I think, her love of animals began turning into a mission. She started talking about Dian Fossey and about how she wanted to do that kind of work when she grew up, and when I suggested to her that with her brains she could grow up to be the first woman president of the United States, she dismissed it with: "Do you want me to get shot, Dad?" Zoos became an enemy force—a different camera angle on cans of lighter fluid glinting in the moonlight—jails, torture chambers, experimental labs.

10   We still visited zoos occasionally, but with her mission in mind. I remember she went to the Houston Zoo once and came back with

voluminous notes—*investigative* notes—about the way the chimps were treated. She compiled her notes and photographs and wrote a 40-page report that she spent her allowance photocopying. She sent copies to anybody with any juice in Houston, and even though she didn't get any responses besides condescending bureaucratic ones, she was pleased with herself.

11   She refused to wear any leather and moved from the study of one species to another: silverbacks to chimps to dolphins to manatees to birds. She spent her entire allowance on things like The Digit Fund and the Animal Liberation Front. She adopted whales and gorillas. And then she became a vegetarian, trying not to frown at her brother as he scarfed his third cheeseburger, letting us glimpse, occasionally, a searing and held-in anger.

12   In some ways, it was the stuff that tried a family's harmony and patience. We couldn't talk during walks anymore, because we'd disturb the birds. She got crazy one day because we wouldn't allow her to get closer than six feet to a group of (rabid?) raccoons. She looked at the aged, suburbia-worn sneakers that I favored and informed me that they were made out of baby kangaroo and I realized I was not the kind of man or father who could resist that kind of Moral Imperative: bye-bye sneakers.

13   I realized, too, that she was not alone in this, that she was part of a children's army that bore this same searing and held-in anger. There were mothers all over Marin who could no longer wear their furs, brothers who had to answer questions about why a baseball *had* to be leather. A household pet was no longer a household pet; he or she was part of the family, to be treated equally. If the Chihuahua was allowed inside the house all the time, it was unfair to keep the Newfoundland *out* much of the time. It would be just as unfair, she pointed out to me, if I allowed her brother inside the house and not her. For a moment, I debated telling her that she didn't break everything inside the house, but that the damn newfie did.

14   I found myself becoming a co-conspirator. She spent much of her time on a vacation in Hawaii going to fur shops and sticking deadly little antifur missives into the pockets. Her mother was a trifle jittery about this—maybe it was simply that she hadn't planned on spending her vacation on the lookout for security guards—but I found myself assuring her that it was okay. We had good lawyers and we'd bail her out. Fast. Besides, it was a misdemeanor.

15   On a visit to Florida, she ran across a roadside "zoo" featuring an alligator named Big Joe. It was a sleazy little place that had been around for about 40 years—owned, we discovered, by a man who was

a political bigwig in the county. She took photographs and notes, and when we got home she made a list of politicos and animal-welfare agencies in the state. She wrote a rough draft of a letter describing the things that were wrong and the way Big Joe was living in filth, and asked me to help her rewrite it. So I did, working with her for three days, trimming, adding, until the letter was just right, realizing as I was doing it that if this worked . . . *if we nailed this bastard* . . . I would be as proud of this piece of rewriting as I was of the letter her brother and I had written to Ted Williams, a letter that had gotten us an autographed baseball card in the mail.

16   She made many copies of the letter and the photographs, wheedled a big allowance advance out of me, and we waited for the bastard to get nailed. I wasn't so sure, of course—I well knew the power of petty bosses. And when she got the usual responses—"It's wonderful that a girl of your age shares our concerns"—she wrote more letters and got another advance. Until, somehow, one of the letters was passed from a Florida animal-rights agency to a national one and then to the Department of Agriculture . . . and we were notified that there would be a hearing . . . a government hearing . . . all because of her.

17   She was twelve years old then, and became a kind of notable among people and organizations devoting themselves to her concerns. She got a phone call one day from a county commissioner in Florida who'd heard about her and said he wanted her to help him with his efforts to save the manatees. The next time she was in Florida, could she go up and see him? They would like her to make a speech and wanted to hold a day in her honor.

18   So the next time we were in Florida, we drove into the boonies for four hours and got to this little town and sat down with the commissioner and his wife. A great many things had been planned for the next day, the commissioner explained to us. Suzi would make a speech to the commissioners and Suzi would swim with the manatees and oh, incidentally, he had invited reporters and TV people from as far away as Tampa and they were all coming up at eight o'clock in the morning to see this California thirteen-year-old. And oh, by the way, he was running for re-election, and in the middle of a rough campaign, and he wanted to make sure that she would stay close to him when all those TV guys and reporters were "doing their thing."

19   *Oh boy. Oh boy oh boy oh boy.*

20   She saw through it, of course. She cried when we got back to the hotel. He's using me, she said. He's just using me for his re-election. It's not about the manatees. It's about politics, isn't it, Dad?

21   I didn't know what to say to her. She had been so excited coming up here. She'd looked forward to swimming with the manatees so much.

22   Your choice, kid. We can stay or we can split.

23   We left at six o'clock the next morning, telling the commissioner that there was an emergency in the family. She was heartbroken, but in the van she smiled at the notion of what the commissioner would say when all those reporters showed up and she wasn't there.

24   I wanted to tell her that if she really did wind up devoting her life to the welfare of *animals,* she'd have to spend a good part of it dealing with *people* who either didn't care, pretended to care or had pocket-book agendas of their own. I didn't tell her. Something told me she knew all about people and that was one of the reasons she was so fond of animals.

Facts and Judgments

GEORGE F. WILL

The Looters of Corporate America

The "looters" referred to in the title of this selection turn out to be the chief executive officers (CEOs) of the very same corporations they head. Columnist George F. Will examines the salaries and additional compensation of people in these positions and concludes that it is "generally disproportionate" in relation to other employees and organizations and "often ludicrous" when considered in relation to the performance of the CEOs own organization. The author reviews selected examples of this situation, and then expresses concern regarding their implications for the nation's business world.

Notice how the author does an excellent job of including many facts, especially statistics, to support his judgments.

1    $\mathbf{A}$mericans' exhilaration about communism's collapse is mingled with dismay about facets of their capitalism. Americans are not toppling statues of tycoons—there aren't many—the way Russians are venting their anger against Lenin's statues. But there is anger, about the BCCI and Salomon Brothers scandals, the S&L debacle and soon perhaps about the way some corporate leaders are paying themselves.

2   The compensation of chief executive officers (CEOs) is generally disproportionate and often ludicrous in light of corporate performance. Often it is difficult to determine how much CEOs are paid. But America's CEOs are paid two to three times more than Japan's or Germany's.

3   In Japan, the compensation of major CEOs is 17 times that of the average worker; in France and Germany, 23–25 times; in Britain, 35 times; in America, between 85 and 100-plus times. The American CEO/worker disparity doubled during the 1980s—while the top income-tax rate was cut and workers' tax burdens increased because

of Social Security taxes. (Japan, Germany and Britain have more progressive tax rates than America.)

4   In 1990, CEO pay rose 7 percent while corporate profits fell 7 percent. How does this happen? CEO compensation is approved by company directors the CEO helps to choose. Sixty percent of all outside directors of the 1,000 largest corporations are themselves chief executive officers.

5   Economists puzzle about this: How do you define, measure and appropriately reward individuals' contributions at the pinnacle of complex, sprawling bureaucratized corporations? How do you distinguish between money earned and money merely taken? The slogan "pay for performance" does not take us far.

6   Madonna made $25 million last year? Fine. Her pay is directly a function of performances. If Roger Clemens stops winning, his $5-million salary will stop. Not so with CEOs.

7   The CEO of Eagle-Picher Industries got a 38 percent raise while profits were falling 27 percent and the company was seeking bankruptcy protection. Because times are hard for the auto industry, Ford's CEO took a pay cut last year. But Chrysler's Lee Iacocca took a 25 percent raise—while earnings were falling 17 percent and workers, suppliers and shareholders were being asked to sacrifice.

8   According to Business Week, in 1990 Walt Disney Co.'s chief executive made more in a day than the average Disney employee made in the year. Is there an economic or moral justification for that, or just a power explanation?

9   Business Week further reports that since 1988, Reebok's CEO has received $40.9 million. But $100 invested in Reebok stock in 1988 was worth only $117 by 1990. Nike, which passed Reebok as leader in the sneaker industry as Reebok profits were growing just 1 percent last year, has a CEO who made a three-year total of $1 million in 1988–90 while Nike's return on equity averaged a robust 23 percent a year.

10   Perhaps Reebok's CEO was worth $14.8 million in 1990, but why, precisely? He would have done his job less well for a piddling, oh, $7 million? He would have left the company if paid less? Would the company have done worse with a $7 million—or even $1 million—replacement? Time may tell: his new contract limits his pay, or at least cash pay, to $2 million.

11   Topping Business Week's annual survey of executive compensation for 1990 is United Airlines' CEO. He received $18.3 million (1,200 times what a new flight attendant makes) in salary, bonuses and a stock-based incentive plan. United's profits fell 71 percent.

12   The word "incentives" is prominent in CEO compensation packages. Incentives to do what, exactly? One's job? One's job well? Or better than one would unless lethargy were conquered by lots of cash?

13   Economists worry that many incentive plans encourage a short-term focus on a few numerical goals, such as stock prices. Those can be floated up by a general market rise unrelated to executive performances.

14   Congress is considering requiring better disclosure of compensation and strengthening stockholders' powers to control it. But stockholder democracy is a weak reed to lean on, at least until large institutional investors get angry and involved.

15   Public anger could provoke at least caution in the clubby corporate culture. And anti-business fever does flare periodically in America.

16   The fever's causes include resentment of government-conferred wealth (for example, from protective tariffs), fear of monopoly and hugeness (which gave rise to "trust-busting" at the turn of this century), dislike of dependency (such as farmers felt regarding unregulated railroads in the 19th Century), disgust with rapaciousness and vulgarity (as in the Gilded Age).

17   The looting—it sometimes looks like that—of companies by some CEOs could cause another bout of business-bashing.

QUESTIONS AND EXERCISES

VOCABULARY
   1. exhilaration (paragraph 1)
   2. facets (1)
   3. tycoons (1)
   4. debacle (1)
   5. ludicrous (2)
   6. disparity (3)
   7. bureaucratized (5)
   8. incentives (12)
   9. lethargy (12)
  10. tariffs (16)

LANGUAGE AND RHETORIC
   1. The author states his thesis explicitly and emphatically early in this article. What is that thesis and where is it stated? Restate it in your own words.
   2. There are many facts, especially statistics, included to support the author's thesis. Select one of the paragraphs containing statistics and show how the author uses them and for that purpose.

3. With the exception of the reference to *Business Week* in paragraphs 8–11, there are no sources of information provided for these facts and figures. In the absence of identified sources, what does the reader have to rely on to assess the credibility of the information provided in this selection?
4. Since this article first appeared as a newspaper column, many of the paragraphs are broken up into smaller units than they would be in book format. Review each paragraph and see which ones may be combined without losing clarity or coherence.

DISCUSSION AND WRITING

1. Based on your own work experience, discuss the compensation rates of employees in a setting that you know. In what ways have you found those rates to be reasonable? In what ways unreasonable? What specific changes, if any, would you propose to improve the situation and why?
2. If you have ever worked at a job where you personally felt grossly underpaid or overpaid, write a paper explaining the circumstances and how they affected you.
3. If you have ever worked in a situation where you had "incentives," for example, commissions, bonuses, a percentage of profits, or any other kind of rewards in addition to the usual salary, write a paper explaining the arrangements and your reaction to them.
4. Given the comparison and contrast between Reebok and Nike in paragraphs 9 and 10, what conclusion do you come to regarding Nike's CEO? In your judgment, is he a more effective CEO or less effective? Does he deserve additional compensation? Support your answers with specific reasons.
5. The author argues that top executive pay is often out of line by three measures. Which of his three measures seems most appropriate and defensible to you? On what basis? Write a paper justifying your choice or offer another alternative.

JOSHUA ZIMMERMAN

Blitzed: Alcoholics Anonymous and Me

This nation has been increasingly and understandably concerned about widespread abuse of alcohol, particularly among young people. But in the following essay, Joshua Zimmerman is equally concerned about the attitudes and assumptions that lead us to label as alcoholics even those who might well be considered moderate drinkers. Zimmerman opens the essay with his personal experience, connects it to what he calls the "alcohol treatment industry," and then documents the coercive treatment that he sees as the embodiment of the currently popular approach to the problem.

This selection is an excellent example of how writers can use factual detail along with personal experience to develop an argument.

1   **M**y name is Josh and I'm *not* an alcoholic.

2   In the past a college student with my drinking habits—a frequent beer or two, a couple of times a year to excess—wouldn't feel compelled to declare this. But when I got ill from drinking last spring at Princeton and was taken to the infirmary, I was told to meet with the school's full-time alcohol counselor. Opening a folder in my name, he began the interview: Do you play drinking games? Have you gotten sick on alcohol before? Do you consume more than fourteen drinks a week? After fifteen minutes of this, he told me that getting sick was "a significant episode" in my "drinking history," that I was teetering on the brink of alcoholism.

3   Subjection to this type of inquisition is an increasing part of the curriculum on America's campuses: 60 percent of colleges have some sort of substance abuse program. And the idea behind it—that a given level of consumption or a major bender means you're a confirmed lush, or close enough to being one to need treatment—now pervades the $2 billion alcohol treatment industry.

4   Today's treatment theories reflect a far broader neo-temperance trend, which first became evident around 1984, when Mothers Against Drunk Driving succeeded in raising the drinking age to 21. In 1988 then Surgeon General C. Everett Koop called (unsuccessfully) for a ban on happy hours. Last January an award-winning edition of *Little Red Riding Hood* was banned for first-graders in the Empire, California, school district because Grandma takes a glass of wine after escaping the wolf. Today's puritans lobby for a whole range of prohibitions, from banning alcohol industry sponsorship of sports events and rock concerts to barring convenience stores, gas stations, and supermarkets from selling booze.

5   The new public awareness about drinking has, of course, helped to reduce the horrendous problems caused by alcohol abuse. Consumption is down, particularly among the young. In 1980, 58 percent of Americans between the ages of 18 and 24 said they drank beer,

according to Simmons Market Research. By 1989, only 47 percent did. The number of deaths attributed to drunk driving has fallen too, from 20,356 in 1982 to 17,849 in 1989—a 12 percent decline in seven years.

6   You'd think such success might moderate the impulse for ever more *means severe* draconian correctives. But if anything, the anti-alcohol severity is increasing. Last summer the Supreme Court found that "the measure of the intrusion on motorists stopped briefly at sobriety checkpoints" is a small price to pay in the effort to reduce the "death and mutilation" caused by drunk drivers. Thirty-nine states now have "dram shop" liability and twenty-four states have "social host" liability, in which bartenders and hosts can be held partially responsible when someone they served gets in an accident.

7   In the treatment industry, the tactics used to intimidate heavy drinkers have become more coercive. An increasingly popular method of alcoholism treatment these days is "intervention." Invented by Dr. Vernon Johnson, a reformed alcoholic who became famous when he pressured Betty Ford into treatment, the method relies upon a team effort. Family, friends, and co-workers "intervene" by confronting the offender in public—sometimes at work, preferably when he is hung over—with a list of grievances and a series of ultimatums. Johnson's transcript of a typical intervention from his recent book, *Chemical Dependence,* includes threats from the victim's wife that she'll leave him if he doesn't seek treatment, and from his boss, who says he'll fire him. A car is supposed to wait outside so the victim can be whisked directly to a treatment center.

8   The Johnson Institute promotes intervention through traveling workshops and a large mail-order business of books, cassettes, and videos. One of Johnson's biggest clients is the national network of Employee Assistance Programs, in-house and regional workplace counselors who specialize in alcohol problems and are currently working with 12,000 corporate and government offices across the country. A supervisor, noticing lagging performance or simply suspecting an alcohol problem, can order an employee to meet with an EAP counselor. The counselor, who doesn't have to meet any national training standards, will tell these presumed alcoholics to go on the wagon. If the employee is caught drinking again—whether or not the drinking is affecting his job performance—his boss is encouraged to send him back for more counseling or fire him.

9   Coercive treatment is essentially an extension of one of the main precepts of Alcoholics Anonymous: alcoholism—a disease over which the

alcoholic has no control—starts with the first drink and leads inexorably to death if the alcoholic does not become perfectly abstinent. It is thus essential to stop alcoholism in its early stages, no matter how scant the evidence. In recent years, however, the disease theory of alcoholism has come under attack. Studies have shown that even many hard-core drinkers are able to control their drinking. Yet virtually every major alcohol treatment program in the country largely adheres to the AA tenets, and now a growing number are using some form of coercion.

10   Drunk drivers, understandably enough, have come under particularly ferocious scrutiny. District Court Judge Albert Kramer of Quincy, Massachusetts, sentences about 400 drunk drivers a year to enroll in Right Turn, a $725, twenty-six-week, out-patient treatment program, and to attend a series of AA meetings. "Everyone is assumed to be having a problem by virtue of their DWI conviction," explains Dr. Steve Valle, director of the program. "Social drinkers are really high-risk problem drinkers." As do most treatment programs, Right Turn uses a questionnaire to determine if you're an alcoholic. Right Turn's test is adapted from one by the National Highway Traffic Safety Administration. Out of curiosity, I took it myself. Sure enough, I scored a 30 out of 47, which meant I was in "the final, deteriorative stage of alcoholism, when most alcoholics outwardly appear to be alcoholic." The test was designed in such a way that each symptom on a night of overindulgence was recorded separately, boosting my score.

11   Across the country convicted drunk drivers are ordered to begin treatment, usually at an AA chapter, or are given a choice between treatment and prison, which is, I suppose, a choice of sorts. But forcing someone to go to AA presents another problem: six of AA's "Twelve Steps" to counter alcoholism allude to God. Last year a Maryland drunk driver, John Norfolk, objected to his court-ordered AA meetings, saying the government was forcing him to participate in a religion. The state yielded—Norfolk was switched to a non-religious program—before a judgment was rendered, avoiding a precedent and letting Maryland continue with court-ordered AA. There are now, though, non-spiritual groups for people with drinking problems, which judges are beginning to use as AA alternatives in sentencing. In contrast with AA, one group, called Rational Recovery, believes everyone has the power to overcome alcohol problems—without undergoing lifelong treatment.

12   The craze for compulsory treatment would make some sense if there were proof that it worked. Yet a 1988 Bureau of Statistics special

report found that nearly half of all inmates convicted of driving while intoxicated had previously been involved with an alcohol treatment program, and one in eleven was in treatment at the time of arrest. A major report issued last spring by the National Academy of Science's Institute of Medicine cites a study in which sanctions (e.g., suspending licenses) were shown to be more effective against recidivism than alcohol treatment.

13   Of course, all this might be an elaborate process of self-denial. After several more sessions with my college alcohol adviser, a couple of compulsory sessions with AA, and an "intervention" organized by TNR[1] interns, maybe I would be forced to admit that, yes, I am an alcoholic. The trouble is, by the time that's all over, I probably will be.

QUESTIONS AND EXERCISES

VOCABULARY
1. inquisition (paragraph 3)
2. neo-temperance (4)
3. horrendous (5)
4. draconian (6)
5. coercive (7)
6. tenets (9)
7. recidivism (12)

LANGUAGE AND RHETORIC
1. What are the dual meanings of the word "blitzed" as used in the title of this selection? How do they relate to the author's subject and central concerns?
2. The author depends heavily on factual information to develop his thesis. He also opens and closes his essay with the first person point of view, using his own perspective to add another dimension to his argument. Evaluate the effectiveness of this technique. Do you find that it strengthens or that it weakens his argument? Support your answer.
3. Does this essay have an explicit thesis? If you believe there is one, point it out. If you do not find one, provide a thesis statement of your own.
4. What is the purpose of paragraph 5? Does it add to or does it detract from the author's argument? Support your answer.
5. Reread the final paragraph (13). What is "all this" referring to in the first sentence? What is the meaning of the last sentence? How does the author's tone help us to understand his intention?

[1] *The New Republic,* the magazine in which this selection was first published.

DISCUSSION AND WRITING

1. How do you respond to the idea of "intervention" as presented in this essay? What is your response to compulsory treatment as explained here? Do you approve or disapprove of such methods? What is the basis for your judgment? Write an essay in which you support or oppose the author's position based on your own experience and/or research.

2. In paragraph 4 the author presents several actions and ideas intended to reduce consumption of alcohol. Review them and discuss their potential effectiveness from your perspective.

3. What do you think of "dram shop" and "social host" liability legislation to combat excessive use of alcohol? Do you believe these are sound measures? Support your answer.

4. Write a paper in which you define alcoholism in your own terms. Be sure to review the sections on definition in Part One to help make the most effective use of this form.

5. Based on your own experience or that of others with whom you are familiar, write a paper in which you recount an incident that provided a significant insight into the problem of excessive drinking.

MARCIA SELIGSON

If It Had a Face, I Won't Eat It

Many, if not most, of us in this country have been eating meat all our lives; and, as with so many other customs, we have adopted this practice without ever really considering either reasons or results. Nevertheless, in recent years many Americans, including Marcia Seligson, have changed to vegetarian diets. In this essay, she explores one significant reason for re-examining our dietary habits and she offers one substantial argument for changing them.

The author makes extensive use of factual details and her personal experience to develop her argument. Consider her use of these methods in terms of both appropriateness and effectiveness.

1 **I** grew up eating red meat three times a day for the first 18 years of my life. Fish was considered some sort of minor hors d'oeuvre—as in fried shrimpballs. Yet my good mother was always deeply committed to health and nutrition. Our refrigerator door was papered with an ever-changing library of newspaper clippings extolling papaya enzyme

and yams and high-colonics. My mother cooked mashed potatoes with heavy cream, and she believed in pure, salted butter, which she scooped—along with Velveeta cheese—onto our egg noodles. Vegetables? Canned peas or creamed spinach. My mother was a Russian immigrant—her soul was dark and robust. Thus, enormous portions of juicy, fatty meat were some of her greatest contributions to her family. I was addicted to heavy peasant foods more than to sweets, and it wasn't until I went away to college that I tasted cereal or peanut butter.

2   A year ago my husband, Tom, and I became vegetarians. This fact utterly astonished my brother, who until recently ate fried salami sandwiches for breakfast. Truly, it still amazes us, too.

3   Like many Americans, I began moving away from red meat several years ago, substituting chicken and fish. I always thought of myself as nutrition conscious, always believed that I am what I eat. I eliminated salt from my cooking, replace "leaded" coffee with decaf, abandoned rich cheeses, and moved from Häagen-Dazs into frozen yogurt.

4   Yet I was forever on a diet or breaking a diet or seeking the perfect diet. At one time Tom was on Nutri/System and I was on Jenny Craig. Our pantry bulged with conflicting astronaut food, and for three months we couldn't share a meal together. My entire relationship to food was one of suffering: I always felt either deprived and virtuous or satisfied and guilt ridden. I longed to get off this painful cycle permanently. I became a vegetarian because I am 53 years old, want to live a very long time in superb health, and have come to believe that the way to do that is to eat a vegetarian diet.

5   The Buddhists say that when you are ready to learn, the teacher shows up at your door. Last July Tom, who's 45, went for his annual physical. He learned that he was 60 pounds overweight and that his cholesterol level had soared to 285. We were shocked and frightened. That same week a friend introduced us to Joe Dillon, a remarkable nutrition and exercise coach.

6   Joe told us that there exists a fairly radical body of knowledge about nutrition, based on extensive new scientific studies. It seems that this information is largely unheeded by or unknown to physicians—who themselves may have little or no nutritional education—and is always disputed by such powers as the National Dairy Council and the meat industry. Indeed, while the American Heart Association recommends keeping blood cholesterol under 200, health revolutionary Nathan Pritikin said that one's blood cholesterol level should total no more than 100 plus one's age. New names in the field are John McDougall, M.D., author of *The McDougall Plan* and *A Challenging Second Opinion;* John Robbins, who wrote *Diet for a New America;* and Dean

Ornish, M.D., who has conducted landmark studies on the reversal of heart disease through lifestyle changes alone and is author of *Dr. Dean Ornish's Program for Reversing Heart Disease.*

7   All of these experts hold with the same guiding principles: barring starvation and infectious diseases, America is one of the unhealthiest countries in the world; more than 50 percent of us die from diseases related to the foods we eat; most of the major causes of death, with the exception of accidents, are the result of choices we make about how we live and eat; and *a fundamental source of illness and death in the Western world is the consumption of animal fat.*

8   I studied the research and was overwhelmed by the evidence. The Framingham Heart Study—in which 5,209 people and their offspring have been tracked for the past 43 years—shows that not one of the subjects who maintained a cholesterol level under 150 has ever had a heart attack. Breast cancer is assuredly linked to fat consumption—it has been observed that Japanese women have low rates of breast cancer consistent with their dietary fat intake but that their rates rise to match ours where they adopt our lifestyle. The fat factor clearly influences the rates of diabetes and hypertension, as well as colon, ovarian, and prostate cancer, all of which are prevalent in countries with high-fat diets and relatively rare in countries with mainly vegetarian, starch-based diets. The fact is that the societies with the least degenerative disease and the greatest longevity on the planet are predominantly vegetarian.

9   Given all the data, I was quite ready to change my life. Joe gave us the good news—the only thing that makes us fat is fat; therefore we could eat as much as we wanted of almost everything else. It was important to keep our blood sugar level steady by never becoming ravenous. We would shed weight slowly, but it would be true fat coming off, not the water or muscle that is lost on fad diets. Our regime would be starch-based but, if we chose, we could eat small amounts of fish or poultry—as condiments. Eliminated completely were beef, pork, egg yolks, shrimp, butter, cheese, milk (except nonfat), ice cream, all sugar, and all oils. Vegetable foods high in fat were also excluded.

10   We began by eating incessantly: pasta, potatoes, bread, cereal, rice, and all manner of previously unexplored grains; beans; peas, and lentils; all fruits and vegetables (except avocados and olives). The amount of food we ingested in a day was embarrassing, yet we lost weight and felt satisfied. We learned that, in our case, eating under 100 milligrams of cholesterol a day (the equivalent of four ounces of skinless grilled chicken breast) would cause our cholesterol to drop continually until it leveled off at approximately 150. Over time we would leach out the fat that clogged our arteries from a lifetime of

abuse. We learned that even vegetable oils can raise cholesterol levels and that the elimination of oils can help prevent many types of cancer.

11 Joe took us to a large supermarket and taught us to read the labels rigorously for fat, sugar, and salt content. I tossed out *Gourmet* and subscribed to *Vegetarian Times.* I began to haunt our local health-food emporium, thrilled to discover oil-free corn chips and sherbet sweetened with fruit juice and no sugar. And I began to cook marvelous yet fast and easy dishes: thick bean soups, Indian rice casseroles, blueberry pancakes, lentil chili.

12 In the beginning, I had aches of deprivation. When I allowed my mind to wander into dangerous territory—"I'll never, ever have another bacon cheeseburger again"—I would go crazy, immediately plotting how and when to cheat. But I learned that if I just think of today, as in "Today I'm not having a pepperoni pizza," I'm fine.

13 I don't look upon eating vegetarian as a diet that I'll be on for a while and abandon. This is it for life. I also find that I'm no longer interested in poultry, and I consume less and less fish all the time—now about ten ounces a week. Though I am just as excited by and attached to food as I ever was, my preferences have changed. I can't tolerate the taste or feel of oily food any longer, and after Tom ate a chocolate cookie as an experiment last month, he got a stomachache.

14 The rewards have been extraordinary: Tom's cholesterol level has dropped from 285 to 175; mine is down from 196 to 151. Tom has lost 45 pounds; I've lost 12. In addition, the cellulite in my thighs has vanished and the fibrocystic lumps in my breasts have lessened dramatically. At the age of 53, my vitality and endurance are as high as when I was in college.

15 Perhaps the most amazing result has been the end of suffering about food. I think it has to do with knowing that everything I eat is enhancing my health. I have a newfound sense of having more control over my body, my wellbeing, the aging process, and, indeed, my future.

Some Myths and Facts About Food and Health

16 Myth: We need some fats for good health.
Fact: This is true. But approximately ten grams of fat a day are sufficient for the average person, and we get that from seven macadamia nuts. Laboratory tests that have cut people's fat intake from the 43 percent of total diet that the typical American eats show that the steeper the cut, even down to 1 percent, the healthier the people. Fat is like protein; it is virtually impossible not to get enough.

17   Myth: We need substantial amounts of protein for good health.
Fact: If we ever needed a lot of protein, it would be during the first two years of life, when we double in size. Yet breast milk, the ideal food for a growing infant, is only 5 percent protein. There is more protein in brown rice than in breast milk. Except for infants and pregnant or nursing mothers, the amount of protein we need is so small that it is impossible not to get enough, unless we are malnourished and not ingesting enough calories. We can be vigorously healthy with as little as 20 grams of protein a day. That can be provided by three glasses of nonfat milk or one and a half cups of kidney beans or four ounces of fish or poultry. Vegetarians should not eat too much protein because processing it drains the body of calcium and can cause kidney stones.

QUESTIONS AND EXERCISES

VOCABULARY
1. *hors d'oeuvre* (paragraph 1)
2. high-colonics (1)
3. robust (1)
4. degenerative (8)
5. longevity (8)
6. condiments (9)
7. incessantly (10)
8. emporium (11)
9. deprivation (12)
10. malnourished (17)

LANGUAGE AND RHETORIC
1. What is the author's purpose in this selection? Is she writing to inform? To explain? To argue? To move the reader to action? Is she pursuing more than one purpose? Support your answer.
2. The author depends to a great extent on her personal experience and her own research to support her judgments. What are the advantages to this approach? What are the disadvantages?
3. The author uses several patterns of development. In addition to fact and judgment, she uses comparison and contrast, cause and effect, and appeal to authority in which she cites sources for her facts. Select one of these patterns, find examples of it, and show how the author uses it to support her thesis.
4. How do you respond to the title of this piece? Does it identify the subject or topic? Does it stimulate you to read the article? Does it suggest a thesis? Present at least one alternative for consideration and justify your choice of title.

5. This piece was first published in *Lear's* magazine and is reprinted here in the same manner. Does it have a conclusion? If so, what is it? Would it benefit from a more definitive conclusion? If so, write a brief conclusion yourself.

DISCUSSION AND WRITING

1. The author bases her conversion to vegetarianism on nutritional and health grounds. Others have argued it on moral grounds, and still others on economic. Which line of reasoning strikes you as most valid and why? After appropriate research, write a paper supporting one of these views. Or write a paper attacking any one or all or them. Use a variety of facts to support your judgments.

2. According to this and other authors, most Americans depend on a meat diet largely because we have been conditioned to believe it is the only way we can fulfill our nutritional needs. Consider your own experience with family, friends, and formal education. Does your experience support this claim? Write a paper recounting your experience and its effect on you.

3. Like the author, more Americans have turned to vegetarianism in recent years. Talk with some people who have done so or do some library research on the subject to see what you can find as the reasons for this development. Write a paper reporting your findings.

4. What are your personal reasons either for eating or not eating meat? Write a paper explaining the basis for your preference.

5. If you have had to struggle to develop any kind of eating pattern that did not come easily or naturally to you, explain the nature of that struggle, how you handled it, and the effect of its outcome on you. Or if you had to struggle with smoking or drinking, use that as your subject and adapt your paper accordingly.

PETER STEINHART

What Can We Do About Environmental Racism?

1 When Frank Villalobos was fifteen, his family was evicted from its East Los Angeles home. The State of California took the house and hundreds of others to clear a path for the new Pomona Freeway. "For a week," Villalobos recalls, "I couldn't go to school for the shame."

2   Today, at forty-five, Villalobos still lives in all-Hispanic East Los
Angeles. He looks out over its sunny streets and modest stucco houses
and lists the burdens neighboring white communities have heaped
upon it. There are five prisons as well as the maintenance yards for
city and county road departments and bus and light-rail systems.
Seven freeways dissect the community into sub-neighborhoods, filling
them with noise and petro-chemical wastes. Where the freeways meet
is the grand-daddy of interchanges, a multilevel concrete pretzel of
road visited by more than a half-million autos a day. Factories elbow
up to the borders of these neighborhoods, bringing additional pollution but no tax revenues. Next door, in the city of Vernon, there are
only one hundred residents but fifteen hundred industries, including
slaughterhouses, meat-packing plants, and medical waste incinerators.
"Just about every type of toxic or fume is experienced here," says
Villalobos. "Prevailing winds are toward East Los Angeles, so every
night we have more than our share of impacts from the freeways and
industries."

3   Villalobos knows that when prisons or hazardous industries are proposed, someone will try to site them in his backyard. Probably 80
percent of the residents of East Los Angeles are immigrants. Most are
young families concentrating on making a living and raising children.
Many speak no English. The local assembly district has the lowest
percentage and lowest number of registered voters in the state: only
57,000 out of a possible 400,000.

4   "Most of our parents were not organized because they had no respect
for government," says Villalobos. They had come from Mexico, where
they were afraid of government, to America, where they were not recognized by government. "And," he adds, "when you don't speak the
language, you don't make waves." So, when other communities won't
accept a factory or a landfill, officials look to East Los Angeles.

5   "The community is said to be dormant politically," says Villalobos.
"And the history of the Latino community in East Los Angeles was
not to stand up to environmental problems."

6   Even when the community resists, it finds the rules for it are different than those for Beverly Hills or Pasadena. In 1985 the state decided
to locate a 4,500-bed, medium-security prison on the edge of East Los
Angeles after the desert suburb of Lancaster had refused it. Governor
George Deukmejian explained that the Lancaster site was unsuitable
because it was within a mile of a school. Villalobos observes, "There
are thirty schools within two miles of the East Los Angeles site."

7   Says Villalobos, "It was a clear case of discrimination." He made
fifty-seven trips to Sacramento to lobby against the prison. In the

capitol, he says, "people would tell us to our faces, 'You're impotent. You don't vote. You don't have money. Why should we listen to you?'"

8   The prison is just one such issue the community has wrestled with. A gas pipeline from Santa Barbara to Carson was routed along Whittier Boulevard, East Los Angeles' commercial center. The state's first commercial-scale toxic waste incinerator, slated to be built in Vernon, was defeated by local opposition but is now being planned for nearby Commerce. And last year, when Southern California communities were sprayed with malathion to control Mediterranean fruit flies, "while everyone else got sprayed one time, we got sprayed four times," says Villalobos.

9   It is a truism in America that freeways, prisons, and waste facilities get foisted off on minority and poor communities. A 1987 study by the United Church of Christ's Commission for Racial Justice declared that three out of every five African-Americans and Hispanics live in a neighborhood with a hazardous waste site, and that race is the most significant variable in differentiating communities with such sites from the communities without them. That, says Benjamin F. Chavis Jr., the commission's executive director, is "environmental racism."

10   Environmental racism does not stop at the boundaries of minority communities. Chavis observes that mainline environmental organizations have few minority group members on their staffs or boards of directors. The Wilderness Society has no non-Whites on its board and only four among the eighty people in professional positions. Only one of the Sierra Club's fifteen directors, and only two of National Audubon Society's thirty-three directors, are members of a minority group. National Audubon has thirty-five nonwhites in a total work force of 320, but only thirteen out of 149 are in professional or managerial positions. At the National Wildlife Federation nineteen of the 283 staff people in professional positions and three of the twenty-nine directors are minority group members. Gerry Stover, director of the Environmental Consortium for Minority Outreach in Washington, D.C., estimates that in the past five years less than two percent of all the field staff and management hirings within the environmental community have been from ethnic minorities.

11   This latter act of discrimination has not been intended. Stover notes that mainline environmental groups tend to recruit future staff members by offering internships to college students and recent graduates. The internships are typically low-paying jobs. White middle-class families may encourage their sons and daughters to take such jobs. But minority students can seldom afford to take them, and once

they graduate, commerce and industry offer them much bigger salaries and better promotion opportunities. The mainline environmental groups were formed at the turn of the century to protect wildlife and natural setting. They were not thinking about minorities. They were moved by trends developing far from the cities.

12 While the main act of American history from 1900 to 1945 was the migration of people from farms to cities, the main act since then has been a migration from cities to suburbs. The postwar migration was a flight from the pollution, crime, and human powerlessness of the industrial world. It abandoned the cities to the narrow logic of corporations and a burgeoning minority group population. But it was explained as a flight upward, into a pastoral grace of tree-lined streets and a society without conflict.

13 In the course of this movement middle-class Whites drew a line and said no dirty industries and, in many cases, no non-Whites beyond this point. They turned their backs on both industry and the urban working class. Today, while we live on the fringes of the great cities and take a proprietary interest in their baseball teams, their mayoral elections, their museums and orchestras, we do not vote, pay taxes, volunteer to work in their schools, or otherwise help to shape their destinies.

14 At the same time we have composed in the suburbs a whole new set of values. At the heart of these values is the view that we are most secure when surrounded by open spaces, greenery, and birdsong. That view has come to be a cornerstone of suburban culture, expressed over and over again in film and literature. Indeed, suburbanites fight over environmental quality in part to assert their cultural identity. The environmental movement of the last forty years largely shaped itself around this suburban culture. And today, when environmental groups seek financial or political support, they look to the suburbs and speak chiefly in the languages of wildlife conservation and wilderness protection.

15 Until recently the mainstream of the environmental movement distinguished between pollution issues and nature issues. Pollution issues were seen as city concerns and by law consigned to health departments, while the laws we designed to protect open space and wildlife were draped around forest, park, and wildlife agencies. In 1970 Audubon produced a booklet on the urban environment for New York City schools. But such interest in the city was rare. Even today the older environmental groups give more attention to the nature issues than to the health issues. In 1978, when Lois Gibbs tried to interest mainline environmental groups in the pollution of her neighborhood in Love Canal, New York, none of them took up her cause.

16   Stover worked for several years for the Trust for Public Land. He points out that most of the executives of environmental groups are middle- and upper-middle-class White males. They are people who grew up in the suburbs and still live there. And the people they rely upon for membership also live in the suburbs. They have only an abstract interest in inner-city problems; and, says Stover, "they see those problems as health problems rather than environmental problems."

17   Since the 1970s, as groundwater pollution found the suburbs, acid rain fell on distant lakes and forests, and urban chemicals devoured the Earth's ozone, the line between nature and pollution issues has narrowed. Now the environmental groups are looking hard at toxic waste facilities and garbage incinerators. And, as they squint across decades of indifference to the plight of the cities, they are seeing the wreckage left behind when their parents and grandparents fled.

18   They are stung by charges that they do a poor job of representing minority group concerns. But they aren't sure what to do about it. There are efforts to bring minority perspectives to environmental groups, by adding minority members to the boards of directors and by offering higher-paying internships to minority candidates. Stover's group is itself sponsored by thirty-one environmental organizations, including National Audubon and the National Wildlife Federation. Another method being attempted is to introduce environmental education programs into the inner cities with the idea that, once exposed to nature, inner-city children will take a greater interest in the issues that preoccupy mainline environmentalists. The Sierra Club takes inner-city children on outings in the wilderness, and Audubon takes its Audubon Adventures program to ten large-city school districts.

19   But bringing nature into inner-city schools is only part of the solution. For at the root of the race gap is a class difference. The flight to the suburbs was a middle-class migration. It is a clichè and a joke of middle-class life that while a working-class person faces adversity with his fists, a middle-class person calls a cop or a lawyer. The middle class learns how to influence political institutions, not only to avoid crooks and crazy people but to obtain economic advantages. They think in terms of lawyers, committees, and lobbying groups. Mainline conservation issues are fought out at this institutional level.

20   The working-class people left behind in the cities are often minorities or recent immigrants whose experience of government is one of oppression. They have little experience of making political institutions work for them. They rely more on resignation or direct complaint. They are less likely to form committees and are often unaware of the work of mainline conservation groups. "These organizations have

never taken the time to explain what they do in a way that's relevant to these communities," says Stover.

21   When working-class communities do respond they are likely to form their own groups out of existing church or civil rights organizations. To fight the prison in East Los Angeles, women from a local church formed Mothers of East Los Angeles; the group got thousands of protesters into the streets but did it without the help of mainline environmentalists. Such groups tend to sort out issues in terms of social justice rather than ecological order. They ask not just how they can avoid the environmental impacts but how they might overcome the social and economic inequalities that led to the injustice in the first place.

22   And they are apt to be quite angry. Suburban environmentalists are often frightened by the anger. A representative of the Citizens Clearing House for Hazardous Wastes recalls an Alabama hearing on the siting of waste facilities at which working-class people got very heated. "It was not polite," he says. "The mainline groups were at the back of the room. They were very uncomfortable with the confrontational nature." Middle-class Whites often leave such confrontations because they are uncomfortable with animosity and reluctant to alienate officials.

23   That middle-class discomfort may keep suburban Whites from seeing the issues of social justice that underlie environmental conflict. But inner-city residents are keenly aware of them. Villalobos recalls how, as Los Angeles grew, the original Spanish-speaking inhabitants were elbowed out. He recalls how Spanish-speaking families were dragged out of their homes to make room for proposed housing projects and how, in the end, they turned around and saw not housing but Dodger Stadium rising on the ruins of their neighborhood. He recalls neighbors who, made homeless by eviction, sneaked back and lived for weeks "in hiding from the world" in the cellar of a boarded-up house. A sadness creeps over his face as he recalls these things. "That sorrow turns into hate," he says. "It is easy to call up that hate."

24   Just trying to show inner-city people what is being lost in the wide-open spaces beyond the city may not bridge the class gap or end decades of mistrust. Suburbanites have to recognize the social issues inside the cities. And city folk have to learn how to sort out authorities and orchestrate the institutions. We have a long way to go before we solve these problems. "It's not going to happen overnight," says Stover. "But you gotta' keep trying."

Comparison and Contrast

ROGER EBERT

Not Being There

The pleasure we derive from watching movies may seem identical to most of us whether we do so in a commercial theater or in a home setting. Not so, says movie reviewer and critic Roger Ebert. Regardless of the similarities between the two situations, there are fundamental differences in the quality and character of the media, and for Ebert, at least, "to experience a movie fully, you have to go to the movies." Here he tells you why.

Ebert develops his thesis largely by means of comparison and contrast, with the emphasis on the latter. As you assess his argument, see to what extent his response to the two experiences matches your own.

1   Like most other people whose tastes began to form before television became the dominant entertainment medium, I have a simple idea of what it means to go to the movies. You buy your ticket and take a seat in a large dark room with hundreds of strangers. You slide down in your seat and make yourself comfortable. On the screen in front of you, the movie image appears—enormous and overwhelming. If the movie is a good one, you allow yourself to be absorbed in its fantasy, and its dreams become part of your memories.

2   Television is not a substitute for that experience, and I have never had a TV-watching experience of emotional intensity comparable to my great movie-going experiences. Television is just not first class. The screen is too small. The image is technically inferior. The sound is disgracefully bad. As the viewer I can contain television—but the movies are so large they can contain me. I can't lose myself in a television image, and neither, I suspect, can most other people. That is why people are forever recreating movie memories in great detail, but hardly ever reminisce about old TV programs.

341

3   I believe, then, that to experience a movie fully you have to go to the movies. I enjoy television for other purposes, and my favorite TV programs are the live ones (sports, news, elections, talk shows), where immediacy helps compensate for the loss in intensity. Unlike a lot of movie buffs, I am not a fan of *The Late Show.* If a movie is good enough to stay up late for, it's too good to be watched through the dilution of television. I'll catch it later at a revival theater or a film society, or, if I never catch it again at least I'll think of it as a *movie* and not as late-night programming.

4   Maybe it's no wonder, then, that, with these personal biases, I was disturbed by some of the things I heard last March during a conference I went to in Colorado. The American Film Institute had taken over the Aspen Institute for three days, and invited forty-five people to gather for a discussion of the future of the feature film. By "feature film," they meant both theatrical and made-for-TV features, the latter including docudramas and TV miniseries.

5   The conference was weighted toward the TV people, among them executives of various pay-cable companies, and although several of us professed an interest in a discussion of content (that is, what movies are *about* these days), most of the talk was about "delivery" (how to sell television programming at a profit). What actually went out on the airwaves or cable systems would presumably take care of itself.

6   Many panelists' remarks were couched in a technological Newspeak that I had trouble understanding at first. *Software,* for example, was the word for TV programming—software to feed the hardware of our new home video entertainment centers. ("Software?" they said. "You know. That's a word for product." "Product?" I asked. "Yeah. Like a movie.") *Television consuming units* was another expression that gave me trouble until I realized it was a reference to human beings. *Windows* was a very interesting word. It referred to the various markets that a new movie could be sold to (or "shown through") once it was made. First there would be the theatrical window, a traditional booking in a movie theater. Then came the network window—sale to commercial television. After that the windows came thick and fast: the pay-cable window, video cassette window, video disc window, airline in-flight window, and so on. In the hierarchy of these windows, the traditional practice of showing the movie in a theater seemed furthest from everybody's mind; the theatrical run was sort of a preliminary before the other markets could be carved up.

7   One of the enticing things about all the windows, I learned, was that a new movie could now be in the position of turning a profit before it

was made. The pre-sales of subsidiary viewing rights would take the risk out of the initial investment.

8   The chilling thought occurred to me that, if a movie was already in profit, actually showing it in theaters could be risky because promotion, advertising, and overhead would be seen as liabilities instead of (in the traditional view) as an investment risk with a hope of profitable return. But no, I was assured, that was wrong. Movies would still have to play in theaters because the theatrical run "legitimized" them: they thus became "real" movies in the eyes of people buying them on cassettes or over pay cable.

9   Wonderful, I thought. The theatrical feature film, the most all-encompassing art form of the twentieth century, has been reduced to a necessary marketing preliminary for software.

10   If this was a pessimistic view, it was mild compared to some of the visions of the future held by the conference participants. An important TV writer-producer, one of the most likable people at the conference, calmly predicted that in ten years people would be sitting at home in front of their wall-size TV screens while (and I am indeed quoting) "marauding bands roam the streets." I thought he was joking, until he repeated the same phrase the next day.

11   What about going out to the movies? Another television executive said he used to go, but he had stopped. "You have to stand in line and be crowded in with all those people. And it's too expensive."

12   Well, apart from the fact that he could no doubt afford to buy a ticket for everyone in line, and that higher ticket prices only reflect general inflation, his view overlooked the fact that video cassettes and pay cable are at least as expensive as going out to the movies, especially when you consider the initial "hardware" investment. And for your money, you get to watch a TV image made up of dots arranged in 625 lines—an image that, even assuming your set has perfect adjustment and color control, does not and cannot approach the quality of an image projected by light through celluloid.

13   But those technical considerations aside, why did this man and some of his colleagues have such a distaste for going out to the movies? I do it all the time. I feel it adds something to a movie-going experience to share it with other people. It's communal. A lot of the fun of seeing a movie such as *Jaws* or *Star Wars* comes, for me, from the massed emotion of the theater audience. When the shark attacks, we all levitate three inches above our seats, and come down screaming and laughing.

14   Watching *Jaws* on network TV isn't a remotely comparable experience. And watching a *comedy* in isolation can actually be a depressing

experience. Our laughter during a movie comedy is an act of communication; an audience roaring with laughter is expressing its shared
opinion about what's funny. I've watched comedies while I was alone
in a room, and I've noticed that I don't laugh at all. Why should I?
Who's to hear? And, perhaps because I don't laugh, those comedies
don't seem as funny. Maybe it's essential to comedy that we're conscious of sharing it with other people; maybe, in human development,
the first communication was a scream and the second was a laugh,
and then they got around to words.

15   I made a modest proposal at Aspen. I suggested that some time and
attention be given to perfecting cheaper and better home 16-mm
movie projection systems, and that 16-mm rental and lending libraries
be set up, like the Fotomat video cassette centers. I've gotten a lot of
enjoyment out of 16-mm movie prints. The picture is larger, sharper,
and brighter than television, so you can get a good idea of what the
director had in mind. My suggestion was received with polite indifference, although, later, there was a lot of enthusiasm about reports that
they're improving those giant-size TV screens you see in bars.

16   As anyone who has seen one knows, giant TV screens aren't the
answer because they further dilute the already washed-out TV image.
The TV signal has only 625 lines to contain its information no matter
how large the screen is, and so a larger screen means a faded picture.
TV retail outlets report that consumers seem to understand this, and
that 17- and 19-inch sets are preferred to 21- and 24-inch screens because of the sharper image.

17   One evening over dinner, I finally got an interesting response to my
suggestion about home 16-mm movie projectors. The problem with
those, I was told, is that they can't be programmed by the pay-TV
systems. You sit in your own house operating your own projector, and
the cable operators don't have access to it. They can't pipe their software into it and charge you for it. Why, you decide for yourself what
and when to watch!

18   What is clearly happening is very alarming.

19   A superior system of technology—motion pictures—is being sold
out in favor of an inferior but more profitable system—pay video
hardware/software combinations. The theatrical motion picture,
which remains such a desirable item that it's used to sell home cassette
systems, is in danger of being held hostage. Truly daring and off beat
film subjects will become increasingly risky because they can't be easily presold for showing through other "windows."

20   The two edges that movies have enjoyed over television are greater quality and impact of image, and greater freedom of subject matter. Now television is poised to absorb and emasculate the movies, all in the name of home entertainment. It will serve us right, as we sit in front of our fuzzy giant-screen home video systems ten or twenty years from now, if there's nothing new or interesting to watch on them. Count me in with the marauding bands.

QUESTIONS AND EXERCISES

VOCABULARY
1. reminisce (paragraph 2)
2. dilution (3)
3. docudramas (4)
4. hierarchy (6)
5. subsidiary (7)
6. marauding (10)
7. levitate (13)
8. emasculate (20)

LANGUAGE AND RHETORIC
1. The title of this essay alludes to the Jerzy Koszinski novel—*Being There*—later made into a motion picture starring Peter Sellers. Does this information enhance your response to the title, or would it be just as effective without your knowing it? Can you suggest other titles that would not depend on such references?
2. The selection is clearly organized into an introduction, body, and conclusion. Which paragraphs comprise each section and how does the author use each to advance his argument?
3. The author, Roger Ebert, is a well-known movie reviewer for both a Chicago daily newspaper and a national television network. The conference he refers to was attended largely by other professionals in the field. What seems to be his intended audience and how can you tell?
4. In paragraph 10, the author quotes a TV writer-producer who refers to "marauding bands" roaming the streets. What is meant by this remark? In the conclusion, Ebert includes himself among those bands. What is the significance of his doing so, and how effective a conclusion does it make? Support your answer.

DISCUSSION AND WRITING
1. Make a point of viewing the same motion picture both in a movie theater and on television. Using Ebert's essay as a basis, carefully compare the two experiences and either validate or refute Ebert's thesis.

2. Discuss Ebert's thesis with your classmates and others to get their ideas on the subject. Then conduct an informal survey of a limited number of students on your campus to determine their opinions. Prepare a written report of your findings.
3. Write a paper in which you make a case for television viewing as superior to movies. Use points of comparison and contrast as one means of supporting your argument.
4. Ebert says that movies have enjoyed an edge over television in terms of "quality and impact of image" and "greater freedom of subject matter." Apply his criteria to the two media yourself and write an essay in which you come to your own conclusions.

ROBIN LAKOFF

You Are What You Say

The language of sexism, like the language of racism, is by now well documented. Yet it is one thing to be an unconscious victim of a society's use of language and quite another to contribute to that condition yourself— whether unwitting or not. Linguist Robin Lakoff shows here how women's language differs from men's. She goes on to reveal that women have not only accepted that difference; they have helped to promote it, and by so doing, have reinforced their second-class status.

This selection originally appeared in Ms *magazine. Consider the implication of that fact for how the author addresses her subject and her audience.*

1   **"W**omen's language" is that pleasant (dainty?), euphemistic, never-aggressive way of talking we learned as little girls. Cultural bias was built into the language we were allowed to speak, the subjects we were allowed to speak about, and the ways we were spoken of. Having learned our linguistic lesson well, we go out in the world, only to discover that we are communicative cripples—damned if we do, and damned if we don't.

2   If we refuse to talk "like a lady," we are ridiculed and criticized for being unfeminine. ("She thinks like a man" is, at best, a left-handed compliment.) If we do learn all the fuzzy-headed, unassertive language of our sex, we are ridiculed for being unable to think clearly, unable to

take part in a serious discussion, and therefore unfit to hold a position of power.

3   It doesn't take much of this for a woman to begin feeling she deserves such treatment because of inadequacies in her own intelligence and education.

4   "Women's language" shows up in all levels of English. For example, women are encouraged and allowed to make far more precise discriminations in naming colors than men do. Words like *mauve, beige, ecru, aquamarine, lavender,* and so on, are unremarkable in a woman's active vocabulary, but largely absent from that of most men. I know of no evidence suggesting that women actually *see* a wider range of colors than men do. It is simply that fine discriminations of this sort are relevant to women's vocabularies, but not to men's; to men, who control most of the interesting affairs of the world, such distinctions are trivial—irrelevant.

5   In the area of syntax, we find similar gender-related peculiarities of speech. There is one construction, in particular, that women use conversationally far more than men: the tag question. A tag is midway between an outright statement and a yes-no question; it is less assertive than the former, but more confident than the latter.

6   A *flat statement* indicates confidence in the speaker's knowledge and is fairly certain to be believed; a *question* indicates a lack of knowledge on some point and implies that the gap in the speaker's knowledge can and will be remedied by an answer. For example, if, at a Little League game, I have had my glasses off, I can legitimately ask someone else: "Was the player out at third?" A *tag question,* being intermediate between statement and question, is used when the speaker is stating a claim, but lacks full confidence in the truth of that claim. So if I say, "Is Joan here?" I will probably not be surprised if my respondent answers "no"; but if I say, "Joan is here, isn't she?" instead, chances are I am already biased in favor of a positive answer, wanting only confirmation. I still want a response, but I have enough knowledge (or think I have) to predict that response. A tag question, then, might be thought of as a statement that doesn't demand to be believed by anyone but the speaker, a way of giving leeway, of not forcing the addressee to go along with the views of the speaker.

7   Another common use of the tag question is in small talk when the speaker is trying to elicit conversation: "Sure is hot here, isn't it?"

8   But in discussing personal feelings or opinions, only the speaker normally has any way of knowing the correct answer. Sentences such as "I have a headache, don't I?" are clearly ridiculous. But there are other examples where it is the speaker's opinions, rather

than perceptions, for which corroboration is sought, as in "The situation in Southeast Asia is terrible, isn't it?"

9   While there are, of course, other possible interpretations of a sentence like this, one possibility is that the speaker has a particular answer in mind—"yes" or "no"—but is reluctant to state it baldly. This sort of tag question is much more apt to be used by women than by men in conversation. Why is this the case?

10   The tag question allows a speaker to avoid commitment, and thereby avoid conflict with the addressee. The problem is that, by so doing, speakers may also give the impression of not really being sure of themselves, or looking to the addressee for confirmation of their views. This uncertainty is reinforced in more subliminal ways, too. There is a peculiar sentence intonation-pattern, used almost exclusively by women, as far as I know, which changes a declarative answer into a question. The effect of using the rising inflection typical of a yes-no question is to imply that the speaker is seeking confirmation, even though the speaker is clearly the only one who has the requisite information, which is why the question was put to her in the first place:

(Q) When will dinner be ready?
(A) Oh . . . around six o'clock . . . ?

It is as though the second speaker were saying, "Six o'clock—if that's okay with you, if you agree." The person being addressed is put in the position of having to provide confirmation. One likely consequence of this sort of speech-pattern in a woman is that, often unbeknownst to herself, the speaker builds a reputation of tentativeness, and others will refrain from taking her seriously or trusting her with any responsibilities, since she "can't make up her mind," and "isn't sure of herself."

11   Such idiosyncrasies may explain why women's language sounds much more "polite" than men's. It is polite to leave a decision open, not impose your mind, or views, or claims, on anyone else. So a tag question is a kind of polite statement, in that it does not force agreement or belief on the addressee. In the same way a request is a polite command, in that it does not force obedience on the addressee, but rather suggests something be done as a favor to the speaker. A clearly stated order implies a threat of certain consequences if it is not followed, and—even more impolite—implies that the speaker is in a superior position and able to enforce the order. By couching wishes in the form of a request, on the other hand, a speaker implies that if the request is not carried out, only the speaker will suffer; noncompliance cannot harm the addressee. So the decision is really left up to [the] addressee. The distinction becomes clear in these examples:

> Close the door.
> Please close the door.
> Will you close the door?
> Will you please close the door?
> Won't you close the door?

12   In the same ways as words and speech patterns used *by* women undermine her image, those used to *describe* women make matters even worse. Often a word may be used of both men and women (and perhaps of things as well); but when it is applied to women, it assumes a special meaning that, by implication rather than outright assertion, is derogatory to women as a group.

13   The use of euphemisms has this effect. A euphemism is a substitute for a word that has acquired a bad connotation by association with something unpleasant or embarrassing. But almost as soon as the new word comes into common usage, it takes on the same old bad connotations, since feelings about the things or people referred to are not altered by a change of name; thus new euphemisms must be constantly found.

14   There is one euphemism for *women* still very much alive. The word of course, is *lady. Lady* has a masculine counterpart, namely *gentleman,* occasionally shortened to *gent.* But for some reason *lady* is very much commoner than *gent(leman).*

15   The decision to use *lady* rather than *woman,* or vice versa, may considerably alter the sense of a sentence, as the following examples show:

> (a) A woman (lady) I know is a dean at Berkeley.
> (b) A woman (lady) I know makes amazing things out of shoelaces and old boxes.

16   The use of *lady* in (a) imparts a frivolous, or nonserious, tone to the sentence: the matter under discussion is not one of great moment. Similarly, in (b), using *lady* here would suggest that the speaker considered the "amazing things" not to be serious art, but merely a hobby or an aberration. If *woman* is used, she might be a serious sculptor. To say *lady doctor* is very condescending, since no one ever says *gentleman* doctor or even *man doctor.* For example, mention in the *San Francisco Chronicle* of January 31, 1972, of Madalyn Murray O'Hair as the *lady atheist* reduces her position to that of scatterbrained eccentric. Even *woman atheist* is scarcely defensible: sex is irrelevant to her philosophical position.

17   Many women argue that, on the other hand, *lady* carries with it overtones recalling the age of chivalry: conferring exalted stature on the person so referred to. This makes the term seem polite at first, but

we must also remember that these implications are perilous: they suggest that a "lady" is helpless, and cannot do things by herself.

18   *Lady* can also be used to infer frivolousness, as in titles of organizations. Those that have a serious purpose (not merely that of enabling "the ladies" to spend time with one another) cannot use the word *lady* in their titles, but less serious ones may. Compare the *Ladies' Auxiliary* of a men's group, or the *Thursday Evening Ladies' Browning and Garden Society* with *Ladies' Liberation* or *Ladies' Strike for Peace*.

19   What is curious about this split is that *lady* is in origin a euphemism—a substitute that puts a better face on something people find uncomfortable—for *women*. What kind of euphemism is it that subtly denigrates the people to whom it refers? Perhaps *lady* functions as a euphemism for *women* because it does not contain the sexual implications present in *woman:* it is not "embarrassing" in that way. If this is so, we may expect that, in the future, *lady* will replace woman as the primary word for the human female, since *woman* will have become too blatantly sexual. That this distinction is already made in some contexts at least is shown in the following examples, where you can try replacing *woman* with *lady:*

> She's only twelve, but she's already a woman.
> After ten years in jail, Harry wanted to find a woman.
> She's my woman, see, so don't mess around with her.

20   Another common substitute for *woman* is *girl*. One seldom hears a man past the age of adolescence referred to as a boy, save in expressions like "going out with the boys," which are meant to suggest an air of adolescent frivolity and irresponsibility. But women of all ages are "girls": one can have a man—not a boy—Friday, but only a girl—never a woman or even a lady—Friday; women have girlfriends, but men do not—in a nonsexual sense—have boyfriends. It may be that this use of *girl* is euphemistic in the same way the use of *lady* is: in stressing the idea of immaturity, it removes the sexual connotations lurking in *woman*. *Girl* brings to mind irresponsibility: you don't send a girl to do a woman's errand (or even, for that matter, a boy's errand). She is a person who is both too immature and too far from real life to be entrusted with responsibilities or with decisions of any serious or important nature.

21   Now let's take a pair of words which, in terms of the possible relationships in an earlier society, were simple male-female equivalents, analogous to *bull: cow*. Suppose we find that, for independent reasons, society has changed in such a way that the original meanings now are

irrelevant. Yet the words have not been discarded, but have acquired new meanings, metaphorically related to their original senses. But suppose these new metaphorical uses are no longer parallel to each other. By seeing where the parallelism breaks down, we discover something about the different roles played by men and women in this culture. One good example of such a divergence through time is found in the pair, *master: mistress.* Once used with reference to one's power over servants, these words have become unusable today in their original master-servant sense as the relationship has become less prevalent in our society. But the words are still common.

22   Unless used with reference to animals, *master* now generally refers to a man who has acquired consummate ability in some field, normally nonsexual. But its feminine counterpart cannot be used this way. It is practically restricted to its sexual sense of "paramour." We start out with two terms, both roughly paraphrasable as "one who has power over another." But the masculine form, once one person is no longer able to have absolute power over another, becomes usable metaphorically in the sense of "having power over *something." Master* requires as its object only the name of some activity, something inanimate and abstract. But *mistress* requires a masculine noun in the possessive to precede it. One cannot say: "Rhonda is a mistress." One must be *someone's* mistress. A man is defined by what he does, a woman by her sexuality, that is, in terms of one particular aspect of her relationship to men. It is one thing to be an *old master* like Hans Holbein, and another to be an *old mistress.*

23   The same is true of the words *spinster* and *bachelor*—gender words for "one who is not married." The resemblance ends with the definition. While *bachelor* is a neuter term, often used as a compliment, *spinster* normally is used pejoratively, with connotations of prissiness, fussiness, and so on. To be a bachelor implies that one has the choice of marrying or not, and this is what makes the idea of a bachelor existence attractive, in the popular literature. He has been pursued and has successfully eluded his pursuers. But a spinster is one who has not been pursued, or at least not seriously. She is old, unwanted goods. The metaphorical connotations of *bachelor* generally suggest sexual freedom; of *spinster,* puritanism or celibacy.

24   These examples could be multiplied. It is generally considered a *faux pas,* in society, to congratulate a woman on her engagement, while it is correct to congratulate her fiancé. Why is this? The reason seems to be that it is impolite to remind people of things that may be uncomfortable to them. To congratulate a woman on her engagement is really to say, "Thank goodness! You had a close call!" For the man,

on the other hand, there was no such danger. His choosing to marry is viewed as a good thing, but not something essential.

25   The linguistic double standard holds throughout the life of the relationship. After marriage, bachelor and spinster become man and wife, not man and woman. The woman whose husband dies remains "John's widow"; John, however, is never "Mary's widower."

26   Finally, why is it that salesclerks and others are so quick to call women customers "dear," "honey," and other terms of endearment they really have no business using? A male customer would never put up with it. But women, like children, are supposed to enjoy these endearments, rather than being offended by them.

27   In more ways than one, it's time to speak up.

QUESTIONS AND EXERCISES

VOCABULARY
 1. euphemistic (paragraph 1)
 2. syntax (5)
 3. elicit (7)
 4. corroboration (8)
 5. subliminal (10)
 6. intonation (10)
 7. inflection (10)
 8. idiosyncrasies (11)
 9. noncompliance (11)
10. frivolous (16)
11. aberration (16)
12. condescending (16)
13. denigrates (19)
14. pejoratively (23)
15. prissiness (23)
16. celibacy (23)
17. *faux pas* (24)

LANGUAGE AND RHETORIC
 1. What indications are there that this essay was initially intended primarily for a female audience? Point out specific evidence in the writing itself.
 2. Lakoff divides her essay into two basic sections. What are they, and how do they relate to one another?
 3. The author brings to bear on this subject both her expertise as a linguist and her experience as a woman. How does she manage to avoid letting that expertise lead to an excessively technical essay for the general reader?

4. Evaluate the title of this selection. In your own words, what does it mean? How does it relate to the subject? Is it an appropriate and effective title, or could you improve it?

DISCUSSION AND WRITING

1. Using this essay as a basis, write a paper defining and illustrating "men's language." Emphasize the contrast between it and "women's language." Use original examples to make your point rather than repeating those provided here.
2. Can you make a case for a "pleasant, euphemistic, never-aggressive" way of talking? Must such a use of language be taken as totally negative? Support your answer in an essay of your own.
3. Examine a dictionary for its use of words associated with male and female. See if in fact the word associations for the former tend to be positive and the latter negative. Write a paper reporting your findings.
4. The language of sexism has received considerable attention in recent years. Investigate the subject in your campus library and develop a list of potential topics for future writing projects.

WILLIAM RASPBERRY

Jousting with the Windmills of Racism

A well-known newspaper columnist and an African-American himself, William Raspberry often writes on racial matters. In this particular selection, he addresses the state of racial relations in our country, contrasting the civil rights movement of the sixties with the anti-racism movement of the nineties. After reviewing these differences, he concludes that there may not be as much cause for concern as many people seem to think.

As you read, notice how heavily the author relies on one primary source, Julius Lester, to define the difference between the racial situation today with that of the sixties. Consider the advantages and disadvantages of his decision to do so.

1   $\mathbf{A}$sk 100 Black Americans about the state of race relations in the country, and maybe 90 of them will tell you that things are getting worse. On the job, in the general society, on the most prestigious of college campuses, you will hear talk—and chapter-and-verse examples—of

growing resurgent racism: ignorant insensitivity, racial slights, open bigotry.

2   Can the country that has seen blacks achieve leadership in industry and in the professions—that has moved so far beyond the question of voting rights that Mississippi has elected a Black member of Congress and Virginia a Black governor—also be a place where racism grows worse with each passing year?

3   Julius Lester, the sixties radical who authored "Look Out, Whitey! Black Power's Gon' Get Your Mama," offers an intriguing explanation of the seeming paradox: Blacks, having achieved the "possible" dream of securing civil rights, are now embarked on a "disastrously divisive and impossible" task of fighting racism.

4   "The first thing to understand about the civil-rights movements," says Lester, now a professor of Jewish studies at the University of Massachusetts, "is that it won. It had set out in the mid-fifties to change the system of racial segregation in public places. With the passage of the 1964 Civil Rights Act, that was accomplished. In the early sixties, the movement set out to ensure that Blacks had access to the voting booth. With the passage of the 1965 Voting Rights Act, that was accomplished. Much is still needed to be done to implement and enforce those acts, but the legal principles of 'freedom and justice for all' had been reiterated and given a new formulation in law."

5   But then something remarkable—but largely unremarked—happened. The civil-rights movement shifted its focus to something called "human rights"—a quest not for constitutional guarantees but for changed attitudes.

6   The new focus "said, in effect, that the opinions, feelings and prejudices of private individuals was a legitimate target of political action," a reorientation that Lester finds not merely inappropriate—"a new statement of totalitarianism"—but dangerous.

7   "The shift from fighting for civil rights to fighting against racism," Lester told a recent audience of the National Forum Foundation in Washington, "was a shift from seeking and finding common ground to a position that has been disastrously divisive. To fight against racism divides humanity into us against them. It leads to a self-definition as 'victim,' and anyone who defines himself as a victim has found a way to keep himself in a perpetual state of self-righteous self-pity and anger. And that, in a nutshell, is the state of Black America today."

8   Has this former revolutionary become so content with his lofty academic position that he cannot see the racism that abounds in America? Does he counsel Black Americans to take no notice of the thoroughgoing racism that is a fact of their daily lives?

9   Not quite. His point is not to deny the existence of racism but to point out the inherently divisive effect of focusing on it, at least in terms of privately held biases.

10   "Racism is an issue in the public domain to the extent that it violates my rights as a citizen," he said. "And the society is still in the midst of trying to determine how we ascertain when that has occurred. This is much of what lies at the center of the debates on affirmative action." But there is no "right not to be bothered by racism. It would be nice. It is certainly desirable. But the fact remains, there is no right to be free from racism, anti-Semitism or sexism."

11   And yet it is the very attempt to force the eradication of "isms" from American life that may account for the racial strife on college campuses and elsewhere. What to Black students seems a reasonable demand—that their campuses be free of racist attitudes—may look to White students as demands for special privilege, special accommodations, special curriculums. As San Jose State's Shelby Steele has observed, there is political power in proving that you are the victim of racist attitudes.

12   But to sustain itself, that power requires that the victims go on celebrating their victimization, and it encourages other groups—women, ethnics, gays, even heterosexual white males—to establish themselves as victims as a means to countervailing political power. The result is to undermine the sense of community on campus.

13   Lester sees it as one of the critical differences between today's racial activism and that of the fifties and sixties.

14   "The impression is given today that the civil-rights movement was a Black movement. It was not. It was an integrated movement, and innumerable Whites also risked their lives and sanity for the principle of 'freedom and justice for all.'"

15   The civil-rights movement was a search for community, and its appeal was to commonality. Today's movement is a search for proof of victimization, and its appeal is to difference. And maybe that's why things seem so much worse than they used to be.

QUESTIONS AND EXERCISES

VOCABULARY
   1. resurgent (paragraph 1)
   2. bigotry (1)
   3. paradox (3)
   4. totalitarianism (6)
   5. perpetual (7)

6. inherently (9)
7. anti-Semitism (10)
8. eradication (11)
9. countervailing (12)
10. commonality (15)

LANGUAGE AND RHETORIC
1. The title of this selection is an allusion to Cervantes' *Don Quixote,* in which the hero confuses illusion with reality and does battle with windmills that he believes to be giants. How is the title relevant to this selection and the author's thesis?
2. The author relies heavily on Julius Lester as a source of, and support for, his own ideas in more than half his paragraphs. What are the advantages of this approach? What are the disadvantages?
3. This selection is included with three others to illustrate the use of comparison and contrast as a pattern of development, but the author also employs appeal to authority as noted in the previous item and the cause and effect pattern. Trace the use of one of these methods to show how the author supports his thesis with it.
4. The concluding paragraph of this selection not only brings it to a close, but it also contains the clearest statement of the author's thesis. Restate it in your own words.

DISCUSSION AND WRITING
1. In his opening paragraph, the author claims that about 90 percent of Black Americans believe that race relations are getting worse in this country rather than better. Several studies conducted on college campuses tend to confirm this view. Do you see any evidence to support it on your campus or in your community? Or do you see evidence that things are getting better? Whatever your response is, prepare a paper to support it. (In assessing the situation, be sure to consider the author's thesis.)
2. The author relies heavily on Julius Lester's ideas to develop his argument that we have shifted from "fighting for civil rights to fighting against racism." How do they define the difference? Write a paper in which you explore that difference and come to your own conclusion. Support it by examples familiar to you personally, library research, or the two in combination.
3. A great deal of research indicates that racial prejudice is learned. If so, what specific methods would you propose to overcome racism? Or, if you think it is impossible to overcome it, what are your reasons for taking that position?
4. If you have ever participated in, or contributed in any way to, a group or activity that might be considered as supporting or opposing racism, write a paper explaining why you did so and what the results were.

5. The author's primary source, Julius Lester, claims that "anyone who defines himself as a victim has found a way to keep himself in a perpetual state of . . . self-pity and anger. And that . . . is the state of Black America today." How do you respond to that statement? Do you agree or disagree? Support your answer with specific reasons and examples.

ALICE WALKER

Am I Blue?

"Ain't these tears in these
eyes tellin' you?"*

1   For about three years my companion and I rented a small house in the country that stood on the edge of a large meadow that appeared to run from the end of our deck straight into the mountains. The mountains, however, were quite far away, and between us and them there was, in fact, a town. It was one of the many pleasant aspects of the house that you never really were aware of this.

2   It was a house of many windows, low, wide, nearly floor to ceiling in the living room, which faced the meadow, and it was from one of these that I first saw our closest neighbor, a large white horse, cropping grass, flipping its mane, and ambling about—not over the entire meadow, which stretched well out of sight of the house, but over the five or so fenced-in acres that were next to the twenty-odd that we had rented. I soon learned that the horse, whose name was Blue, belonged to a man who lived in another town, but was boarded by our neighbor next door. Occasionally, one of the children, usually a stocky teen-ager, but sometimes a much younger girl or boy, could be seen riding Blue. They would appear in the meadow, climb up on his back, ride furiously for ten or fifteen minutes, then get off, slap Blue on the flanks, and not be seen again for a month or more.

3   There were many apple trees in our yard, and one by the fence that Blue could almost reach. We were soon in the habit of feeding him

apples, which he relished, especially because by the middle of summer the meadow grasses—so green and succulent since January—had dried out from lack of rain, and Blue stumbled about munching the dried stalks half-heartedly. Sometimes he would stand very still just by the apple tree, and when one of us came out he would whinny, snort loudly, or stamp the ground. This meant, of course: I want an apple.

4   It was quite wonderful to pick a few apples, or collect those that had fallen to the ground overnight, and patiently hold them, one by one, up to his large, toothy mouth. I remained as thrilled as a child by his flexible dark lips, huge, cubelike teeth that crunched the apples, core and all, with such finality, and his high, broad-breasted *enormity;* beside which, I felt small indeed. When I was a child, I used to ride horses, and was especially friendly with one named Nan until the day I was riding and my brother deliberately spooked her and I was thrown, head first, against the trunk of a tree. When I came to, I was in bed and my mother was bending worriedly over me; we silently agreed that perhaps horseback riding was not the safest sport for me. Since then I have walked, and prefer walking to horseback riding—but I had forgotten the depth of feeling one could see in horses' eyes.

5   I was therefore unprepared for the expression in Blue's. Blue was lonely. Blue was horribly lonely and bored. I was not shocked that this should be the case; five acres to tramp by yourself, endlessly, even in the most beautiful of meadows—and his was—cannot provide many interesting events, and once rainy season turned to dry that was about it. No, I was shocked that I had forgotten that human animals and nonhuman animals can communicate quite well; if we are brought up around animals as children we take this for granted. By the time we are adults we no longer remember. However, the animals have not changed. They are in fact *completed* creations (at least they seem to be, so much more than we) who are not likely *to* change; it is their nature to express themselves. What else are they going to express? And they do. And, generally speaking, they are ignored.

6   After giving Blue the apples, I would wander back to the house, aware that he was observing me. Were more apples not forthcoming then? Was that to be his sole entertainment for the day? My partner's small son had decided he wanted to learn how to piece a quilt; we worked in silence on our respective squares as I thought . . .

7   Well, about slavery: about White children, who were raised by Black people, who knew their first all-accepting love from Black women, and then, when they were twelve or so, were told they must "forget" the

deep levels of communication between themselves and "mammy" that they knew. Later they would be able to relate quite calmly, "My old mammy was sold to another good family" "My old mammy was _____ _____." Fill in the blank. Many more years later a White woman would say: "I can't understand these Negroes, these Blacks. What do they want? They're so different from us."

8   And about the Indians, considered to be "like animals" by the "settlers" (a very benign euphemism for what they actually were), who did not understand their description as a compliment.

9   And about the thousands of American men who marry Japanese, Korean, Filipina, and other non-English-speaking women and of how happy they report they are, "*blissfully,*" until their brides learn to speak English, at which point the marriages tend to fall apart. What then did the men see, when they looked into the eyes of the women they married, before they could speak English? Apparently only their own reflections.

10   I thought of society's impatience with the young. "Why are they playing the music so loud?" Perhaps the children have listened to much of the music of oppressed people their parents danced to before they were born, with its passionate but soft cries for acceptance and love, and they have wondered why their parents failed to hear.

11   I do not know how long Blue had inhabited his five beautiful, boring acres before we moved into our house; a year after we had arrived— and had also traveled to other valleys, other cities, other worlds—he was still there.

12   But then, in our second year at the house, something happened in Blue's life. One morning, looking out the window at the fog that lay like a ribbon over the meadow, I saw another horse, a brown one, at the other end of Blue's field. Blue appeared to be afraid of it, and for several days made no attempt to go near. We went away for a week. When we returned, Blue had decided to make friends and the two horses ambled over galloped along together, and Blue did not come nearly as often to the fence underneath the apple tree.

13   When he did, bringing his new friend with him, there was a different look in his eyes. A look of independence, of self-possession, of inalienable *horse*ness. His friend eventually became pregnant. For months and months there was, it seemed to me, a mutual feeling between me and the horses of justice, of peace. I fed apples to them both. The look in Blue's eyes was one of unabashed "this is *it*ness."

14   It did not, however, last forever. One day, after a visit to the city, I went out to give Blue some apples. He stood waiting, or so I thought,

though not beneath the tree. When I shook the tree and jumped back from the shower of apples, he made no move. I carried some over to him. He managed to half-crunch one. The rest he let fall to the ground. I dreaded looking into his eyes—because I had of course noticed that Brown, his partner, had gone—but I did look. If I had been born into slavery, and my partner had been sold or killed, my eyes would have looked like that. The children next door explained that Blue's partner had been "put with him" (the same expression that old people used, I had noticed, when speaking of an ancestor during slavery who had been impregnated by her owner) so that they could mate and she conceive. Since that was accomplished, she had been taken back by her owner, who lived somewhere else.

15 Will she be back? I asked.

16 They didn't know.

17 Blue was like a crazed person. Blue *was,* to me, a crazed person. He galloped furiously, as if he were being ridden, around and around his five beautiful acres. He whinnied until he couldn't. He tore at the ground with his hooves. He butted himself against his single shade tree. He looked always and always toward the road down which his partner had gone. And then, occasionally, when he came up for apples, or I took apples to him, he looked at me. It was a look so piercing, so full of grief, a look so *human,* I almost laughed (I felt too sad to cry) to think there are people who do not know that animals suffer. People like me who have forgotten, and daily forget, all that animals try to tell us. "Everything you do to us will happen to you; we are your teachers, as you are ours. We are one lesson" is essentially it, I think. There are those who never once have even considered animals' rights: those who have been taught that animals actually want to be used and abused by us, as small children "love" to be frightened, or women "love" to be mutilated and raped. . . . They are the great-grandchildren of those who honestly thought, because someone taught them this: "Women can't think," and "niggers can't faint." But most disturbing of all, in Blue's large brown eyes was a new look, more painful than the look of despair: the look of disgust with human beings, with life; the look of hatred. And it was odd what the look of hatred did. It gave him, for the first time, the look of a beast. And what that meant was that he had put up a barrier within to protect himself from further violence; all the apples in the world wouldn't change that fact.

18 And so Blue remained, a beautiful part of our landscape, very peaceful to look at from the window, white against the grass. Once a friend came to visit and said, looking out on the soothing view: "And

it *would* have to be a *white* horse; the very image of freedom." And I thought, yes, the animals are forced to become for us merely "images" of what they once so beautifully expressed. And we are used to drinking milk from containers showing "contented" cows, whose real lives we want to hear nothing about, eating eggs and drumsticks from "happy" hens, and munching hamburgers advertised by bulls of integrity who seem to command their fate.

19   As we talked of freedom and justice one day for all, we sat down to steaks. I am eating misery, I thought, as I took the first bite. And spit it out.

CHAPTER

Analysis (Division and Classification)

ERICH FROMM

Is Love an Art?

According to Erich Fromm, love is the only satisfactory answer to the problem of human existence, and yet most people have very little understanding of the nature of love. The following section, the first chapter from Dr. Fromm's book The Art of Loving, *considers the premises underlying most popular attitudes about love and urges that love be approached in the same searching spirit and with the same effort of will that characterizes the pursuit of any art.*

In terms of rhetorical techniques, the essay is noteworthy for its coherence, which is achieved in part by a careful enumeration of points and in part by effectively tying one paragraph to another.

1   Is love an art? Then it requires knowledge and effort. Or is love a pleasant sensation, which to experience is a matter of chance, something one "falls into" if one is lucky? This little book is based on the former premise, while undoubtedly the majority of people today believe in the latter.

2   Not that people think that love is not important. They are starved for it; they watch endless numbers of films about happy and unhappy love stories, they listen to hundreds of trashy songs about love—yet hardly anyone thinks that there is anything that needs to be learned about love.

3   This peculiar attitude is based on several premises which either singly or combined tend to uphold it. Most people see the problem of love primarily as that of *being loved,* rather than that of *loving,* of one's capacity to love. Hence the problem to them is how to be loved, how to be lovable. In pursuit of this aim they follow several paths. One,

363

which is especially used by men, is to be successful, to be as powerful and rich as the social margin of one's position permits. Another, used especially by women, is to make oneself attractive, by cultivating one's body, dress, etc. Other ways of making oneself attractive, used both by men and women, are to develop pleasant manners, interesting conversation, to be helpful, modest, inoffensive. Many of the ways to make oneself lovable are the same as those used to make oneself successful, "to win friends and influence people." As a matter of fact, what most people in our culture mean by being lovable is essentially a mixture between being popular and having sex appeal.

4   A second premise behind the attitude that there is nothing to be learned about love is the assumption that the problem of love is the problem of an *object,* not the problem of a faculty. People think that to *love* is simple, but that to find the right object to love—or to be loved— is difficult. This attitude has several reasons rooted in the development of modern society. One reason is the great change which occurred in the twentieth century with respect to the choice of a "love object." In the Victorian age, as in many traditional cultures, love was mostly not a spontaneous personal experience which then might lead to marriage. On the contrary, marriage was contracted by convention—either by the respective families, or by a marriage broker, or without the help of such intermediaries; it was concluded on the basis of social considerations, and love was supposed to develop once the marriage had been concluded. In the last few generations the concept of romantic love has become almost universal in the Western world. In the United States, while considerations of a conventional nature are not entirely absent, to a vast extent people are in search of "romantic love," of the personal experience of love which then should lead to marriage. This new concept of freedom in love must have greatly enhanced the importance of the *object* as against the importance of the *function.*

5   Closely related to this factor is another feature characteristic of contemporary culture. Our whole culture is based on the appetite for buying, on the idea of a mutually favorably exchange. Modern man's happiness consists in the thrill of looking at the shop windows, and in buying all that he can afford to buy, either for cash or on installments. He (or she) looks at people in a similar way. For the man an attractive girl—and for the woman an attractive man—are the prizes they are after. "Attractive" usually means a nice package of qualities which are popular and sought after on the personality market. What specifically makes a person attractive depends on the fashion of the time, physically as well as mentally. During the twenties, a drinking and smoking girl, tough and sexy, was attractive; today the fashion demands more domesticity and coyness. At the end of the nineteenth and the beginning of

this century, a man had to be aggressive and ambitious—today he has to be social and tolerant—in order to be an attractive "package." At any rate, the sense of falling in love develops usually only with regard to such human commodities as are within reach of one's own possibilities for exchange. I am out for a bargain; the object should be desirable from the standpoint of its social value, and at the same time should want me, considering my overt and hidden assets and potentialities. Two persons thus fall in love when they feel they have found the best object available on the market, considering the limitations of their own exchange values. Often, as in buying real estate, the hidden potentialities which can be developed play a considerable role in this bargain. In a culture in which the marketing orientation prevails, and in which material success is the outstanding value, there is little reason to be surprised that human love relations follow the same pattern of exchange which governs the commodity and the labor market.

6   The third error leading to the assumption that there is nothing to be learned about love lies in the confusion between the initial experience of "*falling*" in love, and the permanent state of *being* in love, or as we might better say, of "standing" in love. If two people who have been strangers, as all of us are, suddenly let the wall between them break down, and feel close, feel one, this moment of oneness is one of the most exhilarating, most exciting experiences in life. It is all the more wonderful and miraculous for persons who have been shut off, isolated, without love. This miracle of sudden intimacy is often facilitated if it is combined with, or initiated by, sexual attraction and consummation. However, this type of love is by its very nature not lasting. The two persons become well acquainted, their intimacy loses more and more its miraculous character, until their antagonism, their disappointments, their mutual boredom kill whatever is left of the initial excitement. Yet, in the beginning they do not know all this: in fact, they take the intensity of the infatuation, this being "crazy" about each other, for proof of the intensity of their love, while it may only prove the degree of their preceding loneliness.

7   This attitude—that nothing is easier than to love—has continued to be the prevalent idea about love in spite of the overwhelming evidence to the contrary. There is hardly any activity, any enterprise, which is started with such tremendous hopes and expectations, and yet, which fails so regularly, as love. If this were the case with any other activity, people would be eager to know the reasons for the failure, and to learn how one could do better—or they would give up the activity. Since the latter is impossible in the case of love, there seems to be only one adequate way to overcome the failure of love—to examine the reasons for this failure, and to proceed to study the meaning of love.

8   The first step to take is to become aware that *love is an art,* just as living is an art; if we want to learn how to love we must proceed in the same way we have to proceed if we want to learn any other art, say music, painting, carpentry, or the art of medicine or engineering.

9   What are the necessary steps in learning any art?

10   The process of learning an art can be divided conveniently into two parts: one, the mastery of the theory; the other, the mastery of the practice. If I want to learn the art of medicine, I must first know the facts about the human body, and about various diseases. When I have all this theoretical knowledge, I am by no means competent in the art of medicine. I shall become a master in this art only after a great deal of practice, until eventually the results of my theoretical knowledge and the results of my practice are blended into one—my intuition, the essence of the mastery of any art. But, aside from learning the theory and practice, there is a third factor necessary to becoming a master in any art—the mastery of the art must be a matter of ultimate concern; there must be nothing else in the world more important than the art. This holds true for music, for medicine, for carpentry—and for love. And, maybe, here lies the answer to the question of why people in our culture try so rarely to learn this art, in spite of their obvious failures: in spite of the deep-seated craving for love, almost everything else is considered to be more important than love: success, prestige, money, power—almost all our energy is used for the learning of how to achieve these aims, and almost none to learn the art of loving.

11   Could it be that only those things are considered worthy of being learned with which one can earn money or prestige, and that love, which "only" profits the soul, but is profitless in the modern sense, is a luxury we have no right to spend much energy on?

QUESTIONS AND EXERCISES

VOCABULARY
1. premise (paragraph 1)
2. intermediaries (4)
3. mutually (5)
4. domesticity (5)
5. coyness (5)
6. facilitated (6)
7. consummation (6)
8. antagonism (6)
9. prevalent (7)
10. theoretical (10)

LANGUAGE AND RHETORIC

1. The coherence in this essay is derived in part from the author's constant attempts to clarify relationships by means of analysis. Point out specific examples of this practice.
2. Coherence is also established by the manner in which one paragraph is tied to another. Examine the first sentence of each paragraph, and show how many of these sentences employ transitional devices.
3. Could paragraphs 1 and 2 be combined? Why are they presented as separate paragraphs?
4. Analyze paragraphs 3, 4, and 5 in terms of the topic sentence and the controlling idea for each.

DISCUSSION AND WRITING

1. According to the author, how do most people define love? How does he define it? Write an essay in which you define love as you understand it. You might try using types, steps, or stages to help organize your paper.
2. The author enumerates some of the ways in which people seek to make themselves lovable. What are some of the ways that he does not mention? Develop a list of such ways as a possible source for a paper on the subject.
3. Discuss the advantages and disadvantages of each of the two approaches to marital love mentioned in paragraph 4—the traditional idea of the marriage contract that would hopefully give rise to love and the modern idea of romantic love as a motive for marriage. Write a paper in which you enumerate the reasons why you believe one method is superior to the other.
4. If you are prepared to accept what the author suggests about "the art of loving," what specific things can you do to act in accord with his ideas? How, apart from reading Dr. Fromm's book, might you go about mastering the "art"? Make a list of the things that might be done and use it as the basis for an essay of your own.

JUDY BRADY

Why I Want a Wife

If a woman's "proper place" is in the home as a "housewife," Judy Brady says she would like to take advantage of those services too—but from a male perspective. Why would a woman want a wife? Brady offers a host of reasons as she raises some fundamental questions about sex roles and responsibilities in the American family.

As you read, notice how the author adapts the title as a recurring line to organize her essay, and enumerates the "duties" of a housewife accordingly.

1 **I** belong to that classification of people known as wives. I am A Wife. And, not altogether incidentally, I am a mother.

2 Not too long ago a male friend of mine appeared on the scene from the Midwest fresh from a recent divorce. He had one child, who is, of course, with his ex-wife. He is obviously looking for another wife. As I thought about him while I was ironing one evening, it suddenly occurred to me that I, too, would like to have a wife. Why do I want a wife?

3 I would like to go back to school so that I can become economically independent, support myself, and, if need be, support those dependent upon me. I want a wife who will work and send me to school. And while I am going to school I want a wife to take care of my children. I want a wife to keep track of the children's doctor and dentist appointments. And to keep track of mine, too. I want a wife to make sure my children eat properly and are kept clean. I want a wife who will wash the children's clothes and keep them mended. I want a wife who is a good nurturant attendant to my children, arranges for their schooling, makes sure that they have an adequate social life with their peers, takes them to the park, the zoo, etc. I want a wife who takes care of the children when they are sick, a wife who arranges to be around when the children need special care, because, of course, I cannot miss classes at school. My wife must arrange to lose time at work and not lose the job. It may mean a small cut in my wife's income from time to time, but I guess I can tolerate that. Needless to say, my wife will arrange and pay for the care of the children while my wife is working.

4 I want a wife who will take care of *my* physical needs. I want a wife who will keep my house clean. A wife who will pick up after my children, a wife who will pick up after me. I want a wife who will keep my clothes clean, ironed, mended, replaced when need be, and who will see to it that my personal things are kept in their proper place so that I can find what I need the minute I need it. I want a wife who cooks the meals, a wife who is a *good* cook. I want a wife who will plan the menus, do the necessary grocery shopping, prepare the meals, serve them pleasantly, and then do the cleaning up while I do my studying. I want a wife who will care for me when I am sick and sympathize with my pain and loss of time from school. I want a wife

to go along when our family takes a vacation so that someone can continue to care for me and my children when I need a rest and a change of scene.

5   I want a wife who will not bother me with rambling complaints about a wife's duties. But I want a wife who will listen to me when I feel the need to explain a rather difficult point I have come across in my course of studies. And I want a wife who will type my papers for me when I have written them.

6   I want a wife who will take care of the details of my social life. When my wife and I are invited out by my friends, I want a wife who will take care of the babysitting arrangements. When I meet people at school that I like and want to entertain, I want a wife who will have the house clean, will prepare a special meal, serve it to me and my friends, and not interrupt when I talk about the things that interest me and my friends. I want a wife who will have arranged that the children are fed and ready for bed before my guests arrive so that the children do not bother us. I want a wife who takes care of the needs of my guests so that they feel comfortable, who makes sure that they have an ashtray, that they are passed the hors d'oeuvres, that they are offered a second helping of the food, that their wine glasses are replenished when necessary, that their coffee is served to them as they like it. And I want a wife who knows that sometimes I need a night out by myself.

7   I want a wife who is sensitive to my sexual needs, a wife who makes love passionately and eagerly when I feel like it, a wife who makes sure that I am satisfied. And, of course, I want a wife who will not demand sexual attention when I am not in the mood for it. I want a wife who assumes the complete responsibility for birth control, because I do not want more children. I want a wife who will remain sexually faithful to me so that I do not have to clutter up my intellectual life with jealousies. And I want a wife who understands that *my* sexual needs may entail more than strict adherence to monogamy. I must, after all, be able to relate to people as fully as possible.

8   If, by chance, I find another person more suitable as a wife than the wife I already have, I want the liberty to replace my present wife with another one. Naturally, I will expect a fresh, new life; my wife will take the children and be solely responsible for them so that I am left free.

9   When I am through with school and have acquired a job, I want my wife to quit working and remain at home so that my wife can more fully and completely take care of a wife's duties.

10   My God, who *wouldn't* want a wife?

QUESTIONS AND EXERCISES

VOCABULARY
1. nurturant (paragraph 3)
2. hors d'oeuvres (6)
3. monogamy (7)

LANGUAGE AND RHETORIC
1. What is the tone of this essay? What elements in the essay reflect that tone?
2. The organizational pattern of this piece is based on repetition of the line "I want a wife," followed by a series of clauses. What effect does this technique have on the reader?
3. Review the author's paragraphing. Can you justify the introduction of each new paragraph? Can you suggest any alternatives to the author's pattern?
4. Brady uses sentence fragments in paragraphs 3 and 4. Point them out and comment on their appropriateness. Could she have achieved the same effect in some other way?
5. What is the author's purpose in writing this essay, and to what extent has she succeeded in fulfilling it? Support your answer.

DISCUSSION AND WRITING
1. Consider your family life as you were growing up. To what extent does this essay reflect the role of wife and husband in your household. Write a paper reflecting those roles and relationships in light of Brady's thesis.
2. If you are—or have been—a wife, write a response to this essay in terms of your own experience. If you are—or have been—a husband, write *your* response to it.
3. Write an essay based on this model in which you pursue the reasons why you want a wife or a husband.

JAMES BALDWIN
On Being "White" . . . and Other Lies

The superiority assumed by some White people over other Americans rests in large part on pigmentation. Stated another way, racism in America— whether individual or institutional—is based on skin color. But what in fact is this "White race," where did it come from, who created it, and why? Novelist and essayist James Baldwin raises these questions in the following selection and offers some obvious but easily ignored answers.

Baldwin employs definition as well as analysis to develop his argument, but the latter is the key to his thesis. Examine carefully his specific use of classification for this purpose.

1   The crisis of leadership in the White community is remarkable—and terrifying—because there is, in fact, no White community.

2   This may seem an enormous statement—and it is. I'm willing to be challenged. I'm also willing to attempt to spell it out.

3   My frame of reference is, of course, America, or that portion of the North American continent that calls itself America. And this means I am speaking, essentially, of the European vision of the world—or more precisely, perhaps, the European vision of the universe. It is a vision as remarkable for what it pretends to include as for what it remorselessly diminishes, demolishes or leaves totally out of account.

4   There is, for example—at least, in principle—an Irish community: here, there, anywhere, or, more precisely, Belfast, Dublin and Boston. There is a German community: both sides of Berlin, Bavaria and Yorkville. There is an Italian community: Rome, Naples, the Bank of the Holy Ghost, and Mulberry Street. And there is a Jewish community, stretching from Jerusalem to California to New York. There are English communities. There are French communities. There are Swiss consortiums. There are Poles: in Warsaw (where they would like us to be friends) and in Chicago (where because they are White we are enemies). There are, for that matter, Indian restaurants, and Turkish baths. There is the underworld—the poor (to say nothing of those who intend to become rich) are always with us—but this does not describe a community. It bears terrifying witness to what happened to everyone who got here, and paid the price of the ticket. The price was to become "White." No one was White before he/she came to America. It took generations, and a vast amount of coercion, before this became a White country.

5   It is probable that it is the Jewish community—or more accurately, perhaps, its remnants—that in America has paid the highest and most extraordinary price for becoming White. For the Jews came here from countries where they were not White, and they came here, in part, *because* they were not White; and incontestably—in the eyes of the Black American (and not only in those eyes) American Jews have opted to

become White, and this is how they operate. It was ironical to hear, for example, former Israeli prime minister Menachem Begin declare some time ago that "the Jewish people bow only to God" while knowing that the state of Israel is sustained by a blank check from Washington. Without further pursuing the implication of this mutual act of faith, one is nevertheless aware that the Jewish translation into a White American can sustain the state of Israel in a way that the Black presence, here, can scarcely hope—at least, not yet—to halt the slaughter in South Africa.

6   And there is a reason for that.

7   America became White—the people who, as they claim, "settled" the country became White—because of the necessity of denying the Black presence, and justifying the Black subjugation. No community can be based on such a principle—or, in other words, no community can be established on so genocidal a lie. White men—from Norway, for example, where they were *Norwegians*—became White: by slaughtering the cattle, poisoning the wells, torching the houses, massacring Native Americans, raping Black women.

8   This moral erosion has made it quite impossible for those who think of themselves as White in this country to have any moral authority at all—privately, or publicly. The multitudinous bulk of them sit, stunned, before their TV sets, swallowing garbage that they know to be garbage, and—in a profound and unconscious effort to justify this torpor that disguises a profound and bitter panic—pay a vast amount of attention to athletics: even though they know that the football player (the Son of the Republic, *their* sons!) is merely another aspect of the money-making scheme. They are either relieved or embittered by the presence of the Black boy on the team. I do not know if they remember how long and hard they fought to keep him off it. I know that they do not dare have any notion of the price Black people (mothers and fathers) paid and pay. They do not want to know the meaning, or face the shame, of what they compelled—out of what they took as the necessity of being White—Joe Louis or Jackie Robinson or Cassius Clay (aka Muhammad Ali) to pay. I know that they, themselves, would not have liked to pay it.

9   There has never been a labor movement in this country, the proof being the absence of a Black presence in the so-called father-to-son unions. There are, perhaps, some niggers in the window; but Blacks have no power in the labor unions.

10   Just so does the White community, as a means of keeping itself White, elect, as they imagine, their political (!) representatives. No

nation in the world, including England, is represented by so stunning a pantheon of the relentlessly mediocre. I will not name names—I will leave that to you.

11   But this cowardice, this necessity of justifying a totally false identity and of justifying what must be called a genocidal history, has placed everyone now living into the hands of the most ignorant and powerful people the world has ever seen: And how did they get that way?

12   By deciding that they were White. By opting for safety instead of life. By persuading themselves that a Black child's life meant nothing compared with a White child's life. By abandoning their children to the things White men could buy. By informing their children that Black women, Black men and Black children had no human integrity that those who call themselves White were bound to respect. And in this debasement and definition of Black people, they debased and defined themselves.

13   And have brought humanity to the edge of oblivion; because they think they are White. Because they think they are White, they do not dare confront the ravage and the lie of their history. Because they think they are White, they cannot allow themselves to be tormented by the suspicion that all men are brothers. Because they think they are White, they are looking for, or bombing into existence, stable populations, cheerful natives and cheap labor. Because they think they are White, they believe, as even no child believes, in the dream of safety. Because they think they are White, however vociferous they may be and however multitudinous, they are as speechless as Lot's wife—looking backward, changed into a pillar of salt.

14   However—! White being, absolutely, a moral choice (for there *are* no White people), the crisis of leadership for those of us whose identity has been forged, or branded, as Black is nothing new. We—who were not Black before we got here either, who were defined as Black by the slave trade—have paid for the crisis of leadership in the White community for a very long time, and have resoundingly, even when we face the worst about ourselves, survived and triumphed over it. If we had not survived, and triumphed, there would not be a Black American alive.

15   And the fact that we are still here—even in suffering, darkness, danger, endlessly defined by those who do not dare define, or even confront, themselves—is the key to the crisis in White leadership. The past informs us of various kinds of people—criminals, adventurers and saints, to say nothing, of course, of popes—but it is the Black condition, and only that, which informs us concerning White people.

It is a terrible paradox, but those who believed that they could control and define Black people divested themselves of the power to control and define themselves.

QUESTIONS AND EXERCISES

VOCABULARY
1. remorselessly (paragraph 3)
2. consortiums (4)
3. incontestably (5)
4. subjugation (7)
5. multitudinous (8)
6. pantheon (10)
7. vociferous (13)

LANGUAGE AND RHETORIC
1. What kind of audience do you think Baldwin had in mind for this essay, and how can you tell?
2. Describe the author's tone. Point out specific words, lines, and passages that reveal it to you.
3. Comment on the title of this piece. How do you respond to it, and why? Would another title have been as effective? Suggest at least one of your own.
4. Show how the author employs analysis as a primary method to develop his thesis.

DISCUSSION AND WRITING
1. James Baldwin has been called "an enduring menace to White supremacy." What is meant by that statement? Does this essay reinforce that description? Why or why not?
2. Baldwin argues that there is a "crisis of leadership in the White community" and attributes the source of that problem to the conditions described here. In your opinion, is there any logical basis for him to come to that conclusion? Do you agree with it or not? If yes, write a paper in which you use examples of contemporary White leaders to illustrate your point. If no, write one focusing on a single White leader you believe to be an exception to Baldwin's thesis.
3. Read some of Baldwin's other essays, which should be readily available in your campus library. You might begin with his book *The Fire Next Time*. See if Baldwin is consistent in his thinking on this subject and write a paper in which you classify several of the ideas that are central to his thinking.

MANUEL J. MARTINEZ

The Art of the Chicano Movement, and the Movement of Chicano Art

1   To understand the present cultural values of our people, it is necessary to understand the history of Mexico, to which we are still closely related. Mexican history and artistic expressions that bring life and cultural nationalism within emotional grasp.

2   Unlike many of the styles of contemporary art, many concepts and forms of Chicano art come from its own traditions. This is not to say that Chicano art is an imitation of Indian, Spanish, or Modern Mexican art, in technique or otherwise. The most *ancient* art of our history is purely Indian and is still considered the natural and most vital source of inspiration. Then following the conquest of Mexico came Colonial art which is based fundamentally on Spanish-European principles of the sixteenth and seventeenth centuries. And then came the Modern Mexican art movement dominated by artists who were Mestizo (the offspring of Indian and Spanish blood) and whose work has both Indian and European influences.

3   Chicano art is a newborn baby with Ancient Indian art as a mother, Spanish Colonial art as a father and Modern Mexican art as a midwife. Or we can see it as a branch extending out into the southwest United States from the great Bronze Tree of Mexican art. Taking the roots of that tree for granted as being Indian and Spanish, we can move up to the trunk of the tree which is known as Modern Mexican art.

4   It would be wrong if we first looked up definitions of art in textbooks and then used them to determine the past principles from the modern artistic movement of Mexico. We should start from historical facts, not from abstract definitions.

5   What are some of the historical and artistic facts of the modern art movement in Mexico? Or, from the Mexican point of view what are some of the significant features in the development of this movement? Despite all the conflict, confusion, and bloodshed of the Mexican Revolution, it created a new spirit. A revolutionary spirit that inspired new leadership and began to be felt and expressed by the writers, the musicians, the poets and the painters. Each felt that it was his duty and privilege to share his talents in the social cause of bringing about a new Mexico. Art for art's sake began to die. The new art would no longer serve as a privilege of the rich or a mere decoration. Since

Mexico was largely illiterate, painting had to become the medium of visual education, monumental in size, and become public property.

6   Some of the more advanced artists and pioneers of this new aesthetic concept formed a group in 1922 known as the "Syndicate of painters, sculptors, and intellectual workers." Among those who allied themselves into this group and who brought forth the first original expression of Modern art on this continent were: Ramon Alva de la Canal, Jean Charlot, Fernando Leal, Xavier Guerrero, Carlos Medina, Roberto Montenegro, Jose Clemente Orozco, Fermin Revueltas, Diego Rivera, David Alfaro Sigueiros, and Maximo Pacheco.

7   The open-mindedness and foresight of Jose Vasconcelos, minister of education, must be given credit for opening the doors to the usefulness of monumental painting on the walls of public buildings. Under his program, Vasconcelos patronized the artists and they were given but one instruction: to paint Mexican subjects. It was the first collective attempt at mural painting in Modern art.

8   Then followed the fruits of the "Mexican Renaissance": the rebirth of creative enthusiasm and a time for the people to again recognize human values and their expressions in a creative form.

9   The Mexican painters have shown in their work the long and exciting history of the Mexican people. Great murals were done by men who sought truth and justice for their people and all of humanity. Mexican Modern art was essentially an art of the Revolution. Nowhere else in the world can the people of a country see so much of their own story told pictorially on the big walls of their public buildings.

10   Like the modern art of Mexico, the new Chicano art is essentially an art of social protest. Generally speaking, however, there are two types of Chicano art. The first is an art that makes up the cultural front of the Chicano movement that is sweeping the Southwest, an art that reflects the greatness and sacrifices of our past, an art that clarifies and intensifies the present desires of a people who will no longer be taken for granted as second class citizens and whose time has come to stand up and fight for what is rightfully theirs as human beings.

11   The art of the Chicano movement serves as a shield to preserve and protect our cultural values from the mechanical shark of this society, that has been chewing and spitting out our beautiful language, music, literature, and art for over a hundred years. The artists use their own media in their own way to strengthen the unity of our people and they help to educate us about ourselves since the educational system has failed to do so.

12   The other type of Chicano art is created by artists who find it difficult to allow themselves to be used by any cause, by any institution, or

by any government. They realize that the artist has spent centuries to free himself from the domination of a social hierarchy, the church, or government control. They love the past but refuse to be trapped by it. Their primary interest is to convey a point of view or an idea, whereas the Chicano artist of the movement generally uses any method to achieve his goal.

13   The Chicano artist who refuses to plunge into the movement, yet wishes to deal with social concerns in this society, cannot escape the realities in his life, in the lives of people around him, and in the times in which he lives. These things will inevitably begin to show in his work. Art works that are characterized as works of social protest are really just the product of the artist having to deal with the realities he sees. How does he respond to these realities? He writes a poem, a play, a song; he paints a picture, a mural; or models clay or wax.

14   The Chicano artist will work with his own "raw materials" of his social concerns in his own way. Most importantly, the artist is devoted to his art, and he loves color, form, composition, structure, and rhythm.

15   There are times when the Chicano artist, like other people, attempts to escape his humanness but cannot. His commitment is to himself and to humanity. He loves art and he loves his people. It is this love for humanity that he can reveal to others and in doing so help fulfill their humanness. This does not mean that he is not going to reveal the countless evils of our life but rather to show you that we must get back our humanness if we are to live in this world peacefully.

Analysis (Process)

NATALIE GOLDBERG

Writing as a Practice

In Part One of this textbook, we point out that there are no simple mechanical rules to follow in writing, that a system that works well for one writer may not work well for another. Although for the most part we take a particular structured approach in the overall text ourselves, we recognize there are indeed a variety of valid approaches. In the next four selections, beginning with this one from Natalie Goldberg's Writing down the Bones, *we present some other angles of approach to the writing process.*

The sub-title of the author's book is "Freeing the Writer Within." Think about the relevance of that sub-title as you read.

1 This is the practice school of writing. Like running, the more you do it, the better you get at it. Some days you don't want to run and you resist every step of the three miles, but you do it anyway. You practice whether you want to or not. You don't wait around for inspiration and a deep desire to run. It'll never happen, especially if you are out of shape and have been avoiding it. But if you run regularly, you train your mind to cut through or ignore your resistance. You just do it. And in the middle of the run, you love it. When you come to the end, you never want to stop. And you stop, hungry for the next time.

2 That's how writing is, too. Once you're deep into it, you wonder what took you so long to finally settle down at the desk. Through practice you actually do get better. You learn to trust your deep self more and not give in to your voice that wants to avoid writing. It is odd that we never question the feasibility of a football team practicing long hours for one game; yet in writing we rarely give ourselves the space for practice.

3   When you write, don't say, "I'm going to write a poem." That attitude will freeze you right away. Sit down with the least expectation of
yourself; say, "I am free to write the worst junk in the world." You
have to give yourself the space to write a lot without a destination.
I've had students who said they decided they were going to write the
great American novel and haven't written a line since. If every time
you sat down, you expected something great, writing would always be
a great disappointment. Plus that expectation would also keep you
from writing.

4   My rule is to finish a notebook a month. (I'm always making up
writing guidelines for myself.) Simply to fill it. That is the practice.
My ideal is to write every day. I say it is my ideal. I am careful not to
pass judgment or create anxiety if I don't do that. No one lives up to
his ideal.

5   In my notebooks I don't bother with the side margin or the one at
the top: I fill the whole page. I am not writing anymore for a teacher or
for school. I am writing for myself first and I don't have to stay within
my limits, not even margins. This gives me a psychological freedom
and permission. And when my writing is on and I'm really cooking, I
usually forget about punctuation, spelling, etc. I also notice that my
handwriting changes. It becomes larger and looser.

6   Often I can look around the room at my students as they write and
can tell which ones are really on and present at a given time in their
writing. They are more intensely involved and their bodies are hanging
loose. Again, it is like running. There's little resistance when the run is
good. All of you is moving; there's no you separate from the runner. In
writing, when you are truly on, there's no writer, no paper, no pen, no
thoughts. Only writing does writing—everything else is gone.

7   One of the main aims in writing practice is to learn to trust your
own mind and body; to grow patient and nonaggressive. Art lives in
the Big World. One poem or story doesn't matter one way or the other.
It's the process of writing and life that matters. Too many writers have
written great books and gone insane or alcoholic or killed themselves.
This process teaches about sanity. We are trying to become sane along
with our poems and stories.

8   Chögyam Trungpa, Rinpoche, a Tibetan Buddhist master, said, "We
must continue to open in the face of tremendous opposition. No one is
encouraging us to open and still we must peel away the layers of the
heart." It is the same with this way of practice writing: We must continue to open and trust in our own voice and process. Ultimately, if
the process is good, the end will be good. You will get good writing.

9   A friend once said that when she had a good black-and-white drawing that she was going to add color to, she always practiced first on a few drawings she didn't care about in order to warm up. This writing practice is also a warmup for anything else you might want to write. It is the bottom line, the most primitive, essential beginning of writing. The trust you learn in your own voice can be directed then into a business letter, a novel, a Ph.D. dissertation, a play, a memoir. But it is something you must come back to again and again. Don't think, "I got it! I know how to write. I trust my voice. I'm off to write the great American novel." It's good to go off and write a novel, but don't stop doing writing practice. It is what keeps you in tune, like a dancer who does warmups before dancing or a runner who does stretches before running. Runners don't say, "Oh, I ran yesterday. I'm limber." Each day they warm up and stretch.

10   Writing practice embraces your whole life and doesn't demand any logical form: no Chapter 19 following the action in Chapter 18. It's a place that you can come to wild and unbridled, mixing the dream of your grandmother's soup with the astounding clouds outside your window. It is undirected and has to do with all of you right in your present moment. Think of writing practice as loving arms you come to illogically and incoherently. It's our wild forest where we gather energy before going to prune our garden, write our fine books and novels. It's a continual practice.

11   Sit down right now. Give me this moment. Write whatever's running through you. You might start with "this moment" and end up writing about the gardenia you wore at your wedding seven years ago. That's fine. Don't try to control it. Stay present with whatever comes up, and keep your hand moving.

QUESTIONS AND EXERCISES

VOCABULARY
1. feasibility (paragraph 2)
2. anxiety (4)
3. dissertation (9)
4. memoir (9)
5. unbridled (10)

LANGUAGE AND RHETORIC
1. What does "this" refer to in the opening sentence? In the absence of a larger context, that is, the book from which this selection is taken, can you tell? Is "this" understood as you continue to read?

2. In paragraphs 4–7, the author uses herself as an example. Considering that it comes from a book on writing, does this personal perspective add to or distract from the focus of this particular selection? Support your answer.

3. In addition to process analysis, the author uses comparison as a method of development, specifically the comparison between writing and running. How do the two methods work together to develop the author's ideas?

4. Is the author's purpose to explain the process, to convince you to use it, or both? Could she discuss the process without encouraging you to use it? Could she convince you to use it without explaining the process? Which purpose, then, do you see as central to the selection?

DISCUSSION AND WRITING

1. Some students say they want more structure, feedback, and direction than the "practice school of writing" provides. How do you think the author might respond to them? Since few, if any, teachers read and react to all that you might write under these conditions, what options and alternatives are available?

2. If you have ever kept a diary, journal, or writing notebook, how useful have you found it to be? What purposes did it serve for you? What limitations did it have? Would you recommend keeping one to anyone else? Why or why not?

3. Write a paper in which you explain a process that has helped you improve your writing. Be sure to clarify what the method was intended to achieve, how it was done, and how or why it helped you.

4. Take the author up on her challenge in the last paragraph. Do what she calls for and see what potential it might hold for you. Remember that no single unsustained effort is likely to prove much or be very productive. You'll need to keep practicing. But you've got to start sometime.

PETER ELBOW

Freewriting

Despite the irony of the title and the author's particular desire to help students not enrolled in writing classes, Peter Elbow's book Writing Without Teachers *has had an important influence on writing instructors throughout the nation over the past decade. The first chapter of that brief volume is devoted to freewriting, a process for helping the would-be writer generate words and ideas.*

In this selection from that chapter, Elbow explains the process and how it helps the writer.

Perhaps the best measure of the effectiveness of Elbow's essay might be for you to use his explanation as the basis for practicing some freewriting exercises yourself.

1   The most effective way I know to improve your writing is to do freewriting exercises regularly. At least three times a week. They are sometimes called "automatic writing," "babbling," or "jabbering" exercises. The idea is simply to write for ten minutes (later on, perhaps fifteen or twenty). Don't stop for anything. Go quickly without rushing. Never stop to look back, to cross something out, to wonder how to spell something, to wonder what word or thought to use, or to think about what you are doing. If you can't think of a word or a spelling, just use a squiggle or else write, "I can't think of it." Just put down something. The easiest thing is just to put down whatever is in your mind. If you get stuck it's fine to write "I can't think what to say, I can't think what to say" as many times as you want; or repeat the last word you wrote over and over again; or anything else. The only requirement is that you *never* stop.

2   What happens to a freewriting exercise is important. It must be a piece of writing which, even if someone reads it, doesn't send any ripples back to you. It is like writing something and putting it in a bottle in the sea. The teacherless class helps your writing by providing maximum feedback. Freewritings help you by providing no feedback at all. When I assign one, I invite the writer to let me read it. But also tell him to keep it if he prefers. I read it quickly and make no comments at all and I do not speak with him about it. The main thing is that a freewriting must never be evaluated in any way; in fact there must be no discussion or comment at all.

3   Here is an example of a fairly coherent exercise (sometimes they are very incoherent, which is fine):

> I think I'll write what's on my mind, but the only thing on my mind right now is what to write for ten minutes. I've never done this before and I'm not prepared in any way—the sky is cloudy today, how's that? now I'm afraid I won't be able to think of what to write when I get to the end of the sentence—well, here I am at the end of the sentence—here I am again, again, again, again, at least I'm still writing—Now I ask is there some reason to be

happy that I'm still writing—ah yes! Here comes the question again—What am I getting out of this? What point is there in it? It's almost obscene to always ask it but I seem to question everything that way and I was gonna say something else pertaining to that but I got so busy writing down the first part that I forgot what I was leading into. This is kind of fun oh don't stop writing—cars and trucks speeding by somewhere out the window, pens clittering across peoples' papers. The sky is still cloudy—is it symbolic that I should be mentioning it? Huh? I dunno. Maybe I should try colors, blue, red, dirty words—wait a minute—no can't do that, orange, yellow, arm tired, green pink violet magenta lavender red brown black green—now that I can't think of any more colors—just about done—relief? Maybe.

4   Freewriting may seem crazy but actually it makes simple sense. Think of the difference between speaking and writing. Writing has the advantage of permitting more editing. But that's its downfall too. Almost everybody interposes a massive and complicated series of editings between the time words start to be born into consciousness and when they finally come off the end of the pencil or typewriter onto the page. This is partly because schooling makes us obsessed with the "mistakes" we make in writing. Many people are constantly thinking about spelling and grammar as they try to write. I am always thinking about the awkwardness, wordiness, and general mushiness of my natural verbal product as I try to write down words.

5   But it's not just "mistakes" or "bad writing" we edit as we write. We also edit unacceptable thoughts and feelings, as we do in speaking. In writing there is more time to do it so the editing is heavier: when speaking, there's someone right there waiting for a reply and he'll get bored or think we're crazy if we don't come out with *something*. Most of the time in speaking, we settle for the catch-as-catch-can way in which the words tumble out. In writing, however, there's a chance to try to get them right. But the opportunity to get them right is a terrible burden: you can work for two hours trying to get a paragraph "right" and discover it's not right at all. And then give up.

6   Editing, *in itself,* is not the problem. Editing is usually necessary if we want to end up with something satisfactory. The problem is that editing goes on *at the same time* as producing. The editor is, as it were, constantly looking over the shoulder of the producer and constantly fiddling with what he's doing while he's in the middle of trying to do it. No wonder the producer gets nervous, jumpy, inhibited, and finally can't be coherent. It's an unnecessary burden to try to think of words and also worry at the same time whether they're the right words.

7   The main thing about freewriting is that it is *nonediting*. It is an exercise in bringing together the process of producing words and putting them down on the page. Practiced regularly, it undoes the ingrained habit of editing at the same time you are trying to produce. It will make writing less blocked because words will come more easily. You will use up more paper, but chew up fewer pencils.

8   Next time you write, notice how often you stop yourself from writing down something you were going to write down. Or else cross it out after it's written. "Naturally," you say, "it wasn't any good." But think for a moment about the occasions when you spoke well. Seldom was it because you first got the beginning just right. Usually it was a matter of a halting or even garbled beginning, but you kept going and your speech finally became coherent and even powerful. There is a lesson here for writing: trying to get the beginning just right is a formula for failure—and probably a secret tactic to make yourself give up writing. Make some words, whatever they are, and then grab hold of that line and reel in as hard as you can. Afterwards you can throw away lousy beginnings and make new ones. This is the quickest way to get into good writing.

9   The habit of compulsive, premature editing doesn't just make writing hard. It also makes writing dead. Your voice is damped out by all the interruptions, changes, and hesitations between the consciousness and the page. In your natural way of producing words there is a sound, a texture, a rhythm—a voice—which is the main source of power in your writing. I don't know how it works, but this voice is the force that will make a reader listen to you, the energy that drives the meanings through his thick skull. Maybe you don't *like* your voice; maybe people have made fun of it. But it's the only voice you've got. It's your only source of power. You better get back into it, no matter what you think of it. If you keep writing in it, it may change into something you like better. But if you abandon it, you'll likely never have a voice and never be heard.

10   Freewritings are vacuums. Gradually you will begin to carry over into your regular writing some of the voice, force, and connectedness that creep into those vacuums.

11   I find freewriting offends some people. They accuse it of being an invitation to write garbage.

12   Yes and No.

13   Yes, it produces garbage, but that's all right. What is feared seems to be some kind of infection: "I've struggled so hard to make my writing cleaner, more organized, less chaotic, struggled so hard to be less

helpless and confused in the face of a blank piece of paper. And I've made some progress. If I allow myself to write garbage or randomness *even for short periods,* the chaos will regain a foothold and sneak back to overwhelm me again."

14   Bad writing doesn't infect in this way. It might if you did nothing but freewriting—if you gave up all efforts at care, discrimination, and precision. But no one asks you to give up careful writing. It turns out, in fact, that these brief exercises in not caring help you care better afterward.

15   A word about being "careless." In freewriting exercises you should not stop, go back, correct, or reflect. In a sense this means "be careless." But there is a different kind of carelessness: not giving full attention, focus, or energy. Freewriting helps you pour *more* attention, focus, and energy into what you write. That is why freewriting exercises must be short.

16   If there is any validity to the infectious model of bad writing, it works the other way around: there is garbage in your head; if you don't let it out onto paper, it really will infect everything else up there. Garbage in your head poisons you. Garbage on paper can safely be put in the wastepaper basket.

17   In a sense I'm saying, "Yes, freewriting invites you to write garbage, but it's good for you." But this isn't the whole story. Freewriting isn't just therapeutic garbage. It's also a way to produce bits of writing that are genuinely *better* than usual: less random, more coherent, more highly organized. This may happen soon in your freewriting exercises, or only after you have done them for quite a number of weeks; it may happen frequently or only occasionally; these good bits may be long or short. Everyone's experience is different. But it happens to everyone.

18   It happens because in those portions of your freewriting that are coherent—in those portions where your mind has somehow gotten into high gear and produced a set of words that grows organically out of a thought or feeling or perception—the integration of meanings is at a finer level than you can achieve by conscious planning or arranging. Sometimes when someone speaks or writes about something that is very important to him, the words he produces have this striking integration or coherence: he isn't having to plan and work them out one by one. They are all permeated by his meaning. The meanings have been blended at a finer level, integrated more thoroughly. Not merely manipulated by his mind, but, rather, sifted through his entire self. In such writing you don't feel mechanical cranking, you don't hear the gears change. When there are transitions they are smooth, natural, organic. It is as though every word is permeated by

the meaning of the whole (like a hologram in which each part contains faintly the whole).

19   It boils down to something very simple. If you do freewriting regularly, much or most of it will be far inferior to what you can produce through care and rewriting. But the *good* bits will be much better than anything else you can produce by any other method.

QUESTIONS AND EXERCISES

VOCABULARY
1. interposes (paragraph 4)
2. obsessed (4)
3. inhibited (6)
4. compulsive (9)

LANGUAGE AND RHETORIC
1. Define freewriting in your own words.
2. What does Elbow mean when he says that the most important thing about freewriting is "nonediting"?
3. Why does the author depend upon process rather than definition as the method for developing his ideas? How does it relate to his purpose?
4. Who do you believe is the intended audience for this selection? What clues suggest this to you?
5. What is the author's attitude toward his subject? Point out some specific evidence to support your conclusions.

DISCUSSION AND WRITING
1. Do *not*—repeat *not*—write an essay based on this selection. Instead, practice freewriting exercises as explained here, and share the results of your efforts with your classmates.

WILLIAM STAFFORD

A Way of Writing

All too often we make an unnecessary, and in some senses false, distinction between "creative" writing and other kinds. Happily, poet William Stafford has avoided such premises in this essay and by so doing has produced an explanation of the writing process that should be equally valuable to all writers, whatever form or function their work assumes. His key statement in his opening

*one, in which he tells us that "A writer is not so much someone who has
something to say as he is someone who has found a process that will bring
about new things he would not have thought of if he had not started to say
them." That sentence sets the stage for all that follows.*

*As you read, try to determine whether the process explained here is in fact
applicable to the kinds of writing you do for your composition class.*

1 A writer is not so much someone who has something to say as he is
someone who has found a process that will bring about new things he
would not have thought of if he had not started to say them. That is, he
does not draw on a reservoir; instead, he engages in an activity that
brings to him a whole succession of unforeseen stories, poems, essays,
plays, laws, philosophies, religions, or—but wait!

2 Back in school, from the first when I began to try to write things, I
felt this richness. One thing would lead to another; the world would
give and give. Now, after twenty years or so of trying, I live by that
certain richness, an idea hard to pin, difficult to say, and perhaps
offensive to some. For there are strange implications in it.

3 One implication is the importance of just plain receptivity. When I
write, I like to have an interval before me when I am not likely to be
interrupted. For me, this means usually the early morning, before others are awake. I get pen and paper, take a glance out the window
(often it is dark out there), and wait. It is like fishing. But I do not wait
very long, for there is always a nibble—and this is where receptivity
comes in. To get started I will accept anything that occurs to me.
Something always occurs, of course, to any of us. We can't keep from
thinking. Maybe I have to settle for an immediate impression: it's cold,
or hot, or dark, or bright, or in between! Or—well, the possibilities are
endless. If I put down something, that thing will help the next thing
come, and I'm off. If I let the process go on, things will occur to me
that were not at all in my mind when I started. These things, odd or
trivial as they may be, are somehow connected. And if I let them
string out, surprising things will happen.

4 If I let them string out. . . . Along with initial receptivity, then,
there is another readiness: I must be willing to fail. If I am to keep on
writing, I cannot bother to insist on high standards. I must get into
action and not let anything stop me, or even slow me much. By
"standards" I do not mean "correctness"—spelling, punctuation, and
so on. These details become mechanical for anyone who writes for
a while. I am thinking about what many people would consider

"important" standards, such matters as social significance, positive values, consistency, etc. I resolutely disregard these. Something better, greater, is happening! I am following a process that leads so wildly and originally into new territory that no judgment can at the moment be made about values, significance, and so on. I am making something new, something that has not been judged before. Later others—and maybe I myself—will make judgments. Now, I am headlong to discover. Any distraction may harm the creating.

5   So, receptive, careless of failure, I spin out things on the page. And a wonderful freedom comes. If something occurs to me, it is all right to accept it. It has one justification: it occurs to me. No one else can guide me. I must follow my own weak, wandering, diffident impulses.

6   A strange bonus happens. At times, without my insisting on it, my writings become coherent; the successive elements that occur to me are clearly related. They lead by themselves to new connections. Sometimes the language, even the syllables that happen along, may start a trend. Sometimes the materials alert me to something waiting in my mind, ready for sustained attention. At such times, I allow myself to be eloquent, or intentional, or for great swoops (treacherous! not to be trusted!) reasonable. But I do not insist on any of that; for I know that back of my activity there will be the coherence of my self, and that indulgence of my impulses will bring recurrent patterns and meanings again.

7   This attitude toward the process of writing creatively suggests a problem for me, in terms of what others say. They talk about "skills" in writing. Without denying that I do have experience, wide reading, automatic orthodoxies and maneuvers of various kinds, I still must insist that I am often baffled about what "skill" has to do with the precious little area of confusion when I do not know what I am going to say and then I find out what I am going to say. That precious interval I am unable to bridge by skill. What can I witness about it? It remains mysterious, just as all of us must feel puzzled about how we are so inventive as to be able to talk along through complexities with our friends, not needing to plan what we are going to say, but never stalled for long in our confident forward progress. Skill? If so, it is the skill we all have, something we must have learned before the age of three or four.

8   A writer is one who has become accustomed to trusting that grace, or luck, or—skill.

9   Yet another attitude I find necessary: most of what I write, like most of what I say in casual conversation, will not amount to much. Even I will realize, and even at the time, that it is not negotiable. It will be

like practice. In conversation I allow myself random remarks—in fact, as I recall, that is the way I learned to talk—, so in writing I launch many expendable efforts. A result of this free way of writing is that I am not writing for others, mostly; they will not see the product at all unless the activity eventuates in something that later appears to be worthy. My guide is the self, and its adventuring in the language brings about communication.

10 This process-rather-than-substance view of writing invites a final, dual reflection:

11 1. Writers may not be special—sensitive or talented in any usual sense. They are simply engaged in sustained use of a language skill we all have. Their "creations" come about through confident reliance on stray impulses that will, with trust, find occasional patterns that are satisfying.

12 2. But writing itself is one of the great, free human activities. There is scope for individuality, and elation, and discovery, in writing. For the person who follows with trust and forgiveness what occurs to him, the world remains always ready and deep, an inexhaustible environment, with the combined vividness of an actuality and flexibility of a dream. Working back and forth between experience and thought, writers have more than space and time can offer. They have a whole unexplored realm of human vision.

QUESTIONS AND EXERCISES

VOCABULARY
1. receptivity (paragraph 3)
2. orthodoxies (7)
3. eventuates (9)
4. elation (12)
5. inexhaustible (12)

LANGUAGE AND RHETORIC
1. Why does Stafford place such a premium on receptivity? Why is that quality so important to the writer?
2. How applicable is Stafford's advice to you as a student of composition? Is this essay really that general or is it more appropriately aimed at an audience of creative writers?
3. The author depends upon his own experience to outline the writing process. Could he had reinforced his purpose by also referring to other writers who share similar views and work habits? Why or why not?
4. Where does the author first make his thesis clear? Show how he uses process analysis to develop that thesis. What other methods might he have used?

DISCUSSION AND WRITING
1. Here, as in response to the previous essay, you may wish to try some freewriting. While Stafford may not use that term, the initial step in his process is virtually identical with that proposed by Peter Elbow.
2. Stafford is one of the best known and most respected contemporary American poets. Look for some of his work in your campus library. You might be especially interested in locating a copy of his poem "Traveling Through the Dark" and the essay in which he recalls the source of the poem and the process by which he put it together.

DONALD M. MURRAY

The Maker's Eye: Revising Your Own Manuscripts

1   When students complete a first draft, they consider the job of writing done—and their teachers too often agree. When professional writers complete a first draft, they usually feel that they are at the start of the writing process. When a draft is completed, the job of writing can begin.

2   That difference in attitude is the difference between amateur and professional, inexperience and experience, journeyman and craftsman. Peter F. Drucker, the prolific business writer, calls his first draft "the zero draft"—after that he can start counting. Most writers share the feeling that the first draft, and all of those which follow, are opportunities to discover what they have to say and how best they can say it.

3   To produce a progression of drafts, each of which says more and says it more clearly, the writer has to develop a special kind of reading skill. In school we are taught to decode what appears on the page as finished writing. Writers, however, face a different category of possibility and responsibility when they read their own drafts. To them the words on the page are never finished. Each can be changed and rearranged, can set off a chain reaction of confusion or clarified meaning. This is a different kind of reading, which is possibly more difficult and certainly more exciting.

4   Writers must learn to be their own best enemy. They must accept the criticism of others and be suspicious of it; they must accept the praise of others and be even more suspicious of it. Writers cannot

depend on others. They must detach themselves from their own pages so that they can apply both their caring and their craft to their own work.

5   Such detachment is not easy. Science fiction writer Ray Bradbury supposedly puts each manuscript away for a year to the day and then rereads it as a stranger. Not many writer have the discipline or the time to do this. We must read when our judgment may be at its worst, when we are close to the euphoric moment of creation.

6   Then the writer, counsels novelist Nancy Hale, "should be critical of everything that seems to him most delightful in his style. He should excise what he most admires, because he wouldn't thus admire it if he weren't . . . in a sense protecting it from criticism." John Ciardi, the poet, adds, "The last act of the writing must be to become one's own reader. It is, I suppose, a schizophrenic process, to begin passionately and to end critically, to begin hot and to end cold; and, more important, to be passion-hot and critic-cold at the same time."

7   Most people think that the principal problem is that writers are too proud of what they have written. Actually, a greater problem for most professional writers is one shared by the majority of students. They are overly critical, think everything is dreadful, tear up page after page, never complete a draft, see the task as hopeless.

8   The writer must learn to read critically but constructively, to cut what is bad, to reveal what is good. Eleanor Estes, the children's book author, explains: "The writer must survey his work critically, coolly, as though he were a stranger to it. He must be willing to prune, expertly and hard-heartedly. At the end of each revision, a manuscript may look . . . worked over, torn apart, pinned together, added to, deleted from, words changed and words changed back. Yet the book must maintain its original freshness and spontaneity."

9   Most readers underestimate the amount of rewriting it usually takes to produce spontaneous reading. This is a great disadvantage to the student writer, who sees only a finished product and never watches the craftsman who takes the necessary step back, studies the work carefully, returns to the task, steps back, returns, steps back, again and again. Anthony Burgess, one of the most prolific writers in the English-speaking world, admits, "I might revise a page twenty times." Roald Dahl, the popular children's writer, states, "By the time I'm nearing the end of a story, the first part will have been reread and altered and corrected at least 150 times. . . . Good writing is essentially rewriting. I am positive of this."

10   Rewriting isn't virtuous. It isn't something that ought to be done. It is simply something that most writers find they have to do to discover

what they have to say and how to say it. It is a condition of the writer's life.

11   There are, however, a few writers who do little formal rewriting, primarily because they have the capacity and experience to create and review a large number of invisible drafts in their minds before they approach the page. And some writers slowly produce finished pages, performing all the tasks of revision simultaneously, page by page, rather than draft by draft. But it is still possible to see the sequence followed by most writers most of the time in rereading their own work.

12   Most writers scan their drafts first, reading as quickly as possible to catch the larger problems of subject and form, then move in closer and closer as they read and write, reread and rewrite.

13   The first thing writers look for in their drafts is *information*. They know that a good piece of writing is built from specific, accurate, and interesting information. The writer must have an abundance of information from which to construct a readable piece of writing.

14   Next writers look for *meaning* in the information. The specifics must build to a pattern of significance. Each piece of specific information must carry the reader toward meaning.

15   Writers reading their own drafts are aware of *audience*. They put themselves in the reader's situation and make sure that they deliver information which a reader wants to know or needs to know in a manner which is easily digested. Writers try to be sure that they anticipate and answer the questions a critical reader will ask when reading the piece of writing.

16   Writers make sure that the *form* is appropriate to the subject and the audience. Form, or genre, is the vehicle which carries meaning to the reader, but form cannot be selected until the writer has adequate information to discover its significance and an audience which needs or wants that meaning.

17   Once writers are sure the form is appropriate, they must then look at the *structure,* the order of what they have written. Good writing is built on a solid framework of logic, argument, narrative, or motivation which runs through the entire piece of writing and holds it together. This is the time when many writers find it most effective to outline as a way of visualizing the hidden spine by which the piece of writing is supported.

18   The element on which writers may spend a majority of their time is *development.* Each section of a piece of writing must be adequately developed. It must give readers enough information so that they are satisfied. How much information is enough? That's as difficult as asking how much garlic belongs in a salad. It must be done to taste, but

most beginning writers underdevelop, underestimating the reader's hunger for information.

19   As writers solve development problems, they often have to consider questions of *dimension*. There must be a pleasing and effective proportion among all the parts of the piece of writing. There is a continual process of subtracting and adding to keep the piece of writing in balance.

20   Finally, writers have to listen to their own voices. *Voice* is the force which drives a piece of writing forward. It is an expression of the writer's authority and concern. It is what is between the words on the page, what glues the piece of writing together. A good piece of writing is always marked by a consistent, individual voice.

21   As writers read and reread, write and rewrite, they move closer and closer to the page until they are doing line-by-line editing. Writers read their own pages with infinite care. Each sentence, each line, each clause, each phrase, each word, each mark of punctuation, each section of white space between the type has to contribute to the clarification of meaning.

22   Slowly the writer moves from word to word, looking through language to see the subject. As a word is changed, cut, or added, as a construction is rearranged, all the words used before that moment and all those that follow that moment must be considered and reconsidered.

23   Writers often read aloud at this stage of the editing process, muttering or whispering to themselves, calling on the ear's experience with language. Does this sound right—or that? Writers edit, shifting back and forth from eye to page to ear to page. I find I must do this careful editing in short runs, no more than fifteen or twenty minutes at a stretch, or I become too kind with myself. I begin to see what I hope is on the page, not what actually is on the page.

24   This sounds tedious if you haven't done it, but actually it is fun. Making something right is immensely satisfying, for writers begin to learn what they are writing about by writing. Language leads them to meaning, and there is the joy of discovery, of understanding, of making meaning clear as the writer employs the technical skills of language.

25   Words have double meanings, even triple and quadruple meanings. Each word has its own potential for connotation and denotation. And when writers rub one word against the other, they are often rewarded with sudden insight, an unexpected clarification.

26   The maker's eye moves back and forth from word to phrase to sentence to paragraph to sentence to phrase to word. The maker's eye sees the need for variety and balance, for a firmer structure, for a more

appropriate form. It peers into the interior of the paragraph, looking for coherence, unity, and emphasis, which make meaning clear.

27   I learned something about this process when my first bifocals were prescribed. I had ordered a larger section of the reading portion of the glass because of my work, but even so, I could not contain my eyes within this new limit of vision. And I still find myself taking off my glasses and bending my nose towards the page, for my eyes unconsciously flick back and forth across the page, back to another page, forward to still another, as I try to see each evolving line in relation to every other line.

28   When does this process end? Most writers agree with the great Russian writer Tolstoy, who said, "I scarcely ever reread my published writings, if by chance I come across a page, it always strikes me: all this must be rewritten; this is how I should have written it."

29   The maker's eye is never satisfied, for each word has the potential to ignite new meaning. This article has been twice written all the way through the writing process, and it was published four years ago. Now it is to be republished in a book. The editors make a few small suggestions, and then I read it with my maker's eye. Now it has been re-edited, re-revised, re-read, re-re-edited, for each piece of writing to the writer is full of potential and alternatives.

30   A piece of writing is never finished. It is delivered to a deadline, torn out of the typewriter on demand, sent off with a sense of accomplishment and shame and pride and frustration. If only there were a couple more days, time for just another run at it, perhaps then . . .

Definition

SUZANNE BRITT JORDAN

Fun. Oh, Boy. Fun. You Could Die From It.

Some things just don't sit still for easy definition. Fun, self-respect, happiness—all are equally elusive, and all are subject to scrutiny in the next three reading selections. Abstract aspects of the human condition, they call for a personal perception to be shared before arriving at agreement on their definition. In this first instance, Suzanne Britt Jordan, writing for an audience of The New York Times *readers, appears to be having fun with fun itself. But don't let her title fool you. She treats her topic seriously by working her way through a succession of common examples to arrive at her own definition—yet another example, but this one of her own choosing. The extent to which you can comprehend and accept her definition is up to you.*

While reading this essay, consider what alternative methods might have been employed in search of her definition.

1   Fun is hard to have.

2   Fun is a rare jewel.

3   Somewhere along the line people got the modern idea that fun was there for the asking, that people deserved fun, that if we didn't have a little fun every day we would turn into (sakes alive!) Puritans.

4   "Was it fun?" became the question that overshadowed all other questions: good questions like: Was it moral? Was it kind? Was it honest? Was it beneficial? Was it generous? Was it necessary? And (my favorite) was it selfless?

5   When pleasure got to be the main thing, the fun fetish was sure to follow. Everything was supposed to be fun. If it wasn't fun, then by Jove, we were going to make it fun, or else.

6   Think of all the things that got the reputation of being fun. Family outings were supposed to be fun. Sex was supposed to be fun.

Education was supposed to be fun. Work was supposed to be fun. Walt Disney was supposed to be fun. Church was supposed to be fun. Staying fit was supposed to be fun.

7   Just to make sure that everybody knew how much fun we were having, we put happy faces on flunking test papers, dirty bumpers, sticky refrigerator doors, bathroom mirrors.

8   If a kid, looking at his very happy parents traipsing through that very happy Disney World, said, "This ain't no fun, ma," his ma's heart sank. She wondered where she had gone wrong. Everybody told her what fun family outings to Disney World would be. Golly gee, what was the matter?

9   Fun got to be such a big thing that everybody started to look for more and more thrilling ways to supply it. One way was to step up the level of danger or licentiousness or alcohol or drug consumption so that you could be sure that, no matter what, you would manage to have a little fun.

10   Television commercials brought a lot of fun and fun-loving folks into the picture. Everything that people in those commercials did looked like fun: taking Polaroid snapshots, swilling beer, buying insurance, mopping the floor, bowling, taking aspirin. We all wished, I'm sure, that we could have half as much fun as those rough-and-ready guys around the locker room, flicking each other with towels and pouring champagne. The more commercials people watched, the more they wondered when the fun would start in their own lives. It was pretty depressing.

11   Big occasions were supposed to be fun. Christmas, Thanksgiving and Easter were obviously supposed to be fun. Your wedding day was supposed to be fun. Your wedding night was supposed to be a whole lot of fun. Your honeymoon was supposed to be the epitome of fundom. And so we ended up going through every Big Event we ever celebrated, waiting for the fun to start.

12   It occurred to me, while I was sitting around waiting for the fun to start, that not much is, and that I should tell you just in case you're worried about your fun capacity.

13   I don't mean to put a damper on things. I just mean we ought to treat fun reverently. It is a mystery. It cannot be caught like a virus. It cannot be trapped like an animal. The god of mirth is paying us back for all those years of thinking fun was everywhere by refusing to come to our party. I don't want to blaspheme fun anymore. When fun comes in on little dancing feet, you probably won't be expecting it. In fact, I bet it comes when you're doing your duty, your job, or your work. It may even come on a Tuesday.

14   I remember one day, long ago, on which I had an especially good time. Pam Davis and I walked to the College Village drugstore one Saturday morning to buy some candy. We were about 12 years old (fun ages). She got her Bit-O-Honey. I got my malted milk balls, chocolate stars, Chunkys, and a small bag of M&M's. We started back to her house. I was going to spend the night. We had the whole day to look forward to. We had plenty of candy. It was a long way to Pam's house but every time we got weary Pam would put her hand over her eyes, scan the horizon like a sailor and say, "Oughta reach home by nightfall," at which point the two of us would laugh until we thought we couldn't stand it another minute. Then after we got calm, she'd say it again. You should have been there. It was the kind of day and friendship and occasion that made me deeply regret that I had to grow up.

15   It was fun.

QUESTIONS AND EXERCISES

VOCABULARY
1. fetish (paragraph 5)
2. licentiousness (9)
3. epitome (11)
4. blaspheme (13)

LANGUAGE AND RHETORIC
1. What kind of definition of fun does Jordan offer here? How effective is it? Support your answer.
2. Try your own definition of fun, using several different kinds of definition. Which of the alternatives works best for you and why?
3. How do you respond to the title of this selection? Is it appropriate? Effective? Can you suggest any alternatives?
4. The author concludes with a simple three-word sentence. Do you think it works well as a conclusion? Why or why not?

DISCUSSION AND WRITING
1. Why does the author object to the notion of fun as exemplified in paragraphs 3 through 11? What is your reaction to these items? What is the basis for your reaction?
2. What is your idea of fun? Write an essay in which you define fun by means of a key example the way Jordan did in her last two paragraphs. Try to capture the specific details of your experience as precisely as possible.

SUSAN SARANDON

Let Courage Drive Us

While Susan Sarandon has enjoyed the heights of star status in Hollywood, she has never lost sight of the larger picture. Her public statements, and frequently her films themselves, reflect a continuing concern for the well being of all of us who live on this planet and those yet to come. It is not surprising, then, that when called upon to speak to an audience of New York Women in Film, she presented the following statement, which seeks to redefine heroism, not only in the Hollywood setting but in the larger world as well.

As you read, ask yourself why the author wants to redefine heroism and in what direction she wants to move it.

1 I feel fortunate to be working in this business, to be given the opportunity to move people, transport them, make them laugh or cry, and help them escape a little: to stimulate thought and controversy.

2 Meryl Streep recently pointed out the disparity in salary between women and men in our industry, the disparity in jobs and in roles of substance. I agree with her wholeheartedly, and I am concerned about these inequities. But I am also concerned that in the process of fighting to change these things we not lose sight of other, equally pressing problems. We need to be concerned about the quality of life on all fronts. We can't leave it to someone else. How can we empower ourselves and fight sexism in our industry without addressing our own racism, for instance? Perhaps we need to ask ourselves how we can encourage and create jobs for other women . . . how we can put our energies into projects about women by women. How do we redefine "heroic" for both men and women? How do we reinvent "power" for our sons and daughters? How do we remove manipulation from business? How do we instill respect?

3 It is not only sexism that threatens to strangle and pervert this business; it is greed. The greed that dictates that movies must turn astronomical profits in order to be considered successful. The greed that links violence and sex to turn a profit. The greed that turns a well-intentioned script into pabulum.

4 Let us be aware. As we struggle to attain positions of power let us arm ourselves with knowledge and decency and respect for truth. Let courage drive us.

5 Where do we look to find images of courage? Chances are we will not find them behind the desks we aspire to. And yet these images are within our grasp. There are women all around us, women whose work

and resolute determination for equality have made it possible for us to be in this room. Fannie Lou Hamer, who just 25 years ago stood up with two other black women and refused to compromise her rights in front of an all-white Mississippi congressional delegation. Soon after that the Voting Rights Act was passed. Byllye Avery, who built the National Black Women's Health Project and changed the lives of black women across this country. "Maria," the Salvadoran woman who has lived in the mountains for ten years risking her life to build a new country where children can learn to read.

6   These are women who live extraordinary lives. They are sources of inspiration for many—heroes if you will. But *heroic* is a term that can apply to many. One needn't be known to the masses to be a hero. A single mother of six who through her hard work and determination is able to send a child to college despite all odds is a hero, and so are other women just by virtue of how they carry on, day after day, doing what they must in an honest, dignified way.

7   Let us take on the challenge of telling their stories. Let us take on the challenge of redefining what a hero is. It is possible to be heroic without the use of violence. It is extremely compelling and exciting to see survival in the face of terrible odds. Survival made possible by persistence and strength, not by guns and retribution. There are stories to be told, great stories that we all can tell. Maybe it's time to stop playing with the big boys. Because when we play with the big boys, we are playing by their rules in their ballpark. There are few ways to win, and sooner or later one has to make compromises. We must ask ourselves, Are the compromises worth it? I've seen female power brokers turn blind eyes to sexism in movies they are championing. I've heard the deadly silence of compromise. Perhaps it's time to build our own ballparks and rewrite the rule book.

8   We are communicators of stories, ideas, and images. And our bottom line, our strongest tool, is language. We should be vigilant in our knowledge of words and fierce in our protection of their purity. We must not allow our words and our images to be distorted in order to pacify us. *Kinder* and *gentler*. What a shame to lose those words.

9   The word *accident:* We hear a lot about accidents. Children killed by stray bullets, for example. But the conditions that lead to those killings are not accidents. When a society takes money out of the school budget to pay for missiles, something logically happens to the schools. Poverty is not an accident. Racist violence and intolerance are not accidents. The word *tragedy:* People say that it is a tragedy that there are so many homeless living on the streets. Or that there are so many wounded children in El Salvador. It's not a tragedy. A tornado or a volcano, something beyond our control—that's a tragedy. These

things are crimes, crimes against our humanity. If we are to fight crime, let's fight crime. To be the best women in this business we have to live life fully and confront the truth, not only in the largest sense—that is, globally—but what we see on our doorsteps.

10   If we close our eyes, we close off part of ourselves. If we open our eyes, they will sting, but what we see will propel us to work harder to make this precious, fragile place a little more livable. As Robert Louis Stevenson wrote, "To travel hopefully is a better thing than to arrive, and the true success is to labor."

QUESTIONS AND EXERCISES

VOCABULARY
1. transport (paragraph 1)
2. disparity (2)
3. inequities (2)
4. empower (2)
5. astronomical (3)
6. pabulum (3)
7. persistence (7)
8. retribution (7)
9. championing (7)
10. vigilant (8)

LANGUAGE AND RHETORIC
1. Even if you were unaware of the audience for this speech, there are clues contained in the text that can tell you who that audience was. Point out some of those clues.
2. Throughout this selection, the author suggests ways we can redefine heroism. Why does she want to redefine it? What does she want to move the concept toward? Point out examples of each kind of heroism contained in the text, then write your own definition consistent with the author's purpose and thesis.
3. In paragraph 8, the author says "We must not allow our words and images to be distorted in order to pacify us." She then goes on to say we have lost the words "kinder" and "gentler." Given the fact that President Bush used those terms during his first presidential campaign, how can she say that we have lost them? Support your answer.
4. How does the author's concern for language as expressed in paragraphs 8 through 10 relate to her overall purpose in this speech?

DISCUSSION AND WRITING
1. This speech was first presented to an audience of women in the film industry and later published in *Lear's*, a magazine with a more general

readership, largely women. Do you think it applies to the wider audience? In what ways does the author's statement address all women?

2. How do you define "feminist" or "feminism"? (If you need the assistance of a dictionary, take advantage of it.) In light of your definition, do you consider this speech to be a feminist statement? Why or why not?

3. Have you seen any films in which the author assumes a role that in any way reflects what she says here? If so, point out the relevant idea(s) in the text of the speech and show how you can draw a connection between them and the film(s).

4. The examples that the author uses in paragraphs 5 and 6 are a key to her redefinition of heroism. Using these as a starting point, consider the women that you have known who might also be used as examples. Select an appropriate one and develop a paper in which your chosen subject illustrates the redefinition of heroism.

ELLEN GOODMAN

Parades and Patriotism

Most Americans have little difficulty in advocating or supporting patriotism, but it is considerably more difficult to define what we mean by that term. Some see it exemplified in slogans, flag display, and parades. Others see these as simplistic approaches to something far more complex and demanding, approaches that ultimately may prove to be not only unpatriotic but undemocratic. Whatever your position on the issue, this selection by Ellen Goodman should stimulate serious thinking about the meaning of patriotism.

Look for clues in your reading that tell you when this piece was written, and, therefore, why the issue keeps recurring.

1   **W**e are heading to the country for the holiday. Far away from the prefabricated parades and the made-for-television ticker tape that turns city streets into postwar spectacles.

2   The Pentagon won't send its hardware where we are going. The Fourth of July parade will be homemade and downhome. A patriot is not a missile everywhere.

3   So, we will be spared one last command performance for the Persian Gulf. The red, white and blue all wrapped in yellow. The enthusiasm for a war that was won but isn't over. The endless curtain calls for Schwarzkopf.

4   There is something increasingly artificial in these postwar productions. Do we replay the last hurrahs in order to prove to each other and the "millions watching at home" that we are not experiencing a relapse of Vietnam syndrome? Do we go out in public to do an impression of pride in country?

5   The Fourth of July has always been a special holiday. Never Mondayized, it commemorates a statement of principle, not a day off work. This is the date on which Americans told the world what we stood for: "We hold these truths to be self-evident, that all men are created equal, that they are endowed by their Creator with certain unalienable Rights, that among these are Life, Liberty and the Pursuit of Happiness."

6   But how watered down the current batch of Gulf-infused sentiments seems in contrast. In the wake of a war that liberated Kuwait to hold its kangaroo courts, and conquered a tyrant still very much in charge, our ringing declaration is reduced to: "We're Number One."

7   As the days of glory are covered by ancient sands and arguments, Americans are expected to root for our country as if it were a sporting team whose only obligation was to win the world cup. In our country's third century, we are more like fans than citizens. We prove our allegiance by cheering "USA! USA!" We show our citizenship by joining a parade of approval.

8   How have we become a country of such permissive patriotism? It's as if some perverse child-raising manual was being applied to the relationship between the governed and the government.

9   We, the people, are like parents reluctant to set high standards for their children, to hold them responsible, to criticize them. We have become like parents who quake the first time their children react to discipline with an accusing tone, "You don't love me." We have retreated to the sidelines of civic life where we offer only cheers as proof of our ties.

10   How else to explain the attention to military victory and the inattention to our domestic defeats? How else to explain the din of the parades and the eerie silence about our economic slide? The attendance at postwar parades and the absence of concern about postwar policies?

11   Permissive patriots are easily pleased. We ask little and cheer for less.

12   Thirty years ago, Jack Kennedy told Americans, "Ask not what your country can do for you but what you can do for your country." Now maybe we've learned that lesson too well.

13   We have lowered our expectations, and in return politicians, like children, lowered their performance.

14   On the streets, there is a daily shooting match; in Congress they debate only a waiting period for buying a gun. In family life there is a

work and caretaking crisis; in the government they wrangle over unpaid medical leave. In the country there is poverty and massive deficit; in Washington they argue over John Sununu.

15 Permissive patriotism is deceptively simple. It's too easy to become a point of light along the parade route. But like permissive parenting, it covers up a lack of involvement and even caring. Mindless love—my country right or wrong—is a mushy substitute for duty. The results are spoiled in the process.

16 Real patriotism should be demanding. It should differentiate—my country right AND wrong. It should impose ethical standards higher than being Number One. Patriotism isn't afraid of saying no. It embraces criticism as well as praise.

17 But more than anything else, patriotism is not a spectator sport. It demands that people stay as engaged and committed as that first group who came together—not for a parade but for a daring venture to which they signed their names.

18 "And for the support of this Declaration, with a firm Reliance on the Protection of divine Providence, we mutually pledge to each other our Lives, our Fortunes and our sacred Honor."

QUESTIONS AND EXERCISES

VOCABULARY
1. prefabricated (paragraph 1)
2. relapse (4)
3. syndrome (4)
4. commemorate (5)

LANGUAGE AND RHETORIC
1. The author contrasts her definition of patriotism with the more conventional understanding of the term. As presented here, how is it commonly defined? According to the author, how should it be defined? Support your answers.
2. There are several clues in the author's text that tell you when this essay was written. When was it, and how do you know?
3. Having first appeared as one of the author's regular newspaper columns, this selection is marked by the short paragraphs typical of that format. What paragraphs can you combine without disrupting the continuity and coherence of the essay?
4. In paragraph 5, the author tells us "The Fourth of July has always been a special holiday. Never Monday-ized. . . ." What does she mean by "Monday-ized"? How does that word help her to make her point?

DISCUSSION AND WRITING

1. According to the author, the elements of "patriotism" in its most superficial sense are evident everywhere. Point out some of them in the first six paragraphs of her essay, then develop a brief definition of the term based on them. Having done so, consider the key elements of patriotism as the author sees them in the remainder of the essay; then develop a definition consistent with her perspective.

2. Of the two definitions of patriotism that emerge above, which do you believe to be the most meaningful? What is the basis for your choice? Develop an essay of your own in which you begin with one of the above definitions and go on to illustrate it with examples drawn from your own experience or research.

3. "More than anything else, patriotism is not a spectator sport" says the author in paragraph 17. "It demands that people stay as engaged and committed as [our founders]." What could—or should—we be engaged in or committed to? Think of something you have done, or could do, that might meet the standards of patriotism suggested by the author; then write a paper in which you illustrate that engagement or commitment either through past actions or future plans.

4. If in your judgment the President of this nation is clearly and fundamentally wrong in adopting a particular policy or plan of action, what should you do as a patriotic citizen? Support your answer.

RICHARD REEVES

American Values

1   There was an ad in *The Times* for a designer "classic American hobo suit!" It can be yours for just $2,500 from Martha International on Park Avenue.

2   For $2,500 a woman can look like a bum in a heavy red wool suit decorated or held together with felt patches of many colors. She can wear it downtown and blend in with the crowd at Tompkins Park, where the police are rousting out the homeless these days.

3   History may not be kind to such excess.

4   I had another occasion to think about how others see or will see "American values" when I stopped at a health-food shop for a cup of coffee and a 92-grain muffin of some sort. A small poster caught my

attention: "It will be a great day when our schools get all the money they need and the Air Force has to hold a bake sale to buy a bomber."

5   I laughed but wondered, what are American values today?

6   Certainly the new or real values are not all we say. The ones we talk about most, "family values," are like the weather. Everyone talks about them because we are lost in a nation of shifting relationships, quality time, illegitimate children, and parents who compete with their own children for the joys and toys of youth.

7   Countries with real family values, Italy or India, do not have to talk about them.

8   Our real values are closer to individualism, do your own thing. You're on your own. If that seems harsh, tune in Oprah and Phil, Geraldo and Sally Jessy to find out what your neighbors are doing in their free time—they're not driving their kids to piano lessons.

9   Taste aside, the real value underlying the $2,500 hobo suit is a combination of privacy and privatization: It's a free country, and what you do with your money is nobody's business.

10   Another American value, I'm afraid, is we believe violence is a legitimate and logical solution to almost any problem. That is, more or less, the principal value projected on prime-time TV and most movies. The people who make those things say they're only giving people what they want. I believe that, and worry about it.

11   Take the provocative film "Thelma and Louise," which asks the question Professor Henry Higgins did: "Why can't a woman be more like a man?" Thelma and Louise, like Rambo and Dirty Harry, are make-believe, at least to most adults. But the invasion of Panama and the Gulf War are examples of the same inclination.

12   That done with, we can now show how comfortable we are preaching peace and practicing war. Our leader, President Bush, is simultaneously calling for disarmament in the Middle East and dispatching his most senior assistants there to sell missiles, tanks and attack helicopters to anyone who can afford them.

13   Also, I don't think most Americans believe for a minute that all men are created equal. Perhaps we never did, even when we fought wars and wrote laws under that banner. The real value, at least the one being projected today, is essentially "equal but separate."

14   Give them a chance to make some money, but better they stick with their own kind. That's the real attitude.

15   "Jungle Fever," the new Spike Lee movie, and the beating near to death last weekend of a black Long Island high school student named Alfred Jermaine Ewell after he was seen talking with a white girl indicate that some things never change much. "Why are you talking to that

nigger?" someone said to the girl, and within an hour Ewell was in a coma, beaten with baseball bats.

16   More than 150 years ago, in *Democracy in America,* Alexis de Tocqueville said the same things Lee is trying to articulate: "When one wishes to estimate the equality between different classes, one must always come to the question of how marriages are made. . . . An equality resulting from necessity, courtesy or politics may exist on the surface and deceive the eye. But when one wishes to practice this equality in the intermarriage of families, then one puts one's finger on the sore."

17   That's still the sore.

18   Half of all Asians in America intermarry with another race, usually whites, according to the National Center for Health Statistics.

19   But Blacks and Whites together—almost never.

Cause and Effect

WILLIAM LUTZ

The First Casualty

Professor William Lutz of Rutgers University in New Jersey has spent a major portion of his professional career studying "doublespeak." That word comes from George Orwell's novel 1984 and is generally used as a blanket term for "confusing or deceptive" language. With this selection, Lutz argues that "In war, the first casualty is language. And with the language goes the truth."

While reading, note how the author employs cause and effect as a basic pattern to develop his thesis and provides numerous examples to support it.

1 Senator Hiram Johnson was wrong when in 1917 he observed that in war the first casualty is truth. In war, the first casualty is language. And with the language goes the truth. It was the Vietnam "conflict," not the Vietnam War. It was the Korean "police action," not the Korean War. It was the "pacification" of Gaul by Julius Caesar, not the brutal and bloody subjugation of Gaul. "Where they make a desert, they call it peace," observed the British chieftain Calgacus of the Roman conquest of Britain. War corrupts language.

2 The doublespeak of war consists, as Orwell wrote of all such language, "of euphemism, question-begging, and sheer cloudy vagueness." It is, fundamentally, the language of insincerity, where there is a gap between the speaker's real and declared aims. It is language as an instrument for concealing and preventing thought, not for expressing or extending thought. Such language silences dialogue and blocks communication.

3 During the Vietnam "conflict" we learned that mercenaries paid by the U.S. government were "civilian irregular defense soldiers," refugees fleeing the war were "ambient noncombatant personnel," and

enemy troops who survived bombing attacks were "interdictional non-succumbers." In Vietnam, American warplanes conducted "limited duration protective reaction strikes," during which they achieved an "effective delivery of ordnance." So it went too in the Persian Gulf.

4   Just as officially there was no war in Korea or Vietnam, officially there was no war in the Persian Gulf. After all, Congress didn't declare war, it declared an authorization of the "use of force," a power clearly delegated to Congress in Article I, Section 8, of the Constitution, which now reads: "Congress shall have the power to authorize the use of force." So now we have not war but Operation Desert Storm, or "exercising the military option," or, according to President Bush, an "armed situation."

5   During this "armed situation," massive bombing attacks became "efforts." Thousands of warplanes didn't drop tons of bombs, "weapons systems" or "force packages" "visited a site." These "weapons systems" didn't drop their tons of bombs on buildings and human beings, they "hit" "hard" and "soft targets." During their "visits," these "weapons systems" "degraded," "neutralized," "attrited," "suppressed," "eliminated," "cleansed," "sanitized," "impacted," "decapitated," or "took out" targets; they didn't blow up planes, tanks, trucks, airfields, and the soldiers who were in them, nor did they blow up bridges, roads, factories and other buildings, and the people who happened to be there. A "healthy day of bombing" was achieved when more enemy "assets" were destroyed than expected.

6   If the "weapons systems" didn't achieve "effective results" (blow up their targets) during their first "visit" (bombing attack) as determined by a "damage assessment study" (figuring out if everything was completely destroyed), the "weapons systems" "revisited the site" (bombed it again). Women, children, and other civilians killed or wounded during these "visits," and any schools, hospitals, museums, houses, or other "non-military" targets that were blown up, were "collateral damage"—the undesired damage or casualties produced by the effects from "incontinent ordnance" or "accidental delivery of ordnance equipment"—meaning the bombs and rockets missed their original targets.

7   In order to function as it should and as we expect it to, language must be an accurate reflection of that which it represents. The doublespeak of war is an instance of thought corrupting language, and language corrupting thought.

8   Such language is needed only if, as George Orwell wrote, "one wants to name things without calling up mental pictures of them." Thus the phrase, "traumatic amputation" produces no mental pictures of soldiers with arms or legs blown off. The terms, "light" or "moderate" losses invoke no mental pictures of pilots burned beyond recognition

in the twisted wreckage of their planes, of hundreds of soldiers lying dead on a battlefield or screaming in pain in field hospitals. Killing the enemy becomes the innocuous "servicing the target," which invokes no mental picture of shooting, stabbing, or blowing another human being to small, bloody pieces. Clean-sounding phrases such as "effective delivery of ordnance," "precision bombing," and "surgical air strikes" evoke no mental pictures of thousands of tons of bombs falling on electric power plants, communication centers, railroad lines, and factories, or women, children, and old people huddling in the ruins of their homes and neighborhoods.

9   The new doublespeak of war flowed smoothly as military spokesmen coolly discussed "assets" (everything from men and women soldiers to aircraft carriers and satellites), the "suppression of assets" (bombing everything from enemy soldiers to sewage plants), "airborne sanitation" (jamming enemy radar and radio, blowing up antiaircraft guns and missiles, and shooting down enemy airplanes), "disruption" (bombing), "operations" (bombing), "area denial weapons" (cluster bombs, previously called anti-personnel bombs), "damage" (death and destruction, or the results of bombing), "attrition" (destruction, or the results of bombing).

10   The massive bombing campaign (which included concentrated bombing by massed B-52s dropping thousands of tons of bombs in just one attack) directed against the Republican Guard units of the Iraqi army were considered highly successful by General Norman Schwarzkopf, who based his assessment on "the delivery methods and volume that we've been able to put on them." Returning from a bombing attack, an American pilot said he had "sanitized the area." A Marine general told reporters, "We're prosecuting any target that's out there." And an artillery captain said, "I prefer not to say we are killing other people. I prefer to say we are servicing the target." Even with all this doublespeak, news of the "armed effort" was subject to "security review," not censorship. When language is so corrupted, what becomes of truth?

11   The use of technical, impersonal, bureaucratic, euphemistic language to describe war separates the act of killing from the idea of killing; it separates the word from that which it is supposed to symbolize. Such language is a linguistic cover-up designed to hide an unpleasant reality. It is language that lies by keeping us as far as possible from the reality it pretends to represent. With such language we create a psychological detachment from the horror that is war, and we become numb to the human suffering that is the inevitable result of war. With the doublespeak of war we are not responsible for the results of our actions. And war becomes a "viable" solution for our problems.

QUESTIONS AND EXERCISES

VOCABULARY
1. subjugation (paragraph 1)
2. euphemism (2)
3. mercenaries (3)
4. innocuous (8)
5. linguistic (11)

LANGUAGE AND RHETORIC
1. This selection has a three-part structure. What paragraphs are contained in each part? What is the relationship between and among the parts? How does the author use them to serve his purpose in writing?
2. The author makes extensive use of examples to develop his thesis. Cite some of those that you find especially striking. What do you think the effect might have been on you as a reader if he had limited his article to a handful of examples?
3. In paragraph 7, the author says "The doublespeak of war is an instance of thought corrupting language, and language corrupting thought." What does he mean? Which is the cause and which the effect? Restate the idea in your own words.
4. In addition to cause and effect, which is central to his thesis, the author uses several other means to develop it. Identify three of them and give an example of each.

DISCUSSION AND WRITING
1. What connections can you make between the author's thesis in this essay and the statements Susan Sarandon makes about language in "Let Courage Drive Us" (p. 400)? How does each author view the role of language in public life? Write an essay in which you point out specific references in each selection to support your answer.
2. In his essay on "American Values," (p. 406), Richard Reeves says that one of our values is the belief that "violence is a legitimate and logical solution to almost any problem." How does this selection support that statement?
3. Paragraph 11 outlines a clear relationship of cause and effect between the government's use of language to describe the war and the use of war as a solution to our problems. Can you develop this argument further by providing details, examples, or descriptions from other sources, including personal experience? If so, write an original essay along these lines, supported by those sources and/or that experience.
4. You could, of course, argue that our leaders have little or no choice in this matter. Given the need to take military action, they must do all they can to win, while avoiding opposition at home. Therefore, they must use

the language accordingly. What is your response to that line of reasoning? Write an essay in which you argue one side or the other, using specific details and examples to support your position.

EDWARD ABBEY
Shadows from the Big Woods

The late Edward Abbey spent a lifetime cherishing our natural environment. He urged others to do so largely through his many books, both fiction and non-fiction, including The Journey Home, *from which this selection is taken. Like much of his non-fiction, this piece is what Abbey characterized as a kind of "personal history." In it, he contrasts the marvels and mysteries of the "Big Woods" he knew as a boy with what is left of them in the wake of the "iron monsters" of unrestrained development.*

Note how the author employs a combination of comparison and contrast with cause and effect to develop his thesis.

1   The idea of wilderness needs no defense. It only needs more defenders.
2   In childhood the wilds seemed infinite. Along Crooked Creek in the Allegheny Mountains of western Pennsylvania there was a tract of forest we called the Big Woods. The hemlock, beech, poplar, red oak, white oak, maple, and shagbark hickory grew on slopes so steep they had never been logged. Vines of wild grape trailed from the limbs of ancient druidical oaks—dark glens of mystery and shamanism. My brothers and I, simple-minded farmboys, knew nothing of such mythologies, but we were aware, all the same, of the magic residing among and within those trees. We knew that the Indians had once been here, Seneca and Shawnee, following the same deer paths that wound through fern, moss, yarrow, and mayapple among the massive trunks in the green-gold light of autumn, from spring to stream and marsh. Those passionate warriors had disappeared a century before we were even born, but their spirits lingered, their shades still informed the spirit of the place. We knew they were there. The vanished Indians were reincarnated, for a few transcendent summers, in our bones, within our pale Caucasian skins, in our idolatrous mimicry. We knew all about moccasins and feathers, arrows and bows, the thrill of

sneaking naked through the underbrush, taking care to tread on not a single dry twig. Our lore came from boys' books, but it was the forest that made it real.

3 My brother Howard could talk to trees. Johnny knew how to start a fire without matches, skin a squirrel, and spot the eye of a sitting rabbit. I was an expert on listening to mourning doves, though not on interpretation, and could feel pleasure in the clapperclaw of crows. The wolf was long gone from those woods, and also the puma, but there were still plenty of deer, as well as bobcat and raccoon and gray fox; sometimes a black bear, or the rumor of one, passed through the hills. That was good country then, the country of boyhood, and the woods, the forest, that sultry massed deepness of transpiring green, formed the theater of our play. We invented our boyhood as we grew along; but the forest—in which it was possible to get authentically lost—sustained our sense of awe and terror in ways that fantasy cannot.

4 Now I would not care to revisit those faraway scenes. That forest which seemed so vast to us was only a small thing after all, as the bulldozers, earth movers, and dragline shovels have proved. The woods we thought eternal have been logged by methods formerly considered too destructive, and the very mountainside on which the forest grew has been butchered by the strip miners into a shape of crude symmetry, with spoil banks and head walls and right-angled escarpments where even the running blackberry has a hard time finding a roothold. Stagnant water fills the raw gulches, and the creek below runs sulfur-yellow all year long.

5 Something like a shadow has fallen between present and past, an abyss wide as war that cannot be bridged by any tangible connection, so that memory is undermined and the image of our beginnings betrayed, dissolved, rendered not mythical but illusory. We have connived in the murder of our own origins. Little wonder that those who travel nowhere but in their own heads, reducing all existence to the space of one skull, maintain dreamily that only the pinpoint tip of the moment is real. They are right: A fanatical greed, an arrogant stupidity, has robbed them of the past and transformed their future into a nightmare. They deny the world because the only world they know has denied them.

6 Our cancerous industrialism, reducing all ideological differences to epiphenomena, has generated its own breed of witch doctor. These are men with a genius for control and organization, and the lust to administrate. They propose first to shrink our world to the dimensions of a global village, over which some technological crackpot will erect a geodesic dome to regulate air and light; at the same time the planetary

superintendent of schools will feed our children via endless belt into reinforcement-training boxes where they will be conditioned for their functions in the anthill arcology of the future. The ideal robot, after all, is simply a properly processed human being.

7   The administrators laying out the blueprints for the technological totalitarianism of tomorrow like to think of the earth as a big space capsule, a machine for living. They are wrong: The earth is not a mechanism but an organism, a being with its own life and its own reasons, where the support and sustenance of the human animal is incidental. If man in his newfound power and vanity persists in the attempt to remake the planet in his own image, he will succeed only in destroying himself—not the planet. The earth will survive our most ingenious folly.

8   Meanwhile, though, the Big Woods is gone—or going fast. And the mountains, the rivers, the canyons, the seashores, the swamps, and the deserts. Even our own, the farms, the towns, the cities, all seem to lie helpless before the advance of the technoindustrial juggernaut. We have created an iron monster with which we wage war, not only on small peasant nations over the sea, but even on ourselves—a war against all forms of life, against life itself. In the name of Power and Growth. But the war is only beginning.

9   The Machine may seem omnipotent, but it is not. Human bodies and human wit, active here, there, everywhere, united in purpose, independent in action, can still face that machine and stop it and take it apart and reassemble it—if we wish—on lines entirely new. There is, after all, a better way to live. The poets and the prophets have been trying to tell us about it for three thousand years.

QUESTIONS AND EXERCISES

VOCABULARY
   1. infinite (paragraph 2)
   2. druidical (2)
   3. shamanism (2)
   4. transcendent (2)
   5. idolatrous (2)
   6. mimicry (2)
   7. clapperclaw (3)
   8. sultry (3)
   9. transpiring (3)
   10. technoindustrial (8)
   11. juggernaut (8)
   12. omnipotent (9)

LANGUAGE AND RHETORIC

1. What *are* the "shadows from the Big Woods"? What is the author referring to, and why does he use this image in his title? What would the effect have been if he had called his essay "Mysteries of the Big Woods" or "Memories of the Big Woods"?
2. The author uses his youthful experience and memory of the "Big Woods" as the central example to illustrate his thesis. What does he gain by drawing on personal experience? What does he lose by it?
3. A quick review of the six paragraphs that make up this essay shows us a clear four-part organization. Identify the paragraphs that comprise those four parts. Point out the relationship between and among them, and show how they develop the author's thesis.
4. In his last two paragraphs, the author capitalizes "Power," "Growth," and "Machine." Obviously this is not conventional capitalization. Envision each of the words without a capital. What is the difference? What is the effect that the author is trying to achieve?

DISCUSSION AND WRITING

1. Do you think the author is overly sensitive to the problem he describes here? Has he taken an extreme position? Defend your answer to these questions with specific details, examples, and reasons.
2. If you have known a setting that was especially important to you but has been lost to development, write an essay about your experience. Describe the setting as it was, and explain what it meant to you. Then show it today and explain the effect the change has had on you.
3. Are we Americans as exploitative of our environment as the author seems to contend? Are we in fact using it for commercial purposes without regard to its importance as a source of recreation and renewal? Develop in detail one example you are familiar with that could be used either to challenge or support the author's thesis.

RICHARD REEVES

The Homeless in San Francisco

The plight of the homeless in America has become one of our major national problems over the past several years. Once dominated by middle-age and older men, the homeless population has expanded to include increasing numbers of young men as well as women and children—even entire families. In this selection, Richard Reeves focuses on a mayoral election in San Francisco to address the problem, viewing that event as a significant indicator of things to come elsewhere in the country.

Examine this essay to see how the author uses cause and effect to develop his ideas and insights.

1   Finally the people have spoken about the homeless. They said: Get them out of our sight!

2   Mayor Art Agnos was defeated for re-election in the most liberal of American cities—only a couple of years after being widely hailed as the best and most popular of U.S. mayors.

3   He was defeated by the former chief of police, Frank Jordan, who promised to get panhandlers off the streets.

4   I've always thought Agnos was one of the brighter ornaments on the political tree, but I don't live in this lovely city by the bay. Many who do live here came to think Agnos aloof and arrogant in the two years since his approval rating jumped to more than 70 percent after his energetic response to the problems of people displaced by earthquake.

5   I talked to Agnos a few days before the election, when he knew he was probably going to lose.

6   "I made a mistake, I guess. I thought the homeless were a social problem. But the voters think they're an aesthetic problem."

7   People can't stand seeing them around anymore.

8   It's been more than 10 years—a decade of cutting back on help and compassion, a decade of letting mental cases roam the countryside rather than paying taxes to care for them.

9   The country seems overrun by the grimy and the grotesque, the pathetic and the panhandlers.

10   In places where government has been more decent, more creeps have accumulated.

11   Art Agnos, the old social worker, was very decent, convinced that with a little time and money, San Francisco could provide shelter, medical help and counseling that would nudge many street people back into the mainstream. But few taxpayers agreed such things would work—or were worth waiting for or paying for.

12   San Francisco, the majority of its people seemed to say, is too beautiful to be ruined by the ragged. These people were spoiling the view.

13   They particularly spoiled the view—and the odor—around City Hall, where Mayor Agnos let them pitch tents while they waited for him to find them shelter. People couldn't stand it—that was part of [the voters'] message.

14   They also can't stand it anymore down the coast in Santa Monica, another beautiful California place that tried to be generous to the

homeless over these years and ended up attracting enough of them to turn the oceanside showplace, Palisades Park, into a sewer with a view.

15 Santa Monica, which offered compassion and free meals at City Hall, ended up with at least 1,500 street people. Most seemed to be in local parks, a filthy occupying army. Many taxpayers concluded they were paying these people to ruin their own lives—keeping families away from park and ocean. Now you can feel the pressure building to run out the "invaders."

16 So the bad has won over the good in America.

17 I do not mean Frank Jordan is a bad man. As far as I know, he is the salt of the earth. What I mean is democratic leadership can be judged by whether it brings out the best in people or the worst. For 10 years, people in San Francisco and Santa Monica, in Manhattan and in many other places, tried to do their best, tried to care, tried to be reasonable, tried to be helpful.

18 But they were defeated by the uncaring—particularly by two presidents, Ronald Reagan and George Bush, who saw compassion as weakness.

19 The two presidents managed to persuade most of us that poverty was self-induced, that the most despicable of the poor were the most representative. There was, it seemed, no difference between a threatening beggar in the park, a criminal, and a family that could not quite make it in hard times. They're all guilty of the same crime: no money.

20 So, the caring are giving up or being driven away. People don't want long-term solutions, said Congresswoman Nancy Pelosi, an Agnos supporter, after the mayor's defeat. "They want Band-Aids and miracles."

21 Too harsh, I think. The best of people and the best in people have been defeated. But people are complicated and sensible.

22 Compassion has been defeated—that's obvious—and common sense is telling people the choice is between living with squalor or having it swept away.

23 In San Francisco, the voters decided they wanted this mess picked up, like garbage. I have no doubt that for better or worse, that is what will begin happening all over the country now.

QUESTIONS AND EXERCISES

VOCABULARY
1. liberal (paragraph 2)
2. panhandlers (3)
3. aesthetic (6)
4. grotesque (9)

5. pathetic (9)
6. self-induced (18)
7. despicable (18)
8. squalor (21)

LANGUAGE AND RHETORIC

1. How would you describe the author's attitude toward the homeless? What specific aspects of the essay reveal that attitude?
2. Why does the author focus his attention on San Francisco to deal with this subject? What is there about the timing and setting that make this an appropriate choice?
3. What is the author's purpose in this selection? What does he expect the reader to do in response to his essay?
4. Originally published as a newspaper commentary, this selection reflects the typical length of paragraphs in that context. Review it to see how each new paragraph can be justified. What paragraphs might be successfully combined if this selection were to be published in another context or format?
5. Although this selection is included here for its use of cause and effect as a method of development, the author uses other methods as well. Point out one of them, and show how the author uses it to develop his essay.

DISCUSSION AND WRITING

1. The author quotes Mayor Agnos in paragraph 6 as saying "I thought the homeless were a social problem. But the voters think they're an aesthetic problem." What is the difference? How do you see the situation? What kind of problem is it in your view, and how would you deal with it if you were in a position to make a difference?
2. In paragraph 17 the author states that "democratic leadership can be judged by whether it brings out the best in people or the worst." What do you think of that idea? Is it a reasonable means for measuring leadership in a democracy? Support your answer. By this standard, did Mayor Agnos succeed or fail in his effort to address the problem? Again, support your answer.
3. The author assigns a major share of responsibility for the problem of homelessness on Presidents Reagan and Bush. What is his basis for doing so? What is your response to that argument? Support that response.
4. In his concluding paragraph, the author anticipates that the same kind of thing that happened in San Francisco will take place in other settings around the country. Have you seen any examples or other evidence to support his conclusion? If so, point them out. If not, see if you can attack it.
5. Write a paper in which you assess the homeless situation in your own community. Do you believe there is a problem? If not, how has it been avoided? If there does seem to be one, consider its cause(s) and its most promising solution(s) from your perspective.

THE EDITORIAL STAFF OF
THE NEW YORKER

Magic and AIDS: The Role of Sports Stars in Our National Life

1   The news that Magic Johnson is infected with the HIV virus was met by the country with shock and sadness but with more complicated emotions as well. Some AIDS activists, for example, expressed a certain mordant anger that, when so many people with AIDS were dying around us every day, it took a heterosexual sports star to make the epidemic "real" to America. And when columnists and commentators began talking, almost excitedly, about the "public impact" of Johnson's announcement it only strengthened the feeling that here was one more event to confirm that in America nothing has really happened until it has happened to a celebrity. Yet the reason for the profound effect of Johnson's announcement on the national consciousness is not simply a function of our celebrity obsession; it also has to do with the place that spectator sports—and basketball in particular—have come to occupy in our national life.

2   One of the few positive and heartening developments in the relations between the races in America over the last decade has been the way that Black basketball payers—above all, Magic Johnson and Michael Jordan—have become the idols of American kids everywhere. Of course, there had been dozens of great Black stars and heroes before, but their blackness had always been something defining, and even isolating, about them. To a large extent, they were heroes *because* they were Black—because they had done things that the public had believed Blacks couldn't do. It was expected that, all other things being equal, a White kid would idolize Tom Seaver more than Bob Gibson. Magic and Michael were the first Black stars who transcended everything—their teams, their sport, their race.

3   Johnson's special place was further defined by his relationship to two other figures, each of whom had also come to represent something special in our unduly race-conscious national psyche: Kareem Abdul-Jabbar and Larry Bird. The first time that Johnson, for all his college triumphs, really caught the public's eye was as a sidekick of the aloof and somewhat dour Abdul-Jabbar, the embodiment of an older and (to White people) more intimidating form of Black pride. In a moment replayed on countless sports broadcasts, Magic leaped into the arms of

a startled and alarmed Kareem after some routine narrow Laker victory in an early-season game. Hey, Kareem's face seemed to say as his giant colleague sprang up at him, this is just another game—they make us play eighty of these things. No, no, this is wonderful, worth celebrating, Magic seemed to say in return, and he jumped once again into the arms of the great center. There was nothing phony about this—no playing to the cameras or the crowd or the corporate sponsors. It was a moment of pure joy that Magic had allowed himself, and he wanted to spread it around. And, although Kareem's ingrained surliness and suspicion were themselves authentic emotions, wrought out of hard experience, it was a joy for the rest of us to see, as Kareem melted, that it need not always be that way.

4   The relationship between Johnson and Larry Bird, a driven, proudly unsophisticated White Midwesterner, was also striking. The week of Johnson's press conference, *Sports Illustrated* ran an article about Bird which was accompanied by matching cartoons of the Celtics forward admiring a statue of Magic, way up on a pedestal, and Magic admiring a statue of Bird, way up on another. The article said that Bird, an unrelentingly competitive performer, had developed not a grudging respect but a genuine, spontaneous, unstinting admiration of Johnson. The story was told, too, that last winter Johnson refused to pose for a "dream team" *Sports Illustrated* cover—the five best players in America, ready to go to the Olympics—until he had made certain, through a few dozen phone calls, that Bird (who had decided at that point not to participate in the Olympics and was therefore not invited to pose) wouldn't be offended if Johnson appeared on the cover without him. With the recent deterioration in the daily exchanges between the races in America, these stories and images seemed particularly vivid, and to see Johnson removed now from the arena was to see a diminishment of our civic life.

5   A further reason, perhaps, for the impact of Johnson's announcement on America has to do with the role that we ask our athletes to play in our national drama. People all over the world idolize their sports stars, but we want ours to be heroes in an almost classical sense—not just to be guys who are good at completing passes or dunking baskets but to become the leading characters in our national epics. (Some athletes—Ted Williams, for example—have never accepted such a role, and have preferred to retreat from their overexpectant public; others, like Joe DiMaggio, have become almost frozen in the hero role.) But although we ascribe improbable virtues to certain athletes, we have mixed emotions about the things that can happen to them. We resist the notion of tragedy; we want to argue it out of

existence. Our daydreams are of denial and a new beginning: Joe Jackson invited back into the cornfield, and playing on. We cannot really accept the fact that heroes suffer like the rest of us—and, worse, have to do it in public, with everyone watching.

6   The events of the last week recalled how Kareem Abdul-Jabbar would never call Earvin Johnson by the name Magic. (Neither would Pat Riley, Johnson's former coach.) "Earvin," he would always say, making the unmistakable point that Johnson was a man, not a child or a cartoon character. It is part of Johnson's specialness, though, that he could meet the role of hero with so much ardor and good humor that even now we continue to call him Magic, without a trace of irony. It is part of his generosity of spirit, it seems, that instead of trying to withdraw from our too intense scrutiny he is offering himself to us as a character in a new story. All over America last week, columnists and editorialists and ordinary people were trying to come up with the proper role for Magic. He should come out for safe sex at all times, or for no sex at any time. He should convince us that it is not only homosexuals who get AIDS, or should declare his solidarity with those homosexuals who do have AIDS. He should lobby for more education, or should stress the pointlessness of more education in the absence of more research. He should speak primarily to the minority community, or he should speak for us all. We want Magic to be a hero still, but we have kept AIDS at arm's length for so long that we don't know yet what we want from this story. We will have to make it up as we go along.

INDEXES

Index to Reading Selections by Subject Matter
(Most selections are listed under more than one subject.)

Index to Reading Selections by Basic Rhetorical Type

Index to Questions on Language and Rhetoric
(Selections are indexed in order of appearance in the text.)

Copyrights and Acknowledgments
The authors wish to thank the following for permission to reprint the material listed:

432